SUNDAY SERVICE BOOK

Services authorized for use
in the Church of England from
The Alternative Service Book 1980
and from *The Book of Common Prayer*
together with *The Parish Psalter*

Oxford University Press
A. R. Mowbray & Co Ltd

Sunday Service Book
compilation © Oxford University Press and A. R. Mowbray & Co
Ltd 1988

For further information about copyright see p. 488

Published by:
Oxford University Press, Walton Street, Oxford, OX2 6DP
and
A. R. Mowbray & Co Ltd, Saint Thomas House, Becket Street,
Oxford, OX1 1SJ

Printed in Great Britain at the University Printing House, Oxford by
David Stanford, Printer to the University.

ISBN 0–19–14–61563 (Oxford University Press)
ISBN 0–264–66666–6 (Mowbray)

AUTHORIZATION

The Services of *The Book of Common Prayer* are authorized without
time limit.

The Services of *The Alternative Service Book 1980*, together with the
Calendar, Rules to Order the Service, and Lectionary, are
authorized pursuant to Canon B2 of the Canons of the Church of
England for use from the date of publication of *The Alternative
Service Book 1980* until 31 December 2000.

Decisions as to which of the authorized services are to be used
(other than occasional offices) shall be taken jointly by the
incumbent and the parochial church council; in the case of occasional
offices (other than Confirmation and Ordination), the decision is to
be made by the minister conducting the service, subject to the right
of any of the persons concerned to object beforehand to its use; in
the case of Confirmation and Ordination services, the decision lies
with the confirming or presiding bishop.

The Prayer Book Psalter (reproduced here with the pointing of
The Parish Psalter) is authorized for use in conjunction with the
services both of the Book of Common Prayer and of *The Alternative
Service Book 1980*.

CONTENTS

CONTENTS

PREFACE

by The Most Revd and Rt Hon. John S. Habgood, DD

When *The Alternative Service Book 1980* was being
planned, it was envisaged that other arrangements of
liturgical material would be published once the main book
had had time to become established. That time has now
come, and I am happy to welcome the *Sunday Service Book*
as a helpful compendium of the material most frequently
used Sunday by Sunday in most parishes.

Two of the most persistent complaints about the *ASB*
have been, first its size, and secondly its exclusion of
services from *The Book of Common Prayer*. In 1980 there
were compelling reasons for both. The size of the *ASB* was
largely determined by the inclusion of the complete text of
all the Eucharistic lections. This was done in an attempt to
ensure that, in an age when there are many translations of
the Bible, congregations become familiar with particular
texts by hearing them read repeatedly. In using a shorter
book this advantage could be lost unless care is taken still to
adhere to the *ASB* lections.

Material from *The Book of Common Prayer* was
excluded from the *ASB* on the grounds that its publishers
could not guarantee to continue publishing complete
Prayer Books if its most widely used services were available
elsewhere. That threat now seems to have receded. The
inclusion of the main 1662 services in the *Sunday Service
Book* is a welcome sign that old and new can co-exist, and
that both can be part of any parish church's worship, as has
been the intention from the start.

The next major revision of the *ASB* will not take effect
until the year 2000. It is likely, therefore, that a publication
in 1988 will have a useful life of some fifteen to twenty years.
This is long enough to mould the pattern of worship of a
complete generation, and I welcome the part which the

PREFACE

Sunday Service Book will play in this process by making more generally accessible the full richness of our liturgical tradition.

JOHN EBOR

New Year's Day
1988

THE ALTERNATIVE
SERVICE BOOK

General Notes

1 **Distinctions in the Text** Sections of services with numbers in blue may be omitted. Where a number of options are included in a mandatory part of a service, the rubric governing the options is numbered in black, but the texts themselves are numbered in blue. Texts in bold type are to be said by the congregation.

2 **Saying and Singing** Where rubrics indicate that a section is to be 'said', this must be understood to include 'or sung' and vice versa.

3 **Posture** Wherever a certain posture is particularly appropriate, it is indicated in the left-hand margin. At all other points local custom may be established and followed.

4 **Biblical Passages** The sentences, psalms, and readings may be read in any duly authorized version.

5 **Prayer Book Texts** Where parts of a service are sung to well-known settings, the traditional words for which they were composed may be used.

6 **The Lord's Prayer** On any occasion the Lord's Prayer may be used in its modern form (as in Holy Communion Rite A), or in its modified form (as in Holy Communion Rite B), or in its traditional form (as in the Book of Common Prayer).

7 **Collects** On any occasion when more than one collect is provided (ASB pp. 398 ff.), only one need be used.

8 **Collect Endings** In the case of any collect ending with the words 'Christ our Lord', the Minister may at his discretion add the longer ending:
'who is alive and reigns with you and the Holy Spirit, one God, now and for ever.'

9 **Hymns** Various points are indicated for the singing of hymns; but, if occasion requires, they may be sung at other points also.

10 **Chanting Psalms and Canticles**

(a) Breath is to be taken at asterisks, and at the end of lines except where the pointing clearly forbids it, or when the sign ⌣ is used to indicate a 'carry-over'.

A shorter break, or 'mental comma', made without taking breath, is indicated by an extra space between words.

(b) The centred dot indicates how the syllables within a bar are to be divided, when there are more than two.

(c) The sign † indicates use of the second half of a double chant.

(d) A double space between verses indicates that a change of chant is appropriate.

(e) The final 'ed' should not be pronounced as a separate syllable unless marked with an accent (e.g. blessèd).

(f) Verses enclosed within square brackets may be omitted.

(g) The Jewish doxologies which conclude Books 1 to 4 of the Psalter (see Psalms 41, 72, 89, 106) are enclosed within brackets. When a Christian doxology is used, they may be omitted.

Morning Prayer
and
Evening Prayer

NOTES

1 **Interchangeability** Either form of Morning Prayer and of Evening Prayer may be used on Sundays or weekdays; but the full form is recommended for use on Sundays.

2 **Sentences** Sentences for use on Sundays, other Holy Days and special occasions are included with the collects and readings (ASB pp. 398ff.). There is a further selection on ASB pages 37–42.

3 **Penitence** Sections 3–7 see pp. 10, 11 (ASB pp. 48, 49), 26–30 see pp. 23, 24 (ASB pp. 61, 62), may be used at a later point in the service after the collects.

4 **The Absolution** In the absence of a priest, 'us' and 'our' are said instead of 'you' and 'your' at sections 6, 29, and 66.

5 **Venite** The whole of Psalm 95 may be said instead of the form at section 9.

6 **The Psalms** The psalms to be read each day are as appointed in Table 1 (ASB pp. 983 ff.), or Table 2 (ASB pp.1047, 1048).*

When The Parish Psalter is used some verse numbers will require adjustment.

7 **The Readings** The readings should be announced in the order: book, chapter, verse.

8 **Readings at Holy Communion** If Holy Communion is to follow immediately, two or three readings may be used. When three readings are used, the New Testament reading will be read at sections 13 or 36, and the Gospel after sections 15 or 38. The Sermon will follow the Gospel.

9 **Canticles in Advent and Lent** Saviour of the World and the last five verses of Te Deum are particularly suitable for use in Advent and Lent.

10 **The Litany** The Litany see pp. 34–37 (ASB pp. 99–102) may be said instead of sections 17–23 or 40–46 followed by the Lord's Prayer, the Collect of the Day, and the Grace.

Sentences

GENERAL

Seek the Lord while he may be found; call upon him while he is near. *Isaiah 55.6*

God is spirit, and those who worship him must worship in spirit and in truth. *John 4.24*

In everything make your requests known to God in prayer and petition with thanksgiving. *Philippians 4.6*

Through Jesus let us continually offer up to God the sacrifice of praise, that is, the tribute of lips which acknowledge his name. *Hebrews 13.15*

To God, the only God, who saves us through Jesus Christ our Lord, be glory and majesty, dominion and authority, before all time and now and for ever. *Jude 25*

TIMES OF THANKSGIVING

Give thanks to the Lord, and call upon his name; tell the nations all that he has done. *Psalm 105.1*

Let the nations be glad and sing; for God judges the people with righteousness and governs the nations upon earth. *Psalm 67.4*

TIMES OF TROUBLE

God is our refuge and strength, an ever present help in trouble. *Psalm 46.1*

Morning Prayer

1 **Stand**

The minister may say

> We have come together as the family of God
>   in our Father's presence
> to offer him praise and thanksgiving,
> to hear and receive his holy word,
> to bring before him the needs of the world,
> to ask his forgiveness of our sins,
> and to seek his grace,
> that through his Son Jesus Christ
> we may give ourselves to his service.

2 A SENTENCE OF SCRIPTURE may be said (see p. 8/ASB p. 46) A HYMN may be sung.

3 The minister may say

> If we say we have no sin, we deceive ourselves,
> and the truth is not in us. If we confess our sins,
> God is faithful and just, and will forgive us our
> sins, and cleanse us from all unrighteousness.

or the sentences for Ash Wednesday to Lent 5 may be used.

4 The minister may say

> Let us confess our sins to almighty God.

5 **Kneel**

All **Almighty God, our heavenly Father,**
we have sinned against you and against our
** fellow men,**
in thought and word and deed,
through negligence, through weakness,
through our own deliberate fault.

We are truly sorry
and repent of all our sins.
For the sake of your Son Jesus Christ, who
died for us,
forgive us all that is past;
and grant that we may serve you in newness
of life
to the glory of your name. Amen.

6   Priest   Almighty God,
who forgives all who truly repent,
have mercy upon *you*,
pardon and deliver *you* from all *your* sins,
confirm and strengthen *you* in all goodness,
and keep *you* in life eternal;
through Jesus Christ our Lord. **Amen.**

7   Instead of section 5 one of the alternative Confessions may
be used (see pp. 94, 95/ASB pp. 165, 166).

8   **Stand**
Minister   O Lord, open our lips;
People   **and our mouth shall proclaim your praise.**

Minister   Let us worship the Lord.
People   **All praise to his name.**

All   **Glory to the Father, and to the Son,**
and to the Holy Spirit:
as it was in the beginning, is now,
and shall be for ever. Amen.

9   VENITE, or JUBILATE, or THE EASTER ANTHEMS (which
shall always be used on Easter Day)

VENITE
1   **O come let us sing | out · to the | Lord:**
let us shout in triumph to the | rock of | our sal | vation.

2   Let us come before his | face with | thanksgiving:
         and cry | out to · him | joyfully · in | psalms.

3   For the Lord is a | great | God:
         and a great | king a·bove | all | gods.

4   In his hand are the | depths · of the | earth:
         and the peaks of the | mountains · are | his | also.

†5   The sea is his and | he | made it:
         his hands | moulded | dry | land.

6   Come let us worship and | bow | down:
         and kneel be|fore the | Lord our | maker.

7   For he is the | Lord our | God:
         we are his | people · and the | sheep of · his |
         pasture.

8   If only you would hear his | voice to |day:
         for he | comes to | judge the | earth.

9   He shall judge the | world with | righteousness:
         and the | peoples | with his | truth.

      Glory to the Father and | to the | Son:
      and | to the | Holy | Spirit;
      as it was in the be|ginning is | now:
      and shall be for | ever. | A |men.

JUBILATE

1   O shout to the Lord in triumph | all the | earth:
         serve the Lord with gladness
         and come before his | face with | songs of | joy.

2   Know that the Lord | he is | God:
         it is he who has made us and we are his
         we are his | people · and the | sheep of · his |
         pasture.

3   Come into his gates with thanksgiving
         and into his | courts with | praise:
         give thanks to him and | bless his | holy | name.

4   For the Lord is good * his loving mercy | is for | ever:
         his faithfulness through|out all | gener|ations.

Glory to the Father and | to the | Son:
    and | to the | Holy | Spirit;
as it was in the be|ginning is | now:
    and shall be for ˻ ever. ˻A|men.

THE EASTER ANTHEMS

1   **Christ our passover has been | sacri·ficed | for us:**
    so let us ˻ cele|brate the | feast,

2   **not with the old leaven of cor|ruption · and | wickedness:**
    but with the unleavened | bread of · sin|cerity · and |
    truth.

3   **Christ once raised from the dead | dies no | more:**
    death has no | more do|minion | over him.

4   **In dying he died to sin | once for | all:**
    in | living · he | lives to | God.

5   **See yourselves therefore as | dead to | sin:**
    and alive to God in | Jesus | Christ our | Lord.

6   **Christ has been | raised · from the | dead:**
    the | firstfruits · of | those who | sleep.

7   **For as by | man came | death:**
    by man has come also the resur|rection | of the | dead;

8   **for as in | Adam · all | die:**
    even so in Christ shall | all be | made a|live.

    Glory to the Father and | to the | Son:
        and | to the | Holy | Spirit;
    as it was in the be|ginning is | now:
        and shall be for ˻ ever. ˻A|men.

10 THE PSALMS appointed
    Each psalm or group of psalms ends with

    Glory to the Father and | to the | Son:
        and | to the | Holy | Spirit;
    as it was in the be|ginning is | now:
        and shall be for ˻ ever. ˻A|men.

    For Parish Psalter version (see pp. 254–265).

11 **Sit**
THE FIRST READING, from the Old Testament

At the end the reader may say

This is the word of the Lord.
All **Thanks be to God.**

Silence may be kept.

12 **Stand**
BENEDICTUS, or A SONG OF CREATION,
or GREAT AND WONDERFUL

BENEDICTUS (The Song of Zechariah)

1 **Blessèd be the Lord the | God of | Israel:**
    for he has come to his | people · and | set them | free.

2 **He has raised up for us a | mighty | saviour:**
    born of the | house · of his | servant | David.

3 **Through his holy prophets he | promised · of | old:**
    that he would save us from our enemies
    from the | hands of | all that | hate us.

4 **He promised to show | mercy · to our | fathers:**
    and to re|member · his | holy | covenant.

5 **This was the oath he swore to our | father | Abraham:**
    to set us | free · from the | hands of · our | enemies,

6 **free to worship him with|out | fear:**
    holy and righteous in his sight | all the | days of ·
    our | life.

7 **You my child shall be called the prophet of the |**
    Most | High:
    for you will go before the | Lord · to pre|pare his | way,

8 **to give his people knowledge | of sal|vation:**
    by the for|giveness · of | all their | sins.

9 **In the tender compassion | of our | God:**
    the dawn from on | high shall | break up|on us,

10   to shine on those who dwell in darkness and the | shadow · of | death:
      and to guide our feet | into · the | way of | peace.

Glory to the Father and | to the | Son:
      and | to the | Holy | Spirit;
as it was in the be|ginning is | now:
      and shall be for | ever. | A|men.

A SONG OF CREATION
On weekdays vv. 4-17 may be omitted.

1   **Bless the Lord all cre|ated | things:**
      sing his | praise · and ex|alt him · for | ever.

2   **Bless the | Lord you | heavens:**
      sing his | praise · and ex|alt him · for | ever.

3   **Bless the Lord you | angels · of the | Lord:**
      bless the | Lord all | you his | hosts;

4   **bless the Lord you waters a|bove the | heavens:**
      sing his | praise · and ex|alt him · for | ever.

5   **Bless the Lord | sun and | moon:**
      bless the | Lord you | stars of | heaven;

6   **bless the Lord all | rain and | dew:**
      sing his | praise · and ex|alt him · for | ever.

7   **Bless the Lord all | winds that | blow:**
      bless the | Lord you | fire and | heat;

8   **bless the Lord scorching wind and | bitter | cold:**
      sing his | praise · and ex|alt him · for | ever.

9   **Bless the Lord dews and | falling | snows:**
      bless the | Lord you | nights and | days;

10   **bless the Lord | light and | darkness:**
      sing his | praise · and ex|alt him · for | ever.

11   **Bless the Lord | frost and | cold:**
      bless the | Lord you | ice and | snow;

12   **bless the Lord | lightnings · and | clouds:**
      sing his | praise · and ex|alt him · for | ever.

13 **O let the earth ᛁ bless the ᛁ Lord:**
    bless the ᛁ Lord you ᛁ mountains · and ᛁ hills;

14 **bless the Lord all that ᛁ grows · in the ᛁ ground:**
    sing his ᛁ praise · and ex ᛁ alt him · for ᛁ ever.

15 **Bless the ᛁ Lord you ᛁ springs:**
    bless the ᛁ Lord you ᛁ seas and ᛁ rivers;

16 **bless the Lord you whales and all that ᛁ swim · in the ᛁ waters:**
    sing his ᛁ praise · and ex ᛁ alt him · for ᛁ ever.

17 **Bless the Lord all ᛁ birds · of the ᛁ air:**
    bless the ᛁ Lord you ᛁ beasts and ᛁ cattle;

18 **bless the Lord all ᛁ men · on the ᛁ earth:**
    sing his ᛁ praise · and ex ᛁ alt him · for ᛁ ever.

19 **O People of God ᛁ bless the ᛁ Lord:**
    bless the ᛁ Lord you ᛁ priests · of the ᛁ Lord;

20 **bless the Lord you ᛁ servants · of the ᛁ Lord:**
    sing his ᛁ praise · and ex ᛁ alt him · for ᛁ ever.

21 **Bless the Lord all men of ᛁ upright ᛁ spirit:**
    bless the Lord you that are ᛁ holy · and ᛁ humble · in ᛁ heart.

   Bless the Father the Son and the ᛁ Holy ᛁ Spirit:
    sing his ᛁ praise · and ex ᛁ alt him · for ᛁ ever.

GREAT AND WONDERFUL
 1 **Great and wonderful are your deeds Lord ᛁ God · the Al ᛁ mighty:**
    just and true are your ᛁ ways O ᛁ King · of the ᛁ nations.

 2 **Who shall not revere and praise your ᛁ name O ᛁ Lord?**
    for ᛁ you a ᛁ lone are ᛁ holy.

 3 **All nations shall come and worship ᛁ in your ᛁ presence:**
    for your just ᛁ dealings · have ᛁ been re ᛁ vealed.

   To him who sits on the throne ᛁ and · to the ᛁ Lamb:
    be praise and honour glory and might
    for ever and ᛁ ever. ᛁ A ᛁ men.

16

13 **Sit**
THE SECOND READING, from the New Testament

At the end the reader may say

This is the word of the Lord.
All **Thanks be to God.**

Silence may be kept.

14 A SERMON may be preached here, or at the end of the service.

15 **Stand**
TE DEUM, or GLORIA IN EXCELSIS or, in Lent, SAVIOUR OF THE WORLD

TE DEUM
Verses 14-18 may be omitted.

1 **You are** **God · and we** **praise you:**
you are the **Lord and** **we ac**|**claim you;**

2 **you are the e**|**ternal** **Father:**
all cre|**ation** **worships** **you.**

3 **To you all angels * all the** **powers of** **heaven:**
cherubim and seraphim **sing in** **endless** **praise,**

4 **Holy holy holy Lord * God of** **power and** **might:**
heaven and **earth are** **full of · your** **glory.**

5 **The glorious company of ap**|**ostles** **praise you:**
the noble fellowship of prophets praise you
the white-robed **army · of** **martyrs** **praise you.**

6 **Throughout the world the holy** **Church ac**|**claims you:**
Father of **majes**|**ty un**|**bounded;**

(†) 7 **your true and only Son * worthy of** **all** **worship:**
and the Holy **Spirit** **advocate · and** **guide.**

8 **You Christ are the** **King of** **glory:**
the e|**ternal** **Son · of the** **Father.**

9   When you became man to | set us | free:
      you did not ab | hor the | Virgin's | womb.

10   You overcame the | sting of | death:
      and opened the kingdom of | heaven · to | all be | lievers.

11   You are seated at God's right | hand in | glory:
      we believe that you will | come and | be our | judge.

12   Come then Lord and | help your | people:
      bought with the | price of | your own | blood;

13   and bring us | with your | saints:
      to | glory | ever | lasting.

14   Save your people Lord and | bless · your in | heritance:
      govern and up | hold them | now and | always.

15   Day by | day we | bless you:
      we | praise your | name for | ever.

16   Keep us today Lord from | all | sin:
      have mercy | on us | Lord have | mercy.

17   Lord show us your | love and | mercy:
      for we | put our | trust in | you.

(†) 18   In you Lord | is our | hope:
      let us not be con | founded | at the | last.

GLORIA IN EXCELSIS

1   Glory to | God · in the | highest:
      and | peace · to his | people · on | earth.

2   Lord God | heaven·ly | King:
      al | mighty | God and | Father,

3   we worship you we | give you | thanks:
      we | praise you | for your | glory.

4   Lord Jesus Christ only | Son · of the | Father:
      Lord | God | Lamb of | God,

5   you take away the | sin · of the | world:
      have | mercy | on | us;

18   *56 Morning Prayer*

6   you are seated at the right hand | of the | Father:
       re | ceive | our | prayer.

7   For you a | lone · are the | Holy One:
       you a | lone | are the | Lord,

8   you alone are the Most High
    Jesus Christ with the | Holy | Spirit:
       in the glory of God the | Father. | A | men.

SAVIOUR OF THE WORLD

1   Jesus saviour of the world * come to us | in your | mercy:
       we look to | you to | save and | help us.

2   By your cross and your life laid down
    you set your | people | free:
       we look to | you to | save and | help us.

3   When they were ready to perish you |
    saved · your dis | ciples:
       we look to | you to | come to · our | help.

4   In the greatness of your mercy loose us | from our |
    chains:
       forgive the | sins of | all your | people.

5   Make yourself known as our saviour and |
    mighty · de | liverer:
       save and | help us · that | we may | praise you.

6   Come now and dwell with us | Lord Christ | Jesus:
       hear our | prayer · and be | with us | always.

(†)7   And when you | come in · your | glory:
       make us to be one with you * and to | share the |
       life of · your | kingdom.

· 16   THE APOSTLES' CREED

    All   I believe in God, the Father almighty,
               creator of heaven and earth.

               I believe in Jesus Christ, his only Son,
               our Lord.

He was conceived by the power of the
    Holy Spirit
and born of the Virgin Mary.
He suffered under Pontius Pilate,
was crucified, died, and was buried.
He descended to the dead.
On the third day he rose again.
He ascended into heaven,
and is seated at the right hand
    of the Father.
He will come again to judge the living
    and the dead.

I believe in the Holy Spirit,
the holy catholic Church,
the communion of saints,
the forgiveness of sins,
the resurrection of the body,
and the life everlasting. **Amen.**

17 **Kneel**
The minister may say

	Lord, have mercy upon us.
People	**Christ, have mercy upon us.**
Minister	Lord, have mercy upon us.

18 **All**

Our Father in heaven,	or	Our Father, who art in heaven,
hallowed be your name,		hallowed be thy name;
your kingdom come,		thy kingdom come;
your will be done,		thy will be done;
on earth as in heaven.		on earth as it is in heaven.
Give us today our daily bread.		Give us this day our daily bread.
Forgive us our sins		And forgive us our trespasses,
as we forgive those		as we forgive those
who sin against us.		who trespass against us.
Lead us not into temptation		And lead us not into temptation;
but deliver us from evil.		but deliver us from evil.
For the kingdom, the power,		For thine is the kingdom,
and the glory are yours		the power, and the glory,
now and for ever. Amen.		for ever and ever. Amen.

19   These versicles and responses may be said.

    Minister   Show us your mercy, O Lord;
    People   **and grant us your salvation.**

    Minister   O Lord, save the Queen;
    People   **and teach her counsellors wisdom.**

    Minister   Let your priests be clothed with righteousness;
    People   **and let your servants shout for joy.**

    Minister   O Lord, make your ways known upon the earth;
    People   **let all nations acknowledge your saving power.**

    Minister   Give your people the blessing of peace;
    People   **and let your glory be over all the world.**

    Minister   Make our hearts clean, O God;
    People   **and renew a right spirit within us.**

20   THE COLLECT OF THE DAY

21   THIS COLLECT may be said.

    O God, the author of peace
    and lover of concord,
    to know you is eternal life,
    to serve you is perfect freedom.
    Defend us your servants
    from all assaults of our enemies;
    that we may trust in your defence,
    and not fear the power of any adversaries;
    through Jesus Christ our Lord. **Amen.**

22   ONE OF THESE COLLECTS is said.

Almighty and everlasting Father,
we thank you that you have brought us safely
to the beginning of this day.
Keep us from falling into sin
or running into danger;
order us in all our doings;
and guide us to do always
what is right in your eyes;
through Jesus Christ our Lord. **Amen.**

or   Eternal God and Father,
you create us by your power
and redeem us by your love:
guide and strengthen us by your Spirit,
that we may give ourselves in love and service
to one another and to you;
through Jesus Christ our Lord. **Amen.**

23   Here may be read the State Prayers, occasional prayers and
thanksgivings, or other forms of prayer. The prayers may
conclude with one of the Endings (see p. 42/ASB p. 107). A
sermon may be preached, hymns may be sung, and the
service may end with a blessing.

Evening Prayer

24 **Stand**
The minister may say

> We have come together as the family of God
>   in our Father's presence
> to offer him praise and thanksgiving,
> to hear and receive his holy word,
> to bring before him the needs of the world,
> to ask his forgiveness of our sins,
> and to seek his grace,
>   that through his Son Jesus Christ
> we may give ourselves to his service.

25 A SENTENCE OF SCRIPTURE may be said (see p. 8/ASB
p. 46) A HYMN may be sung.

26 The minister may say

> If we say we have no sin, we deceive ourselves,
> and the truth is not in us. If we confess our sins,
> God is faithful and just, and will forgive us our
> sins, and cleanse us from all unrighteousness.

or the sentences for Ash Wednesday to Lent 5 may be used.

27 The minister may say

> Let us confess our sins to almighty God.

28 **Kneel**
All   **Almighty God, our heavenly Father,**
we have sinned against you and against our
**   fellow men,**
in thought and word and deed,
through negligence, through weakness,
through our own deliberate fault.
We are truly sorry
and repent of all our sins.

For the sake of your Son Jesus Christ, who
   died for us,
forgive us all that is past;
and grant that we may serve you in newness
   of life
to the glory of your name. Amen.

29 Priest   Almighty God,
          who forgives all who truly repent,
          have mercy upon *you*,
          pardon and deliver *you* from all *your* sins,
          confirm and strengthen *you* in all goodness,
          and keep *you* in life eternal;
          through Jesus Christ our Lord. **Amen.**

30 Instead of section 28 one of the alternative Confessions may
   be used (see pp. 94, 95/ASB pp. 165, 166).

31 **Stand**
   Minister   O Lord, open our lips;
   People   and our mouth shall proclaim your praise.

   Minister   Let us worship the Lord.
   People   All praise to his name.

   **All   Glory to the Father, and to the Son,
              and to the Holy Spirit:
              as it was in the beginning, is now,
              and shall be for ever. Amen.**

32 PSALM 134, or O GLADSOME LIGHT,
   or THE EASTER ANTHEMS

   PSALM 134
 1 **Come bless the Lord   all you | servants · of the | Lord:
     you that by night | stand · in the | house of · our | God.**

 2 **Lift up your hands toward the holy place and |
   bless the | Lord:
     may the Lord bless you from Zion
     the | Lord who · made | heaven · and | earth.**

Glory to the Father and ¦ to the ¦ Son:
   and ¦ to the ¦ Holy ¦ Spirit;
as it was in the be¦ginning is ¦ now:
   and shall be for ¦ ever. ¦ A ¦men.

O GLADSOME LIGHT

1 **O gladsome light, O grace**
   Of God the Father's face,
   The eternal splendour wearing;
   Celestial, holy, blest,
   Our Saviour Jesus Christ,
   Joyful in thine appearing.

2 **Now, ere day fadeth quite,**
   We see the evening light,
   Our wonted hymn outpouring;
   Father of might unknown,
   Thee, his incarnate Son,
   And Holy Spirit adoring.

3 **To thee of right belongs**
   All praise of holy songs,
   O Son of God, lifegiver;
   Thee, therefore, O Most High,
   The world doth glorify,
   And shall exalt for ever.

Other translations of the original may be used.

THE EASTER ANTHEMS

1 **Christ our passover has been ¦ sacri·ficed ¦ for us:**
   so let us ¦ cele¦brate the ¦ feast,

2 **not with the old leaven of cor¦ruption · and ¦ wickedness:**
   but with the unleavened ¦ bread of · sin¦cerity · and ¦ truth.

3 **Christ once raised from the dead ¦ dies no ¦ more:**
   death has no ¦ more do¦minion ¦ over him.

4 **In dying he died to sin ¦ once for ¦ all:**
   in ¦ living · he ¦ lives to ¦ God.

5 **See yourselves therefore as | dead to | sin:**
   and alive to God in | Jesus | Christ our | Lord.

6 **Christ has been | raised · from the | dead:**
   the | firstfruits · of | those who | sleep.

7 **For as by | man came | death:**
   by man has come also the resur|rection | of the | dead:

8 **for as in | Adam · all | die:**
   even so in Christ shall | all be | made a|live.

   Glory to the Father and | to the | Son:
   and | to the | Holy | Spirit;
   as it was in the be|ginning is | now:
   and shall be for ⌐ ever. ⌐ A|men.

33 THE PSALMS appointed
   Each psalm or group of psalms ends with

   Glory to the Father and | to the | Son:
   and | to the | Holy | Spirit;
   as it was in the be|ginning is | now:
   and shall be for ⌐ ever. ⌐ A|men.

   For Parish Psalter version (see pp. 254–265).

34 **Sit**
   THE FIRST READING, from the Old Testament

   At the end the reader may say

              This is the word of the Lord.
   All   **Thanks be to God.**

   Silence may be kept.

35 **Stand**
   MAGNIFICAT, or BLESS THE LORD

   MAGNIFICAT (The Song of Mary)

1 **My soul proclaims the | greatness · of the | Lord:**
   my spirit re|joices · in | God my | saviour;

2   for he has looked with favour on his | lowly | servant:
       from this day all gener|ations · will | call me |
       blessèd;

†3   the Almighty has done | great things | for me:
       and | holy | is his | name.

4   He has mercy on | those who | fear him:
       in | every | gener|ation.

5   He has shown the | strength · of his | arm:
       he has scattered the | proud in | their con|ceit.

6   He has cast down the mighty | from their | thrones:
       and has | lifted | up the | lowly.

7   He has filled the hungry with | good | things:
       and the rich he has | sent a|way | empty.

8   He has come to the help of his | servant | Israel:
       for he has re|membered · his | promise · of | mercy,

9   the promise he | made · to our | fathers:
       to Abraham | and his | children · for|ever.

Glory to the Father and | to the | Son:
and | to the | Holy | Spirit;
as it was in the be|ginning is | now:
and shall be for | ever. | A|men.

BLESS THE LORD

1   Bless the Lord the | God of · our | fathers:
       sing his | praise · and ex|alt him · for | ever.

2   Bless his holy and | glori·ous | name:
       sing his | praise · and ex|alt him · for | ever.

3   Bless him in his holy and | glori·ous | temple:
       sing his | praise · and ex|alt him · for | ever.

4   Bless him who be|holds the | depths:
       sing his | praise · and ex|alt him · for | ever.

5   Bless him who sits be|tween the | cherubim:
       sing his | praise · and ex|alt him · for | ever.

6 **Bless him on the | throne of · his | kingdom:**
sing his | praise · and ex | alt him · for | ever.

7 **Bless him in the | heights of | heaven:**
sing his | praise · and ex | alt him · for | ever.

Bless the Father the Son and the | Holy | Spirit:
sing his | praise · and ex | alt him · for | ever.

36 **Sit**
THE SECOND READING, from the New Testament

At the end the reader may say

This is the word of the Lord.
All   Thanks be to God.

Silence may be kept.

37 A SERMON may be preached here, or at the end of
the service.

38 **Stand**
NUNC DIMITTIS, or THE SONG OF CHRIST'S GLORY,
or GLORY AND HONOUR

NUNC DIMITTIS (The Song of Simeon)

1 **Lord now you let your servant | go in | peace:**
your | word has | been ful | filled.

2 **My own eyes have | seen the · sal | vation:**
which you have prepared in the | sight of |
every | people;

(†)3 **a light to re | veal you · to the | nations:**
and the | glory · of your | people | Israel.

Glory to the Father and | to the | Son:
and | to the | Holy | Spirit;
as it was in the be | ginning is | now:
and shall be for | ever. | A | men.

THE SONG OF CHRIST'S GLORY

1 Christ Jesus was in the | form of | God:
    but he did not | cling · to e | quality · with | God.

2 He emptied himself * taking the | form · of a | servant:
    and was | born · in the | likeness · of | men.

3 Being found in human form he | humbled · him | self:
    and became obedient unto death | even |
    death · on a | cross.

4 Therefore God has | highly · ex | alted him:
    and bestowed on him the | name a · bove | every | name,

5 that at the name of Jesus every | knee should | bow:
    in heaven and on | earth and | under · the | earth;

6 and every tongue confess that Jesus | Christ is | Lord:
    to the | glory · of | God the | Father.

Glory to the Father and | to the | Son:
    and | to the | Holy | Spirit;
as it was in the be | ginning is | now:
    and shall be for | ever. | A | men.

GLORY AND HONOUR

1 Glory and | honour · and | power:
    are yours by | right O | Lord our | God;

2 for you cre | ated | all things:
    and by your | will they | have their | being.

3 Glory and | honour · and | power:
    are yours by | right O | Lamb · who was | slain;

4 for by your blood you ransomed | men for | God:
    from every race and language * from | every |
    people · and | nation,

5 to make them a | kingdom · of | priests:
    to stand and | serve be | fore our | God.

To him who sits on the throne | and · to the | Lamb:
    be praise and honour glory and might * for ever and |
    ever. | A | men.

All   I believe in God, the Father almighty,
       creator of heaven and earth.

       I believe in Jesus Christ, his only Son,
         our Lord.
       He was conceived by the power of the
         Holy Spirit
       and born of the Virgin Mary.
       He suffered under Pontius Pilate,
       was crucified, died, and was buried.
       He descended to the dead.
       On the third day he rose again.
       He ascended into heaven,
       and is seated at the right hand
         of the Father.
       He will come again to judge the living
         and the dead.

       I believe in the Holy Spirit,
       the holy catholic Church,
       the communion of saints,
       the forgiveness of sins,
       the resurrection of the body,
       and the life everlasting. Amen.

40   **Kneel**
      The minister may say

                 Lord, have mercy upon us.
      People   **Christ, have mercy upon us.**
      Minister   Lord, have mercy upon us.

41   **All**

Our Father in heaven,   or   Our Father, who art in heaven,
hallowed be your name,   hallowed be thy name;
your kingdom come,   thy kingdom come;
your will be done,   thy will be done;
on earth as in heaven.   on earth as it is in heaven.
Give us today our daily bread.   Give us this day our daily bread.
Forgive us our sins   And forgive us our trespasses,
as we forgive those   as we forgive those
   who sin against us.   who trespass against us.

Lead us not into temptation but deliver us from evil.	And lead us not into temptation; but deliver us from evil.
For the kingdom, the power, and the glory are yours now and for ever. Amen.	For thine is the kingdom, the power, and the glory, for ever and ever. Amen.

42 These versicles and responses may be said.

Minister   Show us your mercy, O Lord;
People   and grant us your salvation.

Minister   O Lord, save the Queen;
People   and teach her counsellors wisdom.

Minister   Let your priests be clothed with righteousness;
People   and let your servants shout for joy.

Minister   O Lord, make your ways known upon the earth;
People   let all nations acknowledge your saving power.

Minister   Give your people the blessing of peace;
People   and let your glory be over all the world.

Minister   Make our hearts clean, O God;
People   and renew a right spirit within us.

43   THE COLLECT OF THE DAY

44   THIS COLLECT may be said.

O God,
the source of all good desires,
all right judgements, and all just works:
give to your servants that peace
    which the world cannot give;
that our hearts may be set to obey
    your commandments,
and that freed from fear of our enemies,
we may pass our time in rest and quietness;
through Jesus Christ our Lord. **Amen.**

45 THIS COLLECT is said.

> Lighten our darkness,
> Lord, we pray;
> and in your mercy defend us
> from all perils and dangers of this night;
> for the love of your only Son,
> our Saviour Jesus Christ. **Amen.**

46 Here may be read the State Prayers, occasional prayers and thanksgivings, or other forms of prayer. The prayers may conclude with one of the Endings (see p. 42/ASB p. 107). A sermon may be preached, hymns may be sung, and the service may end with a blessing.

Prayers for Various Occasions

1 THE LITANY

Sections I and VI must always be used, but a selection of appropriate suffrages may be made from Sections II, III, IV and V.

I

Let us pray.

God the Father,
have mercy on us.

God the Son,
have mercy on us.

God the Holy Spirit,
have mercy on us.

Holy, blessed, and glorious Trinity,
have mercy on us.

II

From all evil and mischief;
from pride, vanity, and hypocrisy;
from envy, hatred, and malice;
and from all evil intent,
Good Lord, deliver us.

From sloth, worldliness, and love of money;
from hardness of heart
and contempt for your word and your laws,
Good Lord, deliver us.

From sins of body and mind;
from the deceits of the world, the flesh,
    and the devil,
Good Lord, deliver us.

From famine and disaster;
from violence, murder, and dying unprepared,
Good Lord, deliver us.

In all times of sorrow;
in all times of joy;
in the hour of death,
and at the day of judgement,
Good Lord, deliver us.

By the mystery of your holy incarnation;
by your birth, childhood, and obedience;
by your baptism, fasting, and temptation,
Good Lord, deliver us.

By your ministry in word and work;
by your mighty acts of power;
and by your preaching of the kingdom,
Good Lord, deliver us.

By your agony and trial;
by your cross and passion;
and by your precious death and burial,
Good Lord, deliver us.

By your mighty resurrection;
by your glorious ascension;
and by your sending of the Holy Spirit,
Good Lord, deliver us.

III

Hear our prayers, O Lord our God.
Hear us, good Lord.

Govern and direct your holy Church; fill it with
love and truth; and grant it that unity which is
your will.
Hear us, good Lord.

Give us boldness to preach the gospel in all the
world, and to make disciples of all the nations.
Hear us, good Lord.

Enlighten your ministers with knowledge and
understanding, that by their teaching and their
lives they may proclaim your word.
Hear us, good Lord.

Give your people grace to hear and receive your word, and to bring forth the fruit of the Spirit.
Hear us, good Lord.

Bring into the way of truth all who have erred and are deceived.
Hear us, good Lord.

Strengthen those who stand; comfort and help the fainthearted; raise up the fallen; and finally beat down Satan under our feet.
Hear us, good Lord.

IV

Guide the leaders of the nations into the ways of peace and justice.
Hear us, good Lord.

Guard and strengthen your servant Elizabeth our Queen, that she may put her trust in you, and seek your honour and glory.
Hear us, good Lord.

Endue the High Court of Parliament and all the Ministers of the Crown with wisdom and understanding.
Hear us, good Lord.

Bless those who administer the law, that they may uphold justice, honesty, and truth.
Hear us, good Lord.

Teach us to use the fruits of the earth to your glory, and for the good of all mankind.
Hear us, good Lord.

Bless and keep all your people.
Hear us, good Lord.

V

Help and comfort the lonely, the bereaved, and the oppressed.
Lord, have mercy.

Keep in safety those who travel, and all who are in danger.
Lord, have mercy.

Heal the sick in body and mind, and provide for the homeless, the hungry, and the destitute.
Lord, have mercy.

Show your pity on prisoners and refugees, and all who are in trouble.
Lord, have mercy.

Forgive our enemies, persecutors, and slanderers, and turn their hearts.
Lord, have mercy.

Hear us as we remember those who have died in the peace of Christ, both those who have confessed the faith and those whose faith is known to you alone, and grant us with them a share in your eternal kingdom.
Lord, have mercy.

VI

Give us true repentance;
forgive us our sins of negligence and ignorance and our deliberate sins;
and grant us the grace of your Holy Spirit to amend our lives according to your holy word.
Holy God,
holy and strong,
holy and immortal,
have mercy upon us.

One of the prayers (sections 13 and 14), and the Lord's Prayer may be added.
When the Litany is said instead of the Prayers at Morning or Evening Prayer, the Lord's Prayer, the Collect of the Day, and the Grace are added here.

STATE PRAYERS

2   Almighty God, the fountain of all goodness,
bless our Sovereign Lady, Queen Elizabeth, and
all who are in authority under her; that they may
order all things in wisdom and equity,
righteousness and peace, to the honour of your
name, and the good of your Church and people;
through Jesus Christ our Lord. **Amen.**

3   Almighty God, the fountain of all goodness,
bless, we pray, Elizabeth the Queen Mother,
Philip Duke of Edinburgh, the Prince and
Princess of Wales, and all the Royal Family.
Endue them with your Holy Spirit; enrich them
with your heavenly grace; prosper them with all
happiness; and bring them to your everlasting
kingdom; through Jesus Christ our Lord. **Amen.**

4   Almighty and everlasting God, the only worker
of great marvels, send down upon our bishops
and other pastors and all congregations
committed to their care the spirit of your saving
grace; and that they may truly please you, pour
upon them the continual dew of your blessing.
Grant this, O Lord, for the honour of our
advocate and mediator, Jesus Christ. **Amen.**

A GENERAL INTERCESSION

5   O God, the creator and preserver of all
mankind, we pray for men of every race, and in
every kind of need: make your ways known on
earth, your saving power among all nations.
(Especially we pray for . . .)
Lord, in your mercy
hear our prayer.

          We pray for your Church throughout the world:
guide and govern us by your Holy Spirit, that
all who profess and call themselves Christians

may be led into the way of truth, and hold the
faith in unity of spirit, in the bond of peace, and
in righteousness of life. (Especially we pray for . . .)
Lord, in your mercy
hear our prayer.

We commend to your fatherly goodness all who
are anxious or distressed in mind or body;
comfort and relieve them in their need; give them
patience in their sufferings, and bring good
out of their troubles. (Especially we pray for . . .)
Merciful Father,
accept these prayers
for the sake of your Son,
our Saviour Jesus Christ. Amen.

A GENERAL THANKSGIVING

6

Almighty God, Father of all mercies,
we your unworthy servants give you most
    humble and hearty thanks
for all your goodness and loving kindness
to us and to all men.
We bless you for our creation, preservation,
    and all the blessings of this life;
but above all for your immeasurable love
in the redemption of the world by our
    Lord Jesus Christ,
for the means of grace, and for the hope of glory.
And give us, we pray, such a sense of all
    your mercies
that our hearts may be unfeignedly thankful,
and that we show forth your praise,
not only with our lips but in our lives,
by giving up ourselves to your service,
and by walking before you in holiness
    and righteousness all our days;
through Jesus Christ our Lord,
to whom, with you and the Holy Spirit,
    be all honour and glory,
for ever and ever. Amen.

A PRAYER OF DEDICATION

7   This may be used at the end of Morning or Evening Prayer,
     or at a service of Ante-Communion.

> Almighty God,
> we thank you for the gift of your holy word.
> May it be a lantern to our feet,
> a light to our paths,
> and a strength to our lives.
> Take us and use us
> to love and serve all men
> in the power of the Holy Spirit
> and in the name of your Son,
> Jesus Christ our Lord. Amen.

CONCLUDING PRAYERS

8   Almighty God, you have given us grace at this
     time with one accord to make our common
     supplication to you; and you have promised that
     when two or three are gathered together in your
     name you will grant their requests. Fulfil now, O
     Lord, the desires and petitions of your servants,
     as may be most expedient for them, granting us
     in this world knowledge of your truth, and in
     the world to come, life everlasting. **Amen.**

9   Heavenly Father, you have promised through
     your Son Jesus Christ, that when we meet in his
     name, and pray according to his mind, he will be
     among us and will hear our prayer. In your love
     and wisdom fulfil our desires, and give us your
     greatest gift, which is to know you, the only true
     God, and Jesus Christ our Lord; who is alive and
     reigns with you and the Holy Spirit, one God,
     now and for ever. **Amen.**

10   Be with us, Lord, in all our prayers, and direct
our way toward the attainment of salvation; that
among the changes and chances of this mortal
life, we may always be defended by your
gracious help; through Jesus Christ our
Lord. **Amen.**

11   Almighty and eternal God, sanctify and govern
our hearts and bodies in the ways of your laws
and the works of your commandments; that
under your protection, now and ever, we may
be preserved in body and soul; through Jesus
Christ our Lord. **Amen.**

12   Guide us, Lord, in all our doings with your
gracious favour, and further us with your
continual help; that in all our works begun,
continued, and ended in you, we may glorify
your holy name, and by your mercy attain
everlasting life; through Jesus Christ our
Lord. **Amen.**

13   Almighty God, the fountain of all wisdom, you
know our needs before we ask, and our
ignorance in asking; have compassion on our
weakness, and give us those things which for
our unworthiness we dare not, and for our
blindness we cannot ask, for the sake of your
Son, Jesus Christ our Lord. **Amen.**

14   Almighty God, you have promised to hear the
prayers of those who ask in your Son's name; we
pray that what we have asked faithfully we may
obtain effectually; through Jesus Christ our
Lord. **Amen.**

ENDINGS

15   The grace of our Lord Jesus Christ, and the love
of God, and the fellowship of the Holy Spirit be
with us all evermore. **Amen.**

16   Now to him who is able to do immeasurably
more than all we can ask or conceive, by the
power which is at work among us, to him be
glory in the Church and in Christ Jesus
throughout all ages. **Amen.**

17   The Lord be with you
and also with you.

    Let us bless the Lord.
Thanks be to God.

BLESSINGS

18   The Lord bless you and watch over you,
the Lord make his face shine upon you
and be gracious to you,
the Lord look kindly on you
    and give you peace;
and the blessing of God almighty,
the Father, the Son, and the Holy Spirit,
be among you and remain with you always.
Amen.

19   The love of the Lord Jesus
draw you to himself,
the power of the Lord Jesus
strengthen you in his service,
the joy of the Lord Jesus fill your hearts;
and the blessing of God almighty,
the Father, the Son, and the Holy Spirit,
be among you and remain with you always.
Amen.

The Order for Holy Communion

also called
The Eucharist
and
The Lord's Supper

Rite A

NOTES

1 **Preparation** Careful devotional preparation before the service is recommended for every communicant.

2 **The President** The president (who, in accordance with the provisions of Canon B12 'Of the ministry of the Holy Communion', must have been episcopally ordained priest) presides over the whole service. He says the opening Greeting, the Collect, the Absolution, the Peace, and the Blessing; he himself must take the bread and the cup before replacing them on the holy table, say the Eucharistic Prayer, break the consecrated bread, and receive the sacrament on every occasion. The remaining parts of the service he may delegate to others. When necessity dictates, a deacon or lay person may preside over the Ministry of the Word.

When the Bishop is present, it is appropriate that he should act as president. He may also delegate sections 32-49 to a priest.

3 **Posture** When a certain posture is particularly appropriate, it is indicated in the margin. For the rest of the service local custom may be established and followed. The Eucharistic Prayer (sections 38, 39, 40, and 41) is a single prayer, the unity of which may be obscured by changes of posture in the course of it.

4 **Seasonal Material** The seasonal sentences and blessings are optional. Any other appropriate scriptural sentences may be read at sections 1 and 50 at the discretion of the president and 'Alleluia' may be added to any sentence from Easter Day until Pentecost.

5 **Greetings** (section 2 etc.) In addition to the points where greetings are provided, at other suitable points (e.g. before the Gospel and before the Blessing and Dismissal) the minister may say 'The Lord be with you' and the congregation reply 'and also with you'.

6   **Prayers of Penitence** These are used either after section 4 or section 23 (but see Note 22 below for occasions when the Order following the pattern of the Book of Common Prayer is used).

7   **Kyrie eleison** (section 9) This may be used in English or Greek. Alternative versions are set out in section 79.

8   **Gloria in excelsis** (sections 10 and 73) This canticle may be appropriately omitted during Advent and Lent, and on weekdays which are not Principal or Greater Holy Days. It may also be used at sections 1 and 16.

9   **The Collect** (section 11) The Collect may be introduced by the words 'Let us pray' and a brief bidding, after which silence may be kept.

10   **Readings** Where one of the three readings is to be omitted, provision for this is found in Table 3A, ASB pp. 1049–60. See ASB p. 981, note 2.

11   **The Gospel in Holy Week** (section 17) From Palm Sunday to the Wednesday in Holy Week, and on Good Friday, the Passion Gospel may be introduced: 'The Passion of our Lord Jesus Christ according to N', and concluded: 'This is the Passion of the Lord'. No responses are used.

12   **The Sermon** (section 18) The sermon is an integral part of the Ministry of the Word. A sermon should normally be preached at all celebrations on Sundays and other Holy Days.

13   **Proper Prefaces** The Proper Prefaces are set out in section 76. They are obligatory when this is indicated in the seasonal propers but may be used on other suitable occasions. The Sunday Prefaces (31), (32), and (33) are for use with the Fourth Eucharistic Prayer and the Order following the pattern of the Book of Common Prayer.

14   **Second Eucharistic Prayer** (section 39) The three paragraphs
      beginning 'For he is your living Word' and ending 'a people
      for your own possession' may be omitted if a Proper Preface
      is used.

15   **Acclamations** These are optional. They may be introduced
      by the president with the words 'Let us proclaim the mystery
      of faith' or with other suitable words or they may be used
      without introduction.

16   **Manual Acts** In addition to the taking of the bread and the
      cup at section 36 the president may use traditional manual
      acts during the Eucharistic Prayers.

17   **Words of Invitation** (section 45) The words provided are to
      be used at least on Sundays and other Holy Days, and those
      in section 85 may be added. On other days those in section 85
      may be substituted.

18   **The Blessing** (section 54) In addition to the blessings
      provided here and in section 77 the president may at his
      discretion use others.

19   **Notices** Banns of marriage and other notices may be
      published after section 2, section 19, or section 53.

20   **Hymns, Canticles, the Peace, the Collection and
      Presentation of the Offerings of the People, and the
      Preparation of the Gifts of Bread and Wine** Points are
      indicated for these, but if occasion requires they may occur
      elsewhere.

21   **Silence** After sections 6, 13, 15, 17, 18, 26, before sections 42
      and 51, and after the biddings in section 21, silence may
      be kept.

22 **The Order following the pattern of the Book of Common Prayer** (sections 22 and 57-75) When this Order is being followed the Prayers of Penitence should not be used at section 4, as they are requisite at section 59. The Order provided should then be followed in its entirety.

23 **Ministry to the Sick** When Holy Communion is ministered to the sick, the Laying on of Hands or Anointing may follow the Absolution (section 28); the alternative Eucharistic Prayer for use with the sick (section 84) may be used; and the service may be shortened if the needs of the patient require it.

24 **A Service without Communion** When there is no communion, the minister reads the service as far as the Absolution (section 28), and then adds the Lord's Prayer, the General Thanksgiving, and/or other prayers (see section 86) at his discretion, ending with the Grace. When such a service is led by a deacon or lay person, 'us' is said instead of 'you' in the Absolution.

The Order for Holy Communion Rite A

THE PREPARATION

1   At the entry of the ministers AN APPROPRIATE SENTENCE may be used; and A HYMN, A CANTICLE, or A PSALM may be sung.

2   The president welcomes the people using these or other appropriate words.

>   The Lord be with you or The Lord is here.
> **All**   **and also with you.**   **His Spirit is with us.**

    or Easter Day to Pentecost

>   Alleluia! Christ is risen.
> **All**   **He is risen indeed. Alleluia!**

3   This prayer may be said.

> **All**   **Almighty God,**
> **to whom all hearts are open,**
> **all desires known,**
> **and from whom no secrets are hidden:**
> **cleanse the thoughts of our hearts**
> **by the inspiration of your Holy Spirit,**
> **that we may perfectly love you,**
> **and worthily magnify your holy name;**
> **through Christ our Lord. Amen.**

PRAYERS OF PENITENCE

4   THE PRAYERS OF PENITENCE (sections 5-8) may be said here, or after section 23; if they are said here, sections 6-8 are always used.
Alternative confessions may be used (see section 80).

5   THE COMMANDMENTS (section 78) or the following SUMMARY OF THE LAW may be said.

Minister   Our Lord Jesus Christ said: The first commandment is this: 'Hear, O Israel, the Lord our God is the only Lord. You shall love the Lord your God with all your heart, with all your soul, with all your mind, and with all your strength.' The second is this: 'Love your neighbour as yourself.' There is no other commandment greater than these.

All   **Amen. Lord, have mercy.**

6   The minister invites the congregation to confess their sins in these or other suitable words (see section 25).

God so loved the world that he gave his only Son Jesus Christ to save us from our sins, to be our advocate in heaven, and to bring us to eternal life.

Let us confess our sins, in penitence and faith, firmly resolved to keep God's commandments and to live in love and peace with all men.

7   All   **Almighty God, our heavenly Father,**
we have sinned against you and against our
    fellow men,
in thought and word and deed,
through negligence, through weakness,
through our own deliberate fault.
We are truly sorry
and repent of all our sins.

For the sake of your Son Jesus Christ, who
    died for us,
forgive us all that is past;
and grant that we may serve you in newness
    of life
to the glory of your name. Amen.

8   President   Almighty God,
who forgives all who truly repent,
have mercy upon *you*,
pardon and deliver *you* from all *your* sins,
confirm and strengthen *you* in all goodness,
and keep *you* in life eternal;
through Jesus Christ our Lord. **Amen.**

---

9   KYRIE ELEISON may be said (see also section 79).

Lord, have mercy.
Lord, have mercy.

Christ, have mercy.
Christ, have mercy.

Lord, have mercy.
Lord, have mercy.

10   GLORIA IN EXCELSIS may be said.

All   **Glory to God in the highest,
and peace to his people on earth.**

**Lord God, heavenly King,
almighty God and Father,
we worship you, we give you thanks,
we praise you for your glory.**

Lord Jesus Christ, only Son of the Father,
Lord God, Lamb of God,
you take away the sin of the world:
have mercy on us;
you are seated at the right hand of the Father:
receive our prayer.

For you alone are the Holy One,
you alone are the Lord,
you alone are the Most High,
Jesus Christ,
with the Holy Spirit,
in the glory of God the Father. Amen.

11 The president says THE COLLECT.

THE MINISTRY OF THE WORD

12 Either two or three readings from scripture follow, the last of
which is always the Gospel.

13 **Sit**
OLD TESTAMENT READING

At the end the reader may say

This is the word of the Lord.
All   **Thanks be to God.**

14 A PSALM may be used.

15 **Sit**
NEW TESTAMENT READING (EPISTLE)

At the end the reader may say

This is the word of the Lord.
All   **Thanks be to God.**

16 A CANTICLE, A HYMN, or A PSALM may be used.

17 **Stand**
THE GOSPEL. When it is announced

All   **Glory to Christ our Saviour.**

At the end the reader says

                This is the Gospel of Christ.
All   **Praise to Christ our Lord.**

18 **Sit**
THE SERMON

19 **Stand**
THE NICENE CREED is said on Sundays and other Holy
Days, and may be said on other days.

All   **We believe in one God,**
                the Father, the almighty,
                maker of heaven and earth,
                of all that is,
                seen and unseen.

                We believe in one Lord, Jesus Christ,
                the only Son of God,
                eternally begotten of the Father,
                God from God, Light from Light,
                true God from true God,
                begotten, not made,
                of one Being with the Father.
                Through him all things were made.
                For us men and for our salvation
                he came down from heaven;
                by the power of the Holy Spirit
                he became incarnate of the Virgin Mary,
                     and was made man.
                For our sake he was crucified under
                     Pontius Pilate;
                he suffered death and was buried.

On the third day he rose again
in accordance with the Scriptures;
he ascended into heaven
and is seated at the right hand of the Father.
He will come again in glory
to judge the living and the dead,
and his kingdom will have no end.

We believe in the Holy Spirit,
the Lord, the giver of life,
who proceeds from the Father and the Son.
With the Father and the Son he is worshipped
    and glorified.
He has spoken through the Prophets.

We believe in one holy catholic
    and apostolic Church.
We acknowledge one baptism for the
    forgiveness of sins.
We look for the resurrection of the dead,
and the life of the world to come. Amen.

THE INTERCESSION

20   INTERCESSIONS AND THANKSGIVINGS are led by the
      president, or by others. The form below, or one of those in
      section 81, or other suitable words, may be used.

21   This form may be used
      (a) with the insertion of specific subjects between the
      paragraphs;
      (b) as a continuous whole with or without brief biddings.

      Not all paragraphs need be used on every occasion.
      Individual names may be added at the places indicated.
      This response may be used before or after each paragraph.

      Minister   Lord, in your mercy
      All   hear our prayer.

Let us pray for the Church and for the world,
and let us thank God for his goodness.

Almighty God, our heavenly Father, you
promised through your Son Jesus Christ to hear
us when we pray in faith.

Strengthen *N* our bishop and all your Church in
the service of Christ; that those who confess your
name may be united in your truth, live together
in your love, and reveal your glory in the world.

Bless and guide Elizabeth our Queen; give
wisdom to all in authority; and direct this and
every nation in the ways of justice and of peace;
that men may honour one another, and seek the
common good.

Give grace to us, our families and friends, and to
all our neighbours; that we may serve Christ in
one another, and love as he loves us.

Comfort and heal all those who suffer in body,
mind, or spirit . . .; give them courage and hope
in their troubles; and bring them the joy of your
salvation.

Hear us as we remember those who have died in
the faith of Christ . . .; according to your
promises, grant us with them a share in your
eternal kingdom.

Rejoicing in the fellowship of (*N* and of) all your
saints, we commend ourselves and all Christian
people to your unfailing love.

Merciful Father,
All   **accept these prayers
for the sake of your Son,
our Saviour Jesus Christ. Amen.**

22   The Order following the pattern of the Book of Common
Prayer continues at section 57.

PRAYERS OF PENITENCE

23 THE PRAYERS OF PENITENCE (sections 24-28) are said
    here, if they have not been said after section 4; if they are said
    here, sections 26-28 are always used.
    Alternative confessions may be used (see section 80).

24 THE COMMANDMENTS (section 78) or the following
    SUMMARY OF THE LAW may be said.

> Minister Our Lord Jesus Christ said: The first
>   commandment is this: 'Hear, O Israel, the Lord
>   our God is the only Lord. You shall love the Lord
>   your God with all your heart, with all your soul,
>   with all your mind, and with all your strength.'
>   The second is this: 'Love your neighbour as
>   yourself.' There is no other commandment
>   greater than these.
> All   **Amen. Lord, have mercy.**

25 The minister may say

> God so loved the world that he gave his only
> Son Jesus Christ to save us from our sins, to be
> our advocate in heaven, and to bring us to
> eternal life.

or one or more of these SENTENCES.

> Hear the words of comfort our Saviour Christ
> says to all who truly turn to him:
> Come to me, all who labour and are heavy
> laden, and I will give you rest *Matthew 11.28*

> God so loved the world that he gave his only
> Son, that whoever believes in him should not
> perish but have eternal life *John 3.16*

Hear what Saint Paul says:
This saying is true and worthy of full
acceptance, that Christ Jesus came into the
world to save sinners. *1 Timothy 1.15*

Hear what Saint John says:
If anyone sins, we have an advocate with the
Father, Jesus Christ the righteous; and he
is the propitiation for our sins. *1 John 2.1*

26   Minister   Let us confess our sins, in penitence and faith,
firmly resolved to keep God's commandments
and to live in love and peace with all men.

27   All   **Almighty God, our heavenly Father,
we have sinned against you and against our
    fellow men,
in thought and word and deed,
through negligence, through weakness,
through our own deliberate fault.
We are truly sorry
and repent of all our sins.
For the sake of your Son Jesus Christ, who
    died for us,
forgive us all that is past;
and grant that we may serve you in newness
    of life
to the glory of your name. Amen.**

28   President   Almighty God,
who forgives all who truly repent,
have mercy upon *you*,
pardon and deliver *you* from all *your* sins,
confirm and strengthen *you* in all goodness,
and keep *you* in life eternal;
through Jesus Christ our Lord. **Amen.**

> We do not presume
> to come to this your table, merciful Lord,
> trusting in our own righteousness,
> but in your manifold and great mercies.
> We are not worthy
> so much as to gather up the crumbs under
>   your table.
> But you are the same Lord
> whose nature is always to have mercy.
> Grant us therefore, gracious Lord,
> so to eat the flesh of your dear Son
>   Jesus Christ
> and to drink his blood,
> that we may evermore dwell in him
> and he in us. Amen.

The alternative prayer at section 82 may be used.

THE MINISTRY OF THE SACRAMENT

THE PEACE

30 **Stand**
The president says either of the following or other suitable
words (see section 83).

> Christ is our peace.
> He has reconciled us to God
>   in one body by the cross.
> We meet in his name and share his peace.

or   We are the Body of Christ.
>   In the one Spirit we were all baptized into
>   one body.
>   Let us then pursue all that makes for peace
>   and builds up our common life.

He then says

> The peace of the Lord be always with you
All **and also with you.**

31 The president may say

> Let us offer one another a sign of peace.

and all may exchange a sign of peace.

THE PREPARATION OF THE GIFTS

32 The bread and wine are placed on the holy table.

33 The president may praise God for his gifts in appropriate
words to which all respond

Blessed be God for ever.

34 The offerings of the people may be collected and presented.
These words may be used.

> **Yours, Lord, is the greatness, the power,**
> **the glory, the splendour, and the majesty;**
> **for everything in heaven and on earth is yours.**
> **All things come from you,**
> **and of your own do we give you.**

35 At the preparation of the gifts A HYMN may be sung.

THE EUCHARISTIC PRAYER

THE TAKING OF THE BREAD AND CUP AND THE GIVING OF THANKS

36 The president takes the bread and cup into his hands and replaces them on the holy table.

37 The president uses one of the four EUCHARISTIC PRAYERS which follow.

---

38 **FIRST EUCHARISTIC PRAYER**

President   The Lord be with you or The Lord is here.
All   **and also with you.**   **His Spirit is with us.**

President   Lift up your hearts.
All   **We lift them to the Lord.**

President   Let us give thanks to the Lord our God.
All   **It is right to give him thanks and praise.**

President   It is indeed right,
it is our duty and our joy,
at all times and in all places
to give you thanks and praise,
holy Father, heavenly King,
almighty and eternal God,
through Jesus Christ your only Son our Lord.

For he is your living Word;
through him you have created all things from
    the beginning,
and formed us in your own image.

Through him you have freed us from the
    slavery of sin,
giving him to be born as man and to die upon
    the cross;
you raised him from the dead
and exalted him to your right hand on high.

Through him you have sent upon us
your holy and life-giving Spirit,
and made us a people for your own possession.

PROPER PREFACE, when appropriate (section 76)

Therefore with angels and archangels,
and with all the company of heaven,
we proclaim your great and glorious name,
for ever praising you and saying:

All   **Holy, holy, holy Lord,**
God of power and might,
heaven and earth are full of your glory.
Hosanna in the highest.

This ANTHEM may also be used.

Blessed is he who comes in the name of the Lord.
Hosanna in the highest.

President   Accept our praises, heavenly Father,
through your Son our Saviour Jesus Christ;
and as we follow his example and obey
    his command,
grant that by the power of your Holy Spirit
these gifts of bread and wine
may be to us his body and his blood;

Who in the same night that he was betrayed,
took bread and gave you thanks;
he broke it and gave it to his disciples,
    saying,
Take, eat; this is my body which is given
    for you;
do this in remembrance of me.
In the same way, after supper
he took the cup and gave you thanks;
he gave it to them, saying,
Drink this, all of you;
this is my blood of the new covenant,
which is shed for you and for many for the
    forgiveness of sins.
Do this, as often as you drink it,

in remembrance of me.

All **Christ has died:**
Christ is risen:
Christ will come again.

President Therefore, heavenly Father,
we remember his offering of himself
made once for all upon the cross,
and proclaim his mighty resurrection and
glorious ascension.
As we look for his coming in glory,
we celebrate with this bread and this cup
his one perfect sacrifice.

Accept through him, our great high priest,
this our sacrifice of thanks and praise;
and as we eat and drink these holy gifts
in the presence of your divine majesty,
renew us by your Spirit,
inspire us with your love,
and unite us in the body of your Son,
Jesus Christ our Lord.

Through him, and with him, and in him,
by the power of the Holy Spirit,
with all who stand before you in earth
and heaven,
we worship you, Father almighty,
in songs of everlasting praise:

All **Blessing and honour and glory and power**
be yours for ever and ever. Amen.

Silence may be kept.

The service continues with THE LORD'S PRAYER at
section 42 on p. 71/ASB p. 142.

President	The Lord be with you or The Lord is here.
All	**and also with you.** **His Spirit is with us.**

President	Lift up your hearts.
All	**We lift them to the Lord.**

President	Let us give thanks to the Lord our God.
All	**It is right to give him thanks and praise.**

President It is indeed right,
it is our duty and our joy,
at all times and in all places
to give you thanks and praise,
holy Father, heavenly King,
almighty and eternal God,
through Jesus Christ your only Son our Lord.

The following may be omitted if a Proper Preface is used.

For he is your living Word;
through him you have created all things from
the beginning,
and formed us in your own image.

Through him you have freed us from the
slavery of sin,
giving him to be born as man and to die upon
the cross;
you raised him from the dead
and exalted him to your right hand on high.

Through him you have sent upon us
your holy and life-giving Spirit,
and made us a people for your own possession.

PROPER PREFACE, when appropriate (section 76)

Therefore with angels and archangels,
and with all the company of heaven,
we proclaim your great and glorious name,
for ever praising you and saying:

All	Holy, holy, holy Lord,
	God of power and might,
	heaven and earth are full of your glory.
	Hosanna in the highest.

This ANTHEM may also be used.

> Blessed is he who comes in the name of
>   the Lord.
> Hosanna in the highest.

President	Hear us, heavenly Father,
	through Jesus Christ your Son our Lord,
	through him accept our sacrifice of praise;
	and grant that by the power of your
	Holy Spirit
	these gifts of bread and wine
	may be to us his body and his blood;

Who in the same night that he was betrayed,
took bread and gave you thanks;
he broke it and gave it to his disciples,
   saying,
Take, eat; this is my body which is given
   for you;
do this in remembrance of me.
In the same way, after supper
he took the cup and gave you thanks;
he gave it to them, saying,
Drink this, all of you;
this is my blood of the new covenant,
which is shed for you and for many for the
   forgiveness of sins.
Do this, as often as you drink it,
in remembrance of me.

All	Christ has died:
	Christ is risen:
	Christ will come again.

President   Therefore, Lord and heavenly Father,
having in remembrance his death once for all
   upon the cross,
his resurrection from the dead,
and his ascension into heaven,
and looking for the coming of his kingdom,
we make with this bread and this cup
the memorial of Christ your Son our Lord.

Accept through him this offering of our duty
   and service;
and as we eat and drink these holy gifts
in the presence of your divine majesty,
fill us with your grace and heavenly blessing;
nourish us with the body and blood of your Son,
that we may grow into his likeness
and, made one by your Spirit,
become a living temple to your glory.

Through Jesus Christ our Lord,
by whom, and with whom, and in whom,
in the unity of the Holy Spirit,
all honour and glory be yours, almighty Father,
from all who stand before you in earth
   and heaven,
now and for ever. **Amen.**

Silence may be kept.

The service continues with THE LORD'S PRAYER at
section 42 on p. 71/ASB p. 142.

| President | The Lord be with you or The Lord is here. |
| **All** | **and also with you.   His Spirit is with us.** |

| President | Lift up your hearts. |
| **All** | **We lift them to the Lord.** |

| President | Let us give thanks to the Lord our God. |
| **All** | **It is right to give him thanks and praise.** |

President   Father, we give you thanks and praise
through your beloved Son Jesus Christ,
your living Word through whom you have
created all things;

Who was sent by you, in your great goodness,
to be our Saviour;
by the power of the Holy Spirit he took flesh
and, as your Son, born of the blessed Virgin,
was seen on earth
and went about among us;

He opened wide his arms for us on the cross;
he put an end to death by dying for us
and revealed the resurrection by rising to
new life;
so he fulfilled your will and won for you a
holy people.

PROPER PREFACE, when appropriate (section 76)

Therefore with angels and archangels,
and with all the company of heaven,
we proclaim your great and glorious name,
for ever praising you and saying:

All   **Holy, holy, holy Lord,**
God of power and might,
heaven and earth are full of your glory.
Hosanna in the highest.

This ANTHEM may also be used.

> **Blessed is he who comes in the name of the Lord.**
> **Hosanna in the highest.**

President   Lord, you are holy indeed, the source of
all holiness;
grant that, by the power of your Holy Spirit,
and according to your holy will,
these your gifts of bread and wine
may be to us the body and blood of our Lord
Jesus Christ;

Who in the same night that he was betrayed,
took bread and gave you thanks;
he broke it and gave it to his disciples,
saying,
Take, eat; this is my body which is given
for you;
do this in remembrance of me.
In the same way, after supper
he took the cup and gave you thanks;
he gave it to them, saying,
Drink this, all of you;
this is my blood of the new covenant,
which is shed for you and for many for the
forgiveness of sins.
Do this, as often as you drink it,
in remembrance of me.

All   **Christ has died:**
Christ is risen:
Christ will come again.

President   And so, Father, calling to mind his death on
the cross,
his perfect sacrifice made once for the sins
of all men,
rejoicing at his mighty resurrection and
glorious ascension,
and looking for his coming in glory,
we celebrate this memorial of our redemption;

We thank you for counting us worthy
to stand in your presence and serve you;
we bring before you this bread and this cup;

We pray you to accept this our duty
and service,
a spiritual sacrifice of praise and
thanksgiving;

Send the Holy Spirit on your people
and gather into one in your kingdom
all who share this one bread and one cup,
so that we, in the company of all the saints,
may praise and glorify you for ever,
through him from whom all good things come,
Jesus Christ our Lord;

By whom, and with whom, and in whom,
in the unity of the Holy Spirit,
all honour and glory be yours, almighty Father,
for ever and ever. **Amen.**

Silence may be kept.

The service continues with THE LORD'S PRAYER at
section 42 on p. 71/ASB p. 142.

41 **FOURTH EUCHARISTIC PRAYER**

President	The Lord be with you or The Lord is here.
All	**and also with you. His Spirit is with us.**

President	Lift up your hearts.
All	**We lift them to the Lord.**

President	Let us give thanks to the Lord our God.
All	**It is right to give him thanks and praise.**

President   It is indeed right,
            it is our duty and our joy,
            at all times and in all places
            to give you thanks and praise,
            holy Father, heavenly King,
            almighty and eternal God,
            creator of heaven and earth,
            through Jesus Christ our Lord:

PROPER PREFACE, when appropriate (section 76)

The following is used when no Proper Preface is provided.

> For he is the true high priest,
> who has loosed us from our sins
> and has made us to be a royal priesthood
>   to you,
> our God and Father.

> Therefore with angels and archangels,
> and with all the company of heaven,
> we proclaim your great and glorious name,
> for ever praising you and saying:

All   **Holy, holy, holy Lord,**
            God of power and might,
            heaven and earth are full of your glory.
            Hosanna in the highest.

This ANTHEM may also be used.

**Blessed is he who comes in the name of
the Lord.
Hosanna in the highest.**

President   All glory to you, our heavenly Father:
in your tender mercy
you gave your only Son Jesus Christ
to suffer death upon the cross for
    our redemption;
he made there
a full atonement for the sins of the
    whole world,
offering once for all his one sacrifice
    of himself;
he instituted,
and in his holy gospel commanded us
    to continue,
a perpetual memory of his precious death
until he comes again.

Hear us, merciful Father, we humbly pray,
and grant that by the power of your
    Holy Spirit
we who receive these gifts of your creation,
this bread and this wine,
according to your Son our Saviour Jesus
    Christ's holy institution,
in remembrance of the death that he suffered,
may be partakers of his most blessed body
    and blood;

Who in the same night that he was betrayed,
took bread and gave you thanks;
he broke it and gave it to his disciples,
    saying,
Take, eat; this is my body which is given
    for you;
do this in remembrance of me.
In the same way, after supper
he took the cup and gave you thanks;
he gave it to them, saying,

Drink this, all of you;
this is my blood of the new covenant,
which is shed for you and for many for the
    forgiveness of sins.
Do this, as often as you drink it,
in remembrance of me.

All   **Christ has died:**
Christ is risen:
Christ will come again.

President   Therefore, Lord and heavenly Father,
in remembrance of the precious death
    and passion,
the mighty resurrection and glorious ascension
of your dear Son Jesus Christ,
we offer you through him this sacrifice of
    praise and thanksgiving.

Grant that by his merits and death,
and through faith in his blood,
we and all your Church may receive forgiveness
    of our sins
and all other benefits of his passion.
Although we are unworthy, through our
    many sins,
to offer you any sacrifice,
yet we pray that you will accept this,
the duty and service that we owe;
do not weigh our merits, but pardon
    our offences,
and fill us all who share in this
    holy communion
with your grace and heavenly blessing.

Through Jesus Christ our Lord,
by whom, and with whom, and in whom,
in the unity of the Holy Spirit,
all honour and glory be yours, almighty Father,
now and for ever. **Amen.**

Silence may be kept.

THE COMMUNION

THE BREAKING OF THE BREAD AND
THE GIVING OF THE BREAD AND CUP

42 THE LORD'S PRAYER is said either as follows or in its
traditional form.

President   As our Saviour taught us, so we pray.

All	Our Father in heaven,	or	Our Father, who art in heaven,
	hallowed be your name,		hallowed be thy name;
	your kingdom come,		thy kingdom come;
	your will be done,		thy will be done;
	on earth as in heaven.		on earth as it is in heaven.
	Give us today our daily bread.		Give us this day our daily bread.
	Forgive us our sins		And forgive us our trespasses,
	as we forgive those		as we forgive those
	who sin against us.		who trespass against us.
	Lead us not into temptation		And lead us not into temptation;
	but deliver us from evil.		but deliver us from evil.
	For the kingdom, the power,		For thine is the kingdom,
	and the glory are yours		the power, and the glory,
	now and for ever. Amen.		for ever and ever. Amen.

43 The president breaks the consecrated bread, saying

We break this bread
to share in the body of Christ.

All **Though we are many, we are one body,
because we all share in one bread.**

44 Either here or during the distribution one of the following
anthems may be said.

**Lamb of God, you take away the sins of
the world:
have mercy on us.**

**Lamb of God, you take away the sins of
the world:
have mercy on us.**

> Lamb of God, you take away the sins of
>   the world:
> grant us peace.

or   **Jesus, Lamb of God: have mercy on us.**
      Jesus, bearer of our sins: have mercy on us.
      Jesus, redeemer of the world: give us
        your peace.

45   Before the distribution the president says

> Draw near with faith. Receive the body of our
> Lord Jesus Christ which he gave for you, and his
> blood which he shed for you.
>
> Eat and drink in remembrance that he died for
> you, and feed on him in your hearts by faith with
> thanksgiving.

Additional words of invitation may be used (see section 85).

46   The president and people receive the communion. At the
distribution the minister says to each communicant

> The body of Christ keep you in eternal life.
> The blood of Christ keep you in eternal life.

or   The body of Christ.
      The blood of Christ.

The communicant replies each time **Amen**, and then
receives.

Alternative words of distribution may be found in section 66.

47   During the distribution HYMNS and ANTHEMS may be
sung.

48   If either or both of the consecrated elements be likely to
      prove insufficient, the president himself returns to the holy
      table and adds more, saying these words.

> Father, giving thanks over the bread and the cup
> according to the institution of your Son Jesus
> Christ, who said, Take, eat; this is my body
> (*and/or* Drink this; this is my blood), we pray
> that this bread/wine also may be to us his
> body/blood, to be received in remembrance of
> him.

49   Any consecrated bread and wine which is not required for
      purposes of communion is consumed at the end of the
      distribution or after the service.

AFTER COMMUNION

50   AN APPROPRIATE SENTENCE may be said and A HYMN
      may be sung.

51   Either or both of the following prayers or other suitable
      prayers are said (see section 86).

52   President   Father of all, we give you thanks and praise, that
                   when we were still far off you met us in your Son
                   and brought us home. Dying and living, he
                   declared your love, gave us grace, and opened
                   the gate of glory. May we who share Christ's
                   body live his risen life; we who drink his cup
                   bring life to others; we whom the Spirit lights
                   give light to the world. Keep us firm in the hope
                   you have set before us, so we and all your
                   children shall be free, and the whole earth live to
                   praise your name; through Christ our Lord.
                   Amen.

or

53 **All** **Almighty God,**
we thank you for feeding us
with the body and blood of your Son
Jesus Christ.
Through him we offer you our souls and bodies
to be a living sacrifice.
Send us out
in the power of your Spirit
to live and work
to your praise and glory. Amen.

THE DISMISSAL

54 The president may say this or an alternative BLESSING (section 77).

The peace of God, which passes all understanding, keep your hearts and minds in the knowledge and love of God, and of his Son Jesus Christ our Lord; and the blessing of God almighty, the Father, the Son, and the Holy Spirit, be among you, and remain with you always. **Amen.**

55 President Go in peace to love and serve the Lord.
All **In the name of Christ. Amen.**

or

President Go in the peace of Christ.
All **Thanks be to God.**

From Easter Day to Pentecost 'Alleluia! Alleluia!' may be added after both the versicle and the response.

56 The ministers and people depart.

The Order following the pattern of the Book of Common Prayer

(continued from section 22)

57 The priest prepares the bread and wine on the holy table, the offerings of the people may be presented, and A HYMN may be sung.

58 THE COMMANDMENTS (section 78) or the following SUMMARY OF THE LAW may be said.

Minister   Our Lord Jesus Christ said: The first commandment is this: 'Hear, O Israel, the Lord our God is the only Lord. You shall love the Lord your God with all your heart, with all your soul, with all your mind, and with all your strength.' The second is this: 'Love your neighbour as yourself.' There is no other commandment greater than these.

All   **Amen. Lord, have mercy.**

59 The priest invites the congregation to confess their sins in these or other suitable words (see section 25). Alternative confessions may be used (see section 80).

Let us confess our sins, in penitence and faith, firmly resolved to keep God's commandments and to live in love and peace with all men.

60 All   **Almighty God, our heavenly Father,**
we have sinned against you and against our
    fellow men,
in thought and word and deed,
through negligence, through weakness,
through our own deliberate fault.
We are truly sorry,
and repent of all our sins.
For the sake of your Son Jesus Christ, who
    died for us,

> forgive us all that is past;
> and grant that we may serve you in newness
>   of life
> to the glory of your name. **Amen.**

61 Priest   Almighty God,
              who forgives all who truly repent,
              have mercy upon *you*,
              pardon and deliver *you* from all *your* sins,
              confirm and strengthen *you* in all goodness,
              and keep *you* in life eternal;
              through Jesus Christ our Lord. **Amen.**

62 The priest says these SENTENCES.

              Hear the words of comfort our Saviour Christ
              says to all who truly turn to him:
              Come to me, all who labour and are heavy
              laden, and I will give you rest. *Matthew 11.28*

              God so loved the world that he gave his only
              Son, that whoever believes in him should not
              perish but have eternal life. *John 3.16*

              Hear what Saint Paul says:
              This saying is true and worthy of full
              acceptance, that Christ Jesus came into the
              world to save sinners. *1 Timothy 1.15*

              Hear what Saint John says:
              If anyone sins, we have an advocate with the
              Father, Jesus Christ the righteous; and he
              is the propitiation for our sins. *1 John 2.1*

63 Priest   Lift up your hearts.
    All   **We lift them to the Lord.**

    Priest   Let us give thanks to the Lord our God.
    All   **It is right to give him thanks and praise.**

76   147 *Holy Communion A*

| Priest | It is indeed right,
| | it is our duty and our joy,
| | at all times and in all places
| | to give you thanks and praise,
| | holy Father, heavenly King,
| | almighty and eternal God,
| | through Jesus Christ our Lord.

PROPER PREFACE, when appropriate (section 76)

Therefore with angels and archangels,
and with all the company of heaven,
we proclaim your great and glorious name,
for ever praising you and saying:

All　　　**Holy, holy, holy Lord,**
God of power and might,
heaven and earth are full of your glory.
Hosanna in the highest.

64　**All**　　**We do not presume**
to come to this your table, merciful Lord,
trusting in our own righteousness,
but in your manifold and great mercies.
We are not worthy
so much as to gather up the crumbs under
**　　your table.**
But you are the same Lord
whose nature is always to have mercy.
Grant us therefore, gracious Lord,
so to eat the flesh of your dear Son
**　　Jesus Christ**
and to drink his blood,
that we may evermore dwell in him
and he in us. Amen.

65　Priest　　Almighty God, our heavenly Father,
in your tender mercy
you gave your only Son Jesus Christ
to suffer death upon the cross for
　　our redemption;
he made there

a full atonement for the sins of the
    whole world,
offering once for all his one sacrifice
    of himself;
he instituted,
and in his holy gospel commanded us
    to continue,
a perpetual memory of his precious death
until he comes again.

Hear us, merciful Father,
we humbly pray,
and grant that we who receive these gifts of
    your creation,
this bread and this wine,
according to your Son our Saviour Jesus
    Christ's holy institution,
in remembrance of the death that he suffered,
may be partakers of his most blessed body
    and blood;

Who in the same night that he was betrayed,
Here the priest takes the paten.
took bread and gave you thanks;
he broke it,*Here he breaks the bread.*
and gave it to his disciples, saying,
Take, eat;
Here he lays his hand on all the bread.
this is my body which is given for you;
do this in remembrance of me.
In the same way, after supper
Here he takes the cup.
he took the cup and gave you thanks;
he gave it to them, saying,
Drink this, all of you;
*Here he lays his hand on all the vessels of wine to be
consecrated.*
this is my blood of the new covenant,
which is shed for you and for many for the
    forgiveness of sins.
Do this, as often as you drink it,
in remembrance of me. **Amen.**

149   Holy Communion A

66 The priest and people receive the communion. At the distribution the minister says to the communicants the following words, or those in sections 45 and 46.

> The body of our Lord Jesus Christ, which was given for you, preserve your body and soul to eternal life. Take and eat this in remembrance that Christ died for you, and feed on him in your heart by faith with thanksgiving.

> The blood of our Lord Jesus Christ, which was shed for you, preserve your body and soul to eternal life. Drink this in remembrance that Christ's blood was shed for you, and be thankful.

67 If either or both of the consecrated elements be likely to prove insufficient, the priest himself returns to the holy table and adds more, and consecrates according to the form in section 65, beginning, 'Our Saviour Christ in the same night . . .', for the bread, and at 'In the same way, after supper our Saviour . . .', for the cup.

68 Any consecrated bread and wine which is not required for purposes of communion is consumed at the end of the distribution or after the service.

69 THE LORD'S PRAYER is said either as follows or in its traditional form.

Priest   As our Saviour taught us, so we pray.

All   **Our Father in heaven,**   or   **Our Father, who art in heaven,**
      hallowed be your name,   **hallowed be thy name;**
      your kingdom come,   **thy kingdom come;**
      your will be done,   **thy will be done;**
      on earth as in heaven.   **on earth as it is in heaven.**
      Give us today our daily bread.   **Give us this day our daily bread.**
      Forgive us our sins   **And forgive us our trespasses,**
      as we forgive those   **as we forgive those**
      **   who sin against us.**   **   who trespass against us.**

Lead us not into temptation but deliver us from evil.	And lead us not into temptation; but deliver us from evil.
For the kingdom, the power, and the glory are yours now and for ever. Amen.	For thine is the kingdom, the power, and the glory, for ever and ever. Amen.

70 One or other of the following prayers or one of those at sections 52 and 53 is used.

71 Lord and heavenly Father, we your servants entirely desire your fatherly goodness mercifully to accept this our sacrifice of praise and thanksgiving, and to grant that, by the merits and death of your Son Jesus Christ, and through faith in his blood, we and your whole Church may receive forgiveness of our sins and all other benefits of his passion.

And here we offer and present to you, O Lord, ourselves, our souls and bodies, to be a reasonable, holy, and living sacrifice, humbly beseeching you that all we who are partakers of this holy communion may be fulfilled with your grace and heavenly benediction.

And although we are unworthy, through our many sins, to offer you any sacrifice, yet we pray that you will accept this, the duty and service that we owe, not weighing our merits but pardoning our offences, through Jesus Christ our Lord; by whom and with whom, in the unity of the Holy Spirit, all honour and glory are yours, Father almighty, now and for ever. **Amen.**

or

72 Almighty and everliving God, we heartily thank you that you graciously feed us, who have duly received these holy mysteries, with the spiritual food of the most precious body and blood of

your Son our Saviour Jesus Christ, and assure
us thereby of your favour and goodness towards
us and that we are true members of the mystical
body of your Son, the blessed company of all
faithful people, and are also heirs, through
hope, of your eternal kingdom, by the merits of
the most precious death and passion of your
dear Son. And we humbly beseech you,
heavenly Father, so to assist us with your grace,
that we may continue in that holy fellowship,
and do all such good works as you have
prepared for us to walk in; through Jesus Christ
our Lord, to whom, with you and the Holy
Spirit, be all honour and glory, now and for
ever. **Amen.**

73   GLORIA IN EXCELSIS or A HYMN may be sung.

All   **Glory to God in the highest,**
            and peace to his people on earth.

            Lord God, heavenly King,
            almighty God and Father,
            we worship you, we give you thanks,
            we praise you for your glory.

            Lord Jesus Christ, only Son of the Father,
            Lord God, Lamb of God,
            you take away the sin of the world:
            have mercy on us;
            you are seated at the right hand of the Father:
            receive our prayer.

            For you alone are the Holy One,
            you alone are the Lord,
            you alone are the Most High,
            Jesus Christ,
            with the Holy Spirit,
            in the glory of God the Father. Amen.

74 Priest The peace of God, which passes all
understanding, keep your hearts and minds in
the knowledge and love of God, and of his Son
Jesus Christ our Lord; and the blessing of God
almighty, the Father, the Son, and the Holy
Spirit, be among you, and remain with you
always. **Amen.**

75 The ministers and people depart.

Appendices

76 PROPER PREFACES

Suitable for use with all Eucharistic Prayers (sections 38, 39, 40, and 41) and the Order following the pattern of the Book of Common Prayer (section 63), except that Preface (3) is not suitable for use with the Third Eucharistic Prayer.

Advent

1 And now we give you thanks because in his coming as man the day of our deliverance has dawned; and through him you will make all things new, as he comes in power and triumph to judge the world.

2 And now we give you thanks because you prepared the way of your Son Jesus Christ by the preaching of your servant John the Baptist, who proclaimed him as the Lamb of God, our Saviour.

The Incarnation

3 And now we give you thanks because by the power of the Holy Spirit he took our nature upon him and was born of the Virgin Mary his mother, that being himself without sin he might make us clean from all sin.

4 And now we give you thanks because in the incarnation of the Word a new light has dawned upon the world; you have become one with us that we might become one with you in your glorious kingdom.

5 And now we give you thanks because in coming to dwell among us as man, he revealed the radiance of your glory, and brought us out of darkness into your own marvellous light.

6 And now we give you thanks because in choosing the blessed Virgin Mary to be the mother of your Son you have exalted the humble and meek. Your angel hailed her as most highly favoured; with all generations we call her blessed, and with her we rejoice and magnify your holy name.

7 And now we give you thanks because in his earthly
childhood you entrusted him to the care of a human family.
In Mary and Joseph you give us an example of love and
devotion to him, and also a pattern of family life.

Lent
8 And now we give you thanks because through him you
have given us the spirit of discipline, that we may triumph
over evil and grow in grace.

The Cross
9 And now we give you thanks because for our sins he was
lifted high upon the cross that he might draw the whole
world to himself; and, by his suffering and death, became
the source of eternal salvation for all who put their trust in
him.

10 And now we give you thanks because for our salvation
he was obedient even to death on the cross. The tree of
shame was made the tree of glory; and where life was lost,
there life has been restored.

Maundy Thursday
11 And now we give you thanks because when his hour had
come, in his great love he gave this supper to his disciples,
that we might proclaim his death, and feast with him in his
kingdom.

The Blessing of the Oils
12 And now we give you thanks because by your Holy Spirit
you anointed your only Son to be servant of all and ordained
that he should enter into his kingdom through suffering. In
your wisdom and love you call your Church to serve the
world, to share in Christ's suffering and to reveal his glory.

The Resurrection
13 And now we give you thanks because you raised him
gloriously from the dead. For he is the true Paschal
Lamb who was offered for us and has taken away the sin of
the world. By his death he has destroyed death, and by his
rising again he has restored to us eternal life.

14 And now we give you thanks because in his victory over the grave a new age has dawned, the long reign of sin is ended, a broken world is being renewed, and man is once again made whole.

15 And now we give you thanks because through him you have given us eternal life, and delivered us from the bondage of sin and the fear of death into the glorious liberty of the children of God.

16 And now we give you thanks because through him you have given us the hope of a glorious resurrection; so that, although death comes to us all, yet we rejoice in the promise of eternal life; for to your faithful people life is changed, not taken away; and when our mortal flesh is laid aside, an everlasting dwelling place is made ready for us in heaven.

The Ascension
17 And now we give you thanks because you have highly exalted him, and given him the name which is above all other names, that at the name of Jesus every knee shall bow.

Pentecost: Baptism and Confirmation
18 And now we give you thanks because by the Holy Spirit you lead us into all truth, and give us power to proclaim your gospel to the nations, and to serve you as a royal priesthood.

Trinity Sunday
19 And now we give you thanks because you have revealed your glory as the glory of your Son and of the Holy Spirit: three persons equal in majesty, undivided in splendour, yet one Lord, one God, ever to be worshipped and adored.

The Transfiguration
20 And now we give you thanks because the divine glory of the incarnate Word shone forth upon the holy mountain; and your own voice from heaven proclaimed your beloved Son.

St Michael and All Angels

21 Through him the archangels sing your praise, the angels fulfil your commands, the cherubim and seraphim continually proclaim your holiness; the whole company of heaven glorifies your name and rejoices to do your will. Therefore we pray that our voices may be heard with theirs, for ever praising you and saying:

All   **Holy, holy, holy Lord . . .**

All Saints' Day

22 And now we give you thanks for the hope to which you call us in your Son, that following in the faith of all your saints, we may run with perseverance the race that is set before us, and with them receive the unfading crown of glory.

Apostles and Evangelists

23 And now we give you thanks because your Son Jesus Christ after his resurrection sent forth his apostles and evangelists to preach the gospel to all nations and to teach us the way of truth.

Martyrs

24 And now we give you thanks that in the witness of your martyrs who followed Christ even to death you revealed your power made perfect in our human weakness.

Saints' Days

25 And now we give you thanks for the work of your grace in the life of Saint *N* and that by the same grace you lead us in the way of holiness setting before us the vision of your glory.

Dedication

26 And now we give you thanks for your blessing on this house of prayer, where through your grace we offer you the sacrifice of praise, and are built by your Spirit into a temple made without hands, even the body of your Son Jesus Christ.

Marriage

27 And now we give you thanks because you have made the union between Christ and his Church a pattern for the marriage between husband and wife.

Ordination

28 And now we give you thanks because within the royal priesthood of your Church you ordain ministers to proclaim the word of God, to care for your people and to celebrate the sacraments of the new covenant.

Unity

29 And now we give you thanks because of the unity that you have given us in your Son and that you are the God and Father of us all, above all and through all and in all.

Baptism

30 And now we give you thanks because through baptism we have been buried with Christ so that we may rise with him to the new life.

Suitable for use with the Fourth Eucharistic Prayer (section 41) and the Order following the pattern of the Book of Common Prayer (section 63).

Sundays

31 And now we give you thanks because you are the source of light and life; you made us in your image, and called us to new life in him.

32 And now we give you thanks because on the first day of the week he overcame death and the grave and opened to us the way of everlasting life.

33 And now we give you thanks because by water and the Holy Spirit you have made us in him a new people to show forth your glory.

Advent
Christ the Sun of Righteousness shine upon you and scatter
the darkness from before your path; and the blessing . . .

Christmas
Christ, who by his incarnation gathered into one all things
earthly and heavenly, fill you with his joy and peace; and the
blessing . . .

or

Christ the Son of God, born of Mary, fill you with his grace to
trust his promises and obey his will; and the blessing . . .

Epiphany
Christ the Son of God gladden your hearts with the good
news of his kingdom; and the blessing . . .

Ash Wednesday to Lent 4
Christ give you grace to grow in holiness, to deny
yourselves, take up your cross, and follow him; and the
blessing . . .

Lent 5 and Holy Week
Christ crucified draw you to himself, to find in him a sure
ground for faith, a firm support for hope, and the assurance
of sins forgiven; and the blessing . . .

Easter
The God of peace, who brought again from the dead our
Lord Jesus, that great shepherd of the sheep, through
the blood of the eternal covenant, make you perfect in every
good work to do his will, working in you that which is
well-pleasing in his sight; and the blessing . . .

or

The God of peace, who brought again from the dead our
Lord Jesus, that great shepherd of the sheep, make you
perfect in every good work to do his will; and the blessing . . .

or

God the Father, by whose glory Christ was raised from the
dead, strengthen you to walk with him in his risen life; and
the blessing . . .

or

God, who through the resurrection of our Lord Jesus Christ
has given us the victory, give you joy and peace in your faith;
and the blessing . . .

Ascension
Christ our king make you faithful and strong to do his will,
that you may reign with him in glory; and the blessing . . .

Pentecost
The Spirit of truth lead you into all truth, give you grace to
confess that Jesus Christ is Lord, and to proclaim the word
and works of God; and the blessing . . .

Trinity Sunday
God the Holy Trinity make you strong in faith and love,
defend you on every side, and guide you in truth and peace;
and the blessing . . .

Saints' Days
God give you grace to follow his saints in faith and hope and
love; and the blessing . . .

or

God give you grace to follow his saints in faith and truth and
gentleness; and the blessing . . .

or

God give you grace to share the inheritance of his saints in
glory; and the blessing . . .

Unity

Christ the Good Shepherd, who laid down his life for the sheep, draw you and all who hear his voice to be one within one fold; and the blessing . . .

General

The God of all grace who called you to his eternal glory in Christ Jesus, establish, strengthen and settle you in the faith; and the blessing . . .

or

God, who from the death of sin raised you to new life in Christ, keep you from falling and set you in the presence of his glory; and the blessing . . .

or

Christ who has nourished us with himself the living bread, make you one in praise and love, and raise you up at the last day; and the blessing . . .

or

The God of peace fill you with all joy and hope in believing; and the blessing . . .

78 THE COMMANDMENTS

Either A:

Minister   Our Lord Jesus Christ said, If you love me, keep my commandments; happy are those who hear the word of God and keep it. Hear then these commandments which God has given to his people, and take them to heart.

I am the Lord your God: you shall have no other gods but me.
You shall love the Lord your God with all your heart, with all your soul, with all your mind, and with all your strength.

All   Amen. Lord, have mercy.

Minister	You shall not make for yourself any idol.
	God is spirit, and those who worship him
	must worship in spirit and in truth.
All	**Amen. Lord, have mercy.**

Minister	You shall not dishonour the name of the Lord
	your God.
	You shall worship him with awe and reverence.
All	**Amen. Lord, have mercy.**

Minister	Remember the Lord's day and keep it holy.
	Christ is risen from the dead: set your
	minds on things that are above, not on
	things that are on the earth.
All	**Amen. Lord, have mercy.**

Minister	Honour your father and mother.
	Live as servants of God; honour all men;
	love the brotherhood.
All	**Amen. Lord, have mercy.**

Minister	You shall not commit murder.
	Be reconciled to your brother; overcome evil
	with good.
All	**Amen. Lord, have mercy.**

Minister	You shall not commit adultery.
	Know that your body is a temple of the
	Holy Spirit.
All	**Amen. Lord, have mercy.**

Minister	You shall not steal.
	Be honest in all that you do and care for
	those in need.
All	**Amen. Lord, have mercy.**

Minister	You shall not be a false witness.
	Let everyone speak the truth.
All	**Amen. Lord, have mercy.**

Minister	You shall not covet anything which belongs to your neighbour. Remember the words of the Lord Jesus: It is more blessed to give than to receive. Love your neighbour as yourself, for love is the fulfilling of the law.
All	**Amen. Lord, have mercy.**

or B:

Minister	God spoke all these words, saying, I am the Lord your God (who brought you out of the land of Egypt, out of the house of bondage). You shall have no other gods before me.
All	**Amen. Lord, have mercy.**
Minister	You shall not make for yourself a graven image (or any likeness of anything that is in heaven above, or that is in the earth beneath, or that is in the water under the earth; you shall not bow down to them or serve them; for I the Lord your God am a jealous God, visiting the iniquity of the fathers upon the children to the third and the fourth generation of those who hate me, but showing steadfast love to thousands of those who love me and keep my commandments).
All	**Amen. Lord, have mercy.**
Minister	You shall not take the name of the Lord your God in vain (for the Lord will not hold him guiltless who takes his name in vain).
All	**Amen. Lord, have mercy.**
Minister	Remember the sabbath day, to keep it holy. (Six days you shall labour, and do all your work; but the seventh day is a sabbath to the Lord your God; in it you shall not do any work, you, or your son, or your daughter, your manservant, or your maidservant, or your cattle, or the sojourner who is within your gates; for in

	six days the Lord made heaven and earth, the sea, and all that is in them, and rested the seventh day; therefore the Lord blessed the sabbath day and hallowed it.)
All	**Amen. Lord, have mercy.**
Minister	Honour your father and your mother (that your days may be long in the land which the Lord your God gives you).
All	**Amen. Lord, have mercy.**
Minister	You shall not kill.
All	**Amen. Lord, have mercy.**
Minister	You shall not commit adultery.
All	**Amen. Lord, have mercy.**
Minister	You shall not steal.
All	**Amen. Lord, have mercy.**
Minister	You shall not bear false witness against your neighbour.
All	**Amen. Lord, have mercy.**
Minister	You shall not covet (your neighbour's house; you shall not covet your neighbour's wife, or his manservant, or his maidservant, or his ox, or his ass, or) anything that is your neighbour's.
All	**Lord, have mercy on us, and write all these your laws in our hearts.**

79 KYRIE ELEISON

Section 9 may be said in one of the following forms.

Lord, have mercy (upon us.)	Kyrie eleison.
Lord, have mercy (upon us.)	**Kyrie eleison.**
Lord, have mercy (upon us.)	Kyrie eleison.

Christ, have mercy (upon us.)	**Christe eleison.**
Christ, have mercy (upon us.)	Christe eleison.
Christ, have mercy (upon us.)	**Christe eleison.**

Lord, have mercy (upon us.)	Kyrie eleison.
Lord, have mercy (upon us.)	**Kyrie eleison.**
Lord, have mercy (upon us.)	Kyrie eleison.

80 **ALTERNATIVE CONFESSIONS**

Either A:

All   Almighty God, our heavenly Father,
         we have sinned against you and against our
             fellow men,
         in thought and word and deed,
         in the evil we have done
         and in the good we have not done,
         through ignorance, through weakness,
         through our own deliberate fault.
         We are truly sorry,
         and repent of all our sins.
         For the sake of your Son Jesus Christ, who
             died for us,
         forgive us all that is past;
         and grant that we may serve you in newness
             of life
         to the glory of your name. Amen.

or B:

All   Almighty God, our heavenly Father,
         we have sinned against you,
         through our own fault,
         in thought and word and deed,
         and in what we have left undone.
         For your Son our Lord Jesus Christ's sake,
         forgive us all that is past;
         and grant that we may serve you in newness
             of life
         to the glory of your name. Amen.

or C:

All
Father eternal, giver of light and grace,
we have sinned against you and against our
  fellow men,
in what we have thought,
in what we have said and done,
through ignorance, through weakness,
through our own deliberate fault.
We have wounded your love,
and marred your image in us.
We are sorry and ashamed,
and repent of all our sins.
For the sake of your Son Jesus Christ, who
  died for us,
forgive us all that is past;
and lead us out from darkness
to walk as children of light. Amen.

81 ALTERNATIVE FORMS OF INTERCESSION

Either A:

Minister
Let us pray for the whole Church of God in
Christ Jesus, and for all men according to their
needs.

O God, the creator and preserver of all
mankind, we pray for men of every race, and in
every kind of need: make your ways known on
earth, your saving power among all nations.
(Especially we pray for . . .)
Lord, in your mercy

All
hear our prayer.

Minister
We pray for your Church throughout the world:
guide and govern us by your Holy Spirit, that
all who profess and call themselves Christians

may be led into the way of truth, and hold the faith in unity of spirit, in the bond of peace, and in righteousness of life.
(Especially we pray for . . .)
Lord, in your mercy

All   **hear our prayer.**

Minister   We commend to your fatherly goodness all who are anxious or distressed in mind or body; comfort and relieve them in their need; give them patience in their sufferings, and bring good out of their troubles.
(Especially we pray for . . .)
Merciful Father,

All   **accept these prayers**
for the sake of your Son,
our Saviour Jesus Christ. Amen.

or B:

Minister   In the power of the Spirit and in union with Christ, let us pray to the Father.

Hear our prayers, O Lord our God.

All   **Hear us, good Lord.**

Minister   Govern and direct your holy Church; fill it with love and truth; and grant it that unity which is your will.

All   **Hear us, good Lord.**

Minister   Give us boldness to preach the gospel in all the world, and to make disciples of all the nations.

All   **Hear us, good Lord.**

Minister   Enlighten your ministers with knowledge and understanding, that by their teaching and their lives they may proclaim your word.

All   **Hear us, good Lord.**

Minister	Give your people grace to hear and receive your word, and to bring forth the fruit of the Spirit.
All	**Hear us, good Lord.**
Minister	Bring into the way of truth all who have erred and are deceived.
All	**Hear us, good Lord.**
Minister	Strengthen those who stand; comfort and help the faint-hearted; raise up the fallen; and finally beat down Satan under our feet.
All	**Hear us, good Lord.**
Minister	Guide the leaders of the nations into the ways of peace and justice.
All	**Hear us, good Lord.**
Minister	Guard and strengthen your servant Elizabeth our Queen, that she may put her trust in you, and seek your honour and glory.
All	**Hear us, good Lord.**
Minister	Endue the High Court of Parliament and all the Ministers of the Crown with wisdom and understanding.
All	**Hear us, good Lord.**
Minister	Bless those who administer the law, that they may uphold justice, honesty, and truth.
All	**Hear us, good Lord.**
Minister	Teach us to use the fruits of the earth to your glory, and for the good of all mankind.
All	**Hear us, good Lord.**
Minister	Bless and keep all your people.
All	**Hear us, good Lord.**

Minister	Help and comfort the lonely, the bereaved, and the oppressed.
All	**Lord, have mercy.**
Minister	Keep in safety those who travel, and all who are in danger.
All	**Lord, have mercy.**
Minister	Heal the sick in body and mind, and provide for the homeless, the hungry, and the destitute.
All	**Lord, have mercy.**
Minister	Show your pity on prisoners and refugees, and all who are in trouble.
All	**Lord, have mercy.**
Minister	Forgive our enemies, persecutors, and slanderers, and turn their hearts.
All	**Lord, have mercy.**
Minister	Hear us as we remember those who have died in the peace of Christ, both those who have confessed the faith and those whose faith is known to you alone, and grant us with them a share in your eternal kingdom.
All	**Lord, have mercy.**
Minister	Father, you hear those who pray in the name of your Son: grant that what we have asked in faith we may obtain according to your will; through Jesus Christ our Lord. **Amen.**

ALTERNATIVE PRAYER OF HUMBLE ACCESS (section 29)

> Most merciful Lord,
> your love compels us to come in.
> Our hands were unclean,
> our hearts were unprepared;
> we were not fit
> even to eat the crumbs from under your table.
> But you, Lord, are the God of our salvation,
> and share your bread with sinners.
> So cleanse and feed us
> with the precious body and blood of your Son,
> that he may live in us and we in him;
> and that we, with the whole company of Christ,
> may sit and eat in your kingdom. Amen.

83 **A SELECTION OF OTHER INTRODUCTORY WORDS
TO THE PEACE** (section 30)

Advent, Christmas, Epiphany
Our Saviour Christ is the Prince of Peace; of the increase of
his government and of peace there shall be no end.

Lent
Being justified by faith, we have peace with God through
our Lord Jesus Christ.

Easter, Ascension
The risen Christ came and stood among his disciples and
said, Peace be with you. Then they were glad when they saw
the Lord.

Pentecost
The fruit of the Spirit is love, joy, peace. If we live in the
Spirit, let us walk in the Spirit.

Saints' Days
We are fellow-citizens with the saints, and of the household
of God, through Christ our Lord who came and preached
peace to those who were far off and those who were near.

President The Lord be with you or The Lord is here.
All   **and also with you.   His Spirit is with us.**

President Lift up your hearts.
All   **We lift them to the Lord.**

President Let us give thanks to the Lord our God.
All   **It is right to give him thanks and praise.**

President It is indeed right,
it is our duty and our joy,
to give you thanks, holy Father,
through Jesus Christ our Lord.

Through him you have created us in your image;
through him you have freed us from sin
  and death;
through him you have made us your own people
  by the gift of the Holy Spirit.

Hear us, Father,
through Christ your Son our Lord,
and grant that by the power of your
  Holy Spirit
these gifts of bread and wine
may be to us his body and his blood;

Who in the same night that he was betrayed,
took bread and gave you thanks;
he broke it and gave it to his disciples,
  saying,
Take, eat; this is my body which is given
  for you;
do this in remembrance of me.
In the same way, after supper
he took the cup and gave you thanks;
he gave it to them, saying,
Drink this, all of you;
this is my blood of the new covenant,

which is shed for you and for many for the
forgiveness of sins.
Do this, as often as you drink it,
in remembrance of me.

Therefore, Father,
proclaiming his saving death and resurrection
and looking for his coming in glory,
we celebrate with this bread and this cup
his one perfect sacrifice.

Accept through him, our great high priest,
this our sacrifice of thanks and praise,
and grant that we who eat this bread and
drink this cup
may be renewed by your Spirit and grow into
his likeness;

Through Jesus Christ our Lord,
by whom, and with whom, and in whom,
all honour and glory be yours, Father,
now and for ever. **Amen.**

85 **ADDITIONAL WORDS OF INVITATION TO
COMMUNION**
which may be used after section 45

Either A:

President Jesus is the Lamb of God
who takes away the sins of the world.
Happy are those who are called to his supper.
All **Lord, I am not worthy to receive you,
but only say the word, and I shall be healed.**

or B:

President The gifts of God for the people of God.
All **Jesus Christ is holy,
Jesus Christ is Lord,
to the glory of God the Father.**

or C: Easter Day to Pentecost

President: Alleluia! Christ our Passover is sacrificed for us.
All   Alleluia! Let us keep the feast.

86   **ALTERNATIVE FINAL PRAYER**
Especially suitable for a service without Communion

**All   Almighty God,
             we offer you our souls and bodies,
             to be a living sacrifice,
             through Jesus Christ our Lord.
             Send us out into the world
             in the power of your Spirit,
             to live and work
             to your praise and glory. Amen.**

The Order for
Holy Communion

Rite B

NOTES

1 **Seasonal Material** The seasonal sentences (sections 1, 43) and blessings (section 54) are optional. Any other appropriate scriptural sentences may be read at sections 1 and 43 at the discretion of the priest and 'Alleluia' may be added to any sentence from Easter Day until Pentecost (Whit Sunday).

2 **1662 Material** It is permitted to use the 1662 text of the Gloria (sections 5, 48), the Creed (section 14), the Intercession (sections 17, 18), the Confession (section 21), the Absolution (section 22), and the Lord's Prayer (sections 33, 36, 44) instead of the texts printed here.

3 **Gloria in excelsis** (section 5) This canticle is also appropriate at sections 1, 11, and 48.

4 **Collects and Readings** The collects and readings are either those set out in this book or those in the Book of Common Prayer, together with any others approved by the General Synod.

5 **The Sermon** The sermon (section 13) is an integral part of the Ministry of the Word. A sermon should normally be preached at all celebrations on Sundays and other Holy Days.

6 **The Peace** The priest may accompany the words of the Peace (sections 24, 25) with a handclasp or similar action; and both the words and the action may be passed through the congregation.

7 **The Prayers of Intercession and The Thanksgiving** (sections 17, 18, and 30, 31) The use of the first Intercession does not presume the use of the first Thanksgiving. Either Prayer of Intercession may be used with either Thanksgiving.

8   **Proper Prefaces** The Proper Prefaces set out for use in the
    first Thanksgiving and those for Christmas, Passiontide,
    Easter and Ascension in the second Thanksgiving are
    obligatory.

9   **The First Thanksgiving** (section 30) The Prayer of Humble
    Access may, if desired, be said after the Sanctus; and the
    Thanksgiving may end after the words, 'Do this, as oft as ye
    shall drink it, in remembrance of me'; in which case the
    people then say **Amen.**

10 **The Blessing** (section 49) In addition to the blessings
    provided here and at section 54 the priest may at his
    discretion use others.

11 **Notices** Banns of marriage and other notices may be
    published after section 1, section 12, or section 42, if they are
    not published at section 15.

12 **Hymns, Canticles, The Peace, The Collection and
    Presentation of the Offerings of the People, and The
    Preparation of the Gifts of Bread and Wine** Points are indicated
    for these, but if occasion requires they may occur elsewhere.

13 **Silence** After sections 8, 10, 12, 13, 20, 43 and after the
    biddings in sections 17, 18 silence may be kept.

14 **A Service without Communion** When there is no
    communion the minister reads the service as far as the
    Absolution (section 22) and then adds the Lord's Prayer
    (section 36), the General Thanksgiving, and/or other prayers
    at his discretion, ending with the Grace. When such a
    service is led by a deacon or lay person, 'us' is said instead of
    'you' in the Absolution.

The Order for Holy Communion Rite B

THE WORD AND THE PRAYERS

THE PREPARATION

1 At the entry of the ministers A SENTENCE may be used; and A HYMN, A CANTICLE, or A PSALM may be sung.

2 The minister may say

> The Lord be with you
> **All** **and with thy spirit.**

3 This prayer may be said.

> **All** **Almighty God,**
> **unto whom all hearts be open,**
> **all desires known,**
> **and from whom no secrets are hid:**
> **cleanse the thoughts of our hearts**
> **by the inspiration of thy Holy Spirit,**
> **that we may perfectly love thee,**
> **and worthily magnify thy holy name;**
> **through Christ our Lord. Amen.**

4 One of the following may be used.

Either THE COMMANDMENTS (section 55);
or THE SUMMARY OF THE LAW (section 56);
or KYRIE ELEISON in English or Greek (section 57),
each petition being said once, twice, or three times.

5   GLORIA IN EXCELSIS may be said.

All   **Glory be to God on high,**
              and in earth peace, good will towards men.

              We praise thee, we bless thee,
              we worship thee, we glorify thee,
              we give thanks to thee for thy great glory,
              O Lord God, heavenly King,
              God the Father almighty.

              O Lord, the only-begotten Son, Jesus Christ:
              O Lord God, Lamb of God, Son of the Father,
              that takest away the sins of the world,
              have mercy upon us.
              Thou that takest away the sins of the world,
              receive our prayer.
              Thou that sittest at the right hand of God
                the Father,
              have mercy upon us.

              For thou only art holy;
              thou only art the Lord;
              thou only, O Christ,
              with the Holy Ghost,
              art the Most High,
              in the glory of God the Father. Amen.

6   THE COLLECT

THE MINISTRY OF THE WORD

7   Either two or three readings from scripture follow, the last of
which is always the Gospel.

8   **Sit**
      OLD TESTAMENT READING

      At the end the reader may say

              This is the word of the Lord.
All   **Thanks be to God.**

9   A PSALM may be used.

10   **Sit**
       NEW TESTAMENT READING (EPISTLE)

       At the end the reader may say

               This is the word of the Lord.
       All   **Thanks be to God.**

11   A CANTICLE, A HYMN, or A PSALM may be used.

12   **Stand**
       THE GOSPEL. When it is announced

       All   **Glory be to thee, O Lord.**

       At the end the reader says

               This is the Gospel of Christ.
       All   **Praise be to thee, O Christ.**

13   **Sit**
       THE SERMON

14   **Stand**
       THE NICENE CREED is said on Sundays and other Holy
       Days, and may be said on other days.

       All   **I believe in one God**
                   the Father almighty,
                   maker of heaven and earth,
                   and of all things visible and invisible:

                   And in one Lord Jesus Christ,
                   the only-begotten Son of God,
                   begotten of his Father before all worlds,
                   God of God, Light of Light,
                   very God of very God,
                   begotten, not made,
                   being of one substance with the Father,
                   by whom all things were made;

who for us men and for our salvation
came down from heaven,
and was incarnate by the Holy Ghost
    of the Virgin Mary,
and was made man,
and was crucified also for us
    under Pontius Pilate.
He suffered and was buried,
and the third day he rose again
according to the scriptures,
and ascended into heaven,
and sitteth on the right hand of the Father.
And he shall come again with glory
to judge both the quick and the dead:
whose kingdom shall have no end.

And I believe in the Holy Ghost,
the Lord, the Giver of life,
who proceedeth from the Father
    and the Son,
who with the Father and the Son together
    is worshipped and glorified,
who spake by the prophets.
And I believe one holy catholic and
    apostolic Church.
I acknowledge one baptism for the
    remission of sins.
And I look for the resurrection
    of the dead,
and the life of the world to come. Amen.

PRAYERS OF INTERCESSION

15 Banns of marriage and other notices may be published;
the offerings of the people may be collected and presented;
a hymn may be sung; and verses of scripture may be read.

16 INTERCESSIONS are led by the priest, or by others. These
may be introduced by biddings.

It is not necessary to include specific subjects in any section
of the following prayers.

The set passages may follow one another as a continuous whole, or this versicle and response may be used after each paragraph.

Minister   Lord, in thy mercy
All   hear our prayer.

Either section 17 or section 18 is used.

17   FIRST INTERCESSION

Minister   Let us pray for the whole Church of God
                  in Christ Jesus,
            and for all men according to their needs.

Almighty and everliving God, who by thy holy apostle hast taught us to make prayers and supplications, and to give thanks, for all men: we humbly beseech thee most mercifully *(to accept our alms and oblations, and) to receive these our prayers, which we offer unto thy divine majesty; beseeching thee to inspire continually the universal Church with the spirit of truth, unity, and concord; and grant that all they that do confess thy holy name may agree in the truth of thy holy word, and live in unity and godly love.

We beseech thee also to lead all nations in the way of righteousness and peace; and so to direct all kings and rulers, that under them thy people may be godly and quietly governed. And grant unto thy servant Elizabeth our Queen and to all that are put in authority under her, that they may truly and impartially administer justice, to the punishment of wickedness and vice, and to the maintenance of thy true religion and virtue. Give grace, O heavenly Father, to all bishops, priests, and deacons, especially to thy servant N our bishop, that they may both by their life and

*If the offerings of the people have not been presented these words in brackets are omitted.

doctrine set forth thy true and lively word and rightly and duly administer thy holy sacraments.

Guide and prosper, we pray thee, those who are labouring for the spread of thy gospel among the nations, and enlighten with thy Spirit all places of education and learning; that the whole world may be filled with the knowledge of thy truth.

And to all thy people give thy heavenly grace; and specially to this congregation here present, that with meek heart and due reverence, they may hear and receive thy holy word; truly serving thee in holiness and righteousness all the days of their life.

And we most humbly beseech thee of thy goodness, O Lord, to comfort and succour all them who in this transitory life are in trouble, sorrow, need, sickness, or any other adversity.

And we commend to thy gracious keeping, O Lord, all thy servants departed this life in thy faith and fear, beseeching thee, according to thy promises, to grant them refreshment, light, and peace.

And here we give thee most high praise and hearty thanks for all thy saints, who have been the chosen vessels of thy grace, and lights of the world in their several generations; and we pray that, rejoicing in their fellowship and following their good examples, we may be partakers with them of thy heavenly kingdom.

Grant this, O Father, for Jesus Christ's sake, our only mediator and advocate, who liveth and reigneth with thee in the unity of the Holy Spirit, one God, world without end. **Amen.**

The service continues at either section 19 or section 20.

Minister   Let us pray for the whole Church of God
in Christ Jesus,
and for all men according to their needs.

Almighty God, who hast promised to hear the
prayers of those who ask in faith:

Here he may pray for the Church throughout
the world, especially for the diocese and its
bishop; and for any particular needs of the
Church.

Grant that we and all who confess thy name may
be united in thy truth, live together in thy love,
and show forth thy glory in the world.

Here he may pray for the nations of the world,
for this kingdom, and for all men in their various
callings.

Give wisdom to all in authority, bless Elizabeth
our Queen, and direct this nation and all nations
in the ways of justice and of peace; that men may
honour one another, and seek the common
good.

Here he may pray for the local community; for
families, friends, and particular persons.

Give grace to us, our families and friends, and to
all our neighbours in Christ, that we may serve
him in one another, and love as he loves us.

Here he may pray for the sick, the poor, and
those in trouble, and for the needs of particular
persons.

Save and comfort those who suffer, that they
may hold to thee through good and ill, and trust
in thy unfailing love.

Here he may commemorate the departed; he
may commend them by name.

Hear us as we remember those who have died in
faith, and grant us with them a share in thy
eternal kingdom.

Merciful Father,
All   **accept these prayers,**
for the sake of thy Son,
our Saviour Jesus Christ. Amen.

PRAYERS OF PENITENCE

19   The minister may say one or more of
THE COMFORTABLE WORDS.

Hear what comfortable words our Saviour
Christ says to all who truly turn to him:
Come unto me, all that travail, and are heavy
laden, and I will refresh you. *Matthew 11.28*

So God loved the world, that he gave his
only-begotten Son, to the end that all that
believe in him should not perish, but have
everlasting life. *John 3.16*

Hear what Saint Paul says:
This is a true saying and worthy of all men to be
received, that Christ Jesus came into the world
to save sinners. *1 Timothy 1.15*

Hear what Saint John says:
If any man sin, we have an advocate with the
Father, Jesus Christ the righteous; and he is the
propitiation for our sins. *1 John 2.1*

20	Minister	*(Ye that do truly and earnestly repent you of your sins, and are in love and charity with your neighbours, and intend to lead a new life, following the commandments of God, and walking from henceforth in his holy ways;) draw near with faith, and take this holy sacrament to your comfort; and make your humble confession to almighty God (meekly kneeling upon your knees).
	or	Seeing we have a great high priest who has passed into the heavens, Jesus the Son of God, let us draw near with a true heart, in full assurance of faith, and make our confession to our heavenly Father.

21 **Kneel
All**
Almighty God, our heavenly Father,
we have sinned against thee,
through our own fault,
in thought, and word, and deed,
and in what we have left undone.
We are heartily sorry
and repent of all our sins.
For thy Son our Lord Jesus Christ's sake,
forgive us all that is past;
and grant that we may serve thee in newness
of life,
to the glory of thy name. Amen.

22 Priest
Almighty God,
who forgives all who truly repent,
have mercy upon *you*,
pardon and deliver *you* from all *your* sins,
confirm and strengthen *you* in all goodness,
and keep *you* in life eternal;
through Jesus Christ our Lord. **Amen.**

*The words in brackets may be omitted.

We do not presume
to come to this thy table, O merciful Lord,
trusting in our own righteousness,
but in thy manifold and great mercies.
We are not worthy
so much as to gather up the crumbs under
   thy table.
But thou art the same Lord
whose nature is always to have mercy.
Grant us therefore, gracious Lord,
so to eat the flesh of thy dear Son
   Jesus Christ
and to drink his blood,
* (that our sinful bodies may be made clean
   by his body
and our souls washed through his most
   precious blood, and)
that we may evermore dwell in him
and he in us. Amen.

* The words in brackets may be omitted.

THE MINISTRY OF THE SACRAMENT

THE PEACE

24 **Stand**

Priest   We are the Body of Christ.
                By one Spirit we were all baptized into
                    one body.
                Endeavour to keep the unity of the Spirit
                    in the bond of peace.

He then says

                The peace of the Lord be always with you
All   **and with thy spirit.**

25 All may exchange a sign of peace.

THE PREPARATION OF THE BREAD AND WINE

26 The priest begins THE OFFERTORY.

The bread and the wine are placed on the holy table.

27 The offerings of the people may be collected and presented if
this has not already been done.
These words may be used.

> **Thine, O Lord, is the greatness and
>   the power
> and the glory and the victory and
>   the majesty.
> All that is in heaven and earth is thine.
> All things come of thee, O Lord,
> and of thine own do we give thee.**

28 At the preparation of the gifts A HYMN may be sung.

THE THANKSGIVING

29   The priest says THE PRAYER OF CONSECRATION using either section 30 or section 31.

30   FIRST THANKSGIVING

Priest	The Lord be with you
All	**and with thy spirit.**

Priest	Lift up your hearts.
All	**We lift them up unto the Lord.**

Priest	Let us give thanks unto the Lord our God.
All	**It is meet and right so to do.**

Priest   It is very meet, right, and our bounden duty,
that we should at all times and in all places
    give thanks unto thee,
O Lord, holy Father,
almighty, everlasting God,
Creator of heaven and earth,

PROPER PREFACE, when appropriate (section 52)

The following is used when no Proper Preface is provided.

through Jesus Christ our Lord; for he is the true
High Priest, who has washed us from our sins,
and has made us to be a kingdom and priests
unto thee, our God and Father.

Therefore with angels and archangels,
and with all the company of heaven,
we laud and magnify thy glorious name,
evermore praising thee and saying:

**Holy, holy, holy, Lord God of Hosts,
heaven and earth are full of thy glory.
Glory be to thee, O Lord most high. (Amen.)**

**(Blessed is he that cometh in the name of
    the Lord.
Hosanna in the highest.)**

All glory be to thee,
almighty God, our heavenly Father,
who of thy tender mercy
didst give thine only Son Jesus Christ
to suffer death upon the cross
     for our redemption;
who made there,
by his one oblation of himself once offered,
a full, perfect, and sufficient sacrifice,
     oblation, and satisfaction
for the sins of the whole world;
and did institute,
and in his holy gospel command us to continue,
a perpetual memory of that his precious death,
until his coming again.

Hear us, O merciful Father,
we most humbly beseech thee;
and grant that by the power of thy Holy Spirit,
we receiving these thy creatures
     of bread and wine,
according to thy Son our Saviour
     Jesus Christ's holy institution,
in remembrance of his death and passion,
may be partakers
     of his most blessed body and blood.
Who, in the same night that he was betrayed,
took bread;
Here the priest is to take the paten into his hands.
and when he had given thanks,
he brake it, *Here he may break the bread.*
and gave it to his disciples, saying, Take, eat;
Here he is to lay his hand upon the bread.
this is my body which is given for you:
do this in remembrance of me.
Likewise after supper he took the cup;
Here he is to take the cup into his hand.
and when he had given thanks,
he gave it to them, saying, Drink ye all of this;
Here to lay his hand upon the cup.
for this is my blood of the New Testament,
which is shed for you and for many

for the remission of sins:
do this, as oft as ye shall drink it,
in remembrance of me.

Wherefore, O Lord and heavenly Father,
we thy humble servants,
having in remembrance
the precious death and passion of thy dear Son,
his mighty resurrection and glorious ascension,
entirely desire thy fatherly goodness
mercifully to accept this our sacrifice
    of praise and thanksgiving;
most humbly beseeching thee to grant that
by the merits and death of thy Son Jesus Christ,
and through faith in his blood,
we and all thy whole Church
may obtain remission of our sins,
and all other benefits of his passion.
And although we be unworthy
    through our manifold sins
to offer unto thee any sacrifice,
yet we beseech thee to accept
    this our bounden duty and service,
not weighing our merits
    but pardoning our offences.
We pray that all we who are partakers
    of this holy communion
may be fulfilled with thy grace
    and heavenly benediction.
Through Jesus Christ our Lord,
by whom, and with whom, and in whom,
in the unity of the Holy Spirit,
all honour and glory be unto thee,
O Father almighty,
world without end. **Amen.**

Silence may be kept.

The service continues at either section 32 or section 33 or
section 34.

| Priest | The Lord be with you |
| **All** | **and with thy spirit.** |

| Priest | Lift up your hearts. |
| **All** | **We lift them up unto the Lord.** |

| Priest | Let us give thanks unto the Lord our God. |
| **All** | **It is meet and right so to do.** |

| Priest | It is very meet, right, and our bounden duty, |

that we should at all times and in all places
   give thanks unto thee,
O Lord, holy Father,
almighty, everlasting God,
through Jesus Christ
   thine only Son our Lord.

Because through him thou hast created
   all things from the beginning,
and fashioned us men in thine own image;

through him thou didst redeem us
   from the slavery of sin,
giving him to be born as man,
   to die upon the cross,
and to rise again for us;

through him thou hast made us a people
   for thine own possession,
exalting him to thy right hand on high,
and sending forth through him
   thy holy and life-giving Spirit.

PROPER PREFACE, when appropriate (section 53)

Therefore with angels and archangels,
and with all the company of heaven,
we laud and magnify thy glorious name,
evermore praising thee and saying,

Holy, holy, holy, Lord God of hosts,
heaven and earth are full of thy glory.
Glory be to thee, O Lord most high.

(Blessed is he that cometh in the name of
the Lord.
Hosanna in the highest.)

Hear us, O Father,
through Christ thy Son our Lord;
through him accept our sacrifice of praise;
and grant that by the power of thy Holy Spirit
these gifts of bread and wine
may be unto us his body and blood.

Who, in the same night that he was betrayed,
took bread;
Here the priest is to take the bread into his hands.
and when he had given thanks to thee,
he broke it,
and gave it to his disciples, saying, Take, eat;
this is my body which is given for you:
do this in remembrance of me.

Likewise after supper he took the cup;
Here he is to take the cup into his hands.
and when he had given thanks to thee,
he gave it to them saying, Drink ye all of this;
for this is my blood of the new covenant,
which is shed for you and for many
for the remission of sins:
do this, as oft as ye shall drink it,
in remembrance of me.

Wherefore, O Lord and heavenly Father,
with this bread and this cup
we make the memorial of his saving passion,
his resurrection from the dead,
and his glorious ascension into heaven,
and we look for the coming of his kingdom.
We pray thee to accept this
our duty and service,

and grant that we may so eat and drink
    these holy things
in the presence of thy divine majesty,
that we may be filled with thy grace
    and heavenly blessing.

Through Jesus Christ our Lord,
by whom, and with whom, and in whom,
in the unity of the Holy Spirit,
all honour and glory be unto thee,
O Father almighty,
world without end. **Amen.**

Silence may be kept.

---

32   THE BENEDICTUS may follow, if it has not already
been said.

> **Blessed is he that cometh in the name of
> the Lord.
> Hosanna in the highest.**

33   The priest and people together say THE LORD'S PRAYER
either here or at section 36, or at section 44. (The text is
printed at section 36.)

THE COMMUNION

THE BREAKING OF THE BREAD AND
THE GIVING OF THE BREAD AND CUP

34   The priest breaks the consecrated bread, if he has not already
done so, saying

> We break this bread
> to share in the body of Christ.

All   **Though we are many, we are one body,
because we all share in one bread.**

35   Either here or during the distribution this anthem may be said.

> **O Lamb of God,**
> **that takest away the sins of the world,**
> **have mercy upon us.**
>
> **O Lamb of God,**
> **that takest away the sins of the world,**
> **have mercy upon us.**
>
> **O Lamb of God,**
> **that takest away the sins of the world,**
> **grant us thy peace.**

36   The priest and people may say THE LORD'S PRAYER, if it
      has not already been said.

Priest   As our Saviour has taught us, so we pray.
All   **Our Father, who art in heaven,**
          hallowed be thy name;
          thy kingdom come;
          thy will be done;
          on earth as it is in heaven.
          Give us this day our daily bread.
          And forgive us our trespasses,
          as we forgive those who trespass
          against us.
          And lead us not into temptation;
          but deliver us from evil.

          For thine is the kingdom, the power,
          and the glory,
          for ever and ever. Amen.

37   The priest and people receive the communion.

      The communion may be administered in one of the
      following ways:

38　The minister says to each communicant

> The body of our Lord Jesus Christ, which was given for you, preserve your body and soul unto everlasting life. Take and eat this in remembrance that Christ died for you, and feed on him in your heart by faith with thanksgiving.

> The blood of our Lord Jesus Christ, which was shed for you, preserve your body and soul unto everlasting life. Drink this in remembrance that Christ's blood was shed for you, and be thankful.

39　or
The priest first says to all the communicants

> Draw near and receive the body of our Lord Jesus Christ, which was given for you, and his blood, which was shed for you. Take this in remembrance that Christ died for you, and feed on him in your hearts by faith with thanksgiving.

One of the ministers then delivers the bread to each communicant, saying

> The body of Christ.

or
> The body of Christ preserve your body and soul unto everlasting life.

or
> The body of our Lord Jesus Christ, which was given for you, preserve your body and soul unto everlasting life.

One of the ministers then delivers the cup to each communicant, saying

> The blood of Christ.

or The blood of Christ preserve your body and soul unto everlasting life.

or The blood of our Lord Jesus Christ, which was shed for you, preserve your body and soul unto everlasting life.

The communicant may reply each time **Amen**, and then receives.

40 During the distribution HYMNS and ANTHEMS may be sung.

41 If either or both of the consecrated elements are likely to prove insufficient, the priest returns to the holy table and adds more, with these words.

> Having given thanks to thee, O Father, over the bread and the cup according to the institution of thy Son Jesus Christ, who said, Take, eat; this is my body (*and/or* Drink this; this is my blood) we pray that this bread/wine also may be to us his body/blood, and be received in remembrance of him.

42 Any consecrated bread and wine which is not required for purposes of communion is consumed at the end of the distribution, or after the service.

AFTER COMMUNION

43 AN APPROPRIATE SENTENCE may be said (ASB pp. 42, 43) and A HYMN may be sung.

44 The priest and people say THE LORD'S PRAYER, if it has not already been said. (The text is printed at section 36.)

45 Either or both of the following PRAYERS or either of those in the Appendices (section 58) are said.

46 Priest Almighty and everliving God, we most heartily thank thee, for that thou dost vouchsafe to feed us, who have duly received these holy mysteries, with the spiritual food of the most precious body and blood of thy Son our Saviour Jesus Christ; and dost assure us thereby of thy favour and goodness towards us; and that we are very members incorporate in the mystical body of thy Son, which is the blessed company of all faithful people, and are also heirs through hope of thy everlasting kingdom, by the merits of the most precious death and passion of thy dear Son. And we most humbly beseech thee, O heavenly Father, so to assist us with thy grace, that we may continue in that holy fellowship, and do all such good works as thou hast prepared for us to walk in; through Jesus Christ our Lord, to whom, with thee and the Holy Spirit, be all honour and glory, world without end. **Amen.**

47 **All**   **Almighty God,**
we thank thee for feeding us
with the body and blood of thy Son
        Jesus Christ our Lord.
Through him we offer thee our souls
        and bodies
to be a living sacrifice.
Send us out
in the power of thy Spirit,
to live and work
to thy praise and glory. Amen.

48 GLORIA IN EXCELSIS may be used, if it has not been used already (the text is printed at section 5); or some other suitable canticle or hymn may be sung.

THE DISMISSAL

49 The priest may say this or an alternative BLESSING (section 54).

> The peace of God, which passes all understanding, keep your hearts and minds in the knowledge and love of God, and of his Son Jesus Christ our Lord; and the blessing of God almighty, the Father, the Son, and the Holy Spirit, be among you and remain with you always. **Amen.**

50 Priest   Go in peace and serve the Lord.
     All   **In the name of Christ. Amen.**

    or

    Priest   Go in the peace of Christ.
     All   **Thanks be to God.**

51 The ministers and people depart.

Appendices

PROPER PREFACES FOR THE FIRST THANKSGIVING

Christmas, Presentation, and Annunciation
because thou didst give Jesus Christ thine only Son to be born for our salvation: who, by the operation of the Holy Spirit, was made true man of the substance of the Virgin Mary his mother: and that without spot of sin, to make us clean from all sin.

Epiphany
through Jesus Christ our Lord: who in substance of our mortal flesh manifested forth his glory: that he might bring all men out of darkness into his own marvellous light.

Thursday before Easter
through Jesus Christ our Lord: who having loved his own that were in the world loved them unto the end; and on the night before he suffered, sitting at meat with his disciples, did institute these holy mysteries; that we, redeemed by his death and quickened by his resurrection, might be partakers of his divine nature.

Easter
but chiefly we are bound to praise thee for the glorious resurrection of thy Son Jesus Christ our Lord: for he is the true Paschal Lamb which was offered for us, and has taken away the sin of the world; who by his death has destroyed death, and by his rising to life again has restored to us everlasting life.

Ascension
through thy most dearly beloved Son Jesus Christ our Lord: who after his most glorious resurrection manifestly appeared to all his apostles; and in their sight ascended up into heaven to prepare a place for us; that where he is, thither we might also ascend, and reign with him in glory.

Pentecost

through Jesus Christ our Lord: who after he had ascended
up far above all the heavens, and was set down at the right
hand of thy majesty, did as at this time send forth upon the
universal Church thy holy and life-giving Spirit: that
through his glorious power the joy of the everlasting gospel
might go forth into all the world; whereby we have been
brought out of darkness and error into the clear light and
true knowledge of thee, and of thy Son our Saviour
Jesus Christ.

Trinity Sunday

who with thine only-begotten Son and the Holy Spirit art
one God, one Lord in trinity of Persons and in unity of
substance: for that which we believe of thy glory, O Father,
the same we believe of thy Son and of the Holy Spirit,
without any difference or inequality.

Transfiguration

because the divine glory of the incarnate Word shone forth
upon the holy mount before the chosen witnesses of his
majesty; and thine own voice from heaven proclaimed thy
beloved Son.

Saints' Days

who in the righteousness of thy saints hast given us an
example of godly living, and in their blessedness a glorious
pledge of the hope of our calling, that, being encompassed
about with so great a cloud of witnesses, we may run with
patience the race that is set before us, and with them receive
the crown of glory that fadeth not away.

Consecration or Dedication of a Church

who, though the heaven of heavens cannot contain thee,
and thy glory is in all the world, dost deign to hallow places
for thy worship, and in them dost pour forth gifts of grace
upon thy faithful people.

Funerals

because through thy Son Jesus Christ our Lord, thou hast given us eternal life, and delivered us from the bondage of sin and the fear of death into the glorious liberty of the children of God.

or

because through thy Son Jesus Christ our Lord, thou hast given us the hope of a glorious resurrection, so that although death comes to us all, yet we rejoice in the promise of eternal life; for to thy faithful people life is changed, not taken away, and when our mortal flesh is laid aside, an everlasting dwelling place is made ready for us in heaven.

53 PROPER PREFACES FOR THE SECOND THANKSGIVING

Advent

And now we give thee thanks, because the day of our deliverance has dawned; and through him thou wilt make all things new, as he comes in power and triumph to judge the world.

Christmas, Presentation, and Annunciation

And now we give thee thanks, for by the operation of the Holy Spirit, he was made man of the Virgin Mary his mother; and that without spot of sin, to make us clean from all sin.

Epiphany

And now we give thee thanks, because in coming to dwell among us as man, he revealed the radiance of his glory, and brought us out of darkness into his own marvellous light.

Lent

And now we give thee thanks, because through him thou hast given us the spirit of discipline, that we may triumph over evil and grow in grace.

Passiontide

And now we give thee thanks, because for our salvation he was obedient even to death on the cross. The tree of defeat became the tree of glory: and where life was lost, there life has been restored.

Thursday before Easter

And now we give thee thanks, because having loved his own that were in the world he loved them unto the end; and on the night before he suffered, sitting at meat with his disciples, did institute these holy mysteries; that we, redeemed by his death and quickened by his resurrection, might be partakers of his divine nature.

Easter

And now we give thee thanks, for his glorious resurrection from the dead. For he is the true Paschal Lamb which was offered for us, and has taken away the sin of the world; who by his death has destroyed death, and by his rising to life again has restored to us everlasting life.

Ascension

And now we give thee thanks, because in his risen body he appeared to his disciples and in their sight was taken into heaven, to reign with thee in glory.

Pentecost

And now we give thee thanks, because by the same Spirit we are led into all truth and are given power to proclaim thy gospel to the nations and to serve thee as a royal priesthood.

Trinity Sunday

And now we give thee thanks, because thou hast revealed thy glory as the glory of thy Son and of the Holy Spirit: three persons equal in majesty, undivided in splendour, yet one Lord, one God, ever to be worshipped and adored.

Transfiguration

And now we give thee thanks, because the divine glory of the incarnate Word shone forth upon the holy mount before the chosen witnesses of his majesty; and thine own voice from heaven proclaimed thy beloved Son.

Saints' Days

And now we give thee thanks, for the glorious pledge of the hope of our calling which thou hast given us in thy saints; that following their example and strengthened by their fellowship, we may run with perseverance the race that is set before us, and with them receive the unfading crown of glory.

Dedication

And now we give thee thanks, for thy blessings on this house of prayer, where we are stirred to faithful witness, and are built up by thy Spirit into a temple made without hands, even the body of thy Son Jesus Christ.

Funerals

And now we give thee thanks, because through him thou hast given us eternal life, and delivered us from the bondage of sin and the fear of death into the glorious liberty of the children of God.

or

And now we give thee thanks, because through him thou hast given us the hope of a glorious resurrection, so that although death comes to us all, yet we rejoice in the promise of eternal life; for to thy faithful people life is changed, not taken away, and when our mortal flesh is laid aside, an everlasting dwelling place is made ready for us in heaven.

54 ALTERNATIVE BLESSINGS

Advent

Christ the Sun of righteousness shine upon you and scatter the darkness from before your path: and the blessing . . .

Christmas

Christ the Son of God gladden your hearts with the good
news of his kingdom: and the blessing . . .

Lent

Christ give you grace to grow in holiness, to deny
yourselves, and to take up your cross, and follow him: and
the blessing . . .

Passiontide

Christ crucified draw you to himself, so that you find in him
a sure ground for faith, a firm support for hope, and the
assurance of sins forgiven: and the blessing . . .

Easter

The God of peace, who brought again from the dead our
Lord Jesus, that great shepherd of the sheep, make you
perfect in every good work to do his will: and the blessing . . .

Ascension

Christ our king make you faithful and strong to do his will,
that you may reign with him in glory: and the blessing . . .

Pentecost

The Spirit of truth lead you into all truth, give you grace to
confess that Jesus Christ is Lord, and to proclaim the word
and works of God: and the blessing . . .

Trinity Sunday

God the Holy Trinity make you strong in faith and love,
defend you on every side, and guide you in truth and peace:
and the blessing . . .

Saints' Days

God give you grace to follow his saints in faith and hope and
love: and the blessing . . .

Unity

Christ the Good Shepherd, who laid down his life for his
sheep, draw you and all who hear his voice to be one within
one fold: and the blessing . . .

Minister God spake these words and said:
I am the Lord thy God, thou shalt have none
other gods but me.
All **Lord, have mercy upon us,**
and incline our hearts to keep this law.

Minister Thou shalt not make to thyself any graven
image, nor the likeness of anything that is in
heaven above, or in the earth beneath, or in the
water under the earth. Thou shalt not bow down
to them, nor worship them.
All **Lord, have mercy upon us,**
and incline our hearts to keep this law.

Minister Thou shalt not take the name of the Lord thy
God in vain.
All **Lord, have mercy upon us,**
and incline our hearts to keep this law.

Minister Remember that thou keep holy the Sabbath day.
Six days shalt thou labour, and do all that thou
hast to do; but the seventh day is the Sabbath of
the Lord thy God.
All **Lord, have mercy upon us,**
and incline our hearts to keep this law.

Minister Honour thy father and thy mother.
All **Lord, have mercy upon us,**
and incline our hearts to keep this law.

Minister Thou shalt do no murder.
All **Lord, have mercy upon us,**
and incline our hearts to keep this law.

Minister Thou shalt not commit adultery.
All **Lord, have mercy upon us,**
and incline our hearts to keep this law.

Minister	Thou shalt not steal.
All	**Lord, have mercy upon us,**
	and incline our hearts to keep this law.

Minister	Thou shalt not bear false witness.
All	**Lord, have mercy upon us,**
	and incline our hearts to keep this law.

Minister	Thou shalt not covet.
All	**Lord, have mercy upon us,**
	and write all these thy laws in our hearts,
	we beseech thee.

56 THE SUMMARY OF THE LAW

Minister	Our Lord Jesus Christ said: Hear, O Israel, the Lord our God is one Lord; and thou shalt love the Lord thy God with all thy heart, and with all thy soul, and with all thy mind, and with all thy strength. This is the first commandment. And the second is like, namely this: Thou shalt love thy neighbour as thyself. There is none other commandment greater than these. On these two commandments hang all the law and the prophets.
All	**Lord, have mercy upon us,**
	and write all these thy laws in our hearts,
	we beseech thee.

57 KYRIE ELEISON

Lord, have mercy (upon us.)	Kyrie eleison.
Lord, have mercy (upon us.)	**Kyrie eleison.**
Lord, have mercy (upon us.)	Kyrie eleison.

Christ, have mercy (upon us.)	**Christe eleison.**
Christ, have mercy (upon us.)	Christe eleison.
Christ, have mercy (upon us.)	**Christe eleison.**

Lord, have mercy (upon us.)	Kyrie eleison.
Lord, have mercy (upon us.)	**Kyrie eleison.**
Lord, have mercy (upon us.)	Kyrie eleison.

Either of the following prayers may be used instead of those
in sections 46 and 47.

Priest   O Lord and heavenly Father, we thy humble
           servants entirely desire thy fatherly goodness
           mercifully to accept this our sacrifice of praise
           and thanksgiving; most humbly beseeching
           thee to grant that by the merits and death of thy
           Son Jesus Christ, and through faith in his blood,
           we and all thy whole Church may obtain
           remission of our sins, and all other benefits of
           his passion. And here we offer and present unto
           thee, O Lord, ourselves, our souls and bodies, to
           be a reasonable, holy, and lively sacrifice unto
           thee; humbly beseeching thee, that all we, who
           are partakers of this Holy Communion, may be
           fulfilled with thy grace and heavenly
           benediction. And although we be unworthy,
           through our manifold sins, to offer unto thee
           any sacrifice, yet we beseech thee to accept this
           our bounden duty and service, not weighing our
           merits, but pardoning our offences; through
           Jesus Christ our Lord, by whom, and with
           whom, in the unity of the Holy Ghost, all
           honour and glory be unto thee, O Father
           almighty, world without end. **Amen.**

All   **Almighty Lord, and everlasting God,**
           we offer and present unto thee ourselves,
           **   our souls and bodies,**
           to be a reasonable, holy, and living
           **   sacrifice unto thee:**
           humbly beseeching thee,
           that all we, who are partakers of this Holy
           **   Communion,**
           may be fulfilled with thy grace and heavenly
           **   benediction.**
           And although we be unworthy, through our
           **   manifold sins,**

to offer unto thee any sacrifice,
yet we beseech thee to accept this our bounden
   duty and service,
not weighing our merits, but pardoning our
   offences;
through Jesus Christ our Lord,
to whom, with thee and the Holy Ghost,
be all honour and glory, world without end.
Amen.

The Baptism of Children

NOTES

1 **The Administration of Baptism** Holy Baptism is normally administered by the parish priest in the course of public worship on Sunday; but it may be administered at other times, and he may delegate its administration to other lawful ministers. Where rubrics indicate that a passage is to be said by 'the priest', this must be understood to include any other minister authorized to administer Holy Baptism.

2 **The Answering of the Questions** When children who are old enough to respond are baptized, the parents and godparents answer the questions (sections 48 and 53), and at the discretion of the priest the children may also answer them.

3 **The Signing with the Cross** The signing with the cross may take place either at section 49 or at section 56. The sign of the cross may be made in oil blessed for this purpose.

4 **The Giving of a Candle** A lighted candle, which may be the paschal candle, may be made ready so that other candles may be lighted from it.

5 **The Use of the Candidate's Name** At the signing with the cross and the giving of a candle, the priest or other minister may address the candidate by name.

6 **The People's Responses** At the signing with the cross it is sufficient if the people join in and say their part (sections 49 and 56) once only, when all have been signed; and if a candle is given to those who have been baptized, it is sufficient if the people join in and say their part (section 57) once only, when all have received a candle.

7 **The Attendance of the People** This order of service should normally be used at Holy Communion or Morning or Evening Prayer. At other times representatives of the

regular congregation should attend the service, so that they may welcome the newly baptized (section 58) and be put in mind of their own baptism.

8 **Hymns** If occasion requires, hymns may be sung at points other than those which are indicated in this order.

9 **The Administration of the Water** A threefold administration of water (whether by dipping or pouring) is a very ancient practice of the Church, and is commended as testifying to the faith of the Trinity in which candidates are baptized. Nevertheless, a single administration is also lawful and valid.

10 **Alternative Readings** Section 45 may be omitted and either Matthew 28.16-20 or John 3.1-8 read in its place.

The Baptism of Children

THE DUTIES OF PARENTS AND GODPARENTS

42   The priest says

> Children who are too young to profess the
> Christian faith are baptized on the
> understanding that they are brought up as
> Christians within the family of the Church.
>
> As they grow up, they need the help and
> encouragement of that family, so that they learn
> to be faithful in public worship and private
> prayer, to live by trust in God, and come to
> confirmation.
>
> Parents and godparents, the *children* whom you
> have brought for baptism *depend* chiefly on you
> for the help and encouragement *they need*. Are
> you willing to give it to *them* by your prayers, by
> your example, and by your teaching?

Parents and godparents

I am willing.

43   And if the *child is* old enough to understand, the priest
speaks to *him* in these or similar words.

> *N*, when you are baptized, you become *a member*
> of a new family. God takes you for his own *child*,
> and all Christian people will be your brothers
> and sisters.

THE MINISTRY OF THE WORD

Sections 44, 45, and 46 may be omitted when Baptism is administered at Holy Communion or at Morning or Evening Prayer.

44 Priest   The Lord is loving to everyone;
   All   **and his mercy is over all his works.**

45 Priest

God is the creator of all things, and by the birth of children he gives to parents a share in the work and joy of creation. But we who are born of earthly parents need to be born again. For in the Gospel Jesus tells us that unless a man has been born again, he cannot see the Kingdom of God. And so God gives us the way to a second birth, a new creation and life in union with him.

Baptism is the sign and seal of this new birth. In St Matthew's Gospel we read of the risen Christ commanding his followers to make disciples of all nations and to baptize men everywhere; and in the Acts of the Apostles we read of St Peter preaching in these words: 'Repent and be baptized in the name of Jesus Christ for the forgiveness of sins; and you shall receive the gift of the Holy Spirit. For the promise is to you and your children and to all that are afar off, everyone whom the Lord calls to him.'

In obedience to this same command we ourselves were baptized and now bring *these children* to baptism.

46 Priest   We thank God therefore for our baptism to life in Christ, and we pray for *these children (N)* and say together
   All   **Heavenly Father, in your love**
   you have called us to know you,
   led us to trust you,
   and bound our life with yours.
   Surround *these children* **with your love;**
   protect *them* **from evil;**
   fill *them* **with your Holy Spirit;**

and receive *them* into the family of your Church;
that *they* may walk with us in the way of Christ
and grow in the knowledge of your love. Amen.

THE DECISION

47 The parents and godparents stand, and the priest says
to them

Those who bring children to be baptized must
affirm their allegiance to Christ and their
rejection of all that is evil.

It is your duty to bring up *these children* to fight
against evil and to follow Christ.

48 Therefore I ask these questions which you must
answer for yourselves and for *these children*.

Do you turn to Christ?
Answer **I turn to Christ.**

Do you repent of your sins?
Answer **I repent of my sins.**

Do you renounce evil?
Answer **I renounce evil.**

49 Either here or at section 56 the priest makes THE SIGN OF
THE CROSS on the forehead of each child, saying to each

I sign you with the cross, the sign of Christ.

After the signing of each or all, he says

Do not be ashamed to confess the faith of Christ
crucified.
All **Fight valiantly under the banner of Christ**
against sin, the world, and the devil,
and continue his faithful *soldiers* and *servants*
to the end of your *lives*.

50	Priest	May almighty God deliver you from the powers of darkness, and lead you in the light and obedience of Christ. **Amen.**

51 A HYMN or PSALM may be sung.

THE BAPTISM

52 The priest stands before the water of baptism and says

	Praise God who made heaven and earth,
All	**who keeps his promise for ever.**

Priest	Almighty God, whose Son Jesus Christ
	was baptized in the river Jordan:
	we thank you for the gift of water
	to cleanse us and revive us;
	we thank you that through the waters of the
	Red Sea, you led your people out of slavery
	to freedom in the promised land;
	we thank you that through the deep waters
	of death you brought your Son, and raised
	him to life in triumph.
	Bless this water, that your *servants* who *are*
	washed in it may be made one with Christ
	in his death and in his resurrection,
	to be cleansed and delivered from all sin.
	Send your Holy Spirit upon *them* to bring
	them to new birth in the family of your
	Church, and raise *them* with Christ to full
	and eternal life.
	For all might, majesty, authority, and power
	are yours, now and for ever. **Amen.**

53 The priest says to the parents and godparents

You have brought *these children* to baptism. You
must now declare before God and his Church

the Christian faith into which *they are* to be baptized, and in which you will help *them* to grow. You must answer for yourselves and for *these children*.

Do you believe and trust in God the Father, who made the world?

Answer **I believe and trust in him.**

Do you believe and trust in his Son Jesus Christ, who redeemed mankind?

Answer **I believe and trust in him.**

Do you believe and trust in his Holy Spirit, who gives life to the people of God?

Answer **I believe and trust in him.**

54 The priest turns to the congregation and says

This is the faith of the Church.

All **This is our faith.**
We believe and trust in one God,
Father, Son, and Holy Spirit.

55 The parents and godparents being present with each child, the priest baptizes *him*. He dips *him* in the water or pours water on *him*, addressing *him* by name.

N, I baptize you in the name of the Father, and of the Son, and of the Holy Spirit.

And each one of *his* sponsors answers

Amen.

56 The priest makes THE SIGN OF THE CROSS on the forehead of each child if he has not already done so. The appropriate words are printed at section 49.

57 The priest or other person may give to a parent or godparent
for each child A LIGHTED CANDLE, saying to each

> Receive this light.

And when a candle has been given to each one, he says

> This is to show that you have passed
> from darkness to light.
All **Shine as a light in the world**
to the glory of God the Father.

THE WELCOME

58 The priest and the congregation, representing the whole
Church, welcome the newly baptized.

Priest   God has received you by baptism into
his Church.
All   **We welcome you into the Lord's Family.**
We are members together of the body of Christ;
we are children of the same heavenly Father;
we are inheritors together of the kingdom
of God.
We welcome you.

THE PRAYERS

59 The prayers that follow are omitted when Baptism
is administered at Holy Communion; and may be
omitted when Baptism is administered at Morning or
Evening Prayer.

Priest   Lord God our Father, maker of heaven and
earth, we thank you that by your Holy Spirit
these children have been born again into new life,
adopted for your own, and received into the
fellowship of your Church:
grant that *they* may grow in the faith
into which *they have* been baptized,
that *they* may profess it for *themselves*

when *they come* to be confirmed,
and that all things belonging to the Spirit
may live and grow in *them*. **Amen.**

60 Priest Heavenly Father, we pray for the parents of *these children*; give them the spirit of wisdom and love, that their *homes* may reflect the joy of your eternal kingdom. **Amen.**

61 Priest Almighty God, we thank you for our fellowship in the household of faith with all those who have been baptized in your name. Keep us faithful to our baptism, and so make us ready for that day when the whole creation shall be made perfect in your Son, our Saviour Jesus Christ. **Amen.**

62 Priest Jesus taught us to call God our Father, and so in faith and trust we say

All   **Our Father in heaven,**   or   **Our Father, who art in heaven,**
hallowed be your name,   **hallowed be thy name;**
your kingdom come,   **thy kingdom come;**
your will be done,   **thy will be done;**
on earth as in heaven.   **on earth as it is in heaven.**
Give us today our daily bread.   **Give us this day our daily bread.**
Forgive us our sins   **And forgive us our trespasses,**
as we forgive those   **as we forgive those**
** who sin against us.**   ** who trespass against us.**
Lead us not into temptation   **And lead us not into temptation;**
but deliver us from evil.   **but deliver us from evil.**

For the kingdom, the power,   **For thine is the kingdom,**
** and the glory are yours**   ** the power, and the glory,**
now and for ever. Amen.   **for ever and ever. Amen.**

63 Priest The grace of our Lord Jesus Christ, and the love of God, and the fellowship of the Holy Spirit be with us all evermore. **Amen.**

The Baptism of Children at Holy Communion

Section numbers refer to Holy Communion Rite A, but the corresponding sections of Holy Communion Rite B may be used in place of these.

Order	Service	Section
Seasonal Sentence	Holy Communion	1
Preparation	Holy Communion	2-11
Ministry of the Word	Holy Communion	12-18
Duties of Parents and Godparents	Baptism	42, 43
(Ministry of the Word	Baptism	44-46 optional)
Decision	Baptism	47-51
Baptism	Baptism	52-57
The Welcome	Baptism	58

The service then follows the Holy Communion service from the Peace (section 30).

These special forms are used.

SENTENCE
For anyone who is in Christ, there is a new creation; the old order has gone, and a new order has already begun.
2 Corinthians 5.17

PROPER PREFACE
And now we give you thanks because through baptism we have been buried with Christ so that we may rise with him to the new life.

POSTCOMMUNION SENTENCE
Through faith you are all the children of God in union with Christ Jesus. Baptized into union with him, you have all put on Christ as a garment. *Galatians 3.26, 27*

The Baptism of Children at Morning or Evening Prayer

The service follows this order.

1   Morning or Evening Prayer, to the end of the second reading.

2   The Baptism of Children:
    The Duties of Parents and Godparents, sections 42, 43.
    The Ministry of the Word, sections 44-46 (optional).
    The Decision, sections 47-51.
    The Baptism, sections 52-57.
    The Welcome, section 58.
    The Prayers, sections 59-61 (optional).

3   Morning or Evening Prayer, from the canticle after the second reading to the end of the service.

4   At the end of the service the prayers in The Baptism of Children, sections 59-61, may be said.

When it is appropriate, the service of Morning Prayer or Evening Prayer may be abbreviated.

THE BOOK OF
COMMON PRAYER

THE ORDER FOR
MORNING PRAYER,
DAILY THROUGHOUT THE YEAR.

¶ *At the beginning of Morning Prayer the Minister shall read with a loud voice some one or more of these Sentences of the Scriptures that follow. And then he shall say that which is written after the said Sentences.*

WHEN the wicked man turneth away from his wickedness that he hath committed, and doeth that which is lawful and right, he shall save his soul alive. *Ezekiel* xviii. 27.

I acknowledge my transgressions, and my sin is ever before me. *Psalm* li. 3.

Hide thy face from my sins, and blot out all mine iniquities. *Psalm* li. 9.

The sacrifices of God are a broken spirit: a broken and a contrite heart, O God, thou wilt not despise. *Psalm* li. 17.

Rend your heart, and not your garments, and turn unto the Lord your God: for he is gracious and merciful, slow to anger, and of great kindness, and repenteth him of the evil. *Joel* ii. 13.

To the Lord our God belong mercies and forgivenesses, though we have rebelled against him: neither have we obeyed the voice of the Lord our God, to walk in his laws which he set before us. *Dan.* ix. 9, 10.

O Lord, correct me, but with judgement; not in thine anger, lest thou bring me to nothing.

Jer. x. 24. *Psalm* vi. 1.

Repent ye; for the Kingdom of heaven is at hand. St. Matthew iii. 2.

I will arise, and go to my father, and will say unto him, Father, I have sinned against heaven, and before thee, and am no more worthy to be called thy son. St. Luke xv. 18, 19.

Enter not into judgement with thy servant, O Lord; for in thy sight shall no man living be justified. Psalm cxliii. 2.

If we say that we have no sin, we deceive ourselves, and the truth is not in us: but, if we confess our sins, he is faithful and just to forgive us our sins, and to cleanse us from all unrighteousness. 1 St. John i. 8, 9.

DEARLY beloved brethren, the Scripture moveth us in sundry places to acknowledge and confess our manifold sins and wickedness; and that we should not dissemble nor cloke them before the face of Almighty God our heavenly Father; but confess them with an humble, lowly, penitent, and obedient heart; to the end that we may obtain forgiveness of the same, by his infinite goodness and mercy. And although we ought at all times humbly to acknowledge our sins before God; yet ought we most chiefly so to do, when we assemble and meet together to render thanks for the great benefits that we have received at his hands, to set forth his most worthy praise, to hear his most holy Word, and to ask those things which are requisite and necessary, as well for the body as the soul. Wherefore I pray and beseech you, as many as are here present, to accompany me with a pure heart, and humble voice, unto the throne of the heavenly grace, saying after me;

¶ *A general Confession to be said of the whole Congregation after the Minister, all kneeling.*

ALMIGHTY and most merciful Father; We have erred, and strayed from thy ways like lost sheep. We have followed too much the devices and desires of our own hearts. We have offended against thy holy laws. We have left undone those things which we ought to have done; And we have done those things which we ought not to have done; And there is no health in us. But thou, O Lord, have mercy upon us, miserable offenders. Spare thou them, O God, which confess their faults. Restore thou them that are penitent; According to thy promises declared unto mankind in Christ Jesu our Lord. And grant, O most merciful Father, for his sake; That we may hereafter live a godly, righteous, and sober life, To the glory of thy holy Name. Amen.

¶ *The Absolution, or Remission of sins, to be pronounced by the Priest alone, standing; the people still kneeling.*

ALMIGHTY God, the Father of our Lord Jesus Christ, who desireth not the death of a sinner, but rather that he may turn from his wickedness, and live; and hath given power, and commandment, to his Ministers, to declare and pronounce to his people, being penitent, the Absolution and Remission of their sins: He pardoneth and absolveth all them that truly repent, and unfeignedly believe his holy Gospel. Wherefore let us beseech him to grant us true repentance, and his holy Spirit, that those things may please him, which we do at this present; and that the rest of our life hereafter may be pure, and holy; so that at the last we may come to his eternal joy; through Jesus Christ our Lord.

¶ *The people shall answer here, and at the end of all other prayers,*
Amen.

¶ Then the Minister shall kneel, and say the Lord's Prayer with an audible voice; the people also kneeling, and repeating it with him, both here, and wheresoever else it is used in Divine Service.

OUR Father, which art in heaven, Hallowed be thy Name. Thy kingdom come. Thy will be done, in earth as it is in heaven. Give us this day our daily bread. And forgive us our trespasses, As we forgive them that trespass against us. And lead us not into temptation; But deliver us from evil: For thine is the kingdom, The power, and the glory, For ever and ever. Amen.

¶ Then likewise he shall say,

O Lord, open thou our lips.

Answer. And our mouth shall shew forth thy praise.

Priest. O God, make speed to save us.

Answer. O Lord, make haste to help us.

¶ Here all standing up, the Priest shall say,

Glory be to the Father, and to the Son : and to the Holy Ghost;

Answer. As it was in the beginning, is now, and ever shall be : world without end. Amen.

Priest. Praise ye the Lord.

Answer. The Lord's Name be praised.

¶ Then shall be said or sung this Psalm following: except on Easter-Day, upon which another Anthem is appointed; and on the Nineteenth day of every Month it is not to be read here, but in the ordinary Course of the Psalms.

VENITE, EXULTEMUS DOMINO.

Psalm xcv.

O COME, let us sing unto the Lord : let us heartily rejoice in the strength of our salvation.

Let us come before his presence with thanksgiving : and shew ourselves glad in him with Psalms.

For the Lord is a great God : and a great King above all gods.

In his hand are all the corners of the earth : and the strength of the hills is his also.

The sea is his, and he made it : and his hands prepared the dry land.

O come, let us worship, and fall down : and kneel before the Lord our Maker.

For he is the Lord our God : and we are the people of his pasture, and the sheep of his hand.

To day if ye will hear his voice, harden not your hearts : as in the provocation, and as in the day of temptation in the wilderness ;

When your fathers tempted me : proved me, and saw my works.

Forty years long was I grieved with this generation, and said : It is a people that do err in their hearts, for they have not known my ways.

Unto whom I sware in my wrath : that they should not enter into my rest.

Glory be to the Father, and to the Son : and to the Holy Ghost ;

As it was in the beginning, is now, and ever shall be : world without end. Amen.

¶ *Then shall follow the Psalms in order as they be appointed. And at the end of every Psalm throughout the Year, and likewise at the end of* Benedicite, Benedictus, Magnificat, *and* Nunc dimittis, *shall be repeated,*

Glory be to the Father, and to the Son : and to the Holy Ghost ;

Answer. As it was in the beginning, is now, and ever shall be : world without end. Amen.

¶ *Then shall be read distinctly with an audible voice the First Lesson, taken out of the Old Testament, as is appointed in the Calendar, except there be proper Lessons assigned for that day: He that readeth so standing and turning himself, as he may best be heard of all such as are present. And after that, shall be said or sung, in* English, *the Hymn called* Te Deum Laudamus, *daily throughout the Year.*

¶ Note, *That before every Lesson the Minister shall say,* Here beginneth such a Chapter, *or* Verse of such a Chapter, of such a Book: *And after every Lesson,* Here endeth the First, *or* the Second Lesson.

TE DEUM LAUDAMUS.

WE praise thee, O God : we acknowledge thee to be the Lord.

All the earth doth worship thee : the Father everlasting.

To thee all Angels cry aloud : the Heavens, and all the Powers therein.

To thee Cherubin, and Seraphin : continually do cry,

Holy, Holy, Holy : Lord God of Sabaoth ;

Heaven and earth are full of the Majesty : of thy Glory.

The glorious company of the Apostles : praise thee.

The goodly fellowship of the Prophets : praise thee.

The noble army of Martyrs : praise thee.

The holy Church throughout all the world : doth acknowledge thee ;

The Father : of an infinite Majesty ;

Thine honourable, true : and only Son ;

Also the Holy Ghost : the Comforter.

Thou art the King of Glory : O Christ.

Thou art the everlasting Son : of the Father.

When thou tookest upon thee to deliver man : thou didst not abhor the Virgin's womb.

When thou hadst overcome the sharpness of death : thou didst open the Kingdom of Heaven to all believers.

Thou sittest at the right hand of God : in the Glory of the Father.

We believe that thou shalt come : to be our Judge.

We therefore pray thee, help thy servants : whom thou hast redeemed with thy precious blood.

Make them to be numbered with thy Saints : in glory everlasting.

O Lord, save thy people : and bless thine heritage.

Govern them : and lift them up for ever.

Day by day : we magnify thee ;

And we worship thy Name : ever world without end.

Vouchsafe, O Lord : to keep us this day without sin.

O Lord, have mercy upon us : have mercy upon us.

O Lord, let thy mercy lighten upon us : as our trust is in thee.

O Lord, in thee have I trusted : let me never be confounded.

¶ *Or this Canticle,*

BENEDICITE, OMNIA OPERA.

O ALL ye Works of the Lord, bless ye the Lord : praise him, and magnify him for ever.

O ye Angels of the Lord, bless ye the Lord : praise him, and magnify him for ever.

O ye Heavens, bless ye the Lord : praise him, and magnify him for ever.

O ye Waters that be above the Firmament, bless ye the Lord : praise him, and magnify him for ever.

O all ye Powers of the Lord, bless ye the Lord : praise him, and magnify him for ever.

O ye Sun, and Moon, bless ye the Lord : praise him, and magnify him for ever.

O ye Stars of Heaven, bless ye the Lord : praise him, and magnify him for ever.

O ye Showers, and Dew, bless ye the Lord : praise him, and magnify him for ever.

O ye Winds of God, bless ye the Lord : praise him, and magnify him for ever.

O ye Fire and Heat, bless ye the Lord : praise him, and magnify him for ever.

O ye Winter and Summer, bless ye the Lord : praise him, and magnify him for ever.

O ye Dews, and Frosts, bless ye the Lord : praise him, and magnify him for ever.

O ye Frost and Cold, bless ye the Lord : praise him, and magnify him for ever.

O ye Ice and Snow, bless ye the Lord : praise him, and magnify him for ever.

O ye Nights, and Days, bless ye the Lord : praise him, and magnify him for ever.

O ye Light and Darkness, bless ye the Lord : praise him, and magnify him for ever.

O ye Lightnings, and Clouds, bless ye the Lord : praise him, and magnify him for ever.

O let the Earth bless the Lord : yea, let it praise him, and magnify him for ever.

O ye Mountains, and Hills, bless ye the Lord : praise him, and magnify him for ever.

O all ye Green Things upon the Earth, bless ye the Lord : praise him, and magnify him for ever.

O ye Wells, bless ye the Lord : praise him, and magnify him for ever.

O ye Seas, and Floods, bless ye the Lord : praise him, and magnify him for ever.

O ye Whales, and all that move in the Waters, bless ye the Lord : praise him, and magnify him for ever.

O all ye Fowls of the Air, bless ye the Lord : praise him, and magnify him for ever.

O all ye Beasts, and Cattle, bless ye the Lord : praise him, and magnify him for ever.

O ye Children of Men, bless ye the Lord : praise him, and magnify him for ever.

O let Israel bless the Lord : praise him, and magnify him for ever.

O ye Priests of the Lord, bless ye the Lord : praise him, and magnify him for ever.

O ye Servants of the Lord, bless ye the Lord : praise him, and magnify him for ever.

O ye Spirits and Souls of the Righteous, bless ye the Lord : praise him, and magnify him for ever.

O ye holy and humble Men of heart, bless ye the Lord : praise him, and magnify him for ever.

O Ananias, Azarias, and Misael, bless ye the Lord : praise him, and magnify him for ever.

Glory be to the Father, and to the Son : and to the Holy Ghost ;

As it was in the beginning, is now, and ever shall be : world without end.   Amen.

¶ *Then shall be read in like manner the Second Lesson, taken out of the New Testament. And after that, the Hymn following; except when that shall happen to be read in the Chapter for the Day, or for the Gospel on* St. John Baptist's *Day.*

BENEDICTUS.

St. Luke i. 68.

BLESSED be the Lord God of Israel : for he hath visited, and redeemed his people ;

And hath raised up a mighty salvation for us : in the house of his servant David ;

As he spake by the mouth of his holy Prophets : which have been since the world began ;

That we should be saved from our enemies : and from the hands of all that hate us ;

To perform the mercy promised to our forefathers : and to remember his holy Covenant ;

To perform the oath which he sware to our forefather Abraham : that he would give us ;

That we being delivered out of the hands of our enemies : might serve him without fear ;

In holiness and righteousness before him : all the days of our life.

And thou, child, shalt be called the Prophet of the Highest : for thou shalt go before the face of the Lord to prepare his ways ;

To give knowledge of salvation unto his people : for the remission of their sins,

Through the tender mercy of our God : whereby the day-spring from on high hath visited us ;

To give light to them that sit in darkness, and in the shadow of death : and to guide our feet into the way of peace.

Glory be to the Father, and to the Son : and to the Holy Ghost;

As it was in the beginning, is now, and ever shall be : world without end.   Amen.

¶ *Or this Psalm,*

JUBILATE DEO.

Psalm c.

O BE joyful in the Lord, all ye lands : serve the Lord with gladness, and come before his presence with a song.

Be ye sure that the Lord he is God : it is he that hath made us, and not we ourselves; we are his people, and the sheep of his pasture.

O go your way into his gates with thanksgiving, and into his courts with praise : be thankful unto him, and speak good of his Name.

For the Lord is gracious, his mercy is everlasting : and his truth endureth from generation to generation.

Glory be to the Father, and to the Son : and to the Holy Ghost;

As it was in the beginning, is now, and ever shall be : world without end.   Amen.

¶ *Then shall be sung or said the Apostles' Creed by the Minister and the people, standing: except only such days as the Creed of* St. Athanasius *is appointed to be read.*

I BELIEVE in God the Father Almighty, Maker of heaven and earth :

And in Jesus Christ his only Son our Lord, Who was conceived by the Holy Ghost, Born of the Virgin Mary, Suffered under Pontius Pilate, Was crucified, dead, and buried, He descended into hell;

The third day he rose again from the dead, He ascended into heaven, And sitteth on the right hand of God the Father Almighty; From thence he shall come to judge the quick and the dead.

I believe in the Holy Ghost; The holy Catholick Church; The Communion of Saints; The Forgiveness of sins; The Resurrection of the body; And the life everlasting. Amen.

¶ *And after that, these Prayers following, all devoutly kneeling; the Minister first pronouncing with a loud voice,*

The Lord be with you.
Answer. And with thy spirit.
Minister. Let us pray.
Lord, have mercy upon us.
Christ, have mercy upon us.
Lord, have mercy upon us.

¶ *Then the Minister, Clerks, and people, shall say the Lord's Prayer with a loud voice.*

OUR Father, which art in heaven, Hallowed be thy Name. Thy kingdom come. Thy will be done, in earth as it is in heaven. Give us this day our daily bread. And forgive us our trespasses, As we forgive them that trespass against us. And lead us not into temptation; But deliver us from evil. Amen.

¶ *Then the Priest standing up shall say,*

O Lord, shew thy mercy upon us.
Answer. And grant us thy salvation.
Priest. O Lord, save the Queen.
Answer. And mercifully hear us when we call upon thee.

Priest. Endue thy Ministers with righteousness.

Answer. And make thy chosen people joyful.

Priest. O Lord, save thy people.

Answer. And bless thine inheritance.

Priest. Give peace in our time, O Lord.

Answer. Because there is none other that fighteth for us, but only thou, O God.

Priest. O God, make clean our hearts within us.

Answer. And take not thy holy Spirit from us.

¶ *Then shall follow three Collects; the first of the Day, which shall be the same that is appointed at the Communion; the second for Peace; the third for Grace to live well. And the two last Collects shall never alter, but daily be said at Morning Prayer throughout all the Year, as followeth; all kneeling.*

THE SECOND COLLECT, FOR PEACE.

O GOD, who art the author of peace and lover of concord, in knowledge of whom standeth our eternal life, whose service is perfect freedom; Defend us thy humble servants in all assaults of our enemies; that we, surely trusting in thy defence, may not fear the power of any adversaries, through the might of Jesus Christ our Lord. *Amen.*

THE THIRD COLLECT, FOR GRACE.

O LORD, our heavenly Father, Almighty and everlasting God, who hast safely brought us to the beginning of this day; Defend us in the same with thy mighty power; and grant that this day we fall into no sin, neither run into any kind of danger; but that all our doings may be ordered by thy governance, to do always that is righteous in thy sight; through Jesus Christ our Lord. *Amen.*

¶ *In Quires and Places where they sing, here followeth the Anthem.*

¶ *Then these five Prayers following are to be read here, except when the Litany is read ; and then only the two last are to be read, as they are there placed.*

A PRAYER FOR THE QUEEN'S MAJESTY.

O LORD our heavenly Father, high and mighty, King of kings, Lord of lords, the only Ruler of princes, who dost from thy throne behold all the dwellers upon earth; Most heartily we beseech thee with thy favour to behold our most gracious Sovereign Lady, Queen *ELIZABETH*; and so replenish her with the grace of thy Holy Spirit, that she may alway incline to thy will, and walk in thy way: Endue her plenteously with heavenly gifts; grant her in health and wealth long to live; strengthen her that she may vanquish and overcome all her enemies; and finally, after this life, she may attain everlasting joy and felicity; through Jesus Christ our Lord. *Amen.*

A PRAYER FOR THE ROYAL FAMILY.

A L M I G H T Y God, the fountain of all goodness, we humbly beseech thee to bless *Elizabeth* the Queen Mother, *Philip* Duke of *Edinburgh*, the Prince and Princess of *Wales*, and all the Royal Family: Endue them with thy holy Spirit; enrich them with thy heavenly grace; prosper them with all happiness; and bring them to thine everlasting kingdom; through Jesus Christ our Lord. *Amen.*

A PRAYER FOR THE CLERGY AND PEOPLE.

A LMIGHTY and everlasting God, who alone workest great marvels; Send down upon our Bishops, and Curates, and all Congregations committed to their charge, the healthful Spirit of thy grace; and that they may truly please thee, pour upon them the continual dew of thy blessing. Grant this, O Lord, for the honour of our Advocate and Mediator, Jesus Christ. *Amen.*

A PRAYER OF ST. CHRYSOSTOM.

ALMIGHTY God, who hast given us grace at this time with one accord to make our common supplications unto thee; and dost promise, that when two or three are gathered together in thy Name thou wilt grant their requests: Fulfil now, O Lord, the desires and petitions of thy servants, as may be most expedient for them; granting us in this world knowledge of thy truth, and in the world to come life everlasting. *Amen.*

2 *Cor.* xiii.

THE grace of our Lord Jesus Christ, and the love of God, and the fellowship of the Holy Ghost, be with us all evermore. *Amen.*

Here endeth the Order of Morning Prayer throughout the Year.

167

THE ORDER FOR

EVENING PRAYER,

DAILY THROUGHOUT THE YEAR.

¶ *At the beginning of Evening Prayer the Minister shall read with
a loud voice some one or more of these Sentences of the Scriptures that
follow. And then he shall say that which is written after the said
Sentences.*

WHEN the wicked man turneth away from his
wickedness that he hath committed, and
doeth that which is lawful and right, he shall save
his soul alive.   Ezekiel xviii. 27.

I acknowledge my transgressions, and my sin is
ever before me.   Psalm li. 3.

Hide thy face from my sins, and blot out all mine
iniquities.   Psalm li. 9.

The sacrifices of God are a broken spirit: a
broken and a contrite heart, O God, thou wilt not
despise.   Psalm li. 17.

Rend your heart, and not your garments, and
turn unto the Lord your God: for he is gracious
and merciful, slow to anger, and of great kindness,
and repenteth him of the evil.   Joel ii. 13.

To the Lord our God belong mercies and forgivenesses, though we have rebelled against him: neither
have we obeyed the voice of the Lord our God, to
walk in his laws which he set before us.   Dan. ix. 9, 10.

O Lord, correct me, but with judgement; not in
thine anger, lest thou bring me to nothing.

                                          Jer. x. 24; Psalm vi. 1.

Repent ye; for the Kingdom of heaven is at hand. St. Matthew iii. 2.

I will arise, and go to my father, and will say unto him, Father, I have sinned against heaven, and before thee, and am no more worthy to be called thy son. St. Luke xv. 18, 19.

Enter not into judgement with thy servant, O Lord; for in thy sight shall no man living be justified. Psalm cxliii. 2.

If we say that we have no sin, we deceive ourselves, and the truth is not in us: but, if we confess our sins, he is faithful and just to forgive us our sins, and to cleanse us from all unrighteousness.
1 St. John i. 8, 9.

DEARLY beloved brethren, the Scripture moveth us in sundry places to acknowledge and confess our manifold sins and wickedness; and that we should not dissemble nor cloke them before the face of Almighty God our heavenly Father; but confess them with an humble, lowly, penitent, and obedient heart; to the end that we may obtain forgiveness of the same, by his infinite goodness and mercy. And although we ought at all times humbly to acknowledge our sins before God; yet ought we most chiefly so to do, when we assemble and meet together to render thanks for the great benefits that we have received at his hands, to set forth his most worthy praise, to hear his most holy Word, and to ask those things which are requisite and necessary, as well for the body as the soul. Wherefore I pray and beseech you, as many as are here present, to accompany me with a pure heart, and humble voice, unto the throne of the heavenly grace, saying after me;

¶ *A general Confession to be said of the whole Congregation after the Minister, all kneeling.*

ALMIGHTY and most merciful Father; We have erred, and strayed from thy ways like lost sheep. We have followed too much the devices and desires of our own hearts. We have offended against thy holy laws. We have left undone those things which we ought to have done; And we have done those things which we ought not to have done; And there is no health in us. But thou, O Lord, have mercy upon us, miserable offenders. Spare thou them, O God, which confess their faults. Restore thou them that are penitent; According to thy promises declared unto mankind in Christ Jesu our Lord. And grant, O most merciful Father, for his sake; That we may hereafter live a godly, righteous, and sober life, To the glory of thy holy Name. Amen.

¶ *The Absolution, or Remission of sins, to be pronounced by the Priest alone, standing; the people still kneeling.*

ALMIGHTY God, the Father of our Lord Jesus Christ, who desireth not the death of a sinner, but rather that he may turn from his wickedness, and live; and hath given power, and commandment, to his Ministers, to declare and pronounce to his people, being penitent, the Absolution and Remission of their sins: He pardoneth and absolveth all them that truly repent, and unfeignedly believe his holy Gospel. Wherefore let us beseech him to grant us true repentance, and his holy Spirit, that those things may please him, which we do at this present; and that the rest of our life hereafter may be pure, and holy; so that at the last we may come to his eternal joy; through Jesus Christ our Lord. *Amen.*

¶ *Then the Minister shall kneel, and say the Lord's Prayer; the people also kneeling, and repeating it with him.*

OUR Father, which art in heaven, Hallowed be thy Name. Thy kingdom come. Thy will be done, in earth as it is in heaven. Give us this day our daily bread. And forgive us our trespasses, As we forgive them that trespass against us. And lead us not into temptation; But deliver us from evil: For thine is the kingdom, The power, and the glory, For ever and ever. Amen.

¶ *Then likewise he shall say,*

O Lord, open thou our lips.

Answer. And our mouth shall shew forth thy praise.

Priest. O God, make speed to save us.

Answer. O Lord, make haste to help us.

¶ *Here all standing up, the Priest shall say,*

Glory be to the Father, and to the Son: and to the Holy Ghost;

Answer. As it was in the beginning, is now, and ever shall be: world without end. Amen.

Priest. Praise ye the Lord.

Answer. The Lord's Name be praised.

¶ *Then shall be said or sung the Psalms in order as they be appointed. Then a Lesson of the Old Testament, as is appointed. And after that,* Magnificat *(or the Song of the blessed Virgin* Mary*) in English, as followeth.*

MAGNIFICAT.

St. Luke i.

MY soul doth magnify the Lord : and my spirit hath rejoiced in God my Saviour.

For he hath regarded : the lowliness of his hand-maiden.

For behold, from henceforth : all generations shall call me blessed.

For he that is mighty hath magnified me : and holy is his Name.

And his mercy is on them that fear him : throughout all generations.

He hath shewed strength with his arm : he hath scattered the proud in the imagination of their hearts.

He hath put down the mighty from their seat : and hath exalted the humble and meek.

He hath filled the hungry with good things : and the rich he hath sent empty away.

He remembering his mercy hath holpen his servant Israel : as he promised to our forefathers, Abraham and his seed, for ever.

Glory be to the Father, and to the Son : and to the Holy Ghost;

As it was in the beginning, is now, and ever shall be : world without end. Amen.

¶ *Or else this Psalm; except it be on the Nineteenth Day of the Month, when it is read in the ordinary Course of the Psalms.*

CANTATE DOMINO.

Psalm xcviii.

O SING unto the Lord a new song : for he hath done marvellous things.

With his own right hand, and with his holy arm : hath he gotten himself the victory.

The Lord declared his salvation : his righteousness hath he openly shewed in the sight of the heathen.

He hath remembered his mercy and truth toward

the house of Israel : and all the ends of the world have seen the salvation of our God.

Shew yourselves joyful unto the Lord, all ye lands : sing, rejoice, and give thanks.

Praise the Lord upon the harp : sing to the harp with a psalm of thanksgiving.

With trumpets also and shawms : O shew yourselves joyful before the Lord the King.

Let the sea make a noise, and all that therein is : the round world, and they that dwell therein.

Let the floods clap their hands, and let the hills be joyful together before the Lord : for he cometh to judge the earth.

With righteousness shall he judge the world : and the people with equity.

Glory be to the Father, and to the Son : and to the Holy Ghost ;

As it was in the beginning, is now, and ever shall be : world without end. Amen.

¶ *Then a Lesson of the New Testament, as it is appointed. And after that, Nunc dimittis (or the Song of Simeon) in English, as followeth.*

NUNC DIMITTIS.

St. Luke ii. 29.

LORD, now lettest thou thy servant depart in peace : according to thy word.

For mine eyes have seen : thy salvation,

Which thou hast prepared : before the face of all people ;

To be a light to lighten the Gentiles : and to be the glory of thy people Israel.

Glory be to the Father, and to the Son : and to the Holy Ghost ;

As it was in the beginning, is now, and ever shall be : world without end. Amen.

¶ *Or else this Psalm; except it be on the Twelfth Day of the Month.*

DEUS MISEREATUR.

Psalm lxvii.

GOD be merciful unto us, and bless us : and shew us the light of his countenance, and be merciful unto us :

That thy way may be known upon earth : thy saving health among all nations.

Let the people praise thee, O God : yea, let all the people praise thee.

O let the nations rejoice and be glad : for thou shalt judge the folk righteously, and govern the nations upon earth.

Let the people praise thee, O God : yea, let all the people praise thee.

Then shall the earth bring forth her increase : and God, even our own God, shall give us his blessing.

God shall bless us : and all the ends of the world shall fear him.

Glory be to the Father, and to the Son : and to the Holy Ghost ;

As it was in the beginning, is now, and ever shall be : world without end.   Amen.

¶ *Then shall be said or sung the Apostles' Creed by the Minister and the people, standing.*

I BELIEVE in God the Father Almighty, Maker of heaven and earth :

And in Jesus Christ his only Son our Lord, Who was conceived by the Holy Ghost, Born of the Virgin Mary, Suffered under Pontius Pilate, Was crucified, dead, and buried, He descended into hell ;

The third day he rose again from the dead, He ascended into heaven, And sitteth on the right hand of God the Father Almighty; From thence he shall come to judge the quick and the dead.

I believe in the Holy Ghost; The holy Catholick Church; The Communion of Saints; The Forgiveness of sins; The Resurrection of the body, And the life everlasting. Amen.

¶ *And after that, these Prayers following, all devoutly kneeling; the Minister first pronouncing with a loud voice,*

> The Lord be with you.
> *Answer.* And with thy spirit.
> *Minister.* Let us pray.
> Lord, have mercy upon us.
> *Christ, have mercy upon us.*
> Lord, have mercy upon us.

¶ *Then the Minister, Clerks, and people, shall say the Lord's Prayer with a loud voice.*

OUR Father, which art in heaven, Hallowed be thy Name. Thy kingdom come. Thy will be done, in earth as it is in heaven. Give us this day our daily bread. And forgive us our trespasses, As we forgive them that trespass against us. And lead us not into temptation; But deliver us from evil. Amen.

¶ *Then the Priest standing up shall say,*

O Lord, shew thy mercy upon us.
Answer. And grant us thy salvation.
Priest. O Lord, save the Queen.
Answer. And mercifully hear us when we call upon thee.

Priest. Endue thy Ministers with righteousness.

Answer. And make thy chosen people joyful.

Priest. O Lord, save thy people.

Answer. And bless thine inheritance.

Priest. Give peace in our time, O Lord.

Answer. Because there is none other that fighteth for us, but only thou, O God.

Priest. O God, make clean our hearts within us.

Answer. And take not thy holy Spirit from us.

¶ *Then shall follow three Collects; the first of the Day; the second for Peace; the third for Aid against all Perils, as hereafter followeth: which two last Collects shall be daily said at Evening Prayer without alteration.*

THE SECOND COLLECT AT EVENING PRAYER.

O GOD, from whom all holy desires, all good counsels, and all just works do proceed; Give unto thy servants that peace which the world cannot give; that both our hearts may be set to obey thy commandments, and also that by thee we being defended from the fear of our enemies may pass our time in rest and quietness; through the merits of Jesus Christ our Saviour. *Amen.*

THE THIRD COLLECT, FOR AID AGAINST ALL PERILS.

L IGHTEN our darkness, we beseech thee, O Lord; and by thy great mercy defend us from all perils and dangers of this night; for the love of thy only Son, our Saviour, Jesus Christ. *Amen.*

¶ *In Quires and Places where they sing, here followeth the Anthem.*

A PRAYER FOR THE QUEEN'S MAJESTY.

O LORD our heavenly Father, high and mighty, King of kings, Lord of lords, the only Ruler of princes, who dost from thy throne behold all the dwellers upon earth; Most heartily we beseech thee with thy favour to behold our most gracious Sovereign Lady, Queen *ELIZABETH*; and so replenish her with the grace of thy Holy Spirit, that she may alway incline to thy will, and walk in thy way: Endue her plenteously with heavenly gifts; grant her in health and wealth long to live; strengthen her that she may vanquish and overcome all her enemies; and finally, after this life, she may attain everlasting joy and felicity; through Jesus Christ our Lord. *Amen.*

A PRAYER FOR THE ROYAL FAMILY.

A LMIGHTY God, the fountain of all goodness, we humbly beseech thee to bless *Elizabeth* the Queen Mother, *Philip* Duke of *Edinburgh*, the Prince and Princess of *Wales*, and all the Royal Family: Endue them with thy holy Spirit; enrich them with thy heavenly grace; prosper them with all happiness; and bring them to thine everlasting kingdom; through Jesus Christ our Lord. *Amen.*

A PRAYER FOR THE CLERGY AND PEOPLE.

A LMIGHTY and everlasting God, who alone workest great marvels; Send down upon our Bishops, and Curates, and all Congregations committed to their charge, the healthful Spirit of thy grace; and that they may truly please thee, pour upon them the continual dew of thy blessing. Grant this, O Lord, for the honour of our Advocate and Mediator, Jesus Christ. *Amen.*

A PRAYER OF ST. CHRYSOSTOM.

ALMIGHTY God, who hast given us grace at this time with one accord to make our common supplications unto thee; and dost promise, that when two or three are gathered together in thy Name thou wilt grant their requests: Fulfil now, O Lord, the desires and petitions of thy servants, as may be most expedient for them; granting us in this world knowledge of thy truth, and in the world to come life everlasting. *Amen.*

2 *Cor.* xiii.

THE grace of our Lord Jesus Christ, and the love of God, and the fellowship of the Holy Ghost, be with us all evermore. *Amen.*

Here endeth the Order of Evening Prayer throughout the Year.

AT MORNING PRAYER.

¶ *Upon these Feasts;* Christmas-day, *the* Epiphany, *Saint* Matthias, Easter-day, Ascension-day, Whitsunday, *Saint* John Baptist, *Saint* James, *Saint* Bartholomew, *Saint* Matthew, *Saint* Simon *and Saint* Jude, *Saint* Andrew, *and upon* Trinity-Sunday, *shall be sung or said at* Morning Prayer, *instead of the Apostles' Creed, this Confession of our Christian Faith, commonly called The Creed of Saint Athanasius, by the Minister and people standing.*

QUICUNQUE VULT

WHOSOEVER will be saved : before all things it is necessary that he hold the Catholick Faith.

Which Faith except every one do keep whole and undefiled : without doubt he shall perish everlastingly.

And the Catholick Faith is this : That we worship one God in Trinity, and Trinity in Unity ;

Neither confounding the Persons : nor dividing the Substance.

For there is one Person of the Father, another of the Son : and another of the Holy Ghost.

But the Godhead of the Father, of the Son, and of the Holy Ghost, is all one : the Glory equal, the Majesty co-eternal.

Such as the Father is, such is the Son : and such is the Holy Ghost.

The Father uncreate, the Son uncreate : and the Holy Ghost uncreate.

The Father incomprehensible, the Son incomprehensible : and the Holy Ghost incomprehensible.

The Father eternal, the Son eternal : and the Holy Ghost eternal.

And yet they are not three eternals : but one eternal.

179

As also there are not three incomprehensibles, nor three uncreated : but one uncreated, and one incomprehensible.

So likewise the Father is Almighty, the Son Almighty : and the Holy Ghost Almighty.

And yet they are not three Almighties : but one Almighty.

So the Father is God, the Son is God : and the Holy Ghost is God.

And yet they are not three Gods : but one God.

So likewise the Father is Lord, the Son Lord : and the Holy Ghost Lord.

And yet not three Lords : but one Lord.

For like as we are compelled by the Christian verity : to acknowledge every Person by himself to be God and Lord ;

So are we forbidden by the Catholick Religion : to say, There be three Gods, or three Lords.

The Father is made of none : neither created, nor begotten.

The Son is of the Father alone : not made, nor created, but begotten.

The Holy Ghost is of the Father and of the Son : neither made, nor created, nor begotten, but proceeding.

So there is one Father, not three Fathers; one Son, not three Sons : one Holy Ghost, not three Holy Ghosts.

And in this Trinity none is afore, or after other : none is greater, or less than another ;

But the whole three Persons are co-eternal together : and co-equal.

So that in all things, as is aforesaid : the Unity in Trinity, and the Trinity in Unity is to be worshipped.

He therefore that will be saved : must thus think of the Trinity.

Furthermore, it is necessary to everlasting salvation : that he also believe rightly the Incarnation of our Lord Jesus Christ.

For the right Faith is, that we believe and confess : that our Lord Jesus Christ, the Son of God, is God and Man ;

God, of the Substance of the Father, begotten before the worlds : and Man, of the Substance of his Mother, born in the world ;

Perfect God, and perfect Man : of a reasonable soul and human flesh subsisting ;

Equal to the Father, as touching his Godhead : and inferior to the Father, as touching his Manhood.

Who although he be God and Man : yet he is not two, but one Christ ;

One ; not by conversion of the Godhead into flesh : but by taking of the Manhood into God ;

One altogether ; not by confusion of Substance : but by unity of Person.

For as the reasonable soul and flesh is one man : so God and Man is one Christ ;

Who suffered for our salvation : descended into hell, rose again the third day from the dead.

He ascended into heaven, he sitteth on the right hand of the Father, God Almighty : from whence he shall come to judge the quick and the dead.

At whose coming all men shall rise again with their bodies : and shall give account for their own works.

And they that have done good shall go into life everlasting : and they that have done evil into everlasting fire.

This is the Catholick Faith : which except a man believe faithfully, he cannot be saved.

Glory be to the Father, and to the Son : and to the Holy Ghost ;

As it was in the beginning, is now, and ever shall be : world without end. Amen.

THE LITANY.

¶ *Here followeth the LITANY, or General Supplication, to be sung or said after Morning Prayer upon* Sundays, Wednesdays, *and* Fridays, *and at other times when it shall be commanded by the Ordinary.*

O GOD the Father of heaven : have mercy upon us miserable sinners.

O God the Father of heaven : have mercy upon us miserable sinners.

O God the Son, Redeemer of the world : have mercy upon us miserable sinners.

O God the Son, Redeemer of the world : have mercy upon us miserable sinners.

O God the Holy Ghost, proceeding from the Father and the Son : have mercy upon us miserable sinners.

O God the Holy Ghost, proceeding from the Father and the Son : have mercy upon us miserable sinners.

O holy, blessed, and glorious Trinity, three Persons and one God : have mercy upon us miserable sinners.

O holy, blessed, and glorious Trinity, three Persons and one God : have mercy upon us miserable sinners.

Remember not, Lord, our offences, nor the offences of our forefathers; neither take thou vengeance of our sins : spare us, good Lord, spare thy people, whom thou hast redeemed with thy most precious blood, and be not angry with us for ever.

Spare us, good Lord.

From all evil and mischief; from sin, from the crafts and assaults of the devil; from thy wrath, and from everlasting damnation,

Good Lord, deliver us.

From all blindness of heart; from pride, vainglory, and hypocrisy; from envy, hatred, and malice, and all uncharitableness,

Good Lord, deliver us.

From fornication, and all other deadly sin; and from all the deceits of the world, the flesh, and the devil,

Good Lord, deliver us.

From lightning and tempest; from plague, pestilence, and famine; from battle and murder, and from sudden death,

Good Lord, deliver us.

From all sedition, privy conspiracy, and rebellion; from all false doctrine, heresy, and schism; from hardness of heart, and contempt of thy Word and Commandment,

Good Lord, deliver us.

By the mystery of thy holy Incarnation; by thy holy Nativity and Circumcision; by thy Baptism, Fasting, and Temptation,

Good Lord, deliver us.

By thine Agony and bloody Sweat; by thy Cross

and Passion; by thy precious Death and Burial; by thy glorious Resurrection and Ascension; and by the coming of the Holy Ghost,

Good Lord, deliver us.

In all time of our tribulation; in all time of our wealth; in the hour of death and in the day of judgement,

Good Lord, deliver us.

We sinners do beseech thee to hear us, O Lord God; and that it may please thee to rule and govern thy holy Church universal in the right way;

We beseech thee to hear us, good Lord.

That it may please thee to keep and strengthen in the true worshipping of thee, in righteousness and holiness of life, thy Servant *ELIZABETH*, our most gracious Queen and Governor;

We beseech thee to hear us, good Lord.

That it may please thee to rule her heart in thy faith, fear, and love, and that she may evermore have affiance in thee, and ever seek thy honour and glory;

We beseech thee to hear us, good Lord.

That it may please thee to be her defender and keeper, giving her the victory over all her enemies;

We beseech thee to hear us, good Lord.

That it may please thee to bless and preserve *Elizabeth* the Queen Mother, *Philip* Duke of *Edinburgh*, the Prince and Princess of *Wales*, and all the Royal Family;

We beseech thee to hear us, good Lord.

That it may please thee to illuminate all Bishops, Priests, and Deacons, with true knowledge and understanding of thy Word; and that both by their preaching and living they may set it forth, and shew it accordingly;

We beseech thee to hear us, good Lord.

That it may please thee to endue the Lords of the Council, and all the Nobility, with grace, wisdom, and understanding;

We beseech thee to hear us, good Lord.

That it may please thee to bless and keep the Magistrates, giving them grace to execute justice, and to maintain truth;

We beseech thee to hear us, good Lord.

That it may please thee to bless and keep all thy people;

We beseech thee to hear us, good Lord.

That it may please thee to give to all nations unity, peace, and concord;

We beseech thee to hear us, good Lord.

That it may please thee to give us an heart to love and dread thee, and diligently to live after thy commandments;

We beseech thee to hear us, good Lord.

That it may please thee to give to all thy people increase of grace to hear meekly thy Word, and to receive it with pure affection, and to bring forth the fruits of the Spirit;

We beseech thee to hear us, good Lord.

That it may please thee to bring into the way of truth all such as have erred, and are deceived;

We beseech thee to hear us, good Lord.

That it may please thee to strengthen such as do stand; and to comfort and help the weak-hearted;

and to raise up them that fall; and finally to beat down Satan under our feet;

We beseech thee to hear us, good Lord.

That it may please thee to succour, help, and comfort, all that are in danger, necessity, and tribulation;

We beseech thee to hear us, good Lord.

That it may please thee to preserve all that travel by land or by water, all women labouring of child, all sick persons, and young children; and to shew thy pity upon all prisoners and captives;

We beseech thee to hear us, good Lord.

That it may please thee to defend, and provide for, the fatherless children, and widows, and all that are desolate and oppressed;

We beseech thee to hear us, good Lord.

That it may please thee to have mercy upon all men;

We beseech thee to hear us, good Lord.

That it may please thee to forgive our enemies, persecutors, and slanderers, and to turn their hearts;

We beseech thee to hear us, good Lord.

That it may please thee to give and preserve to our use the kindly fruits of the earth, so as in due time we may enjoy them;

We beseech thee to hear us, good Lord.

That it may please thee to give us true repentance; to forgive us all our sins, negligences, and ignorances; and to endue us with the grace of thy Holy Spirit to amend our lives according to thy holy Word;

We beseech thee to hear us, good Lord.

Son of God : we beseech thee to hear us.

Son of God : we beseech thee to hear us.

O Lamb of God : that takest away the sins of the world ;

Grant us thy peace.

O Lamb of God : that takest away the sins of the world ;

Have mercy upon us.

O Christ, hear us.

O Christ, hear us.

Lord, have mercy upon us.

Lord, have mercy upon us.

Christ, have mercy upon us.

Christ, have mercy upon us.

Lord, have mercy upon us.

Lord, have mercy upon us.

¶ *Then shall the Priest, and the people with him, say the Lord's Prayer.*

OUR Father, which art in heaven, Hallowed be thy Name. Thy kingdom come. Thy will be done, in earth as it is in heaven. Give us this day our daily bread. And forgive us our trespasses, As we forgive them that trespass against us. And lead us not into temptation ; But deliver us from evil. Amen.

Priest. O Lord, deal not with us after our sins.

Answer. Neither reward us after our iniquities.

Let us pray.

O GOD, merciful Father, that despisest not the sighing of a contrite heart, nor the desire of such as be sorrowful ; Mercifully assist our prayers that we make before thee in all our troubles and adversities, whensoever they oppress us; and graciously hear us, that those evils, which the craft and subtilty of the devil or man worketh against us, be brought to nought; and by the providence of thy goodness they may be dispersed; that we thy servants, being hurt by no persecutions, may evermore give thanks unto thee in thy holy Church; through Jesus Christ our Lord.

O Lord, arise, help us, and deliver us for thy Name's sake.

O GOD, we have heard with our ears, and our fathers have declared unto us, the noble works that thou didst in their days, and in the old time before them.

O Lord, arise, help us, and deliver us for thine honour.

Glory be to the Father, and to the Son : and to the Holy Ghost;

Answer. As it was in the beginning, is now, and ever shall be : world without end. Amen.

From our enemies defend us, O Christ.
Graciously look upon our afflictions.
Pitifully behold the sorrows of our hearts.
Mercifully forgive the sins of thy people.
Favourably with mercy hear our prayers.
O Son of David, have mercy upon us.
Both now and ever vouchsafe to hear us, O Christ.
Graciously hear us, O Christ; graciously hear us, O Lord Christ.

Priest. O Lord, let thy mercy be shewed upon us;
Answer. As we do put our trust in thee.

Let us pray.

WE humbly beseech thee, O Father, mercifully to look upon our infirmities; and for the glory of thy Name turn from us all those evils that we most righteously have deserved; and grant, that in all our troubles we may put our whole trust and confidence in thy mercy, and evermore serve thee in holiness and pureness of living, to thy honour and glory; through our only Mediator and Advocate, Jesus Christ our Lord. *Amen.*

A PRAYER OF ST. CHRYSOSTOM.

ALMIGHTY God, who hast given us grace at this time with one accord to make our common supplications unto thee; and dost promise, that when two or three are gathered together in thy Name thou wilt grant their requests: Fulfil now, O Lord, the desires and petitions of thy servants, as may be most expedient for them; granting us in this world knowledge of thy truth, and in the world to come life everlasting. *Amen.*

2 *Cor.* xiii.

THE grace of our Lord Jesus Christ, and the love of God, and the fellowship of the Holy Ghost, be with us all evermore. *Amen.*

Here endeth the LITANY.

PRAYERS AND THANKSGIVINGS,

UPON SEVERAL OCCASIONS,

¶ *To be used before the two final Prayers of the Litany, or of Morning and Evening Prayer.*

PRAYERS.

For Rain.

O GOD, heavenly Father, who by thy Son Jesus Christ hast promised to all them that seek thy kingdom, and the righteousness thereof, all things necessary to their bodily sustenance; Send us, we beseech thee, in this our necessity, such moderate rain and showers, that we may receive the fruits of the earth to our comfort, and to thy honour; through Jesus Christ our Lord. *Amen.*

For fair Weather.

O ALMIGHTY Lord God, who for the sin of man didst once drown all the world, except eight persons, and afterward of thy great mercy didst promise never to destroy it so again; We humbly beseech thee, that although we for our iniquities have worthily deserved a plague of rain and waters, yet upon our true repentance thou wilt send us such weather, as that we may receive the fruits of the earth in due season; and learn both by thy punishment to amend our lives, and for thy clemency to give thee praise and glory; through Jesus Christ our Lord. *Amen.*

In the time of Dearth and Famine.

O GOD, heavenly Father, whose gift it is, that the rain doth fall, the earth is fruitful, beasts increase, and fishes do multiply; Behold, we beseech thee, the afflictions of thy people; and grant that the scarcity and dearth, which we do now most justly suffer for our iniquity, may through thy goodness be mercifully turned into cheapness and plenty; for the love of Jesus Christ our Lord, to whom with thee and the Holy Ghost be all honour and glory, now and for ever. *Amen.*

Or this.

O GOD, merciful Father, who, in the time of Elisha the prophet, didst suddenly in Samaria turn great scarcity and dearth into plenty and cheapness; Have mercy upon us, that we, who are now for our sins punished with like adversity, may likewise find a seasonable relief: Increase the fruits of the earth by thy heavenly benediction; and grant that we, receiving thy bountiful liberality, may use the same to thy glory, the relief of those that are needy, and our own comfort; through Jesus Christ our Lord. *Amen.*

In the time of War and Tumults.

O ALMIGHTY God, King of all kings, and Governor of all things, whose power no creature is able to resist, to whom it belongeth justly to punish sinners, and to be merciful to them that truly repent; Save and deliver us, we humbly beseech thee, from the hands of our enemies; abate their pride, asswage their malice, and confound

191

their devices; that we, being armed with thy defence, may be preserved evermore from all perils, to glorify thee, who art the only giver of all victory; through the merits of thy only Son, Jesus Christ our Lord. *Amen.*

In the time of any common Plague or Sickness.

O ALMIGHTY God, who in thy wrath didst send a plague upon thine own people in the wilderness, for their obstinate rebellion against Moses and Aaron; and also, in the time of king David, didst slay with the plague of Pestilence threescore and ten thousand, and yet remembering thy mercy didst save the rest; Have pity upon us miserable sinners, who now are visited with great sickness and mortality; that like as thou didst then accept of an atonement, and didst command the destroying Angel to cease from punishing, so it may now please thee to withdraw from us this plague and grievous sickness; through Jesus Christ our Lord. *Amen.*

¶ *In the Ember Weeks, to be said every day, for those that are to be admitted into Holy Orders.*

A LMIGHTY God, our heavenly Father, who hast purchased to thyself an universal Church by the precious blood of thy dear Son; Mercifully look upon the same, and at this time so guide and govern the minds of thy servants the Bishops and Pastors of thy flock, that they may lay hands suddenly on no man, but faithfully and wisely make choice of fit persons to serve in the sacred Ministry of thy Church. And to those which shall be ordained to any holy function give thy grace and heavenly benediction; that both by their life and doctrine they may set forth thy glory, and set forward the salvation of all men; through Jesus Christ our Lord. *Amen.*

Or this.

ALMIGHTY God, the giver of all good gifts, who of thy divine providence hast appointed divers Orders in thy Church; Give thy grace, we humbly beseech thee, to all those who are to be called to any office and administration in the same; and so replenish them with the truth of thy doctrine, and endue them with innocency of life, that they may faithfully serve before thee, to the glory of thy great Name, and the benefit of thy holy Church; through Jesus Christ our Lord. *Amen.*

¶ *A Prayer that may be said after any of the former.*

O GOD, whose nature and property is ever to have mercy and to forgive, receive our humble petitions; and though we be tied and bound with the chain of our sins, yet let the pitifulness of thy great mercy loose us; for the honour of Jesus Christ, our Mediator and Advocate. *Amen.*

¶ *A Prayer for the High Court of Parliament, to be read during their Session.*

MOST gracious God, we humbly beseech thee, as for this Kingdom in general, so especially for the High Court of Parliament, under our most religious and gracious Queen at this time assembled: That thou wouldest be pleased to direct and prosper all their consultations to the advancement of thy glory. the good of thy Church, the safety, honour, and welfare of our Sovereign, and her Dominions; that all things may be so ordered and settled by their endeavours, upon the best and surest foundations, that peace and happiness, truth and justice, religion and piety, may be established among us for all generations. These and all other necessaries, for them, for us, and thy whole Church, we humbly beg in the Name and Mediation of Jesus Christ our most blessed Lord and Saviour. *Amen.*

¶ *A Collect or Prayer for all Conditions of men, to be used at such times when the Litany is not appointed to be said.*

O GOD, the Creator and Preserver of all mankind, we humbly beseech thee for all sorts and conditions of men; that thou wouldest be pleased to make thy ways known unto them, thy saving health unto all nations. More especially, we pray for the good estate of the Catholick Church; that it may be so guided and governed by thy good Spirit, that all who profess and call themselves Christians may be led into the way of truth, and hold the faith in unity of spirit, in the bond of peace, and in righteousness of life. Finally, we commend to thy fatherly goodness all those, who are any ways afflicted, or distressed, in mind, body, or estate; [*especially those for whom our prayers are desired,*] that it may please thee to comfort and relieve them, according to their several necessities, giving them patience under their sufferings, and a happy issue out of all their afflictions. And this we beg for Jesus Christ his sake. *Amen.*

* This to be said when any desire the Prayers of the Congregation.

THANKSGIVINGS.

¶ *A General Thanksgiving.*

ALMIGHTY God, Father of all mercies, we thine unworthy servants do give thee most humble and hearty thanks for all thy goodness and loving-kindness to us, and to all men; [*particularly to those who desire now to offer up their praises and thanksgivings for thy late mercies vouchsafed unto them.] We bless thee for our creation, preservation, and all the blessings of this life; but above all, for thine inestimable love in the redemption of the world by our Lord Jesus Christ; for the means of grace, and for the hope of glory. And, we beseech thee, give us that due sense of all thy mercies, that our hearts may be unfeignedly thankful, and that we shew forth thy praise, not only with our lips, but in our lives; by giving up ourselves to thy service, and by walking before thee in holiness and righteousness all our days; through Jesus Christ our Lord, to whom with thee and the Holy Ghost be all honour and glory, world without end. *Amen.*

* This to be said when any that have been prayed for desire to return praise.

For Rain.

O GOD our heavenly Father, who by thy gracious providence dost cause the former and the latter rain to descend upon the earth, that it may bring forth fruit for the use of man; We give thee humble thanks that it hath pleased thee, in our great necessity, to send us at the last a joyful rain upon thine inheritance, and to refresh it when it was dry, to the great comfort of us thy unworthy servants, and to the glory of thy holy Name; through thy mercies in Jesus Christ our Lord. *Amen.*

For fair Weather.

O LORD God, who hast justly humbled us by thy late plague of immoderate rain and waters, and in thy mercy hast relieved and comforted our souls by this seasonable and blessed change of weather; We praise and glorify thy holy Name for this thy mercy, and will always declare thy loving-kindness from generation to generation; through Jesus Christ our Lord. *Amen.*

For Plenty.

O MOST merciful Father, who of thy gracious goodness hast heard the devout prayers of thy Church, and turned our dearth and scarcity into cheapness and plenty; We give thee humble thanks for this thy special bounty; beseeching thee to continue thy loving-kindness unto us, that our land may yield us her fruits of increase, to thy glory and our comfort; through Jesus Christ our Lord. *Amen.*

For Peace and Deliverance from our Enemies.

O ALMIGHTY God, who art a strong tower of defence unto thy servants against the face of their enemies; We yield thee praise and thanksgiving for our deliverance from those great and apparent dangers wherewith we were compassed: We acknowledge it thy goodness that we were not delivered over as a prey unto them; beseeching thee still to continue such thy mercies towards us, that all the world may know that thou art our Saviour and mighty Deliverer; through Jesus Christ our Lord. *Amen.*

For restoring Publick Peace at Home.

O ETERNAL God, our heavenly Father, who alone makest men to be of one mind in a house, and stillest the outrage of a violent and unruly people; We bless thy holy Name, that it hath pleased thee to appease the seditious tumults which have been lately raised up amongst us; most humbly beseeching thee to grant to all of us grace, that we may henceforth obediently walk in thy holy commandments; and, leading a quiet and peaceable life in all godliness and honesty, may continually offer unto thee our sacrifice of praise and thanksgiving for these thy mercies towards us; through Jesus Christ our Lord. *Amen.*

For Deliverance from the Plague, or other common Sickness.

O LORD God, who hast wounded us for our sins, and consumed us for our transgressions, by thy late heavy and dreadful visitation; and now, in the midst of judgement remembering mercy, hast redeemed our souls from the jaws of death; We offer unto thy fatherly goodness ourselves, our souls and bodies which thou hast delivered, to be a living sacrifice unto thee, always praising and magnifying thy mercies in the midst of thy Church; through Jesus Christ our Lord. *Amen.*

Or this.

WE humbly acknowledge before thee, O most merciful Father, that all the punishments which are threatened in thy law might justly have fallen upon us, by reason of our manifold transgressions and hardness of heart : Yet seeing it hath pleased thee of thy tender mercy, upon our weak and unworthy humiliation, to asswage the contagious sickness wherewith we lately have been sore afflicted, and to restore the voice of joy and health into our dwellings ; We offer unto thy Divine Majesty the sacrifice of praise and thanksgiving, lauding and magnifying thy glorious Name for such thy preservation and providence over us ; through Jesus Christ our Lord. *Amen.*

THE ORDER OF THE
ADMINISTRATION OF THE LORD'S SUPPER,
OR
HOLY COMMUNION.

¶ *SO many as intend to be partakers of the holy Communion shall signify their names to the Curate, at least some time the day before.*

¶ *And if any of those be an open and notorious evil liver, or have done any wrong to his neighbours by word or deed, so that the Congregation be thereby offended; the Curate, having knowledge thereof, shall call him and advertise him, that in any wise he presume not to come to the Lord's Table, until he have openly declared himself to have truly repented and amended his former naughty life, that the Congregation may thereby be satisfied, which before were offended; and that he have recompensed the parties, to whom he hath done wrong; or at least declare himself to be in full purpose so to do, as soon as he conveniently may.*

¶ *The same order shall the Curate use with those betwixt whom he perceiveth malice and hatred to reign; not suffering them to be partakers of the Lord's Table, until he know them to be reconciled. And if one of the parties so at variance be content to forgive from the bottom of his heart all that the other hath trespassed against him, and to make amends for that he himself hath offended; and the other party will not be persuaded to a godly unity, but remain still in his frowardness and malice: the Minister in that case ought to admit the penitent person to the holy Communion, and not him that is obstinate. Provided that every Minister so repelling any, as is specified in this, or the next precedent Paragraph of this Rubrick, shall be obliged to give an account of the same to the Ordinary within fourteen days after at the farthest. And the Ordinary shall proceed against the offending person according to the Canon.*

¶ *The Table, at the Communion-time having a fair white linen cloth upon it, shall stand in the Body of the Church, or in the Chancel, where Morning and Evening Prayer are appointed to be said. And the Priest standing at the north side of the Table shall say the Lord's Prayer, with the Collect following, the people kneeling.*

OUR Father which art in heaven, Hallowed be thy Name. Thy kingdom come. Thy will be done, in earth as it is in heaven. Give us this day our daily bread. And forgive us our trespasses, As we forgive them that trespass against us. And lead us not into temptation; But deliver us from evil. Amen.

THE COLLECT.

ALMIGHTY God, unto whom all hearts be open, all desires known, and from whom no secrets are hid; Cleanse the thoughts of our hearts by the inspiration of thy Holy Spirit, that we may perfectly love thee, and worthily magnify thy holy Name; through Christ our Lord. *Amen.*

¶ *Then shall the Priest, turning to the people, rehearse distinctly all the TEN COMMANDMENTS; and the people still kneeling shall, after every Commandment, ask God mercy for their transgression thereof for the time past, and grace to keep the same for the time to come, as followeth.*

Minister.

GOD spake these words, and said; I am the Lord thy God: Thou shalt have none other gods but me.

People. Lord, have mercy upon us, and incline our hearts to keep this law.

Minister. Thou shalt not make to thyself any graven image, nor the likeness of any thing that is in heaven above, or in the earth beneath, or in the water under the earth. Thou shalt not bow down to them, nor worship them: for I the Lord thy God am a jealous God, and visit the sins of the fathers upon the children unto the third and fourth generation of them that hate me, and shew mercy unto thousands in them that love me, and keep my commandments.

People. Lord, have mercy upon us, and incline our hearts to keep this law.

Minister. Thou shalt not take the Name of the Lord thy God in vain : for the Lord will not hold him guiltless, that taketh his Name in vain.

People. Lord, have mercy upon us, and incline our hearts to keep this law.

Minister. Remember that thou keep holy the Sabbath-day. Six days shalt thou labour, and do all that thou hast to do ; but the seventh day is the Sabbath of the Lord thy God. In it thou shalt do no manner of work, thou, and thy son, and thy daughter, thy man-servant, and thy maid-servant, thy cattle, and the stranger that is within thy gates. For in six days the Lord made heaven and earth, the sea, and all that in them is, and rested the seventh day : wherefore the Lord blessed the seventh day, and hallowed it.

People. Lord, have mercy upon us, and incline our hearts to keep this law.

Minister. Honour thy father and thy mother ; that thy days may be long in the land which the Lord thy God giveth thee.

People. Lord, have mercy upon us, and incline our hearts to keep this law.

Minister. Thou shalt do no murder.

People. Lord, have mercy upon us, and incline our hearts to keep this law.

Minister. Thou shalt not commit adultery.

People. Lord, have mercy upon us, and incline our hearts to keep this law.

Minister. Thou shalt not steal.

People. Lord, have mercy upon us, and incline our hearts to keep this law.

Minister. Thou shalt not bear false witness against thy neighbour.

People. Lord, have mercy upon us, and incline our hearts to keep this law.

Minister. Thou shalt not covet thy neighbour's house, thou shalt not covet thy neighbour's wife, nor his servant, nor his maid, nor his ox, nor his ass, nor any thing that is his.

People. Lord, have mercy upon us, and write all these thy laws in our hearts, we beseech thee.

¶ *Then shall follow one of these two Collects for the Queen, the Priest standing as before, and saying,*

Let us pray.

ALMIGHTY God, whose kingdom is everlasting, and power infinite; Have mercy upon the whole Church; and so rule the heart of thy chosen Servant *ELIZABETH*, our Queen and Governor, that she (knowing whose minister she is) may above all things seek thy honour and glory: and that we, and all her subjects (duly considering whose authority she hath) may faithfully serve, honour, and humbly obey her, in thee, and for thee, according to thy blessed Word and ordinance; through Jesus Christ our Lord, who with thee and the Holy Ghost liveth and reigneth, ever one God, world without end. *Amen.*

Or,

ALMIGHTY and everlasting God, we are taught by thy holy Word, that the hearts of Kings are in thy rule and governance, and that thou dost dispose and turn them as it seemeth best to thy godly wisdom: We humbly beseech thee so to dispose and govern the heart of *ELIZABETH* thy Servant, our Queen and Governor, that, in all her thoughts, words, and works, she may ever seek thy honour and glory, and study to preserve thy people committed to her charge, in wealth, peace, and godliness: Grant this, O merciful Father, for thy dear Son's sake, Jesus Christ our Lord. *Amen.*

¶ *Then shall be said the Collect of the Day. And immediately after the Collect the Priest shall read the Epistle, saying,* The Epistle [*or,* The portion of Scripture appointed for the Epistle] is written in the —— Chapter of —— beginning at the —— Verse. *And the Epistle ended, he shall say,* Here endeth the Epistle. *Then shall he read the Gospel (the people all standing up) saying,* The holy Gospel is written in the —— Chapter of —— beginning at the —— Verse. *And the Gospel ended, shall be sung or said the Creed following, the people still standing, as before.*

I BELIEVE in one God the Father Almighty, Maker of heaven and earth, And of all things visible and invisible:

And in one Lord Jesus Christ, the only-begotten Son of God, Begotten of his Father before all worlds, God of God, Light of Light, Very God of very God, Begotten, not made, Being of one substance with the Father, By whom all things were made: Who for us men, and for our salvation came down from heaven, And was incarnate by the Holy Ghost of the Virgin Mary, And was made man, And was crucified also for us under Pontius Pilate. He suffered and was buried, And the third day he rose again according to the Scriptures, And ascended into heaven, And sitteth on the right hand of the Father. And he shall come again with glory to judge both the quick and the dead: Whose kingdom shall have no end.

And I believe in the Holy Ghost, The Lord and giver of life, Who proceedeth from the Father and the Son, Who with the Father and the Son together is worshipped and glorified, Who spake by the Prophets. And I believe one Catholick and Apostolick Church. I acknowledge one Baptism for the remission of sins. And I look for the Resurrection of the dead, And the life of the world to come. Amen.

¶ *Then the Curate shall declare unto the people what Holy-days, or Fasting-days, are in the Week following to be observed. And then also (if occasion be) shall notice be given of the Communion; and Briefs, Citations, and Excommunications read. And nothing shall be proclaimed or published in the Church, during the time of Divine Service, but by the Minister: nor by him any thing, but what is prescribed in the Rules of this Book, or enjoined by the Queen, or by the Ordinary of the place.*

¶ *Then shall follow the Sermon, or one of the Homilies already set forth, or hereafter to be set forth, by authority.*

¶ *Then shall the Priest return to the Lord's Table, and begin the Offertory, saying one or more of these Sentences following, as he thinketh most convenient in his discretion.*

LET your light so shine before men, that they may see your good works, and glorify your Father which is in heaven.   St. Matth. v.

Lay not up for yourselves treasure upon the earth; where the rust and moth doth corrupt, and where thieves break through and steal: but lay up for yourselves treasures in heaven; where neither rust nor moth doth corrupt, and where thieves do not break through and steal.   St. Matth. vi.

Whatsoever ye would that men should do unto you, even so do unto them; for this is the Law and the Prophets.   St. Matth. vii.

Not every one that saith unto me, Lord, Lord, shall enter into the Kingdom of heaven; but he that doeth the will of my Father which is in heaven.   St. Matth. vii.

Zacchæus stood forth, and said unto the Lord, Behold, Lord, the half of my goods I give to the poor; and if I have done any wrong to any man, I restore four-fold. St. Luke xix.

Who goeth a warfare at any time of his own cost? Who planteth a vineyard, and eateth not of the fruit thereof? Or who feedeth a flock, and eateth not of the milk of the flock? 1 Cor. ix.

If we have sown unto you spiritual things, is it a great matter if we shall reap your worldly things? 1 Cor. ix.

Do ye not know, that they who minister about holy things live of the sacrifice; and they who wait at the altar are partakers with the altar? Even so hath the Lord also ordained, that they who preach the Gospel should live of the Gospel. 1 Cor. ix.

He that soweth little shall reap little; and he that soweth plenteously shall reap plenteously. Let every man do according as he is disposed in his heart, not grudging, or of necessity; for God loveth a cheerful giver. 2 Cor. ix.

Let him that is taught in the Word minister unto him that teacheth, in all good things. Be not deceived, God is not mocked: for whatsoever a man soweth that shall he reap. Gal. vi.

While we have time, let us do good unto all men; and specially unto them that are of the household of faith. Gal. vi.

Godliness is great riches, if a man be content with that he hath: for we brought nothing into the world, neither may we carry any thing out. 1 Tim. vi.

Charge them who are rich in this world, that they be ready to give, and glad to distribute; laying up in store for themselves a good foundation against the time to come, that they may attain eternal life. 1 Tim. vi.

God is not unrighteous, that he will forget your works, and labour that proceedeth of love; which love ye have shewed for his Name's sake, who have ministered unto the saints, and yet do minister.

Heb. vi.

To do good, and to distribute, forget not; for with such sacrifices God is pleased. Heb. xiii.

Whoso hath this world's good, and seeth his brother have need, and shutteth up his compassion from him, how dwelleth the love of God in him?

1 St. John iii.

Give alms of thy goods, and never turn thy face from any poor man; and then the face of the Lord shall not be turned away from thee. Tobit iv.

Be merciful after thy power. If thou hast much, give plenteously: if thou hast little, do thy diligence gladly to give of that little: for so gatherest thou thyself a good reward in the day of necessity.

Tobit iv.

He that hath pity upon the poor lendeth unto the Lord: and look, what he layeth out, it shall be paid him again. Prov. xix.

Blessed be the man that provideth for the sick and needy: the Lord shall deliver him in the time of trouble. Psalm xli.

¶ *Whilst these Sentences are in reading, the Deacons, Church-wardens, or other fit person appointed for that purpose, shall receive the Alms for the Poor, and other devotions of the people, in a decent bason to be provided by the Parish for that purpose; and reverently bring it to the Priest, who shall humbly present and place it upon the holy Table.*

¶ *And when there is a Communion, the Priest shall then place upon the Table so much Bread and Wine, as he shall think sufficient.*

After which done, the Priest shall say,

Let us pray for the whole state of Christ's Church militant here in earth.

ALMIGHTY and everliving God, who by thy holy Apostle hast taught us to make prayers, and supplications, and to give thanks, for all men;

If there be no alms or oblations, then shall the words [of accepting our alms and oblations] be left out unsaid.

We humbly beseech thee most mercifully [*to accept our alms and oblations, and*] to receive these our prayers, which we offer unto thy Divine Majesty; beseeching thee to inspire continually the universal Church with the spirit of truth, unity, and concord: And grant, that all they that do confess thy holy Name may agree in the truth of thy holy Word, and live in unity, and godly love. We beseech thee also to save and defend all Christian Kings, Princes, and Governors; and specially thy Servant *ELIZABETH* our Queen; that under her we may be godly and quietly governed: And grant unto her whole Council, and to all that are put in authority under her, that they may truly and indifferently minister justice, to the punishment of wickedness and vice, and to the maintenance of thy true religion, and virtue. Give grace, O heavenly Father, to all Bishops and Curates, that they may both by their life and doctrine set forth thy true and lively Word, and rightly and duly administer thy holy Sacraments: And to all thy people give thy heavenly grace; and specially to this congregation here present; that, with meek heart and due reverence, they may hear, and receive thy holy Word; truly serving thee in holiness and righteousness all the days of their life. And we most humbly beseech thee of thy goodness, O Lord, to comfort and succour all them, who in this transitory life are in trouble, sorrow, need, sickness, or any other adversity. And we also bless thy holy Name for all thy servants departed this life in thy faith and fear; beseeching thee to give us grace so to follow their good examples, that with them we may be partakers of thy heavenly kingdom: Grant this, O Father, for Jesus Christ's sake, our only Mediator and Advocate. *Amen.*

¶ *When the Minister giveth warning for the celebration of the holy Communion, (which he shall always do upon the Sunday, or some Holy-day, immediately preceding,) after the Sermon or Homily ended, he shall read this Exhortation following.*

DEARLY beloved, on —— day next I purpose, through God's assistance, to administer to all such as shall be religiously and devoutly disposed the most comfortable Sacrament of the Body and Blood of Christ; to be by them received in remembrance of his meritorious Cross and Passion; whereby alone we obtain remission of our sins, and are made partakers of the Kingdom of heaven. Wherefore it is our duty to render most humble and hearty thanks to Almighty God our heavenly Father, for that he hath given his Son our Saviour Jesus Christ, not only to die for us, but also to be our spiritual food and sustenance in that holy Sacrament. Which being so divine and comfortable a thing to them who receive it worthily, and so dangerous to them that will presume to receive it unworthily; my duty is to exhort you in the mean season to consider the dignity of that holy mystery, and the great peril of the unworthy receiving thereof; and so to search and examine your own consciences, (and that not lightly, and after the manner of dissemblers with God; but so) that ye may come holy and clean to such a heavenly Feast, in the marriage-garment required by God in holy Scripture, and be received as worthy partakers of that holy Table.

The way and means thereto is; First, to examine your lives and conversations by the rule of God's commandments; and whereinsoever ye shall perceive yourselves to have offended, either by will, word, or deed, there to bewail your own sinfulness, and to confess yourselves to Almighty God, with full purpose of amendment of life. And if ye shall perceive your offences to be such as are not only against God, but also against your neighbours; then ye shall reconcile yourselves unto them; being ready to make restitution and satisfaction, according to the uttermost of your powers, for all injuries and wrongs done by you to any other; and being likewise ready to forgive others that have offended you, as ye would have forgiveness of your offences at God's hand: for otherwise the receiving of the holy Communion doth nothing else but increase your damnation. Therefore if any of you be a blasphemer of God, an hinderer or slanderer of his Word, an adulterer, or be in malice, or envy, or in any other grievous crime, repent you of your sins, or else come not to that holy Table; lest, after the taking of that holy Sacrament, the devil enter into you, as he entered into Judas, and fill you full of all iniquities, and bring you to destruction both of body and soul.

And because it is requisite, that no man should come to the holy Communion, but with a full trust in God's mercy, and with a quiet conscience; therefore if there be any of you, who by this means cannot quiet his own conscience herein, but requireth further comfort or counsel, let him come to me, or to some other discreet and learned Minister of God's Word, and open his grief; that by the ministry of God's holy Word he may receive the benefit of absolution, together with ghostly counsel and advice, to the quieting of his conscience, and avoiding of all scruple and doubtfulness.

¶ *Or, in case he shall see the people negligent to come to the holy Communion, instead of the former, he shall use this Exhortation.*

DEARLY beloved brethren, on —— I intend, by God's grace, to celebrate the Lord's Supper: unto which, in God's behalf, I bid you all that are here present; and beseech you, for the Lord Jesus Christ's sake, that ye will not refuse to come thereto, being so lovingly called and bidden by God himself. Ye know how grievous and unkind a thing it is, when a man hath prepared a rich feast, decked his table with all kind of provision, so that there lacketh nothing but the guests to sit down; and yet they who are called (without any cause) most unthankfully refuse to come. Which of you in such a case would not be moved? Who would not think a great injury and wrong done unto him? Wherefore, most dearly beloved in Christ, take ye good heed, lest ye, withdrawing yourselves from this holy Supper, provoke God's indignation against you. It is an easy matter for a man to say, I will not communicate, because I am otherwise hindered with worldly business. But such excuses are not so easily accepted and allowed before God. If any man say, I am a grievous sinner, and therefore am afraid to come : wherefore then do ye not repent and amend? When God calleth you, are ye not ashamed to say ye will not come? When ye should return to God, will ye excuse yourselves, and say ye are not ready? Consider earnestly with yourselves how little such feigned excuses will avail before God. They that refused the feast in the Gospel, because they had bought a farm, or would try their yokes of oxen, or because they were married, were not so excused, but counted unworthy of the heavenly feast. I, for my part, shall be ready; and, according to mine Office, I bid you in the Name of God, I call you in Christ's behalf, I exhort you, as ye love your own salvation, that ye will be partakers of this holy Communion. And as the Son of God did vouchsafe to yield up his soul by death upon the Cross for your salvation; so it is your duty to receive the Communion in remembrance of the sacrifice of his death, as he himself hath commanded : which if ye shall neglect to do, consider with yourselves how great injury ye do unto God, and how sore punishment hangeth over your heads for the same ; when ye wilfully abstain from the Lord's Table, and separate from your brethren, who come to feed on the banquet of that most heavenly food. These things if ye earnestly consider, ye will by God's grace return to a better mind : for the obtaining whereof we shall not cease to make our humble petitions unto Almighty God our heavenly Father.

¶ *At the time of the celebration of the Communion, the Communicants being conveniently placed for the receiving of the holy Sacrament, the Priest shall say this Exhortation.*

DEARLY beloved in the Lord, ye that mind to come to the holy Communion of the Body and Blood of our Saviour Christ, must consider how Saint Paul exhorteth all persons diligently to try and examine themselves, before they presume to eat of that Bread, and drink of that Cup. For as the benefit is great, if with a true penitent heart and lively faith we receive that holy Sacrament; (for then we spiritually eat the flesh of Christ, and drink his blood; then we dwell in Christ, and Christ in us; we are one with Christ, and Christ with us;) so is the danger great, if we receive the same unworthily. For then we are guilty of the Body and Blood of Christ our Saviour; we eat and drink our own damnation, not considering the Lord's Body; we kindle God's wrath against us; we provoke him to plague us with divers diseases, and sundry kinds of death. Judge therefore yourselves, brethren, that ye be not judged of the Lord; repent you truly for your sins past; have a lively and stedfast faith in Christ our Saviour; amend your lives, and be in perfect charity with all men; so shall ye be meet partakers of those holy mysteries. And above all things ye must give most humble and hearty thanks to God, the Father, the Son, and the Holy Ghost, for the redemption of the world by the death and passion of our Saviour Christ, both God and man; who did humble himself, even to the death upon the Cross, for us, miserable sinners, who lay in darkness and the shadow of death; that he might make us the children of God, and exalt us to everlasting life. And to the end that we should alway remember the exceeding great love of our Master, and only Saviour, Jesus Christ, thus dying for us, and the innumerable benefits which by his precious blood-shedding he hath obtained to us; he hath instituted and ordained holy mysteries, as pledges of his love, and for a continual remembrance of his death, to our great and endless comfort. To him therefore, with the Father and the Holy Ghost, let us give (as we are most bounden) continual thanks; submitting ourselves wholly to his holy will and pleasure, and studying to serve him in true holiness and righteousness all the days of our life. *Amen.*

¶ *Then shall the Priest say to them that come to receive the holy Communion,*

YE that do truly and earnestly repent you of your sins, and are in love and charity with your neighbours, and intend to lead a new life, following the commandments of God, and walking from henceforth in his holy ways; Draw near with faith, and take this holy Sacrament to your comfort; and make your humble confession to Almighty God, meekly kneeling upon your knees.

¶ *Then shall this general Confession be made, in the name of all those that are minded to receive the holy Communion, by one of the Ministers; both he and all the people kneeling humbly upon their knees, and saying,*

ALMIGHTY God, Father of our Lord, Jesus Christ, Maker of all things, Judge of all men; We acknowledge and bewail our manifold sins and wickedness, Which we, from time to time, most grievously have committed, By thought, word, and deed, Against thy Divine Majesty, Provoking most justly thy wrath and indignation against us. We do earnestly repent, And are heartily sorry for these our misdoings ; The remembrance of them is grievous unto us; The burden of them is intolerable. Have mercy upon us, Have mercy upon us, most merciful Father; For thy Son our Lord Jesus Christ's sake, Forgive us all that is past; And grant that we may ever hereafter Serve and please thee In newness of life, To the honour and glory of thy Name; Through Jesus Christ our Lord.   Amen.

¶ *Then shall the Priest (or the Bishop, being present,) stand up, and turning himself to the people, pronounce this Absolution.*

ALMIGHTY God, our heavenly Father, who of his great mercy hath promised forgiveness of sins to all them that with hearty repentance and true faith turn unto him; Have mercy upon you; pardon and deliver you from all your sins ; confirm and strengthen you in all goodness; and bring you to everlasting life; through Jesus Christ our Lord. *Amen.*

¶ *Then shall the Priest say,*

Hear what comfortable words our Saviour Christ
saith unto all that truly turn to him

COME unto me all that travail and are heavy laden, and I will refresh you.   St. Matth. xi. 28.
So God loved the world, that he gave his only-begotten Son, to the end that all that believe in him should not perish, but have everlasting life.

St. John iii. 16.

Hear also what Saint Paul saith.

This is a true saying, and worthy of all men to be received, That Christ Jesus came into the world to save sinners.   1 Tim. i. 15.

Hear also what Saint John saith.

If any man sin, we have an Advocate with the Father, Jesus Christ the righteous; and he is the propitiation for our sins.   1 St. John ii. 1.

¶ After which the Priest shall proceed, saying,

          Lift up your hearts.

Answer.   We lift them up unto the Lord.

Priest.   Let us give thanks unto our Lord God.

Answer.   It is meet and right so to do.

¶ Then shall the Priest turn to the Lord's Table, and say,

IT is very meet, right, and our bounden duty, that we should at all times, and in all places, give thanks unto thee, O Lord, * Holy Father, Almighty, Everlasting God.

       * *These words* [Holy Father] *must be omitted on* Trinity-Sunday.

¶ Here shall follow the Proper Preface, according to the time, if there be any specially appointed: or else immediately shall follow,

THEREFORE with Angels and Archangels, and with all the company of heaven, we laud and magnify thy glorious Name; evermore praising thee, and saying, Holy, holy, holy, Lord God of hosts, heaven and earth are full of thy glory: Glory be to thee, O Lord most High. Amen.

PROPER PREFACES.

Upon Christmas-day, *and seven days after.*

BECAUSE thou didst give Jesus Christ thine only Son to be born as at this time for us; who, by the operation of the Holy Ghost, was made very man of the substance of the Virgin Mary his mother; and that without spot of sin, to make us clean from all sin. Therefore with Angels, &c.

Upon Easter-day, *and seven days after.*

BUT chiefly are we bound to praise thee for the glorious Resurrection of thy Son Jesus Christ our Lord : for he is the very Paschal Lamb, which was offered for us, and hath taken away the sin of the world ; who by his death hath destroyed death, and by his rising to life again hath restored to us everlasting life. Therefore with Angels, &c.

Upon Ascension-day, *and seven days after.*

THROUGH thy most dearly beloved Son Jesus Christ our Lord ; who after his most glorious Resurrection manifestly appeared to all his Apostles, and in their sight ascended up into heaven to prepare a place for us ; that where he is, thither we might also ascend, and reign with him in glory. Therefore with Angels, &c.

Upon Whit-sunday, *and six days after.*

THROUGH Jesus Christ our Lord ; according to whose most true promise, the Holy Ghost came down as at this time from heaven with a sudden great sound, as it had been a mighty wind, in the likeness of fiery tongues, lighting upon the Apostles, to teach them, and to lead them to all truth ; giving them both the gift of divers languages, and also boldness with fervent zeal constantly to preach the Gospel unto all nations ; whereby we have been brought out of darkness and error into the clear light and true knowledge of thee, and of thy Son Jesus Christ. Therefore with Angels, &c.

Upon the Feast of Trinity *only.*

WHO art one God, one Lord ; not one only Person, but three Persons in one Substance. For that which we believe of the glory of the Father, the same we believe of the Son, and of the Holy Ghost, without any difference or inequality. Therefore with Angels, &c.

¶ *After each of which Prefaces shall immediately be sung or said,*

THEREFORE with Angels and Archangels, and with all the company of heaven, we laud and magnify thy glorious Name; evermore praising thee, and saying, Holy, holy, holy, Lord God of hosts, heaven and earth are full of thy glory: Glory be to thee, O Lord most High. Amen.

¶ *Then shall the Priest, kneeling down at the Lord's Table, say in the name of all them that shall receive the Communion this Prayer following.*

WE do not presume to come to this thy Table, O merciful Lord, trusting in our own righteousness, but in thy manifold and great mercies. We are not worthy so much as to gather up the crumbs under thy Table. But thou art the same Lord, whose property is always to have mercy: Grant us therefore, gracious Lord, so to eat the flesh of thy dear Son Jesus Christ, and to drink his blood, that our sinful bodies may be made clean by his body, and our souls washed through his most precious blood, and that we may evermore dwell in him, and he in us. *Amen.*

¶ *When the Priest, standing before the Table, hath so ordered the Bread and Wine, that he may with the more readiness and decency break the Bread before the people, and take the Cup into his hands, he shall say the Prayer of Consecration, as followeth.*

ALMIGHTY God, our heavenly Father, who of thy tender mercy didst give thine only Son Jesus Christ to suffer death upon the cross for our redemption; who made there (by his one oblation of himself once offered) a full, perfect, and sufficient sacrifice, oblation, and satisfaction, for the sins of the whole world; and did institute, and in his holy Gospel command us to continue, a perpetual memory of that his precious death, until his coming again; Hear us, O merciful Father, we most humbly beseech thee; and grant that we receiving these thy creatures of bread and wine, according to thy Son our Saviour Jesus Christ's holy institution, in remembrance of his death and passion, may be partakers of his most blessed Body and Blood: who, in the same night that he was betrayed, *took Bread; and, when he had given thanks, †he brake it, and gave it to his disciples, saying, Take, eat, ‡this is my Body which is given for you: Do this in remembrance of me. Likewise after supper he § took the Cup; and, when he had given thanks, he gave it to them, saying, Drink ye all of this; for this ‖ is my Blood of the New Testament, which is shed for you and for many for the remission of sins: Do this, as oft as ye shall drink it, in remembrance of me. *Amen.*

* Here the Priest is to take the Paten into his hands:

† And here to break the Bread:

‡ And here to lay his hand upon all the Bread.

§ Here he is to take the Cup into his hand:

‖ And here to lay his hand upon every vessel (be it Chalice or Flagon) in which there is any Wine to be consecrated.

¶ *Then shall the Minister first receive the Communion in both kinds himself, and then proceed to deliver the same to the Bishops, Priests, and Deacons, in like manner, (if any be present,) and after that to the people also in order, into their hands, all meekly kneeling. And, when he delivereth the Bread to any one, he shall say,*

THE Body of our Lord Jesus Christ, which was given for thee, preserve thy body and soul unto everlasting life. Take and eat this in remembrance that Christ died for thee, and feed on him in thy heart by faith with thanksgiving.

¶ *And the Minister that delivereth the Cup to any one shall say,*

THE Blood of our Lord Jesus Christ, which was shed for thee, preserve thy body and soul unto everlasting life. Drink this in remembrance that Christ's Blood was shed for thee, and be thankful.

¶ *If the consecrated Bread or Wine be all spent before all have communicated, the Priest is to consecrate more according to the Form before prescribed; beginning at* [Our Saviour Christ in the same night, &c.] *for the blessing of the Bread; and at* [Likewise after Supper, &c.] *for the blessing of the Cup.*

¶ *When all have communicated, the Minister shall return to the Lord's Table, and reverently place upon it what remaineth of the consecrated Elements, covering the same with a fair linen cloth.*

¶ *Then shall the Priest say the Lord's Prayer, the people repeating after him every Petition.*

OUR Father, which art in heaven, Hallowed be thy Name. Thy kingdom come. Thy will be done, in earth as it is in heaven. Give us this day our daily bread. And forgive us our trespasses, As we forgive them that trespass against us. And lead us not into temptation; But deliver us from evil: For thine is the kingdom, The power, and the glory, For ever and ever. Amen.

¶ *After shall be said as followeth.*

O LORD and heavenly Father, we thy humble servants entirely desire thy fatherly goodness mercifully to accept this our sacrifice of praise and thanksgiving; most humbly beseeching thee to grant, that by the merits and death of thy Son Jesus Christ, and through faith in his blood, we and all thy whole Church may obtain remission of our sins, and all other benefits of his passion. And here we offer and present unto thee, O Lord, ourselves, our souls and bodies, to be a reasonable, holy, and lively sacrifice unto thee; humbly beseeching thee, that all we, who are partakers of this holy Communion, may be fulfilled with thy grace and heavenly benediction. And although we be unworthy, through our manifold sins, to offer unto thee any sacrifice, yet we beseech thee to accept this our bounden duty and service; not weighing our merits, but pardoning our offences, through Jesus Christ our Lord; by whom, and with whom, in the unity of the Holy Ghost, all honour and glory be unto thee, O Father Almighty, world without end. *Amen.*

Or this.

ALMIGHTY and everliving God, we most heartily thank thee, for that thou dost vouchsafe to feed us, who have duly received these holy mysteries, with the spiritual food of the most precious Body and Blood of thy Son our Saviour Jesus Christ; and dost assure us thereby of thy favour and goodness towards us; and that we are very members incorporate in the mystical body of thy Son, which is the blessed company of all faithful people; and are also heirs through hope of thy everlasting kingdom, by the merits of the most precious death and passion of thy dear Son. And we most humbly beseech thee, O heavenly Father, so to assist us with thy grace, that we may continue in that holy fellowship, and do all such good works as thou hast prepared for us to walk in; through Jesus Christ our Lord, to whom, with thee and the Holy Ghost, be all honour and glory, world without end. *Amen.*

¶ Then shall be said or sung,

GLORY be to God on high, and in earth peace, good will towards men. We praise thee, we bless thee, we worship thee, we glorify thee, we give thanks to thee for thy great glory, O Lord God, heavenly King, God the Father Almighty.

O Lord, the only-begotten Son Jesu Christ; O Lord God, Lamb of God, Son of the Father, that takest away the sins of the world, have mercy upon us. Thou that takest away the sins of the world, have mercy upon us. Thou that takest away the sins of the world, receive our prayer. Thou that sittest at the right hand of God the Father, have mercy upon us.

For thou only art holy; thou only art the Lord; thou only, O Christ, with the Holy Ghost, art most high in the glory of God the Father. Amen.

¶ Then the Priest (or Bishop if he be present) shall let them depart with this Blessing.

THE peace of God, which passeth all understanding, keep your hearts and minds in the knowledge and love of God, and of his Son Jesus Christ our Lord: and the blessing of God Almighty, the Father, the Son, and the Holy Ghost, be amongst you and remain with you always. *Amen.*

¶ Collects to be said after the Offertory, when there is no Communion, every such day one or more; and the same may be said also, as often as occasion shall serve, after the Collects either of Morning or Evening Prayer, Communion, or Litany, by the discretion of the Minister.

ASSIST us mercifully, O Lord, in these our supplications and prayers, and dispose the way of thy servants towards the attainment of everlasting salvation; that, among all the changes and chances of this mortal life, they may ever be defended by thy most gracious and ready help; through Jesus Christ our Lord. *Amen.*

O ALMIGHTY Lord, and everlasting God, vouchsafe, we beseech thee, to direct, sanctify, and govern, both our hearts and bodies, in the ways of thy laws, and in the works of thy commandments; that through thy most mighty protection, both here and ever, we may be preserved in body and soul; through our Lord and Saviour Jesus Christ. *Amen.*

GRANT, we beseech thee, Almighty God, that the words, which we have heard this day with our outward ears, may through thy grace be so grafted inwardly in our hearts, that they may bring forth in us the fruit of good living, to the honour and praise of thy Name; through Jesus Christ our Lord. *Amen.*

PREVENT us, O Lord, in all our doings with thy most gracious favour, and further us with thy continual help; that in all our works begun, continued, and ended in thee, we may glorify thy holy Name, and finally by thy mercy obtain everlasting life; through Jesus Christ our Lord. *Amen.*

ALMIGHTY God, the fountain of all wisdom, who knowest our necessities before we ask, and our ignorance in asking; We beseech thee to have compassion upon our infirmities; and those things, which for our unworthiness we dare not, and for our blindness we cannot ask, vouchsafe to give us, for the worthiness of thy Son Jesus Christ our Lord. *Amen.*

222

ALMIGHTY God, who hast promised to hear the petitions of them that ask in thy Son's Name; We beseech thee mercifully to incline thine ears to us that have made now our prayers and supplications unto thee; and grant, that those things, which we have faithfully asked according to thy will, may effectually be obtained, to the relief of our necessity, and to the setting forth of thy glory; through Jesus Christ our Lord. *Amen.*

¶ *Upon the Sundays and other Holy-days (if there be no Communion) shall be said all that is appointed at the Communion, until the end of the general Prayer* [For the whole state of Christ's Church militant here in earth] *together with one or more of these Collects last before rehearsed, concluding with the Blessing.*

¶ *And there shall be no celebration of the Lord's Supper, except there be a convenient number to communicate with the Priest, according to his discretion.*

¶ *And if there be not above twenty persons in the Parish of discretion to receive the Communion; yet there shall be no Communion, except four (or three at the least) communicate with the Priest.*

¶ *And in Cathedral and Collegiate Churches, and Colleges, where there are many Priests and Deacons, they shall all receive the Communion with the Priest every Sunday at the least, except they have a reasonable cause to the contrary.*

¶ *And to take away all occasion of dissension, and superstition, which any person hath or might have concerning the Bread and Wine, it shall suffice that the Bread be such as is usual to be eaten; but the best and purest Wheat Bread that conveniently may be gotten.*

¶ *And if any of the Bread and Wine remain unconsecrated, the Curate shall have it to his own use: but if any remain of that which was consecrated, it shall not be carried out of the Church, but the Priest and such other of the Communicants as he shall then call unto him, shall, immediately after the Blessing, reverently eat and drink the same.*

¶ *The Bread and Wine for the Communion shall be provided by the Curate and the Church-wardens at the charges of the Parish.*

THE COMMUNION.

¶ *And note, that every Parishioner shall communicate at the least three times in the year, of which Easter to be one. And yearly at Easter every Parishioner shall reckon with the Parson, Vicar, or Curate, or his or their Deputy or Deputies; and pay to them or him all Ecclesiastical Duties, accustomably due, then and at that time to be paid.*

¶ *After the Divine Service ended, the money given at the Offertory shall be disposed of to such pious and charitable uses, as the Minister and Church-wardens shall think fit. Wherein if they disagree, it shall be disposed of as the Ordinary shall appoint.*

¶ *Whereas it is ordained in this Office for the Administration of the Lord's Supper, that the Communicants should receive the same kneeling; (which order is well meant, for a signification of our humble and grateful acknowledgement of the benefits of Christ therein given to all worthy Receivers, and for the avoiding of such profanation and disorder in the holy Communion, as might otherwise ensue;) yet, lest the same kneeling should by any persons, either out of ignorance and infirmity, or out of malice and obstinacy, be misconstrued and depraved; It is hereby declared, That thereby no adoration is intended, or ought to be done, either unto the Sacramental Bread or Wine there bodily received, or unto any Corporal Presence of Christ's natural Flesh and Blood. For the Sacramental Bread and Wine remain still in their very natural substances, and therefore may not be adored; (for that were Idolatry, to be abhorred of all faithful Christians;) and the natural Body and Blood of our Saviour Christ are in Heaven, and not here; it being against the truth of Christ's natural Body to be at one time in more places than one.*

THE MINISTRATION OF

PUBLICK BAPTISM OF INFANTS,

TO BE USED IN THE CHURCH.

¶ *The people are to be admonished, that it is most convenient that Baptism should not be administered but upon Sundays, and other Holy-days, when the most number of people come together; as well for that the Congregation there present may testify the receiving of them that be newly baptized into the number of Christ's Church; as also because in the Baptism of Infants every Man present may be put in remembrance of his own profession made to God in his Baptism. For which cause also it is expedient that Baptism be ministered in the vulgar tongue. Nevertheless (if necessity so require,) Children may be baptized upon any other day.*

¶ *And note, that there shall be for every Male-child to be baptized two Godfathers and one Godmother; and for every Female, one Godfather and two Godmothers.*

¶ *When there are Children to be baptized, the Parents shall give knowledge thereof over night, or in the morning before the beginning of Morning Prayer, to the Curate. And then the Godfathers and Godmothers, and the people with the Children, must be ready at the Font, either immediately after the last Lesson at Morning Prayer, or else immediately after the last Lesson at Evening Prayer, as the Curate by his discretion shall appoint. And the Priest coming to the Font, (which is then to be filled with pure Water,) and standing there, shall say,*

HATH this Child been already baptized, or no?

¶ *If they answer,* No: *Then shall the Priest proceed as followeth.*

DEARLY beloved, forasmuch as all men are conceived and born in sin; and that our Saviour Christ saith, None can enter into the kingdom of God, except he be regenerate and born anew of Water and of the holy Ghost; I beseech you to call upon God the Father, through our Lord Jesus Christ, that of his bounteous mercy he will grant to *this Child* that thing which by nature *he* cannot have; that *he* may be baptized with Water and the holy Ghost, and received into Christ's holy Church, and be made *a lively member* of the same.

¶ *Then shall the Priest say.*

Let us pray.

ALMIGHTY and everlasting God, who of thy great mercy didst save Noah and his family in the ark from perishing by water; and also didst safely lead the children of Israel thy people through the Red Sea, figuring thereby thy holy Baptism; and by the Baptism of thy well-beloved Son Jesus Christ, in the river Jordan, didst sanctify Water to the mystical washing away of sin; We beseech thee, for thine infinite mercies, that thou wilt mercifully look upon *this Child*; wash *him* and sanctify *him* with the holy Ghost; that *he*, being delivered from thy wrath, may be received into the ark of Christ's Church: and being stedfast in faith, joyful through hope, and rooted in charity, may so pass the waves of this troublesome world, that finally *he* may come to the land of everlasting life, there to reign with thee world without end ; through Jesus Christ our Lord. *Amen.*

ALMIGHTY and immortal God, the aid of all that need, the helper of all that flee to thee for succour, the life of them that believe, and the resurrection of the dead ; We call upon thee for *this Infant,* that *he,* coming to thy holy Baptism, may receive remission of *his* sins by spiritual regeneration. Receive *him,* O Lord, as thou hast promised by thy well-beloved Son, saying, Ask, and ye shall have ; seek, and ye shall find ; knock, and it shall be opened unto you : So give now unto us that ask ; let us that seek find ; open the gate unto us that knock ; that *this Infant* may enjoy the everlasting benediction of thy heavenly washing, and may come to the eternal kingdom which thou hast promised by Christ our Lord. *Amen.*

¶ *Then shall the people stand up, and the Priest shall say,*

Hear the words of the Gospel, written by Saint *Mark,* in the tenth Chapter, at the thirteenth Verse.

THEY brought young children to Christ, that he should touch them ; and his disciples rebuked those that brought them. But when Jesus saw it, he was much displeased, and said unto them, Suffer the little children to come unto me, and forbid them not ; for of such is the kingdom of God. Verily I say unto you, Whosoever shall not receive the kingdom of God as a little child, he shall not enter therein. And he took them up in his arms, put his hands upon them, and blessed them.

¶ *After the Gospel is read, the Minister shall make this brief Exhortation upon the words of the Gospel.*

BELOVED, ye hear in this Gospel the words of our Saviour Christ, that he commanded the children to be brought unto him ; how he blamed those that would have kept them from him ; how he exhorteth all men to follow their innocency. Ye perceive how by his outward gesture and deed he declared his good will toward them ; for he embraced them in his arms, he laid his hands upon them, and blessed them. Doubt ye not therefore, but earnestly believe, that he will likewise favourably receive *this* present *Infant ;* that he will embrace *him* with the arms of his mercy ; that he will give unto *him* the blessing of eternal life, and make *him partaker* of his everlasting kingdom. Wherefore we being thus persuaded of the good will of our heavenly Father towards *this Infant,* declared by his Son Jesus Christ ; and nothing doubting but that he favourably alloweth this charitable work of our's in bringing *this Infant* to his holy Baptism ; let us faithfully and devoutly give thanks unto him, and say,

ALMIGHTY and everlasting God, heavenly Father, we give thee humble thanks, for that thou hast vouchsafed to call us to the knowledge of thy grace, and faith in thee : Increase this knowledge, and confirm this faith in us evermore. Give thy holy Spirit to *this Infant*, that *he* may be born again, and be made *an heir* of everlasting salvation; through our Lord Jesus Christ, who liveth and reigneth with thee and the Holy Spirit, now and for ever. *Amen.*

¶ *Then shall the Priest speak unto the Godfathers and Godmothers on this wise.*

DEARLY beloved, ye have brought *this Child* here to be baptized, ye have prayed that our Lord Jesus Christ would vouchsafe to receive *him*, to release *him* of *his* sins, to sanctify *him* with the holy Ghost, to give *him* the kingdom of heaven, and everlasting life. Ye have heard also that our Lord Jesus Christ hath promised in his Gospel to grant all these things that ye have prayed for: which promise he, for his part, will most surely keep and perform. Wherefore, after this promise made by Christ, *this Infant* must also faithfully, for *his* part, promise by you that are *his* sureties, (until *he* come of age to take it upon *himself*,) that *he* will renounce the devil and all his works, and constantly believe God's holy Word, and obediently keep his commandments.

I demand therefore,

DOST thou, in the name of this Child, renounce the devil and all his works, the vain pomp and glory of the world, with all covetous desires of the same, and the carnal desires of the flesh, so that thou wilt not follow, nor be led by them?

Answer. I renounce them all.

Minister.

DOST thou believe in God the Father Almighty, Maker of heaven and earth?

And in Jesus Christ his only-begotten Son our Lord? And that he was conceived by the Holy Ghost; born of the Virgin Mary; that he suffered under Pontius Pilate, was crucified, dead, and buried; that he went down into hell, and also did rise again the third day; that he ascended into heaven, and sitteth at the right hand of God the Father Almighty; and from thence shall come again at the end of the world, to judge the quick and the dead?

And dost thou believe in the Holy Ghost; the holy Catholick Church; the Communion of Saints; the Remission of sins; the Resurrection of the flesh; and everlasting life after death?

Answer. All this I stedfastly believe.

Minister.

WILT thou be baptized in this faith?
Answer. That is my desire.

Minister.

WILT thou then obediently keep God's holy will and commandments, and walk in the same all the days of thy life?
Answer. I will.

¶ *Then shall the Priest say,*

O MERCIFUL God, grant that the old Adam in *this Child* may be so buried, that the new man may be raised up in *him*. *Amen.*

Grant that all carnal affections may die in *him*, and that all things belonging to the Spirit may live and grow in *him*. *Amen.*

Grant that *he* may have power and strength to have victory, and to triumph, against the devil, the world, and the flesh. *Amen.*

Grant that whosoever is here dedicated to thee by our office and ministry may also be endued with heavenly virtues, and everlastingly rewarded, through thy mercy, O blessed Lord God, who dost live, and govern all things, world without end. *Amen.*

A LMIGHTY, everliving God, whose most dearly beloved Son Jesus Christ, for the forgiveness of our sins, did shed out of his most precious side both water and blood ; and gave commandment to his disciples, that they should go teach all nations, and baptize them In the Name of the Father, and of the Son, and of the Holy Ghost ; Regard, we beseech thee, the supplications of thy congregation ; sanctify this Water to the mystical washing away of sin ; and grant that *this Child*, now to be baptized therein, may receive the fulness of thy grace, and ever remain in the number of thy faithful and elect children ; through Jesus Christ our Lord. *Amen.*

¶ *Then the Priest shall take the Child into his hands, and shall say to the Godfathers and Godmothers,*

Name this Child.

¶ *And then naming it after them (if they shall certify him that the Child may well endure it) he shall dip it in the Water discreetly and warily, saying,*

N. I baptize thee In the Name of the Father, and of the Son, and of the Holy Ghost. Amen.

¶ *But if they certify that the Child is weak, it shall suffice to pour Water upon it, saying the foresaid words,*

N. I baptize thee In the Name of the Father, and of the Son, and of the Holy Ghost. Amen.

¶ *Then the Priest shall say,*

W E receive this Child into the congregation of Christ's flock, *and do sign *him* with the sign of the Cross, in token that hereafter *he* shall not be ashamed to confess the faith of Christ crucified, and manfully to fight under his banner, against sin, the world, and the devil ; and to continue Christ's faithful soldier and servant unto *his* life's end. Amen.

* Here the Priest shall make a Cross upon the Child's forehead.

¶ *Then shall the Priest say,*

S EEING now, dearly beloved brethren, that *this Child is* regenerate, and grafted into the body of Christ's Church, let us give thanks unto Almighty God for these benefits ; and with one accord make our prayers unto him, that *this Child* may lead the rest of *his* life according to this beginning.

¶ Then shall be said, all kneeling;

OUR Father, which art in heaven, Hallowed be thy Name. Thy kingdom come. Thy will be done, in earth as it is in heaven. Give us this day our daily bread. And forgive us our trespasses, As we forgive them that trespass against us. And lead us not into temptation ; But deliver us from evil. Amen.

¶ Then shall the Priest say,

WE yield thee hearty thanks, most merciful Father, that it hath pleased thee to regenerate *this Infant* with thy holy Spirit, to receive *him* for thine own *Child* by adoption, and to incorporate *him* into thy holy Church. And humbly we beseech thee to grant, that *he*, being dead unto sin, and living unto righteousness, and being buried with Christ in his death, may crucify the old man, and utterly abolish the whole body of sin ; and that, as *he is* made *partaker* of the death of thy Son, *he* may also be *partaker* of his resurrection ; so that finally, with the residue of thy holy Church, *he* may be *an inheritor* of thine everlasting kingdom ; through Christ our Lord. *Amen.*

¶ Then, all standing up, the Priest shall say to the Godfathers and Godmothers this Exhortation following.

FORASMUCH as *this Child hath* promised by you *his* sureties to renounce the devil and all his works, to believe in God, and to serve him ; ye must remember, that it is your parts and duties to see that *this Infant* be taught, so soon as *he* shall be able to learn, what a solemn vow, promise, and profession, *he hath* here made by you. And that *he* may know these things the better, ye shall call upon *him* to hear Sermons ; and chiefly ye shall provide, that *he* may learn the Creed, the Lord's Prayer, and the Ten Commandments, in the vulgar tongue, and all other things which a Christian ought to know and believe to his soul's health ; and that *this Child* may be virtuously brought up to lead a godly and a christian life ; remembering always, that Baptism doth represent unto us our profession ; which is, to follow the example of our Saviour Christ, and to be made like unto him ; that, as he died, and rose again for us, so should we, who are baptized, die from sin, and rise again unto righteousness ; continually mortifying all our evil and corrupt affections, and daily proceeding in all virtue and godliness of living.

¶ Then shall he add and say,

YE are to take care that *this Child* be brought to the Bishop to be confirmed by him, so soon as *he* can say the Creed, the Lord's Prayer, and the Ten Commandments, in the vulgar tongue, and be further instructed in the Church-Catechism set forth for that purpose.

¶ It is certain by God's Word, that Children which are baptized, dying before they commit actual sin, are undoubtedly saved.

¶ To take away all scruple concerning the use of the sign of the Cross in Baptism; the true explication thereof, and the just reasons for the retaining of it, may be seen in the xxxth Canon, first published in the Year MDCIV.

¶ Then shall be read the following.

A SELECTION
OF PRAYERS

PREPARATION

Thou awakest us to delight in Thy praises; for Thou madest us for Thyself, and our heart is restless, until it repose in Thee.

St Augustine, 354–450

My spirit longs for thee
Within my troubled breast,
Though I unworthy be
Of so divine a Guest.

Of so divine a guest
Unworthy though I be,
Yet has my heart no rest
Unless it come from thee.

John Byrom, 1692–1763

O Lord our God, grant us grace to desire thee with our whole heart, that so desiring, we may seek and find thee; and so finding thee we may love thee; and loving thee we may hate those sins from which thou hast redeemed us; for the sake of Jesus Christ.

St Anselm, 1033–1109

Lord, I want to love you, yet I'm not sure.
  I want to trust you, yet I'm afraid of being taken in.
  I know I need you, yet I'm ashamed of the need.
  I want to pray, yet I'm afraid of being a hypocrite.
  I need my independence, yet I fear to be alone.
  I want to belong, yet I must be myself.
  Take me, Lord, yet leave me alone.
  Lord, I believe; help thou my unbelief.
O Lord, if you are there, you do understand, don't you?
Give me what I need but leave me free to choose.
Help me work it out my own way, but don't let me go.
Let me understand myself, but don't let me despair.
  Come unto me, O Lord – I want you there.
  Lighten my darkness – but don't dazzle me.
  Help me to see what I need to do and give me strength to do it.
O Lord, I believe, help thou my unbelief.

Bernard, SSF

233

God be in my head, and in my understanding;
God be in my eyes, and in my looking;
God be in my mouth, and in my speaking;
God be in my heart, and in my thinking;
God be at my end, and at my departing.

Old Sarum Primer

Lord Jesus Christ, Son of the living God,
teach us to walk in your way more trustfully,
to accept your truth more faithfully,
and to share your life more lovingly.
By the power of the Holy Spirit
guide us in our work for the Church,
so that we may come as one family
to the Kingdom of the Father,
where you live for ever.

National Pastoral Congress, Liverpool, 1980

God of our salvation, our rescue, our health: all things are yours
and when we bring our hearts and hands and voices to worship, we
bring you what is yours.

Yet we do not serve you as we should, and the world is racked by
all the tensions and outright conflicts which come from the worship of that which is less than yourself. Our goodwill towards men
has no firm foundation, and crumbles at the first tremor of real
testing. In our personal affairs, and in our communal judgements,
we try to heal deep wounds with superficial cures.

Father, forgive us. Confront us with your way of righting wrong,
your strange work of redemption through the sacrificial love of
Jesus. And help us to love one another as he has loved us.

from Contemporary Prayers for Public Worship, *ed. Caryl Micklem*

St Denis's Prayer
You are wisdom, uncreated and eternal,
    the supreme first cause, above all being,
    sovereign Godhead, sovereign goodness,
    watching unseen the God-inspired wisdom of Christian
      people.
Raise us, we pray, that we may totally respond
    to the supreme, unknown, ultimate and splendid height, of
    your words, mysterious and inspired.
There all God's secret matters lie covered and hidden under
    darkness both profound and brilliant, silent and wise.
You make what is ultimate and beyond brightness secretly to
    shine in all that is most dark.
In your way, ever unseen and intangible, you fill to the full with
    most beautiful splendour those souls who close their eyes
    that they may see.
And I, please, with love that goes on beyond mind to all that is
    beyond mind, seek to gain such for myself through this
    prayer.

from The Cloud of Unknowing, *14th century*

O Holy Spirit, whose presence is liberty, grant us that freedom of
the spirit, which will not fear to tread in unknown ways, nor be
held back by misgivings of ourselves and fear of others. Ever
beckon us forward to the place of thy will which is also the place of
thy power, O ever-leading, ever-loving Lord.   *George Appleton*

O God, early in the morning I cry to you.
Help me to pray
And to concentrate my thoughts on you:
I cannot do this alone.
In me there is darkness,
But with you there is light;
I am lonely, but you do not leave me;
I am feeble in heart, but with you there is help;
I am restless, but with you there is peace.
In me there is bitterness, but with you there is patience;
I do not understand your ways,
But you know the way for me . . .

Restore me to liberty,
And enable me so to live now
That I may answer before you and before me.
Lord, whatever this day may bring,
Your name be praised.

Dietrich Bonhoeffer,
written while awaiting execution in a Nazi prison

Almighty God,
we thank you for the gift of your holy word.
May it be a lantern to our feet,
a light to our paths,
and a strength to our lives.
Take us and use us
to love and serve all men
in the power of the Holy Spirit
and in the name of your Son,
Jesus Christ our Lord.

Heavenly Father, you have promised through your Son Jesus
Christ, that when we meet in his name, and pray according to his
mind, he will be among us and will hear our prayer. In your love and
wisdom fulfil our desires and give us your greatest gift, which is to
know you, the only true God, and Jesus Christ our Lord; who is
alive and reigns with you and the Holy Spirit, one God, now and for
ever.

Be with us, Lord, in all our prayers, and direct our way toward the
attainment of salvation; that among the changes and chances of
this mortal life, we may always be defended by your gracious help;
through Jesus Christ our Lord.

BEFORE WORSHIP

Heavenly Father,
accept our worship
forgive our sins,
bless the people we pray for,
and bless us too,
for Jesus' sake.

Jamie Wallace

LEARNING AND OBEYING GOD'S WILL

Lord God, you have given us your holy word
    to be a lamp to our feet and a light for our path.
Grant us all your Holy spirit,
      that we may from your word learn your will,
      and may, by his help, frame our lives in obedience to it.
So may your name be honoured,
    and our faith increased,
        through Jesus Christ our Lord.

(Ps. 119: 105)   *Edward Dering*

A MODERN VERSION OF THE BIDDING PRAYER FOR A SERVICE OF LESSONS AND CAROLS

Good Christian friends, at this Christmas time let us prepare
ourselves to hear again, in word and song, the good tidings of
God's redeeming love made known to us in the birth of the Holy
Child of Bethlehem; and with the angelic host let us give glory to
God in the highest.

But first let us pray for the needs of the whole world: for
peace and goodwill among all nations; for unity and brotherhood
in this community and in our diocese of . . . .; for love and
harmony in our families and our homes, and for a blessing on all
children dear to us, and on loved ones absent from home.

Let us also remember at this time those for whom Christmas
brings little joy: the poor and homeless, the hungry and destitute,
the unemployed, the sick and those who mourn; and all victims of
tryanny, cruelty, violence and oppression.

Lastly, let us remember with thanksgiving those who shared
our Christmasses in years gone by and who now rejoice in the
greater light of God's heavenly kingdom. To their company, and
to the fellowship of all the citizens above, may God in his mercy
bring us all.

Let us bring together all our prayers in the words our Saviour
Christ taught us:

    'Our Father . . .'

                                      Frank Colquhoun

THE NEEDS OF THE POOR

Lord, as we make ready for Christmas amid so much affluence and abundance, keep us mindful of the poverty-stricken peoples of the world, the vast multitude who at this very time lack the bare necessities of life.

Through the gifts we offer for their relief may we show something of our gratitude for all that you have given us; and may our gifts be acceptable through him who for our sake became poor and was born in a stable, Jesus our Saviour.

(2 Cor. 8: 9)   *Frank Colquhoun*

AROUSING THE CHURCH

O God, rouse your church,
    lest we sleep and miss men's need of you and your yearning
    love for men.
O God, cleanse your church,
    and forgive our lack of zeal for your kingdom.
O God, set your church ablaze with the fire of your Spirit, that we
    may spend and be spent for your gospel, your will,
    and your glory, all our days.
        Through Jesus Christ, our Lord.

                                                   George Appleton

AROUSING OUR FACULTIES

Lord, we have found out so much knowledge and yet possess so little wisdom. We pray that in your mercy you will save us from ourselves. Help us to learn the right use of nature no less quickly than we unlock her new treasures; and give us hearts and wills made new in Christ to dedicate your gifts of knowledge to the service of others and to the praise of your name.

                                              Timothy Dudley-Smith

A SELECTION OF PRAYERS

THE PRESENCE OF THE RISEN LORD

Remind us Father that our daily lives will be wearisome and fruitless unless the risen power and presence of the Lord Jesus transforms us. Grant that in the week ahead we may know his presence with us in all we do, and may be ready to hear and to obey his voice as he calls us to follow him.

J. C.

THE PASTORAL MINISTRY

Pour out your Holy Spirit, O Lord,
on all whom you have called to serve your Church
as pastors and teachers.
Give them wise and understanding hearts;
fill them with a true love for your people;
make them holy and keep them humble;
that they may be faithful shepherds
and feed the flock committed to their care,
ever seeking your glory
and the increase of your kingdom;
through Jesus Christ our Lord.

(Acts. 20: 28; 1 Pet. 5: 2–3)   *Frank Colquhoun*

A CONFESSION FOR THE CHURCH

O God, whose will it is that all your children should be one in Christ, we pray for the unity of your church.

Pardon all our pride and our lack of faith, of understanding and of charity, which are the cause of our divisions.

Deliver us from our narrow-mindedness, from our bitterness, from our prejudices.

Save us from considering as normal that which is a scandal to the world and an offence to your love.

Teach us to recognize the gifts of your grace among all those who call upon you and confess the faith of Jesus Christ our Lord.

Liturgy of the Reformed Church of France

MEN BROUGHT TOGETHER AGAIN

Father, you have given all peoples one common origin,
    and your will is to gather them as one family in yourself.
Fill the hearts of all men
            with the fire of your love
            and the desire to ensure justice for
                all their brothers and sisters.
By sharing the good things you gave us, may we secure
            justice and equality for every human being,
            an end to all division, and
            a human society built on love and peace.
(Eph. 3: 15)   *From the Roman Missal*

INSTRUMENTS OF GOD'S PEACE

Lord, make us instruments of your peace.
    Where there is hatred, let us sow love;
    where there is injury, let there be pardon;
    where there is discord, union;
    where there is doubt, faith;
    where there is despair, hope;
    where there is darkness, light;
    where there is sadness, joy;
    for your mercy and for your truth's sake.
O Divine Master, grant that we may not so much seek
            to be consoled, as to console;
            to be understood, as to understand;
            to be loved, as to love.
For it is in giving that we receive;
            in pardoning that we are pardoned; and
            in dying that we are born to eternal life;
                through our Saviour, Jesus Christ.

After a Franciscan Prayer

A PRAYER FOR THE WHOLE CONGREGATION

Sovereign Lord, help us and all who are baptized into
Christ's death
> to consider ourselves dead to sin;
> to walk in newness of life; and
> to be united in resurrection with him,
>> our Lord and Saviour Jesus Christ.

(Rom. 6: 3–11)   *J. C.*

RESPONSIBILITY OF THE WHOLE CHURCH

We thank you, our God and Father, for those who in confirmation have made confession of their faith and have been
welcomed into the communicant life of the Christian family in this
place.

Help us each one, by our prayers, our friendship and our
example, to encourage them in the way of Christ, that they may
fully grow up into him and continue steadfastly in the worship and
fellowship of the Church, to the glory of your name; through Jesus
Christ our Lord.

Frank Colquhoun

DAILY STRENGTHENING BY THE HOLY SPIRIT

Into your hands, O Lord, we commend ourselves and all who
are dear to us this day.

Be with us as we go out and as we come in; strengthen us for
the work you have prepared for us to do.

Grant that we may be filled with your Holy Spirit, and so may
walk worthy of our high calling and joyfully achieve all you want
us to do; through Jesus Christ our Lord.

Bishop Theodore Woods

PREPARATION FOR THE UNEXPECTED

Go with us, O Lord, into this unknown day, and help us in all the duties and pleasures which lie ahead.

Make us prepared for the unexpected things as well as for those which we know will take place; keep us watchful against the sudden attack of temptation, that it may not take us unawares.

Make us quick to seize every opportunity of helping someone who is in need. Keep us ready for the request we could not foresee, and the problem we did not anticipate.

So grant, O Lord, that this day may be one in which we prove your help in our lives, and find happiness in our hearts, through Jesus Christ our Lord.

John Eddison

OUR DEPENDENCE ON GOD'S GIVING

Lord God, as we so seed, or plant,
    hoping for a rich harvest,
    we pray that we may be delivered from thinking that this comes
        wholly of its own accord, or
        simply due to our efforts.
Teach us again
    that sun and rain are your gifts,
    that by ourselves we can do nothing and
    that we are stewards of your creation.
In your mercy, grant us
    favourable crops,
    trusting and thankful hearts and
    wise and fair use of your gifts,
        for Jesus's sake.

J. C.

MOTHER DAY: THANKSGIVINGS AND INTERCESSIONS

Loving God, we thank you that Jesus enjoyed a mother's love and grew up within a family.

We thank you for the homes where we were born, and for the care and affection of our mothers.

We pray for all mothers today:

> for expectant mothers, especially those awaiting the birth of their first child;
>
> for those who have young or handicapped children, and who get tired and harassed with so much to do;
>
> for those who are anxious because their children are growing up and seem to be growing away from them;
>
> for those who feel a sense of emptiness as their children marry and leave home;
>
> for those who are elderly and may feel unwanted;
>
> for those who have no husband to share their responsibilities—the widowed, the divorced, and the unmarried mothers.

We pray also for those who have been denied the privilege of motherhood—those who cannot have children of their own, and those who have never had the opportunity to marry.

Finally we pray for those who are closest to us: may we love and care for them as we ourselves have been loved and helped.

We ask it for your love's sake.

John Searle

YESTERDAY'S WARS AND TODAY'S NEEDS

O heavenly Lord, in whose hands are the nations and peoples of the earth:

We thank you for the deliverance from evil which you gave through those who fought, suffered, endured and died in two world wars;

We thank you too for all the evidences of your gracious hand upon
    our nation.

We pray for those who still bear the scars of war, in body or mind;
    Help us to show the love of Christ in our attitudes towards
    them;

We pray for all peoples who are now at variance with one another,
    asking that they may be ready
        to admit what is sinful on their own part, and
        to forgive what they think to be sinful in others;

We pray too that they and all men may, by the working of the Holy
        Spirit,
    be brought to know for themselves the whole gospel of Jesus
        Christ,
    who, by dying for our sins,
        showed that no man can have greater love than that of
        laying down his life for others.

All this we ask in the name of him who is the Prince of Peace.
(John 15: 13)   *J. C.*

THE PARISH CHURCH

God our Father, we thank you for this house of prayer in which
    you bless your family on its pilgrimage.

So quicken our consciences by your holiness,
    nourish our minds by your truth,
    purify our imaginations by your beauty, and
    open our hearts to your love
        that, in the surrender of our wills to your purpose, the
        world may be renewed in Christ Jesus our Lord.

After William Temple

A PRAYER OF THE EASTERN CHURCH

Be mindful, O Lord,
    of us your people who are present
        together here in this place, and

of those who are absent
    through age, frailty or sickness.
We commend the children to your care,
    the young to your guidance,
    the married to your enriching,
    the aged to your support,
    the faint-hearted to your strengthening power,
    the scattered to your shepherd's love, and
    the wandering to your call to repent and be
    forgiven.
Journey with all travellers;
  help the bereaved;
  release the addicted;
  heal the sick.
Bring assurance to all who are passing through
    trouble,
    need, or
    anxiety.
Remember for good
  all those who love us,
  those who care nothing for us, and
those who have asked us (unworthy as we are) to pray for them.

There are surely some whom we have forgotten,
  but you, Lord, will surely remember them;
For you are
  the helper of the helpless,
  the saviour of the lost,
  the refuge for the wanderer, and
  the healer of the sick.
Since you know each one's need,
    and hear every prayer,
  we commend each one to
    your merciful grace and
    your everlasting love.
Grant to us that together
  we may praise your great name,
    now and for ever.

Based on the Anaphora of St Basil the Great

245

'THAT THE WORLD MAY BELIEVE'

Lord Jesus Christ, who prayed for your disciples that they may be one, even as you are one with the Father; draw us to yourself, that in common love and obedience to you we may be united to one another, in the fellowship of the one Spirit, that the world may believe that you are Lord, to the glory of God the Father.

(John 17: 21)   *William Temple*

THE COMMUNION OF SAINTS

We give thanks to you, our Father,

for all your servants departed this life in your faith and fear;

for the memory of their words and deeds;

for the sure and certain hope of reunion with them hereafter;

for the joy that is now theirs, free from earth's sin and sorrow; and

for our communion with them in your Son, Jesus Christ our Lord.

© *Frank Colquhoun*

WHO SHALL SEPARATE?

God of hope and giver of all comfort, we commend to your keeping those who mourn the loss of loved ones (and especially those for whom we have been asked to pray).

Give them the peace that passes all understanding, and make them to know that neither death nor life can separate them from your love in Jesus Christ our Lord.

(Phil. 4: 7; Rom. 8: 35–9)   *Frank Colquhoun*

THE DAYS AHEAD

Grant, O Lord, to all who are bereaved the spirit of faith and courage, that they may have strength to meet the days to come with steadfastness and patience; not sorrowing as those without hope, but in thankful remembrance of your great goodness in past years, and in the sure expectation of a joyful reunion in heaven; and this we ask in the name of Jesus Christ our Saviour.

Episcopal Church, U.S.A.

THOSE IN PAIN

Merciful Father, help all who suffer pain of body, or grief of heart, to find in you their help.

As Jesus suffered pain in his body, and healed it in others, help them to find their peace in him, and to be renewed in strength of body and mind; by your mercy.

Dick Williams

THE INCURABLE

Father we bring to you
    the needs of those whose lives are shadowed by
        suffering,
praying especially for those whose sickness has no cure.
        whose sadness finds no
          comfort, and
        whose loneliness can never
          be filled.
Bind up their wounds, O Lord,
    and lift their hearts to you,
as now in silence we remember them in Jesus' name.

© *Frank Colquhoun*

HANDICAPPED CHILDREN

God our Father, we commend to your compassion
    all children who are in need;
        those whose bodies are handicapped by injury or illness;

those whose minds are retarded; and
those whose lives are warped by broken marriages and
unhappy homes.
Enable all who care for them
to minister with tenderness and understanding;
And give them the assurance of your unfailing love;
through Christ our Lord.

© *Frank Colquhoun*

THE BIRTH OF A BABY

Heavenly Father, creator and giver of life, there is much joy in
our hearts at the news of a baby's birth—a most special and
complete gift of your love, a new being and a wonder of creation.
Be with the mother and father of this little baby in their happiness, and accept their praise and ours as we give thanks to you
through Jesus Christ our Lord.

Mothers' Union Prayer Book

ENGAGED COUPLES

Lord Jesus Christ, who by your presence and power brought joy
to the wedding at Cana:
Bless those engaged to be married, that there may be
truth at the beginning of their lives together,
unselfishness all the way, and
perseverance to the end.
May their hopes be realized,
and their love for each other deepen and grow,
that through them your name may be glorified.
(John 2: 1–11) *Mothers' Union Service Book*

AFTER SERVICE

As we have been hearers of your word today,
give us grace, Lord, to be doers of it through this week, for
Christ's sake.
(Jas. 1: 22) *J. C.*

THE
PARISH PSALTER

The Psalms of David Pointed
for Chanting

BY

SYDNEY H. NICHOLSON

ARRANGED ACCORDING TO THE
BOOK OF COMMON PRAYER

(Where Psalms for the day are to be as appointed
in The Alternative Lectionary, see ASB pp. 983–1046
and ASB pp. 1049–1091.)

GENERAL PRINCIPLES

THE purpose of this Psalter is to secure the proper emphasis and rhythm of the words by the simplest means.

The success of the method depends upon the intelligence and thought of the singers rather than on a multiplicity of signs.

Psalms should frequently be read through by the singers in order to secure unanimity in rhythm, before the music is added.

RULES

1. Every word must be pronounced clearly and with natural emphasis, as in deliberate reading.

2. The length and accentuation of each note (or chord) in the chant must be governed entirely by the words, and not vice versa.

3. The final syllable '-ed' should only be pronounced separately where this is indicated by means of a hyphen. The one exception is the word 'blessed' which is always pronounced as two syllables.

4. Breath is to be taken at commas.

SIGNS USED IN POINTING

1. The 'bar-mark' '. This corresponds with the bar-lines in the chant, and indicates which syllables are to be sung to each note (or chord).

(*a*) Where there is one syllable in a bar, two notes of the chant are sung to it, and generally speaking they should be sung quickly, the main emphasis being on the first note. (See Venite vs. 3a, etc.)

(*b*) Where there are two syllables in a bar, they are allotted to the two notes. (See Venite vss. 1b, etc.)

(*c*) Where there are three or more syllables in a bar, the *first* note (or chord) is repeated as many times as necessary, the *last* syllable only being sung to the second note (or chord). (See Venite vss. 1a, 2a, 3b, etc.) This is the general rule; in exceptional cases the syllables to be sung to the first note (or chord) are divided from those to be sung to the second note (or chord) by an inverted dot. (See Venite vss. 4a, 11a.)

(*d*) Where there is a dotted note followed by a crochet in the recitation, the crotchet will be sung to the last syllable before the 'bar-mark'; but if this syllable bears a verbal stress the principal note must be sung to it as well, the crotchet being sung very lightly, or even omitted altogether.

Where crotchets occur in other parts of the chant they are grouped with the minims of which they are subdivisions, and the group is subject to the same rules as apply to the plain chords: where such groups occur on unaccented syllables they must, of course, be sung lightly and quickly.

While this system in no way precludes the use of florid chants, it should be remembered that more dignified as well as more flexible results are obtained with those that are free from such embellishments.

2. The 'single-phrase' sign *. Normally, the colon dividing the verse corresponds with the double bar in the chant, but sometimes a far smoother effect is obtained if the whole chant is treated as a single phrase of seven bars, instead of two phrases of three and four bars respectively. In such cases, the break at the double bar is cancelled, and the whole verse is sung straight through. (See Venite vs. 9.) Where this device is employed, a suitable chant must be selected, and the best effect is usually obtained where the movement of the parts is more or less conjunct; but individual chants should be tested.

3. The 'half-chant' sign, ½. This is employed in a few cases only (e.g. Psalm xv. vs. 7). In these cases the chant is commenced at the double bar. This device is only practicable with single chants.

4. The grouping of the verses follows that in the Prayer Book in all the psalms except Ps. xviii. vs. 1, lxxxix. vs. 50, and civ. vs. 35, where a simple sub-division obviously improves the sense.

In all the above cases of special treatment an alternative is provided in a footnote, for use if preferred.

5. The usual grouping of verses in certain of the Canticles (especially the Te Deum) has been modified in order to make them suitable to ordinary chants.

6. Three Psalms (ci, cxv, and cxlviii) suggest a different form of chant, with fewer notes in the ending; they are given in the

appendix, pointed in this way, with specimen chants, and may be used as an alternative to the ordinary settings. It is suggested that other chants in this form might be written or adapted.

The Canticles

VENITE, EXULTEMUS Psalm 95

f O COME let us ' sing unto the ' Lord : let us heartily rejoice in the ' strength of ' our sal'vation.

2 Let us come before his ' presence with ' thanksgiving : and shew ourselves ' glad in ' him with ' psalms.

3 For the Lord is a ' great ' God : and a great ' King above ' all ' gods.

4 In his hand are all the ' corners · of the ' earth : and the strength of the ' hills is ' his ' also.

2nd Part

5 The sea is his and ' he ' made it : and his hands pre ' pared the ' dry ' land.

p 6 O come let us worship and ' fall ' down : and kneel be'fore the ' Lord our ' Maker.

7 For he is the ' Lord our ' God : and we are the people of his pasture, and the ' sheep of ' his ' hand.

mf 8 To-day if ye will hear his voice, harden ' not your ' hearts : as in the provocation, and as in the day of temp'tation ' in the ' wilderness;

* 9 When your ' fathers ' tempted ' me : ' proved me and ' saw my ' works.

9 When your fathers ' tempted ' me : proved ' me and ' saw my ' works.

10 Forty years long was I grieved with this gene'ration and '
   said : It is a people that do err in their hearts, for they ' have
   not ' known my ' ways;

11 Unto whom I ' sware · in my ' wrath : that they should not '
   enter ' into my ' rest.

Glory be to the Father, and ' to the ' Son : and ' to the ' Holy '
   Ghost;

As it was in the beginning, is now and ' ever ' shall be : world
   without ' end · ' A'men.

EASTER DAY

At Morning Prayer, instead of the Psalm, O come, let us sing,
   etc., *these Anthems shall be sung or said.*

1 CHRIST our passover is ' sacrificed ' for us : therefore ' let
   us ' keep the ' feast;

2 Not with the old leaven, nor with the leaven of ' malice
   and ' wickedness : but with the unleavened bread of sin'-
   ceri'ty and ' truth. *1 Cor. v. 7.*

3 Christ being raised from the dead ' dieth no ' more : death
   hath no ' more do'minion ' over him.

4 For in that he died, he died unto ' sin ' once : but in that he
   liveth, he ' liveth ' unto ' God.

5 Likewise reckon ye also yourselves to be dead indeed '
   unto ' sin : but alive unto God through ' Jesus ' Christ our '
   Lord. *Rom. vi. 9.*

6 Christ is ' risen from the ' dead : and become the ' first-
   fruits of ' them that ' slept.

7 For since by ' man came ' death : by man came also the
   resur'rection ' of the ' dead.

8 For as in Adam ' all ' die : even so in Christ shall ' all be ' made a'live. *1 Cor. xv. 20.*

Glory be to the Father, and ' to the ' Son : and ' to the ' Holy ' Ghost;

As it was in the beginning, is now and ' ever ' shall be : world without ' end. ' A'men.

TE DEUM LAUDAMUS

1 WE praise ' thee O ' God : we acknowledge ' thee to ' be the ' Lord.

2 All the earth doth ' worship ' thee : the ' Father ' ever'lasting.

3 To thee all Angels ' cry a'loud : the Heavens and ' all the ' Powers there'in.

4 To thee ' Cherubin and ' Seraphin : con'tinual'ly do ' cry,

5 Holy ' Holy ' Holy : Lord ' God of ' Saba'oth;

† 6 Heaven and ' earth are ' full : of the ' Majesty ' of thy ' Glory.

7 The glorious company of the Apostles ' praise ' thee : the goodly fellowship of the ' Prophets ' praise ' thee:

8 The noble ' army of ' Martyrs : praise ' — ' — ' thee.

9 The holy Church throughout all the world doth ac'know-ledge ' thee : the Father ' of an ' infinite ' Majesty,

10 Thine honourable true and ' only ' Son : also the ' Holy ' Ghost the ' Comforter.

† *This verse may be sung without any break at the colon.*

256

11 Thou art the King of ' Glory O ' Christ : thou art the ever'lasting ' Son of the ' Father.

12 When thou tookest upon thee to de'liver ' man : thou didst not ab'hor the ' Virgin's ' womb.

2nd Part

13 When thou hadst overcome the ' sharpness of ' death : thou didst open the Kingdom of ' Heaven to ' all be'lievers.

14 Thou sittest at the right ' hand of ' God : in the ' Glory ' of the ' Father.

* 15 We be'lieve that ' thou ' shalt ' come : to ' be our ' judge.

16 We therefore pray thee ' help thy ' servants : whom thou hast redeemed ' with thy ' precious ' blood.

17 Make them to be numbered ' with thy ' Saints : in ' glory ' ever'lasting.

18 O Lord save thy people and ' bless thine ' heritage : govern them and ' lift them ' up for ' ever.

19 Day by day we ' magnify ' thee : and we worship thy Name ' ever ' world without ' end.

20 Vouch'safe O ' Lord : to keep us this ' day with'out ' sin.

21 O Lord have ' mercy up'on us : have ' mer'cy up'on us.

22 O Lord let thy mercy ' lighten up'on us : as our ' trust is ' in ' thee.

23 O Lord in thee ' have I ' trusted : let me ' never ' be con'founded.

Or this Canticle

BENEDICITE, OMNIA OPERA

1 O ALL ye Works of the Lord ' bless ye the ' Lord : praise him and ' magnify ' him for ' ever.

15 We believe that ' thou shalt ' come : to ' be ' our ' judge.

2 O ye Angels of the Lord ' bless ye the ' Lord : praise him and ' magnify ' him for ' ever.

3 O ye Heavens ' bless ye the ' Lord : praise him and ' magnify ' him for ' ever.

4 O ye Waters that be above the Firmament ' bless ye the ' Lord : praise him and ' magnify ' him for ' ever.

5 O all ye Powers of the Lord ' bless ye the ' Lord : praise him and ' magnify ' him for ' ever.

6 O ye Sun and Moon ' bless ye the ' Lord : praise him and ' magnify ' him for ' ever.

7 O ye Stars of Heaven ' bless ye the ' Lord : praise him and ' magnify ' him for ' ever.

8 O ye Showers and Dew ' bless ye the ' Lord : praise him and ' magnify ' him for ' ever.

9 O ye Winds of God ' bless ye the ' Lord : praise him and ' magnify ' him for ' ever.

10 O ye Fire and Heat ' bless ye the ' Lord : praise him and ' magnify ' him for ' ever.

11 O ye Winter and Summer ' bless ye the ' Lord : praise him and ' magnify ' him for ' ever.

12 O ye Dews and Frosts ' bless ye the ' Lord : praise him and ' magnify ' him for ' ever.

13 O ye Frost and Cold ' bless ye the ' Lord : praise him and ' magnify ' him for ' ever.

14 O ye Ice and Snow ' bless ye the ' Lord : praise him and ' magnify ' him for ' ever.

15 O ye Nights and Days ' bless ye the ' Lord : praise him and ' magnify ' him for ' ever.

16 O ye Light and Darkness ' bless ye the ' Lord : praise him and ' magnify ' him for ' ever.

17 O ye Lightnings and Clouds ' bless ye the ' Lord : praise him and ' magnify ' him for ' ever.

18 O let the Earth ' bless the ' Lord : yea let it praise him and ' magnify ' him for ' ever.

19 O ye Mountains and Hills ' bless ye the ' Lord : praise him and ' magnify ' him for ' ever.

20 O all ye Green Things upon the Earth ' bless ye the ' Lord : praise him and ' magnify ' him for ' ever.

21 O ye Wells ' bless ye the ' Lord : praise him and ' magnify ' him for ' ever.

22 O ye Seas and Floods ' bless ye the ' Lord : praise him and ' magnify ' him for ' ever.

23 O ye Whales and all that move in the Waters ' bless ye the ' Lord : praise him and ' magnify ' him for ' ever.

24 O all ye Fowls of the Air ' bless ye the ' Lord : praise him and ' magnify ' him for ' ever.

25 O all ye Beasts and Cattle ' bless ye the ' Lord : praise him and ' magnify ' him for ' ever.

26 O ye Children of Men ' bless ye the ' Lord : praise him and ' magnify ' him for ' ever.

27 O let Israel ' bless the ' Lord : praise him and ' magnify ' him for ' ever.

28 O ye Priests of the Lord ' bless ye the ' Lord : praise him and ' magnify ' him for ' ever.

29 O ye Servants of the Lord ' bless ye the ' Lord : praise him and ' magnify ' him for ' ever.

30 O ye Spirits and Souls of the Righteous ' bless ye the ' Lord : praise him and ' magnify ' him for ' ever.

31 O ye holy and humble Men of heart ' bless ye the ' Lord : praise him and ' magnify ' him for ' ever.

32 O Ananias Azarias and Misael ' bless ye the ' Lord : praise him and ' magnify ' him for ' ever.

Glory be to the Father, and ' to the ' Son : and ' to the ' Holy ' Ghost;

As it was in the beginning, is now and ' ever ' shall be : world without ' end. ' A'men.

BENEDICTUS St Luke i 68

1 BLESSED be the Lord ' God of ' Israel : for he hath ' visited · and re'deemed his ' people;

2 And hath raised up a mighty sal'vation ' for us : in the ' house of his ' servant ' David;

3 As he spake by the mouth of his ' holy ' Prophets : which have been ' since the ' world be'gan;

4 That we should be saved ' from our ' enemies : and from the ' hands of ' all that ' hate us;

5 To perform the mercy promised ' to our ' forefathers : and to re'member his ' holy ' Covenant;

* 6 To per'form the ' oath : which he ' sware to our ' fore · father ' Abraham;

6 To perform the oath which he sware to our ' fore · father ' Abraham : that ' he would ' give ' us;

260

* 7 That he would give us, that we being delivered out of the '
  hand of our ' enemies : might ' serve him with'out ' fear;

8 In holiness and ' righteousness be'fore him : all the ' days
  of ' our ' life.

9 And thou Child shalt be called the ' Prophet of the '
  Highest : for thou shalt go before the face of the Lord ' to
  pre'pare his ' ways;

10 To give knowledge of salvation ' unto his ' people : for the
   re'mission ' of their ' sins,

11 Through the tender mercy of ' our ' God : whereby the day-
   spring ' from on ' high hath ' visited us;

12 To give light to them that sit in darkness, and in the '
   shadow of ' death : and to guide our feet ' into the ' way of '
   peace.

Glory be to the Father, and ' to the ' Son : and ' to the ' Holy '
Ghost;

As it was in the beginning, is now and ' ever ' shall be : world
without ' end. ' A'men.

JUBILATE DEO Psalm 100

1 O be joyful in the Lord ' all ye ' lands : serve the Lord with
  gladness, and come before his ' presence ' with a ' song.

2 Be ye sure that the Lord ' he is ' God : it is he that hath
  made us and not we ourselves, we are his ' people · and the '
  sheep of his ' pasture.

7 That we being delivered out of the ' hand of our ' enemies : might '
serve him with'out ' fear;

3 O go your way into his gates with thanksgiving, and into his ' courts with ' praise : be thankful unto him and ' speak good ' of his ' Name.

4 For the Lord is gracious, his mercy is ' ever'lasting : and his truth endureth from gene'ration to ' gene'ration.

Glory be to the Father, and ' to the ' Son : and ' to the ' Holy ' Ghost;

As it was in the beginning, is now and ' ever ' shall be : world without ' end. ' A'men.

MAGNIFICAT St Luke i

1 My soul doth ' magnify the ' Lord : and my spirit hath re'joiced in ' God my ' Saviour.

2 For he ' hath re'garded : the ' lowliness ' of his ' handmaiden.

3 For be'hold from ' henceforth : all gene'rations shall ' call me ' blessed.

4 For he that is mighty hath ' magnified ' me : and ' holy ' is his ' Name.

5 And his mercy is on ' them that ' fear him : through'out all ' gene'rations.

6 He hath shew-ed ' strength with his ' arm : he hath scattered the proud, in the imagi'nation ' of their ' hearts.

7 He hath put down the mighty ' from their ' seat : and hath ex'alted the ' humble and ' meek.

8 He hath fill-ed the hungry with ' good ' things : and the rich he ' hath sent ' empty a'way.

9 He re'membering his ' mercy : hath ' holpen his ' servant ' Israel.

10 As he promised ' to our ' forefathers : Abraham ' and his '
seed for ' ever.

Glory be to the Father, and ' to the ' Son : and ' to the ' Holy '
Ghost;

As it was in the beginning, is now and ' ever ' shall be : world
without ' end. ' A'men.

CANTATE DOMINO Psalm 98

1 O sing unto the Lord a ' new ' song : for he hath ' done '
marvellous ' things.

2 With his own right hand and with his ' holy ' arm : hath he '
gotten him'self the ' victory.

3 The Lord declared ' his sal'vation : his righteousness hath
he openly ' shewed in the ' sight of the ' heathen.

4 He hath remembered his mercy and truth, toward the '
house of ' Israel : and all the ends of the world have seen the
sal'vation of ' our ' God.

5 Shew yourselves joyful unto the Lord ' all ye ' lands : sing
re'joice and ' give ' thanks.

6 Praise the Lord up'on the ' harp : sing to the ' harp with a '
psalm of ' thanksgiving.

7. With trumpets ' also and ' shawms : O shew yourselves
joyful be'fore the ' Lord the ' King.

8 Let the sea make a noise, and all that ' therein ' is : the
round world and ' they that ' dwell there'in.

9 Let the floods clap their hands, and let the hills be joyful
together be'fore the ' Lord : for he is ' come to ' judge the '
earth.

10 With righteousness shall he ' judge the ' world : and the '
people ' with ' equity.

Glory be to the Father, and ' to the ' Son : and ' to the ' Holy '
Ghost;

As it was in the beginning, is now and ' ever ' shall be : world
without ' end. ' A'men.

NUNC DIMITTIS St Luke ii 29

1 LORD now lettest thou thy servant de'part in ' peace :
ac'cording ' to thy ' word.

2 For mine eyes have ' seen thy sal'vation : which thou hast
prepared before the ' face of ' all ' people.

3 To be a light to ' lighten the ' Gentiles : and to be the '
glory · of thy ' people ' Israel.

Glory be to the Father, and ' to the ' Son : and ' to the ' Holy '
Ghost;

As it was in the beginning, is now and ' ever ' shall be : world
without ' end. ' A'men.

DEUS MISEREATUR Psalm 67

1 God be merciful unto ' us and ' bless us : and shew us the
light of his countenance, and be ' merciful ' unto ' us :

2 That thy way may be ' known upon ' earth : thy saving '
health a'mong all ' nations.

3 Let the people ' praise thee O ' God : yea let ' all the '
people ' praise thee.

4 O let the nations re'joice and be ' glad : for thou shalt judge
the folk righteously, and govern the ' nations up'on ' earth.

264

5 Let the people ' praise thee O ' God : yea let ' all the ' people ' praise thee.

6 Then shall the earth bring ' forth her ' increase : and God even our own ' God shall ' give us his ' blessing.

2nd Part

7 God ' shall ' bless us : and all the ' ends of the ' world shall ' fear him.

Glory be to the Father, and ' to the ' Son : and ' to the ' Holy ' Ghost;

As it was in the beginning, is now and ' ever ' shall be : world without ' end. ' A'men.

The Psalms of David

DAY 1   MORNING

PSALM 1

BLESSED is the man that hath not walked in the counsel of the ungodly, nor stood in the ' way of ' sinners : and hath not ' sat · in the ' seat of the ' scornful.

2 But his delight is in the ' law of the ' Lord : and in his law will he exercise him'self ' day and ' night.

3 And he shall be like a tree planted by the ' water'side : that will bring forth his ' fruit in ' due ' season.

4 His leaf also ' shall not ' wither : and look, whatsoever he ' doeth ' it shall ' prosper.

5 As for the ungodly, it is not ' so with ' them : but they are like the chaff, which the wind scattereth a'way · from the ' face of the ' earth.

6 Therefore the ungodly shall not be able to ' stand · in the ' judgement : neither the sinners in the congre'gation ' of the ' righteous.

2nd Part

7 But the Lord knoweth the ' way · of the ' righteous : and the ' way of · the un'godly shall ' perish.

PSALM 2

Single Chant

WHY do the heathen so furiously ' rage to'gether : and why do the people i'magine a ' vain ' thing?

2 The kings of the earth stand up, and the rulers take ' counsel to'gether : against the ' Lord and a'gainst his A'nointed.

3 Let us break their ' bonds a'sunder : and cast a'way their ' cords ' from us.

4 He that dwelleth in heaven shall ' laugh them to ' scorn : the Lord shall ' have them ' in de'rision.

5 Then shall he speak unto them ' in his ' wrath : and vex them ' in his ' sore dis'pleasure.

6 Yet have I ' set my ' King : upon my ' holy ' hill of ' Sion.

7 I will preach the law, whereof the Lord hath ' said unto ' me : Thou art my Son, this day have ' I be'gotten ' thee.

8 Desire of me, and I shall give thee the heathen for ' thine in'heritance : and the utmost parts of the ' earth for ' thy pos'session.

9 Thou shalt bruise them with a ' rod of ' iron : and break them in pieces ' like a ' potter's ' vessel.

10 Be wise now therefore ' O ye ' kings : be learned, ye that are ' judges ' of the ' earth.

11 Serve the ' Lord in ' fear : and re'joice unto ' him with ' reverence.

12 Kiss the Son lest he be angry, and so ye perish from the ' right ' way : if his wrath be kindled (yea but a little), blessed are all they that ' put their ' trust in ' him.

PSALM 3

p LORD, how are they in'creased that ' trouble me : many are ' they that ' rise a'gainst me.

2 Many one there be that ' say of my ' soul : There is no help '
  for him ' in his ' God.

3 But thou O Lord art ' my de'fender : thou art my worship,
  and the ' lifter ' up of my ' head.

4 I did call upon the Lord ' with my ' voice : and he heard me '
  out of his ' holy ' hill.

5 I laid me down and slept, and rose ' up a'gain : for the '
  Lord sus'tain-ed ' me.

6 I will not be afraid for ten ' thousands · of the ' people : that
  have set themselves a'gainst me ' round a'bout.

f 7 Up Lord and help me ' O my ' God : for thou smitest all
  mine enemies upon the cheek-bone, thou hast broken the '
  teeth of ' the un'godly.

8 Salvation belongeth ' unto the ' Lord : and thy blessing ' is
  up'on thy ' people.

PSALM 4

HEAR me when I call O ' God of my ' righteousness :
  thou hast set me at liberty when I was in trouble,
  have mercy upon me and ' hearken ' unto my '
  prayer.

2 O ye sons of men, how long will ye blas'pheme mine '
  honour : and have such pleasure in vanity and ' seek ' after '
  leasing?

3 Know this also, that the Lord hath chosen to himself the '
  man that is ' godly : when I call upon the ' Lord ' he will '
  hear me.

4 Stand in ' awe and ' sin not : commune with your own
  heart, and in your ' chamber ' and be ' still.

5 Offer the ' sacrifice of ' righteousness : and ' put your ' trust · in the ' Lord.

6 There be ' many that ' say : Who will ' shew us ' any ' good?

7 Lord ' lift thou ' up : the light of thy ' counte'nance up'on us.

8 Thou hast put gladness ' in my ' heart : since the time that their corn and ' wine and ' oil in'creased.

2nd Part

9 I will lay me down in peace and ' take my ' rest : for it is thou Lord only that ' makest me ' dwell in ' safety.

PSALM 5

PONDER my ' words O ' Lord : con'sider my ' medi'tation.

2 O hearken thou unto the voice of my calling, my ' King and my ' God : for unto ' thee will I ' make my ' prayer.

3 My voice shalt thou hear be'times O ' Lord : early in the morning will I direct my prayer unto thee ' and will ' look ' up.

4 For thou art the God that hast no ' pleasure in ' wickedness : neither shall any ' evil ' dwell with ' thee.

5 Such as be foolish shall not ' stand in thy ' sight : for thou ' hatest all ' them that work ' vanity.

6 Thou shalt destroy ' them that speak ' leasing : the Lord will abhor both the bloodthirsty ' and de'ceitful ' man.

2nd Part

7 But as for me I will come into thine house, even upon the multitude of ' thy ' mercy : and in thy fear will I worship ' toward thy ' holy ' temple.

8 Lead me O Lord in thy righteousness, be'cause of mine ' enemies : make thy way ' plain be'fore my ' face.

9 For there is no faithfulness ' in his ' mouth : their inward ' parts are ' very ' wickedness.

10 Their throat is an ' open ' sepulchre : they ' flatter ' with their ' tongue.

11 Destroy thou them O God, let them perish through their own i'magi'nations : cast them out in the multitude of their ungodliness, for ' they have re'belled a'gainst thee.

12 And let all them that put their trust in ' thee re'joice : they shall ever be giving of thanks because thou defendest them, they that love thy Name ' shall be ' joyful in ' thee;

13 For thou Lord wilt give thy blessing ' unto the ' righteous : and with thy favourable kindness wilt thou de'fend him ' as with a ' shield.

DAY 1   EVENING

PSALM 6

p O LORD rebuke me not in thine ' indig'nation : neither ' chasten · me in ' thy dis'pleasure.

2 Have mercy upon me O Lord for ' I am ' weak : O Lord heal me ' for my ' bones are ' vexed.

3 My soul also is ' sore ' troubled : but ' Lord how ' long · wilt thou ' punish me?

4 Turn thee O Lord and de'liver my ' soul : O save me ' for thy ' mercy's ' sake.

5 For in death ' no man re'membereth thee : and who will ' give thee ' thanks in the ' pit?

6 I am weary of my groaning, every night ' wash I my ' bed : and ' water my ' couch with my ' tears.

2nd Part

7 My beauty is gone for ' very ' trouble : and worn away be'cause of ' all mine ' enemies.

f 8 Away from me all ' ye that work ' vanity : for the Lord hath ' heard the ' voice of my ' weeping.

9 The Lord hath ' heard my pe'tition : the ' Lord will re'ceive my ' prayer.

2nd Part

10 All mine enemies shall be confounded and ' sore ' vexed : they shall be turned back and ' put to ' shame ' suddenly.

PSALM 7

p O LORD my God, in thee have I ' put my ' trust : save me from all them that persecute me ' and de'liver ' me;

2 Lest he devour my soul like a lion and ' tear it in ' pieces : while ' there is ' none to ' help.

3 O Lord my God if I have done ' any such ' thing : or if there be any ' wickedness ' in my ' hands;

4 If I have rewarded evil unto him that dealt ' friendly ' with me : yea I have delivered him that with'out · any ' cause is mine ' enemy;

5 Then let mine enemy persecute my ' soul and ' take me :
yea let him tread my life down upon the earth, and lay
mine ' honour ' in the ' dust.

6 Stand up O Lord in thy wrath and lift up thyself, because of
the indignation ' of mine ' enemies : arise up for me in the '
judgement that ' thou hast com'manded.

7 And so shall the congregation of the people ' come a'bout
thee : for their sakes therefore lift ' up thy'self a'gain.

8 The Lord shall judge the people, give sentence with ' me O
' Lord : according to my righteousness, and according to
the ' innocency ' that is ' in me.

9 O let the wickedness of the ungodly ' come to an ' end :
but ' guide ' thou the ' just.

10 For the ' righteous ' God : trieth the ' very ' hearts and '
reins.

f 11 My help ' cometh of ' God : who preserveth ' them that
are ' true of ' heart.

12 God is a righteous Judge ' strong and ' patient : and God is
pro'vok-ed ' every ' day.

13 If a man will not turn he will ' whet his ' sword : he hath
bent his ' bow and ' made it ' ready.

14 He hath prepared for him the ' instruments of ' death : he
ordaineth his ' arrows a'gainst the ' persecutors.

15 Behold he ' travaileth with ' mischief : he hath conceived
sorrow and ' brought ' forth un'godliness.

16 He hath graven and dig-ged ' up a ' pit : and is fallen himself
into the destruction ' that he ' made for ' other.

17 For his travail shall come upon his ' own ' head : and his
wickedness shall ' fall on his ' own ' pate.

18 I will give thanks unto the Lord, ac'cording · to his '
righteousness : and I will praise the ' Name · of the ' Lord
most ' High.

PSALM 8

Single Chant
Unison

O Lord our Governor, how excellent is thy Name in '
all the ' world : thou that hast set thy ' glory a'bove
the ' heavens!

2 Out of the mouth of very babes and sucklings hast thou
ordained strength, be'cause of thine ' enemies : that thou
mightest still the ' enemy ' and the a'venger.

3 For I will consider thy heavens, even the ' works of thy '
fingers : the moon and the stars ' which thou ' hast
or'dained.

4 What is man, that thou art ' mindful of ' him : and the son of
man, that ' thou ' visitest ' him?

5 Thou madest him lower ' than the ' angels : to ' crown him
with ' glory and ' worship.

6 Thou makest him to have dominion of the ' works of thy '
hands : and thou hast put all things in sub'jection ' under
his ' feet;

7 All ' sheep and ' oxen : yea and the ' beasts ' of the ' field;

8 The fowls of the air and the ' fishes of the ' sea : and
whatsoever walketh ' through the ' paths of the ' seas.

273

Unison

9 O ' Lord our ' Governor : how excellent is thy ' Name in '
all the ' world!

DAY 2   MORNING
PSALM 9

I WILL give thanks unto thee O Lord with my ' whole ' heart : I
will speak of ' all thy ' marvellous ' works.

2 I will be glad and re'joice in ' thee : yea my songs will I
make of thy ' Name O ' thou most ' Highest.

3 While mine enemies are ' driven ' back : they shall fall and '
perish ' at thy ' presence.

4 For thou hast maintained my ' right and my ' cause : thou
art set in the ' throne that ' judgest ' right.

5 Thou hast rebuked the heathen, and de'stroyed the
un'godly : thou hast put out their ' name for ' ever and '
ever.

6 O thou enemy, destructions are come to a per'petual ' end :
even as the cities which thou hast destroyed, their
me'morial is ' perish-ed ' with them.

7 But the Lord shall en'dure for ' ever : he hath also
pre'pared his ' seat for ' judgement.

8 For he shall judge the ' world in ' righteousness : and
minister true ' judgement ' unto the ' people.

9 The Lord also will be a defence ' for the op'pressed : even a
refuge in ' due ' time of ' trouble.

10 And they that know thy Name will put their ' trust in ' thee :
for thou Lord hast never ' fail-ed ' them that ' seek thee.

11 O praise the Lord which ' dwelleth in ' Sion : shew the ' people ' of his ' doings.

12 For when he maketh inquisition for blood, he re'membereth ' them : and forgetteth not the com'plaint ' of the ' poor.

13 Have mercy upon me O Lord, consider the trouble which I suffer of ' them that ' hate me : thou that liftest me up ' from the ' gates of ' death.

14 That I may shew all thy praises within the ports of the ' daughter of ' Sion : I will re'joice in ' thy sal'vation.

15 The heathen are sunk down in the pit ' that they ' made : in the same net which they hid privily ' is their ' foot ' taken.

16 The Lord is known to ' execute ' judgement : the ungodly is trapped in the ' work of his ' own ' hands.

17 The wicked shall be turned ' into ' hell : and all the people ' that for'get ' God.

18 For the poor shall not alway ' be for'gotten : the patient abiding of the meek ' shall not ' perish for ' ever.

19 Up Lord, and let not man have the ' upper ' hand : let the heathen be ' judg-ed ' in thy ' sight.

20 Put them in ' fear O ' Lord : that the heathen may know them'selves to ' be but ' men.

PSALM 10

p WHY standest thou so far ' off O ' Lord : and hidest thy face in the ' needful ' time of ' trouble?

2 The ungodly for his own lust doth ' persecute the ' poor : let them be taken in the crafty wiliness ' that they ' have i'magined.

3 For the ungodly hath made boast of his own ' heart's de'sire : and speaketh good of the covetous ' whom ' God ab'horreth.

4 The ungodly is so proud that he careth ' not for ' God : neither is ' God in ' all his ' thoughts.

5 His ways are ' alway ' grievous : thy judgements are far above out of his sight, and therefore de'fieth he ' all his ' enemies.

6 For he hath said in his heart, Tush I shall never be ' cast ' down : there shall no harm ' happen ' unto ' me.

7 His mouth is full of cursing de'ceit and ' fraud : under his ' tongue is un'godliness and ' vanity.

8 He sitteth lurking in the thievish ' corners · of the ' streets : and privily in his lurking dens doth he murder the innocent, his eyes are ' set a'gainst the ' poor.

9 For he lieth waiting secretly, even as a lion lurketh he ' in his ' den : that ' he may ' ravish the ' poor.

10 He doth ' ravish the ' poor : when he ' getteth him ' into his ' net.

11 He falleth down and ' humbleth him'self : that the con-gregation of the poor may fall ' into the ' hands of his ' captains.

12 He hath said in his heart, Tush ' God hath for'gotten : he hideth away his face and ' he will ' never ' see it.

f 13 Arise O Lord God and lift ' up thine ' hand : for'get ' not the ' poor.

14 Wherefore should the wicked blas'pheme ' God : while he doth say in his heart, Tush, ' thou God ' carest not ' for it.

15 Surely ' thou hast ' seen it : for thou be'holdest un'godli-ness and ' wrong.

16 That thou mayest take the matter ' into thy ' hand : the poor committeth himself unto thee, for thou art the ' helper ' of the ' friendless.

17 Break thou the power of the ungodly ' and ma'licious : take away his ungodliness and ' thou shalt ' find ' none.

18 The Lord is King for ' ever and ' ever : and the heathen are ' perished ' out of the ' land.

19 Lord thou hast heard the de'sire of the ' poor : thou preparest their heart, and thine ear ' hearkeneth ' there'to;

20 To help the fatherless and poor ' unto their ' right : that the man of the earth be no ' more ex'alted a'gainst them.

PSALM 11

In the Lord put ' I my ' trust : how say ye then to my soul, that she should flee as a ' bird ' unto the ' hill?

2 For lo the ungodly bend their bow, and make ready their arrows with'in the ' quiver : that they may privily shoot at them ' which are ' true of ' heart.

2nd Part

3 For the foundations will be ' cast ' down : and ' what hath the ' righteous ' done?

4 The Lord is in his ' holy ' temple : the Lord's ' seat ' is in ' heaven.

5 His eyes con'sider the ' poor : and his eyelids ' try the ' children of ' men.

6 The Lord al'loweth the ' righteous : but the ungodly and him that delighteth in wickedness ' doth his ' soul ab'hor.

7 Upon the ungodly he shall rain snares, fire and brimstone ' storm and ' tempest : this shall ' be their ' portion to ' drink.

2nd Part

8 For the righteous Lord ' loveth ' righteousness : his countenance will be'hold the ' thing that is ' just.

DAY 2   EVENING
PSALM 12

HELP me Lord for there is not one ' godly man ' left : for the
faithful are minished from a'mong the ' children of ' men.

2 They talk of vanity every one ' with his ' neighbour : they
   do but flatter with their lips, and dissemble ' in their '
   double ' heart.

3 The Lord shall root out all de'ceitful ' lips : and the tongue
   that ' speaketh ' proud ' things;

4 Which have said, With our tongue will ' we pre'vail : we are
   they that ought to speak, ' who is ' lord over ' us?

5 Now for the comfortless trouble's sake ' of the ' needy : and
   because of the deep ' sighing ' of the ' poor,

6 I will up ' saith the ' Lord : and will help every one from him
   that swelleth against him ' and will ' set him at ' rest.

7 The words of the ' Lord are ' pure words : even as the silver
   which from the earth is tried, and purified ' seven times ' in
   the ' fire.

8 Thou shalt ' keep them O ' Lord : thou shalt preserve him
   from ' this · gene'ration for ' ever.

2nd Part

9 The ungodly walk on ' every ' side : when they are exalted,
the children of ' men are ' put to re'buke.

PSALM 13

p How long wilt thou forget me O ' Lord for ' ever : how
long wilt thou ' hide thy ' face ' from me?

2 How long shall I seek counsel in my soul, and be so vexed '
in my ' heart : how long shall mine ' enemies ' triumph '
over me?

3 Consider and hear me O ' Lord my ' God : lighten mine
eyes that I ' sleep ' not in ' death.

4 Lest mine enemy say, I have pre'vailed a'gainst him : for if
I be cast down, they that trouble me ' will re'joice ' at it.

f 5 But my trust is ' in thy ' mercy : and my heart is ' joyful in '
thy sal'vation.

6 I will sing of the Lord, because he hath dealt so '
lovingly ' with me : yea I will praise the ' Name of the ' Lord
most ' Highest.

PSALM 14

The fool hath said ' in his ' heart : There ' is ' no ' God.

2 They are corrupt, and become abominable ' in their '
doings : there is none that doeth ' good ' no not ' one.

3 The Lord looked down from heaven upon the ' children of '
men : to see if there were any that would understand and '
seek ' after ' God.

4 But they are all gone out of the way, they are altogether be'come a'bominable : there is none that doeth ' good ' no not ' one.

[5 Their throat is an open sepulchre, with their tongues have ' they de'ceived : the poison of ' asps is ' under their ' lips.

6 Their mouth is full of ' cursing and ' bitterness : their feet are ' swift to ' shed ' blood.

7 Destruction and unhappiness is in their ways, and the way of peace have ' they not ' known : there is no fear of ' God be'fore their ' eyes.]

8 Have they no knowledge, that they are all such ' workers of ' mischief : eating up my people as it were bread, and ' call not up'on the ' Lord?

9 There were they brought in great fear, even where ' no fear ' was : for God is in the gene'ration ' of the ' righteous.

10 As for you, ye have made a mock at the counsel ' of the ' poor : because he ' putteth his ' trust in the ' Lord.

2nd Part

11 Who shall give salvation unto Israel ' out of ' Sion? : When the Lord turneth the captivity of his people, then shall Jacob rejoice and ' Israel ' shall be ' glad.

DAY 3   MORNING
PSALM 15

Single Chant

Lord who shall ' dwell in thy ' tabernacle : or who shall rest up'on thy ' holy ' hill?

2 Even he that leadeth an ' uncorrupt ' life : and doeth the thing which is right, and speaketh the ' truth ' from his ' heart.

3 He that hath used no deceit in his tongue, nor done evil ' to his ' neighbour : and ' hath not ' slandered his ' neighbour.

4 He that setteth not by himself, but is lowly in his ' own ' eyes : and maketh much of ' them that ' fear the ' Lord.

· 5 He that sweareth unto his neighbour, and disap'pointeth him ' not : though it ' were to his ' own ' hindrance.

6 He that hath not given his ' money · upon ' usury : nor taken re'ward a'gainst the ' innocent.

Unison

½ 7 Whoso doeth these ' things : shall ' never ' fall.

PSALM 16

PRESERVE ' me O ' God : for in thee ' have I ' put my ' trust.

2 O my soul thou hast said ' unto the ' Lord : Thou art my God, my goods are ' nothing ' unto ' thee.

3 All my delight is upon the saints that are ' in the ' earth : and upon ' such as ex'cel in ' virtue.

4 But they that run after an'other ' god : shall ' have 'great ' trouble.

5 Their drink-offerings of blood will ' I not ' offer : neither make mention of their ' names with'in my ' lips.

6 The Lord himself is the portion of mine inheritance and ' of my ' cup : thou ' shalt main'tain my ' lot.

Ps. 15. vs. 7 Whoso ' doeth these ' things : shall ' ne'ver ' fall.

7 The lot is fallen unto me in a ' fair ' ground : yea I ' have a ' goodly ' heritage.

8 I will thank the Lord for ' giving me ' warning : my reins also chasten me ' in the ' night'season.

9 I have set God ' always be'fore me : for he is on my right hand ' therefore I ' shall not ' fall.

10 Wherefore my heart was glad and my ' glory re'joiced : my flesh ' also shall ' rest in ' hope.

11 For why?, thou shalt not leave my ' soul in ' hell : neither shalt thou suffer thy ' Holy One to ' see cor'ruption.

12 Thou shalt shew me the path of life, in thy presence is the ' fulness of ' joy : and at thy right hand there is ' pleasure for ' ever ' more.

PSALM 17

HEAR the right O Lord, consider ' my com'plaint : and hearken unto my prayer that goeth not ' out of ' feign-ed ' lips.

2 Let my sentence come forth ' from thy ' presence : and let thine eyes look up'on the ' thing that is ' equal.

3 Thou hast proved and visited mine heart in the night-season, thou hast tried me and shalt find no ' wickedness ' in me : for I am utterly purposed that my ' mouth shall ' not of'fend.

4 Because of men's works, that are done against the ' words of thy ' lips : I have kept me from the ' ways of ' the de'stroyer.

282

* 5 O hold thou up my ' goings ' in thy ' paths : ' that my '
   footsteps ' slip not.

6 I have called upon thee O God for ' thou shalt ' hear me :
   incline thine ear to me and ' hearken ' unto my ' words.

7 Shew thy marvellous loving-kindness, thou that art the
   Saviour of them which put their ' trust in ' thee : from such
   as re'sist thy ' right ' hand.

8 Keep me as the ' apple · of an ' eye : hide me under the '
   shadow ' of thy ' wings,

9 From the un'godly that ' trouble me : mine enemies compass me round about to ' take a'way my ' soul.

10 They are inclosed in their ' own ' fat : and their mouth '
    speaketh ' proud ' things.

11 They lie waiting in our way on ' every ' side : turning
    their ' eyes ' down to the ' ground;

12 Like as a lion that is ' greedy · of his ' prey : and as it were a
    lion's whelp ' lurking in ' secret ' places.

13 Up Lord, disappoint him and ' cast him ' down : deliver my
    soul from the ungodly which ' is a ' sword of ' thine;

14 From the men of thy hand O Lord, from the men I say and
    from the ' evil ' world : which have their portion in this life,
    whose bellies thou fillest ' with thy ' hid ' treasure.

15 They have children at ' their de'sire : and leave the rest of
    their ' substance ' for their ' babes.

5 O hold thou up my goings ' in thy ' paths : that my ' footsteps ' slip '
not.

16 But as for me, I will behold thy ' presence in ' righteousness : and when I awake up after thy likeness ' I shall be '
satisfied ' with it.

DAY 3   EVENING

PSALM 18

* I WILL love thee O ' Lord my ' strength : the Lord is my stony '
rock and ' my de'fence.

1a My Saviour my God and my might, in whom ' I will ' trust :
my buckler, the horn also of my sal'vation ' and my '
refuge.

2nd Part

2 I will call upon the Lord which is ' worthy · to be ' praised :
so shall ' I be ' safe from mine ' enemies.

3 The sorrows of ' death ' compassed me : and the overflow-
ings of un'godliness ' made me a'fraid.

4 The pains of hell ' came a'bout me : the snares of ' death '
over'took me.

5 In my trouble I will call up'on the ' Lord : and com'plain '
unto my ' God.

6 So shall he hear my voice out of his ' holy ' temple : and my
complaint shall come before him, it shall enter ' even ' into
his ' ears.

7 The earth ' trembled and ' quaked : the very foundations
also of the hills shook, and were re'moved be'cause he
was ' wroth.

---

* I will love thee O Lord my strength; the Lord is my stony rock
and ' my de'fence : my Saviour my God and my might in whom I will
trust, my buckler, the horn also of my sal'vation ' and my ' refuge.

284

8　There went a smoke out ' in his ' presence : and a consuming fire out of his mouth, so that ' coals were ' kindled ' at it.

9　He bowed the heavens also and ' came ' down : and it was ' dark ' under his ' feet.

10　He rode upon the cherubins ' and did ' fly : he came flying up'on the ' wings of the ' wind.

11　He made darkness his ' secret ' place : his pavilion round about him, with dark water and thick ' clouds to ' cover ' him.

12　At the brightness of his presence his ' clouds re'moved : hail'stones and ' coals of ' fire.

13　The Lord also thundered out of heaven, and the Highest ' gave his ' thunder : hail'stones and ' coals of ' fire.

14　He sent out his ' arrows and ' scattered them : he cast forth ' lightnings ' and de'stroyed them.

15　The springs of waters were seen, and the foundations of the round world were discovered, at thy ' chiding O ' Lord : at the blasting of the ' breath of ' thy dis'pleasure.

16　He shall send down from on ' high to ' fetch me : and shall take me ' out of ' many ' waters.

17　He shall deliver me from my strongest enemy, and from ' them which ' hate me : for they ' are too ' mighty ' for me.

18　They prevented me in the ' day of my ' trouble : but the ' Lord was ' my up'holder.

19　He brought me forth also into a ' place of ' liberty : he brought me forth, even because he had a ' favour ' unto ' me.

20　The Lord shall reward me after my ' righteous ' dealing : according to the cleanness of my hands ' shall he ' recompense ' me.

21 Because I have kept the ' ways of the ' Lord : and have not forsaken my God ' as the ' wicked ' doth.

22 For I have an eye unto ' all his ' laws : and will not cast out ' his com'mandments ' from me.

23 I was also uncor'rupt be'fore him : and es'chewed mine ' own ' wickedness.

24 Therefore shall the Lord reward me after my ' righteous ' dealing : and according unto the cleanness of my ' hands in ' his ' eyesight.

25 With the holy ' thou shalt be ' holy : and with a ' perfect man ' thou shalt be ' perfect.

26 With the clean ' thou shalt be ' clean : and with the ' froward ' thou shalt learn ' frowardness.

27 For thou shalt save the people that are ' in ad'versity : and shalt bring down the ' high ' looks of the ' proud.

28 Thou also shalt ' light my ' candle : the Lord my God shall make my ' darkness ' to be ' light.

29 For in thee I shall discomfit an ' host of ' men : and with the help of my God I shall ' leap ' over the ' wall.

30 The way of God is an unde'fil-ed ' way : the word of the Lord also is tried in the fire, he is the defender of all them that ' put their ' trust in ' him.

31 For who is ' God · but the ' Lord : or who hath any ' strength ex'cept our ' God?

32 It is God that girdeth me with ' strength of ' war : and ' maketh my ' way ' perfect.

33 He maketh my ' feet like ' harts' feet : and ' setteth me ' up on ' high.

34 He teacheth mine ' hands to ' fight : and mine arms shall break ' even a ' bow of ' steel.

35 Thou hast given me the defence of ' thy sal'vation : thy right hand also shall hold me up, and thy loving cor'rection shall ' make me ' great.

36 Thou shalt make room enough under me ' for to ' go : that my ' footsteps ' shall not ' slide.

37 I will follow upon mine enemies and ' over'take them : neither will I turn again ' till I ' have de'stroyed them.

38 I will smite them that they shall not be ' able to ' stand : but ' fall ' under my ' feet.

39 Thou hast girded me with strength ' unto the ' battle : thou shalt throw ' down mine ' enemies ' under me.

40 Thou hast made mine enemies also to turn their ' backs up'on me : and I shall de'stroy ' them that ' hate me.

41 They shall cry, but there shall be ' none to ' help them : yea, even unto the Lord shall they cry ' but he ' shall not ' hear them.

42 I will beat them as small as the dust be'fore the ' wind : I will cast them ' out as the ' clay · in the ' streets.

43 Thou shalt deliver me from the ' strivings · of the ' people : and thou shalt ' make me the ' head of the ' heathen.

* 44 A people ' whom I ' have ' not ' known : shall ' serve ' me.

45 As soon as they hear of me ' they shall o'bey me : but the strange children ' shall dis'semble ' with me.

46 The strange ' children shall ' fail : and be a'fraid ' out of their ' prisons.

44 A people whom I ' have not ' known : shall ' serve ' — ' me.

47 The Lord liveth, and blessed be my ' strong ' helper : and prais-ed be the ' God of ' my sal'vation;

48 Even the God that seeth that I ' be a'venged : and subdueth the ' people ' unto ' me.

49 It is he that delivereth me from my cruel enemies, and setteth me up a'bove mine ' adversaries : thou shalt rid me ' from the ' wicked ' man.

50 For this cause will I give thanks unto thee O Lord a'mong the ' Gentiles : and sing ' praises ' unto thy ' Name.

2nd Part

51 Great prosperity giveth he ' unto his ' King : and sheweth loving-kindness unto David his Anointed, and unto his ' seed for ' ever'more.

DAY 4   MORNING
PSALM 19

Single Chant

THE heavens declare the ' glory of ' God : and the ' firmament ' sheweth his ' handy-work.

2 One day ' telleth an'other : and one night ' certi'fieth an'other.

3 There is neither ' speech nor ' language : but their ' voices are ' heard a'mong them.

4 Their sound is gone out into ' all ' lands : and their words ' into the ' ends of the ' world.

5 In them hath he set a tabernacle ' for the ' sun : which cometh forth as a bridegroom out of his chamber, and rejoiceth as a ' giant to ' run his ' course.

6 It goeth forth from the uttermost part of the heaven, and
   runneth about unto the end of ' it a'gain : and there is
   nothing hid ' from the ' heat there'of.

7 The law of the Lord is an undefiled law con'verting the '
   soul : the testimony of the Lord is sure, and giveth ' wisdom ' unto the ' simple.

8 The statutes of the Lord are right and re'joice the ' heart :
   the commandment of the Lord is pure, and giveth ' light '
   unto the 'eyes.

9 The fear of the Lord is clean and en'dureth for ' ever : the
   judgements of the Lord are true and ' righteous '
   alto'gether.

10 More to be desired are they than gold, yea than ' much
   fine ' gold : sweeter also than ' honey ' and the ' honey-
   comb.

11 Moreover by them is thy ' servant ' taught : and in keeping
   of them ' there is ' great re'ward.

12 Who can tell how ' of the of'fendeth : O cleanse thou me '
   from my ' secret ' faults.

13 Keep thy servant also from presumptuous sins, lest they get
   the do'minion ' over me : so shall I be undefiled and
   innocent ' from the ' great of'fence.

14 Let the words of my mouth and the meditation ' of my '
   heart : be alway ac'ceptable ' in thy ' sight,

½ 15 O Lord : my ' strength and ' my re'deemer.

PSALM 20

THE Lord hear thee in the ' day of ' trouble : the Name
   of the ' God of ' Jacob de'fend thee;

   15 O ' — ' Lord : my ' strength and' my re'deemer.

2 Send thee help ' from the ' sanctuary : and ' strengthen thee ' out of ' Sion;

3 Remember ' all thy ' offerings : and ac'cept thy ' burnt ' sacrifice;

4 Grant thee thy ' heart's de'sire : and ful'fil ' all thy ' mind.

5 We will rejoice in thy salvation, and triumph in the Name of the ' Lord our ' God : the Lord per'form all ' thy pe'titions.

6 Now know I that the Lord helpeth his Anointed, and will hear him from his ' holy ' heaven : even with the wholesome ' strength of ' his right ' hand.

7 Some put their trust in chariots and ' some in ' horses : but we will remember the ' Name of the ' Lord our ' God.

8 They are brought ' down and ' fallen : but we are ' risen and ' stand ' upright.

2nd Part

9 Save Lord and hear us O ' King of ' heaven : when we ' call up'on ' thee.

PSALM 21

The King shall rejoice in thy ' strength O ' Lord : exceeding glad shall he ' be of ' thy sal'vation.

2 Thou hast given him his ' heart's de'sire : and hast not de'nied him the re'quest of his ' lips.

3 For thou shalt prevent him with the ' blessings of ' goodness : and shalt set a crown of pure ' gold up'on his ' head.

* 4 He asked life of thee, and thou ' gavest · him a ' long ' life : ' even for ' ever and ' ever.

  5 His honour is great in ' thy sal'vation : glory and great worship ' shalt thou ' lay up'on him.

  6 For thou shalt give him ever'lasting fe'licity : and make him glad with the ' joy of ' thy ' countenance.

  7 And why?, because the King putteth his ' trust in the ' Lord : and in the mercy of the most Highest ' he shall ' not mis'carry.

  8 All thine enemies shall ' feel thine ' hand : thy right hand shall ' find out ' them that ' hate thee.

  9 Thou shalt make them like a fiery oven in ' time of thy ' wrath : the Lord shall destroy them in his displeasure, and the ' fire ' shall con'sume them.

10 Their fruit shalt thou root ' out of the ' earth : and their seed from a'mong the ' children of ' men.

11 For they intended ' mischief a'gainst thee : and imagined such a device as they are not ' able ' to per'form.

12 Therefore shalt thou ' put them to ' flight : and the strings of thy bow shalt thou make ' ready a'gainst the ' face of them.

2nd Part

13 Be thou exalted Lord in thine ' own ' strength : so will we ' sing and ' praise thy ' power.

DAY 4   EVENING

PSALM 22

p My God, my God, look upon me, why hast ' thou for'saken me : and art so far from my health, and from the ' words of ' my com'plaint?

    4 He asked life of thee, and thou gavest him a ' long ' life : even for ' ever ' and ' ever.

2 O my God I cry in the day-time ' but thou ' hearest not : and in the night-season ' also I ' take no ' rest.

3 And thou con'tinuest ' holy : O ' thou ' worship of ' Israel.

4 Our fathers ' hoped in ' thee : they trusted in thee ' and thou ' didst de'liver them.

5 They called upon thee ' and were ' holpen : they put their trust in thee ' and were ' not con'founded.

6 But as for me, I am a worm and ' no ' man : a very scorn of men and the ' outcast ' of the ' people.

7 All they that see me ' laugh me to ' scorn : they shoot out their lips and ' shake their ' heads ' saying,

8 He trusted in God that ' he would de'liver him : let him de'liver him ' if he will ' have him.

9 But thou art he that took me out of my ' mother's ' womb : thou wast my hope, when I hang-ed yet up'on my ' mother's ' breasts.

10 I have been left unto thee ever since ' I was ' born : thou art my God ' even · from my ' mother's ' womb.

11 O go not from me, for trouble is ' hard at ' hand : and ' there is ' none to ' help me.

12 Many oxen are ' come a'bout me : fat bulls of Basan close me ' in on ' every ' side.

13 They gape upon me ' with their ' mouths : as it were a ' ramping · and a ' roaring ' lion.

14 I am poured out like water, and all my bones are ' out of ' joint : my heart also in the midst of my body is ' even like ' melting ' wax.

15 My strength is dried up like a potsherd, and my tongue ' cleaveth · to my ' gums : and thou shalt bring me ' into the ' dust of ' death.

16 For many dogs are ' come a'bout me : and the council of the wicked ' layeth ' siege a'gainst me.

17 They pierced my hands and my feet, I may tell ' all my ' bones : they stand ' staring and ' looking u'pon me.

18 They part my ' garments a'mong them : and cast ' lots up'on my ' vesture.

19 But be not thou far from ' me O ' Lord : thou art my succour ' haste ' thee to ' help me.

20 Deliver my soul ' from the ' sword : my darling ' from the ' power of the ' dog.

21 Save me from the ' lion's ' mouth : thou hast heard me also from a'mong the ' horns of the ' unicorns.

f 22 I will declare thy Name ' unto my ' brethren : in the midst of the congre'gation ' will I ' praise thee.

23 O praise the Lord ' ye that ' fear him : magnify him all ye of the seed of Jacob, and fear him ' all ye ' seed of ' Israel;

24 For he hath not despised nor abhorred the low e'state of the ' poor : he hath not hid his face from him, but when he called ' unto ' him he ' heard him.

25 My praise is of thee in the great ' congre'gation : my vows will I perform in the ' sight of ' them that ' fear him.

26 The poor shall ' eat and be ' satisfied : they that seek after the Lord shall praise him, your ' heart shall ' live for ' ever.

27 All the ends of the world shall remember themselves, and be turned ' unto the ' Lord : and all the kindreds of the ' nations shall ' worship be'fore him.

28 For the kingdom ' is the ' Lord's : and he is the ' Governor a'mong the ' people.

29 All such as be ' fat upon ' earth : have ' eaten ' and ' worshipped.

30 All they that go down into the dust shall ' kneel be'fore him : and no man hath ' quickened his ' own ' soul.

31 My ' seed shall ' serve him : they shall be counted unto the ' Lord for a ' gene'ration.

32 They shall come, and the heavens shall de'clare his ' right-eousness : unto a people that shall be born ' whom the ' Lord hath ' made.

PSALM 23

THE Lord ' is my ' shepherd : therefore ' can I ' lack ' nothing.

 2 He shall feed me in a ' green ' pasture : and lead me forth be'side the ' waters of ' comfort.

 3 He shall con'vert my ' soul : and bring me forth in the paths of righteousness ' for his ' Name's ' sake.

Cres 4 Yea though I walk through the valley of the shadow of death, I will ' fear no ' evil : for thou art with me, thy ' rod and thy ' staff ' comfort me.

 5 Thou shalt prepare a table before me, against ' them that ' trouble me : thou hast anointed my head with oil ' and my ' cup shall be ' full.

f 6 But thy loving-kindness and mercy shall follow me, all the '
    days of my ' life : and I will dwell in the ' house of the ' Lord
    for ' ever.

DAY 5   MORNING

PSALM 24

THE earth is the Lord's, and all that ' therein ' is : the compass
    of the world and ' they that ' dwell there'in.

2 For he hath founded it up'on the ' seas : and pre'pared it
    up'on the ' floods.

3 Who shall ascend into the ' hill of the ' Lord : or who shall
    rise up ' in his ' holy ' place?

4 Even he that hath clean hands and a ' pure ' heart : and that
    hath not lift up his mind unto vanity, nor ' sworn to
    de'ceive his ' neighbour.

5 He shall receive the blessing ' from the ' Lord : and right-
    eousness from the ' God of ' his sal'vation.

6 This is the generation of ' them that ' seek him : even of
    them that ' seek thy ' face O ' Jacob.

Unison

7 Lift up your heads O ye gates, and be ye lift up ye ever'last-
    ing ' doors : and the King of ' glory ' shall come ' in.

Men

8 Who is the ' King of ' glory : (*Unison*) it is the Lord strong
    and mighty, even the ' Lord ' mighty in ' battle.

Unison

9 Lift up your heads O ye gates, and be ye lift up ye ever'last-
    ing ' doors : and the King of ' glory ' shall come ' in.

Men

10 Who is the ' King of ' glory : (*Unison*) even the Lord of
hosts, ' he is the ' King of ' glory.

PSALM 25

Unto thee O Lord will I lift up my soul, my God I have
put my ' trust in ' thee : O let me not be confounded,
neither let mine ' enemies ' triumph ' over me.

2 For all they that hope in thee shall ' not be a'shamed : but
such as transgress without a cause ' shall be ' put to
con'fusion.

3 Shew me thy ' ways O ' Lord : and ' teach me ' thy ' paths.

4 Lead me forth in thy ' truth and ' learn me : for thou art the
God of my salvation, in thee hath been my ' hope ' all the
day ' long.

5 Call to remembrance O Lord thy ' tender ' mercies : and
thy loving kindnesses, which ' have been ' ever of ' old.

6 O remember not the sins and offences ' of my ' youth : but
according to thy mercy, think thou upon me O ' Lord ' for
thy ' goodness.

7 Gracious and righteous ' is the ' Lord : therefore will he
teach ' sinners ' in the ' way.

8 Them that are meek shall he ' guide in ' judgement : and
such as are gentle ' them shall he ' learn his ' way.

9 All the paths of the Lord are ' mercy and ' truth : unto such
as keep his ' covenant ' and his ' testimonies.

10 For thy Name's ' sake O ' Lord : be merciful unto my ' sin
for ' it is ' great.

11 What man is he that ' feareth the ' Lord : him shall he teach
in the ' way that ' he shall ' choose.

12 His soul shall ' dwell at ' ease : and his ' seed shall in'herit
the ' land.

13 The secret of the Lord is among ' them that ' fear him :
and ' he will ' shew them his ' covenant.

14 Mine eyes are ever looking ' unto the ' Lord : for he shall
pluck my ' feet ' out of the ' net.

15 Turn thee unto me and have ' mercy up'on me : for I am '
desolate ' and in ' misery.

16 The sorrows of my heart ' are en'larged : O ' bring thou
me ' out of my ' troubles.

17 Look upon my ad'versity and ' misery : and for'give me ' all
my ' sin.

18 Consider mine enemies how ' many they ' are : and they
bear a ' tyrannous ' hate a'gainst me.

19 O keep my ' soul and de'liver me : let me not be confounded, for I have ' put my ' trust in ' thee.

20 Let perfectness and righteous dealing ' wait up'on me : for
my ' hope hath ' been in ' thee.

2nd Part

21 Deliver ' Israel O ' God : out of ' all ' his ' troubles.

PSALM 26

BE thou my Judge O Lord, for I have ' walk-ed ' innocently : my trust hath been also in the Lord ' therefore ' shall I not ' fall.

2 Examine me O ' Lord and ' prove me : try out my ' reins '
and my ' heart.

3 For thy loving-kindness is ever be'fore mine ' eyes : and I
will ' walk in ' thy ' truth.

4 I have not dwelt with ' vain ' persons : neither will I have '
fellowship ' with the de'ceitful.

5 I have hated the congregation ' of the ' wicked : and will
not ' sit a'mong the un'godly.

6 I will wash my hands in innocency ' O ' Lord : and ' so will
I ' go to · thine ' altar;

7 That I may shew the ' voice of ' thanksgiving : and tell of '
all thy ' wondrous ' works.

8 Lord, I have loved the habitation ' of thy ' house : and the
place ' where thine ' honour ' dwelleth.

9 O shut not up my soul ' with the ' sinners : nor my life ' with
the ' blood'thirsty;

10 In whose ' hands is ' wickedness : and their right ' hand is '
full of ' gifts.

11 But as for me, I will ' walk ' innocently : O deliver me, and
be ' merciful ' unto ' me.

12 My foot ' standeth ' right : I will praise the ' Lord in the '
Congre'gations.

DAY 5   EVENING

PSALM 27

THE Lord is my light and my salvation, whom then ' shall I '
fear : the Lord is the strength of my life, of whom then '
shall I ' be a'fraid?

2 When the wicked even mine enemies and my foes, came upon me to eat ' up my ' flesh : they ' stumbled ' and ' fell.

3 Though an host of men were laid against me, yet shall not my heart ' be a'fraid : and though there rose up war against me, yet will I ' put my ' trust in ' him.

4 One thing have I desired of the Lord which I ' will re'quire : even that I may dwell in the house of the Lord all the days of my life, to behold the fair beauty of the Lord ' and to ' visit his ' temple.

5 For in the time of trouble he shall hide me ' in his ' taber-nacle : yea in the secret place of his dwelling shall he hide me, and set me up up'on a ' rock of ' stone.

6 And now shall he lift ' up mine ' head : above mine ' enemies ' round a'bout me.

7 Therefore will I offer in his dwelling an oblation with ' great ' gladness : I will sing and speak ' praises ' unto the ' Lord.

8 Hearken unto my voice O Lord, when I cry ' unto thee : have ' mercy up'on me and ' hear me.

9 My heart hath talked of thee, Seek ' ye my ' face : Thy face ' Lord ' will I ' seek.

10 O hide not thou thy ' face ' from me : nor cast thy ' servant a'way in dis'pleasure.

11 Thou hast ' been my ' succour : leave me not neither forsake me O ' God of ' my sal'vation.

12 When my father and my ' mother for'sake me : the ' Lord ' taketh me ' up.

13 Teach me thy ' way O ' Lord : and lead me in the right ' way be'cause of mine ' enemies.

14 Deliver me not over into the ' will of mine ' adversaries : for there are false witnesses risen up against me, and ' such as ' speak ' wrong.

15 I should ' utterly have ' fainted : but that I believe verily to see the goodness of the ' Lord in the ' land of the ' living.

16 O tarry thou the ' Lord's ' leisure : be strong and he shall comfort thine heart, and ' put thou thy ' trust in the ' Lord.

PSALM 28

UNTO thee will I cry O ' Lord my ' strength : think no scorn of me, lest if thou make as though thou hearest not, I become like them that go ' down ' into the ' pit.

2 Hear the voice of my humble petitions, when I cry ' unto ' thee : when I hold up my hands towards the mercy-seat ' of thy ' holy ' temple.

3 O pluck me not away, neither destroy me with the ungodly and ' wicked ' doers : which speak friendly to their neighbours, but imagine ' mischief ' in their ' hearts.

4 Reward them according ' to their ' deeds : and according to the wickedness ' of their ' own in'ventions.

5 Recompense them after the ' work of their ' hands : pay them ' that they ' have de'served.

6 For they regard not in their mind the works of the Lord, nor the operation ' of his ' hands : therefore shall he break them down ' and not ' build them ' up.

7 Praised ' be the ' Lord : for he hath heard the ' voice of my ' humble pe'titions.

8 The Lord is my strength and my shield, my heart hath trusted in him and ' I am ' helped : therefore my heart danceth for joy, and in my ' song ' will I ' praise him.

9 The Lord ' is my ' strength : and he is the wholesome de'fence of ' his A'nointed.

10 O save thy people, and give thy blessing unto ' thine in'heritance : feed them and ' set them ' up for ' ever.

PSALM 29

BRING unto the Lord O ye mighty, bring young rams ' unto the ' Lord : ascribe unto the ' Lord ' worship and ' strength.

2 Give the Lord the honour due ' unto his ' Name : worship the ' Lord with ' holy ' worship.

3 It is the Lord that com'mandeth the ' waters : it is the glorious ' God that ' maketh the ' thunder.

4 It is the Lord that ruleth the sea, the voice of the Lord is mighty in ' oper'ation : the voice of the Lord ' is a ' glorious ' voice.

5 The voice of the Lord ' breaketh the ' cedar-trees : yea the Lord ' breaketh the ' cedars of ' Libanus.

6 He maketh them also to skip ' like a ' calf : Libanus also and Sirion ' like a ' young ' unicorn.

7 The voice of the Lord divideth the flames of fire, the voice of the Lord ' shaketh the ' wilderness : yea the Lord ' shaketh the ' wilderness of ' Cades.

8 The voice of the Lord maketh the hinds to bring forth young, and discovereth the ' thick ' bushes : in his temple doth ' every man ' speak of his ' honour.

9 The Lord sitteth a'bove the ' water-flood : and the Lord re'maineth a ' King for ' ever.

10 The Lord shall give strength ' unto his ' people : the Lord shall give his ' people the ' blessing of ' peace.

DAY 6 MORNING

PSALM 30

I WILL magnify thee O Lord for thou hast ' set me ' up : and not made my ' foes to ' triumph ' over me.

2 O Lord my God I cried ' unto ' thee : and ' thou hast ' heal-ed ' me.

3 Thou Lord hast brought my soul ' out of ' hell : thou hast kept my life from ' them that go ' down to the ' pit.

4 Sing praises unto the Lord O ye ' saints of ' his : and give thanks unto him, for a re'membrance ' of his ' holiness.

5 For his wrath endureth but the twinkling of an eye, and in his ' pleasure is ' life : heaviness may endure for a night, but joy ' cometh ' in the ' morning.

6 And in my prosperity I said, I shall never ' be re'moved : thou Lord of thy goodness hast ' made my ' hill so ' strong.

7 Thou didst turn thy ' face ' from me : and ' I ' was ' troubled.

8 Then cried I unto ' thee O ' Lord : and gat me ' to my ' Lord right ' humbly.

9 What profit is there ' in my ' blood : when I go ' down ' to the ' pit?

10 Shall the dust give thanks ' unto ' thee : or ' shall it de'clare thy ' truth?

2nd Part

11 Hear O Lord and have ' mercy up'on me : Lord be '
thou ' my ' helper.

12 Thou hast turned my heaviness ' into ' joy : thou hast put
off my sackcloth and ' girded ' me with ' gladness.

13 Therefore shall every good man sing of thy praise
with'out ' ceasing : O my God, I will give thanks ' unto '
thee for ' ever.

PSALM 31

IN thee O Lord have I ' put my ' trust : let me never be
put to confusion, de'liver me ' ' in thy ' righteousness.

2 Bow down thine ' ear to ' me : make ' haste · to de-'
liver ' me.

3 And be thou my strong rock and ' house of de'fence :
that ' thou ' mayest ' save me.

4 For thou art my strong rock ' and my ' castle : be thou also
my guide, and lead me ' for thy ' Name's ' sake.

5 Draw me out of the net that they have laid ' privily ' for me :
for ' thou ' art my ' strength.

6 Into thy hands I com'mend my ' spirit : for thou hast
redeemed me O ' Lord thou ' God of ' truth.

7 I have hated them that hold of super'stitious ' vanities : and
my ' trust hath ' been in the ' Lord.

8 I will be glad and re'joice in thy ' mercy : for thou hast
considered my trouble, and hast ' known my ' soul in
ad'versities.

2nd Part

9 Thou hast not shut me up into the ' hand of the ' enemy : but hast set my ' feet in a ' large ' room.

10 Have mercy upon me O Lord for ' I am in ' trouble : and mine eye is consumed for very heaviness, yea my ' soul ' and my ' body.

11 For my life is waxen ' old with ' heaviness : and my ' years ' with ' mourning.

12 My strength faileth me because of ' mine in'iquity : and my ' bones ' are con'sumed.

13 I became a reproof among all mine enemies, but especially a'mong my ' neighbours : and they of mine acquaintance were afraid of me, and they that did see me without con'veyed them'selves ' from me.

14 I am clean forgotten, as a dead man ' out of ' mind : I am become ' like a ' broken ' vessel.

15 For I have heard the blasphemy ' of the ' multitude : and fear is on every side, while they conspire together against me, and take their counsel to ' take a'way my ' life.

16 But my hope hath been in ' thee O ' Lord : I have said ' Thou art ' my ' God.

17 My time is in thy hand, deliver me from the ' hand of mine ' enemies : and from ' them that ' persecute ' me.

18 Shew thy servant the ' light of thy ' countenance : and save me ' for thy ' mercy's ' sake.

19 Let me not be confounded O Lord, for I have ' called up'on thee : let the ungodly be put to confusion, and be put to ' silence ' in the ' grave.

2nd Part

20 Let the lying lips be ' put to ' silence : which cruelly
disdainfully and despitefully ' speak a'gainst the ' righteous.

21 O how plentiful is thy goodness, which thou hast laid up
for ' them that ' fear thee : and that thou hast prepared for
them that put their trust in thee, even be'fore the ' sons of '
men!

22 Thou shalt hide them privily by thine own presence, from
the pro'voking of ' all men : thou shalt keep them secretly
in thy tabernacle ' from the ' strife of ' tongues.

23 Thanks ' be to the ' Lord : for he hath shewed me marvellous great kindness ' in a ' strong ' city.

24 And when I made ' haste I ' said : I am cast out of the ' sight
of ' thine ' eyes.

2nd Part

25 Nevertheless thou heardest the ' voice of my ' prayer :
when I ' cried ' unto ' thee.

26 O love the Lord all ' ye his ' saints : for the Lord preserveth
them that are faithful, and plenteously re'wardeth the '
proud ' doer.

27 Be strong and he shall e'stablish your ' heart : all ye
that ' put your ' trust in the ' Lord.

DAY 6 EVENING

PSALM 32

BLESSED is he whose unrighteousness ' is for'given : and
whose ' sin ' is ' covered.

2 Blessed is the man unto whom the Lord im'puteth no ' sin :
and in whose ' spirit there ' is no ' guile.

3 For while I ' held my ' tongue : my bones consumed
away ' through my ' daily com'plaining.

4 For thy hand is heavy upon me ' day and ' night : and my
moisture is ' like the ' drought in ' summer.

5 I will acknowledge my sin ' unto ' thee : and mine
un'righteousness ' have I not ' hid.

6 I said I will confess my sins ' unto the ' Lord : and so thou
forgavest the ' wickedness ' of my ' sin.

7 For this shall every one that is godly make his prayer unto
thee, in a time when thou ' mayest be ' found : but in the
great water-floods ' they shall ' not come ' nigh him.

8 Thou art a place to hide me in, thou shalt pre'serve me
from ' trouble : thou shalt compass me a'bout with ' songs
of de'liverance.

9 I will inform thee and teach thee in the way wherein ' thou
shalt ' go : and I will ' guide thee ' with mine ' eye.

10 Be ye not like to horse and mule, which have no '
under'standing : whose mouths must be held with bit and
bridle ' lest they ' fall up'on thee.

11 Great plagues remain ' for the un'godly : but whoso putteth his trust in the Lord, mercy embraceth ' him on '
every ' side.

12 Be glad O ye righteous, and rejoice ' in the ' Lord : and be
joyful all ' ye that are ' true of ' heart.

PSALM 33

REJOICE in the Lord ' O ye ' righteous : for it becometh '
well the ' just to be ' thankful.

2 Praise the ' Lord with ' harp : sing praises unto him with the lute, and ' instrument ' of ten ' strings.

3 Sing unto the Lord a ' new ' song : sing praises lustily unto him ' with a ' good ' courage.

4 For the word of the ' Lord is ' true : and ' all his ' works are ' faithful.

5 He loveth ' righteousness and ' judgement : the earth is full of the ' goodness ' of the ' Lord.

6 By the word of the Lord were the ' heavens ' made : and all the hosts of them ' by the ' breath of his ' mouth.

7 He gathereth the waters of the sea together, as it were up'on an ' heap : and layeth up the deep as ' in a ' treasure'house.

8 Let all the earth ' fear the ' Lord : stand in awe of him, all ' ye that ' dwell in the ' world.

9 For he spake and ' it was ' done : he commanded ' and it ' stood ' fast.

10 The Lord bringeth the counsel of the ' heathen to ' nought : and maketh the devices of the people to be of none effect, and casteth ' out the ' counsels of ' princes.

11 The counsel of the Lord shall en'dure for ' ever : and the thoughts of his heart from gene'ration to ' gene'ration.

12 Blessed are the people whose God is the ' Lord Je'hovah : and blessed are the folk, that he hath chosen to him to ' be ' his in'heritance.

13 The Lord looked down from heaven, and beheld all the ' children of ' men : from the habitation of his dwelling he considereth all ' them that ' dwell on the ' earth.

14 He fashioneth ' all the ' hearts of them : and under'standeth ' all their ' works.

15 There is no king that can be saved by the multitude ' of an '
  host : neither is any mighty man de'livered by ' much '
  strength.

16 A horse is counted but a vain thing to ' save a ' man :
  neither shall he deliver any man ' by his ' great ' strength.

17 Behold the eye of the Lord is upon ' them that ' fear him :
  and upon them that ' put their ' trust in his ' mercy;

18 To deliver their ' soul from ' death : and to feed them '
  in the ' time of ' dearth.

19 Our soul hath patiently tarried ' for the ' Lord : for he is
  our ' help and ' our ' shield.

20 For our heart shall re'joice in ' him : because we have
  hop-ed ' in his ' holy ' Name.

2nd Part

21 Let thy merciful kindness O Lord ' be up'on us : like as we
  do ' put our ' trust in ' thee.

PSALM 34

I WILL alway give thanks ' unto the ' Lord : his praise
  shall ' ever be ' in my ' mouth.

 2 My soul shall make her ' boast in the ' Lord : the humble
  shall ' hear there'of and be ' glad.

 3 O praise the ' Lord with ' me : and let us ' magnify
  his ' Name to'gether.

 4 I sought the Lord ' and he ' heard me : yea he delivered
  me ' out of ' all my ' fear.

 5 They had an eye unto him ' and were ' lightened : and
  their ' faces were ' not a'shamed.

6 Lo the poor crieth and the Lord ' heareth ' him : yea and saveth him ' out of ' all his ' troubles.

* 7 The angel of the Lord tarrieth ' round about ' them that ' fear him : and ' — de'livereth ' them.

8 O taste and see how ' gracious the ' Lord is : blessed is the ' man that ' trusteth in ' him.

9 O fear the Lord ye that ' are his ' saints : for they that ' fear him ' lack ' nothing.

10 The lions do lack and ' suffer ' hunger : but they who seek the Lord shall want no ' manner of ' thing that is ' good.

11 Come ye children, and hearken ' unto ' me : I will ' teach you the ' fear of the ' Lord.

12 What man is he that ' lusteth to ' live : and would ' fain see ' good ' days?

13 Keep thy ' tongue from ' evil : and thy lips ' that they ' speak no ' guile.

14 Eschew evil and ' do ' good : seek ' peace ' and en'sue it.

15 The eyes of the Lord are ' over the ' righteous : and his ears are ' open ' unto their ' prayers.

16 The countenance of the Lord is against ' them that do ' evil : to root out the remembrance ' of them ' from the ' earth.

17 The righteous cry and the ' Lord ' heareth them : and delivereth them ' out of ' all their ' troubles.

18 The Lord is nigh unto them that are of a ' contrite ' heart : and will save such as ' be of an ' humble ' spirit.

19 Great are the ' troubles of the ' righteous : but the Lord de'livereth him ' out of ' all.

7 The angel of the Lord tarrieth round about ' them that ' fear him : and ' — de'livereth ' them.

20 He keepeth ' all his ' bones : so that not ' one of ' them is ' broken.

21 But misfortune shall ' slay the un'godly : and they that hate the ' righteous ' shall be ' desolate.

22 The Lord delivereth the ' souls of his ' servants : and all they that put their trust in ' him shall ' not be ' destitute.

DAY 7   MORNING

PSALM 35

PLEAD thou my cause O Lord with ' them that ' strive with me : and fight thou against ' them that ' fight a'gainst me.

2 Lay hand upon thy ' shield and ' buckler : and ' stand ' up to ' help me.

3 Bring forth the spear, and stop the way against ' them that ' persecute me : say unto my soul ' I am ' thy sal'vation.

4 Let them be confounded and put to shame, that seek ' after my ' soul : let them be turned back and brought to confusion, that im'agine ' mischief ' for me.

5 Let them be as the dust be'fore the ' wind : and the angel of the ' Lord ' scattering ' them.

6 Let their way be ' dark and ' slippery : and let the angel of the ' Lord ' persecute ' them.

7 For they have privily laid their net to destroy me with'out a ' cause : yea, even without a cause have they ' made a ' pit for my ' soul.

8 Let a sudden destruction come upon him unawares, and his net that he hath laid privily ' catch him'self : that he may fall ' into his ' own ' mischief.

9 And my soul be joyful ' in the ' Lord : it shall re'joice in ' his sal'vation.

10 All my bones shall say, Lord who is like unto thee, who deliverest the poor from him that ' is too ' strong for him : yea the poor, and him that is in ' misery from ' him that ' spoileth him?

11 False witnesses did ' rise ' up : they laid to my charge ' things that ' I ' knew not.

12 They rewarded me ' evil for ' good : to the great dis'comfort ' of my ' soul.

13 Nevertheless when they were sick I put on sackcloth, and humbled my ' soul with ' fasting : and my prayer shall turn ' into mine ' own ' bosom.

14 I behaved myself as though it had been my friend ' or my ' brother : I went heavily, as one that ' mourneth ' for his ' mother.

15 But in mine adversity they rejoiced, and gathered them'-selves to'gether : yea the very abjects came together against me unawares, making ' mouths at ' me and ' ceased not.

16 With the flatterers were ' busy ' mockers : who gnashed up'on me ' with their ' teeth.

17 Lord how long wilt thou ' look upon ' this : O deliver my soul from the calamities which they bring on me, and my ' darling ' from the ' lions.

18 So will I give thee thanks in the great ' congre'gation : I will ' praise thee a'mong much ' people.

19 O let not them that are mine enemies triumph over ' me un'godly : neither let them wink with their eyes that ' hate me with'out a ' cause.

20 And why? their communing is ' not for ' peace : but they imagine deceitful words against them that are ' quiet ' in the ' land.

21 They gaped upon me with their ' mouths and ' said : Fie on thee, fie on thee, we ' saw it ' with our ' eyes.

22 This thou hast ' seen O ' Lord : hold not thy tongue then, go not ' far from ' me O ' Lord.

23 Awake and stand up to ' judge my ' quarrel : avenge thou my cause my ' God and ' my ' Lord.

24 Judge me O Lord my God according ' to thy ' righteousness : and ' let them not ' triumph ' over me.

25 Let them not say in their hearts, There, there, ' so would we ' have it : neither let them say, ' We ' have de'voured him.

26 Let them be put to confusion and shame together that rejoice ' at my ' trouble : let them be clothed with rebuke and dishonour that ' boast them'selves a'gainst me.

27 Let them be glad and rejoice that favour my ' righteous ' dealing : yea let them say alway, Blessed be the Lord who hath pleasure in the pros'perity ' of his ' servant.

28 And as for my tongue it shall be talking ' of thy ' righteousness : and of thy ' praise ' all the day ' long.

PSALM 36

My heart sheweth me the wickedness ' of the un'godly : that there is no fear of ' God be'fore his ' eyes.

2 For he flattereth himself in his ' own ' sight : until his abominable ' sin be ' found ' out.

3 The words of his mouth are unrighteous and ' full of de'ceit : he hath left off to behave himself wisely ' and to ' do ' good.

4 He imagineth mischief upon his bed, and hath set himself in ' no good ' way : neither doth he abhor ' any thing ' that is ' evil.

5 Thy mercy O Lord reacheth ' unto the ' heavens : and thy ' faithfulness ' unto the ' clouds.

6 Thy righteousness standeth like the ' strong ' mountains : thy judgements are ' like the ' great ' deep.

7 Thou Lord shalt save both man and beast. How excellent is thy ' mercy O ' God : and the children of men shall put their trust under the ' shadow ' of thy ' wings.

8 They shall be satisfied with the plenteousness ' of thy ' house : and thou shalt give them drink of thy ' pleasures as ' out of the ' river.

9 For with thee is the ' well of ' life : and in thy ' light shall ' we see ' light.

10 O continue forth thy loving-kindness unto ' them that ' know thee : and thy righteousness unto ' them that are ' true of ' heart.

11 O let not the foot of pride ' come a'gainst me : and let not the hand of the un'godly ' cast me ' down.

12 There are they fallen ' all that work ' wickedness : they are cast down and shall ' not be ' able to ' stand.

DAY 7 EVENING

PSALM 37

FRET not thyself be'cause of · the un'godly : neither be thou envious a'gainst the ' evil'doers.

313

2 For they shall soon be cut ' down like the ' grass : and be withered ' even . as the ' green ' herb.

3 Put thou thy trust in the Lord and be ' doing ' good : dwell in the land, and ' verily ' thou shalt be ' fed.

4 Delight thou ' in the ' Lord : and he shall ' give thee thy ' heart's de'sire.

5 Commit thy way unto the Lord, and put thy ' trust in ' him : and ' he shall ' bring it to ' pass.

6 He shall make thy righteousness as ' clear as the ' light : and thy just ' dealing ' as the ' noon-day.

7 Hold thee still in the Lord, and abide ' patiently up'on him : but grieve not thyself at him whose way doth prosper, against the man that doeth ' after ' evil ' counsels.

8 Leave off from wrath and let ' go dis'pleasure : fret not thyself, else shalt thou be ' moved to ' do ' evil.

9 Wicked doers shall be ' rooted ' out : and they that patiently abide the Lord ' those shall in'herit the ' land.

10 Yet a little while, and the ungodly shall be ' clean ' gone : thou shalt look after his place and ' he shall ' be a'way.

11 But the meek-spirited shall pos'sess the ' earth : and shall be re'freshed in the ' multitude of ' peace.

12 The ungodly seeketh counsel a'gainst the ' just : and gnasheth up'on him ' with his ' teeth.

13 The Lord shall ' laugh him to ' scorn : for he hath ' seen that his ' day is ' coming.

14 The ungodly have drawn out the sword and have ' bent their ' bow : to cast down the poor and needy, and to slay such as are of a ' right ' conver'sation.

15 Their sword shall go through their ' own ' heart : and their ' bow ' shall be ' broken.

16 A small thing that the ' righteous ' hath : is better than great ' riches ' of the un'godly.

17 For the arms of the ungodly ' shall be ' broken : and the ' Lord up'holdeth the ' righteous.

18 The Lord knoweth the ' days of the ' godly : and their inheritance ' shall en'dure for'ever.

19 They shall not be confounded in the ' perilous ' time : and in the days of dearth ' they shall ' have e'nough.

20 As for the ungodly they shall perish, and the enemies of the Lord shall consume as the ' fat of ' lambs : yea even as the smoke shall ' they con'sume a'way.

21 The ungodly borroweth and payeth ' not a'gain : but the ' righteous is ' merciful and ' liberal.

22 Such as are blessed of God shall pos'sess the ' land : and they that are cursed of him ' shall be ' rooted ' out.

23 The Lord ordereth a ' good man's ' going : and maketh his way ac'ceptable ' to him'self.

24 Though he fall he shall not be ' cast a'way : for the Lord up'holdeth him ' with his ' hand.

25 I have been young and ' now am ' old : and yet saw I never the righteous forsaken, nor his ' seed ' begging their ' bread.

26 The righteous is ever ' merciful and ' lendeth : and ' his ' seed is ' blessed.

27 Flee from evil, and do the ' thing that is ' good : and ' dwell for ' ever'more.

315

28 For the Lord loveth the ' thing that is ' right : he forsaketh
not his that be godly, but ' they are pre'served for ' ever.

29 The unrighteous ' shall be ' punished : as for the seed of the
ungodly ' it shall be ' rooted ' out.

30 The righteous shall in'herit the ' land : and ' dwell there'in
for ' ever.

31 The mouth of the righteous is ' exercised in ' wisdom : and
his ' tongue will be ' talking of ' judgement.

32 The law of his God is ' in his ' heart : and his ' goings ' shall
not ' slide.

33 The ungodly ' seeth the ' righteous : and ' seeketh
oc'casion to ' slay him.

34 The Lord will not leave him ' in his ' hand : nor con'demn
him ' when he is ' judged.

35 Hope thou in the Lord and keep his way, and he shall
promote thee that thou shalt pos'sess the ' land : when the
ungodly shall ' perish ' thou shalt ' see it.

36 I myself have seen the ungodly in ' great ' power : and
flourishing ' like a ' green ' bay-tree.

2nd Part

37 I went by, and ' lo he was ' gone : I sought him, but
his ' place could ' no where be ' found.

38 Keep innocency, and take heed unto the ' thing that
is ' right : for that shall ' bring a man ' peace at the ' last.

39 As for the transgressors they shall ' perish to'gether : and
the end of the ungodly is, they shall be ' rooted ' out at
the ' last.

40 But the salvation of the righteous ' cometh of the ' Lord :
who is also their ' strength in the ' time of ' trouble.

41 And the Lord shall stand by ' them and ' save them : he shall deliver them from the ungodly and shall save them, because they ' put their ' trust in ' him.

DAY 8 MORNING

PSALM 38

PUT me not to rebuke O Lord ' in thine ' anger : neither chasten me ' in thy ' heavy dis'pleasure.

2 For thine arrows stick ' fast in ' me : and thy ' hand ' presseth me ' sore.

3 There is no health in my flesh because of ' thy dis'pleasure : neither is there any rest in my bones by ' reason ' of my ' sin.

4 For my wickednesses are gone ' over my ' head : and are like a sore burden too ' heavy for ' me to ' bear.

* 5 My ' wounds ' stink and ' are cor'rupt : through ' my ' foolishness.

6 I am brought into so great ' trouble and ' misery : that I go ' mourning ' all the day ' long.

7 For my loins are filled with a ' sore dis'ease : and there is no ' whole part ' in my ' body.

8 I am feeble and ' sore ' smitten : I have roared for the very dis'quietness ' of my ' heart.

9 Lord thou knowest all ' my de'sire : and my groaning ' is not ' hid from ' thee.

10 My heart panteth my ' strength hath ' failed me : and the ' sight of mine ' eyes is ' gone from me.

5 My wounds stink and ' are cor'rupt : through ' my ' foolish'ness.

11 My lovers and my neighbours did stand looking up'on my ' trouble : and my kinsmen ' stood a'far ' off.

12 They also that sought after my ' life laid ' snares for me : and they that went about to do me evil talked of wickedness, and imagined deceit ' all the ' day ' long.

13 As for me, I was like a deaf ' man and ' heard not : and as one that is dumb who ' doth not ' open his ' mouth.

14 I became even as a man that ' heareth ' not : and in whose ' mouth are ' no re'proofs.

15 For in thee O Lord have I ' put my ' trust : thou shalt answer for ' me O ' Lord my ' God.

16 I have required that they even mine enemies, should not ' triumph ' over me : for when my foot slipped, they re'joic-ed ' greatly a'gainst me.

17 And I truly am ' set in the ' plague : and my heaviness is ' ever ' in my ' sight.

18 For I will con'fess my ' wickedness : and be ' sorry ' for my ' sin.

19 But mine enemies live ' and are ' mighty : and they that hate me ' wrongfully are ' many in ' number.

20 They also that reward evil for good ' are a'gainst me : because I follow the ' thing that ' good ' is.

21 Forsake me not O ' Lord my ' God : be not ' thou ' far ' from me.

22 Haste ' thee to ' help me : O Lord ' God of ' my sal'vation.

PSALM 39

I SAID I will take heed ' to my ' ways : that I of'fend not ' in my ' tongue.

2 I will keep my mouth as it ' were with a ' bridle : while the un'godly is ' in my ' sight.

3 I held my tongue and ' spake ' nothing : I kept silence, yea even from good words, but it was ' pain and ' grief to ' me.

4 My heart was hot within me, and while I was thus musing the ' fire ' kindled : and at the ' last I ' spake with my ' tongue;

5 Lord let me know mine end and the ' number · of my ' days : that I may be certified how ' long I ' have to ' live.

6 Behold thou hast made my days as it were a ' span ' long : and mine age is even as nothing in respect of thee, and verily every man living is ' alto'gether ' vanity.

7 For man walketh in a vain shadow, and disquieteth him'self in ' vain : he heapeth up riches, and ' cannot tell ' who shall ' gather them.

8 And now Lord ' what is my ' hope : truly my ' hope is ' even in ' thee.

9 Deliver me from all ' mine of'fences : and make me not a re'buke ' unto the ' foolish.

10 I became dumb, and opened ' not my ' mouth : for ' it was ' thy ' doing.

11 Take thy plague a'way ' from me : I am even consumed by the ' means of thy ' heavy ' hand.

12 When thou with rebukes dost chasten man for sin, thou makest his beauty to consume away, like as it were a moth ' fretting a ' garment : every man ' therefore ' is but ' vanity.

13 Hear my prayer O Lord, and with thine ears con'sider my ' calling : hold not thy ' peace ' at my ' tears.

14 For I am a ' stranger with ' thee : and a sojourner as ' all my ' fathers ' were.

2nd Part

15 O spare me a little that I may re'cover my ' strength :
before I go ' hence and be ' no more ' seen.

PSALM 40

I WAITED patiently ' for the ' Lord : and he inclined unto ' me and ' heard my ' calling.

2 He brought me also out of the horrible pit, out of the ' mire
and ' clay : and set my feet upon the rock, and ' ordered '
my ' goings.

3 And he hath put a new ' song in my ' mouth : even
a ' thanks · giving ' unto our ' God.

4 Many shall ' see it and ' fear : and shall ' put their ' trust in
the ' Lord.

5 Blessed is the man that hath set his ' hope in the ' Lord : and
turned not unto the proud, and to such as ' go a'bout with '
lies.

6 O Lord my God, great are the wondrous works which thou
hast done, like as be also thy thoughts which ' are to '
us-ward : and yet there is no man that ' ordereth them '
unto ' thee.

7 If I should de'clare them and ' speak of them : they should
be more than I am ' able ' to ex'press.

8 Sacrifice and meat-offering thou ' wouldest ' not : but
mine ' ears hast ' thou ' opened.

9 Burnt-offerings and sacrifice for sin hast thou ' not
re'quired : then ' said I ' Lo I ' come,

10 In the volume of the book it is written of me, that I should fulfil thy will ' O my ' God : I am content to do it, yea thy law ' is with'in my ' heart.

11 I have declared thy righteousness in the great ' con-gre'gation : lo I will not refrain my lips O ' Lord and ' that thou ' knowest.

12 I have not hid thy righteousness with'in my ' heart : my talk hath been of thy ' truth and of ' thy sal'vation.

2nd Part

13 I have not kept back thy loving ' mercy and truth : from the ' great ' congre'gation.

14 Withdraw not thou thy mercy from ' me O ' Lord : let thy loving-kindness and thy ' truth ' alway pre'serve me.

15 For innumerable troubles are come about me, my sins have taken such hold upon me, that I am not able to ' look ' up : yea they are more in number than the hairs of my head, and my ' heart hath ' fail-ed ' me.

16 O Lord let it be thy ' pleasure · to de'liver me : make ' haste O ' Lord to ' help me.

17 Let them be ashamed and confounded together, that seek after my soul ' to de'stroy it : let them be driven backward and put to re'buke that ' wish me ' evil.

18 Let them be desolate and re'warded with ' shame : that say unto me, Fie up'on thee ' fie up'on thee.

19 Let all those that seek thee be joyful and ' glad in ' thee : and let such as love thy salvation say ' alway The ' Lord be ' praised.

20 As for me I am ' poor and ' needy : but the ' Lord ' careth ' for me.

21 Thou art my helper ′ and re′deemer : make no long ′
tarrying ′ O my ′ God.

DAY 8 EVENING

PSALM 41

BLESSED is he that considereth the ′ poor and ′ needy : the
Lord shall deliver him ′ in the ′ time of ′ trouble.

2 The Lord preserve him and keep him alive, that he may be
blessed up′on ′ earth : and deliver not thou him ′ into the ′
will of his ′ enemies.

3 The Lord comfort him when he lieth sick up′on his ′ bed :
make thou all his ′ bed ′ in his ′ sickness.

4 I said Lord be merciful ′ unto ′ me : heal my soul for ′ I
have ′ sinned a′gainst thee.

5 Mine enemies speak ′ evil ′ of me : When shall he die ′ and
his ′ name ′ perish?

6 And if he come to see me he ′ speaketh ′ vanity : and his
heart conceiveth falsehood within himself, and when he ′
cometh ′ forth he ′ telleth it.

7 All mine enemies whisper to′gether a′gainst me : even
against me do ′ they im′agine this ′ evil.

8 Let the sentence of guiltiness pro′ceed a′gainst him : and
now that he lieth ′ let him rise ′ up no ′ more.

9 Yea even mine own familiar friend ′ whom I ′ trusted : who
did also eat of my bread hath ′ laid great ′ wait for ′ me.

10 But be thou merciful unto ′ me O ′ Lord : raise thou me up
again ′ and I ′ shall re′ward them.

11 By this I know thou ' favourest ' me : that mine enemy '
doth not ' triumph a'gainst me.

12 And when I am in my health ' thou up'holdest me : and
shalt set me be'fore thy ' face for ' ever.

2nd Part Unison

13 Blessed be the Lord ' God of ' Israel : world without ' end. '
A'men.

PSALM 42

LIKE as the hart de'sireth the ' water-brooks : so longeth
my soul ' after ' thee O ' God.

2 My soul is athirst for God, yea even for the ' living ' God :
when shall I come to appear be'fore the ' presence of '
God?

3 My tears have been my meat ' day and ' night : while they
daily say unto me, Where is ' now ' thy ' God?

4 Now when I think thereupon, I pour out my heart ' by
my'self : for I went with the multitude, and brought them
forth ' into the ' house of ' God;

2nd Part

5 In the voice of ' praise and ' thanksgiving : among such as '
keep ' holy ' day.

p 6 Why art thou so full of heaviness ' O my ' soul : and why art
thou ' so dis'quiet · ed with'in me?

f 7 Put thy ' trust in ' God : for I will yet give him ' thanks for
the ' help of his ' countenance.

323

8 My God my soul is ' vexed with'in me : therefore will I
remember thee concerning the land of Jordan, and the '
little ' hill of ' Hermon.

9 One deep calleth another, because of the ' noise of
the ' water pipes : all thy ' waves and ' storms are gone '
over me.

10 The Lord hath granted his loving-kindness ' in the ' day-
time : and in the night-season did I sing of him, and made
my prayer ' unto the ' God of my ' life.

11 I will say unto the God of my strength, Why hast ' thou
for'gotten me : why go I thus heavily, while the ' enemy
op'presseth ' me?

12 My bones are smitten asunder ' as with a ' sword : while
mine enemies that trouble me ' cast me ' in the ' teeth;

13 Namely while they say ' daily ' unto me : Where is ' now '
thy ' God?

p 14 Why art thou so vexed ' O my ' soul : and why art thou ' so
dis'quiet · ed with'in me?

f 15 O put thy ' trust in ' God : for I will yet thank him, which is
the help of my ' countenance ' and my ' God.

PSALM 43

GIVE sentence with me O God, and defend my cause
against the un'godly ' people : O deliver me from the
de'ceitful and ' wicked ' man.

2 For thou art the God of my strength, why hast thou ' put
me ' from thee : and why go I so heavily, while the ' enemy
op'presseth ' me?

3 O send out thy light and thy truth that ' they may ' lead me :
and bring me unto thy holy ' hill and ' to thy ' dwelling.

4 And that I may go unto the altar of God, even unto the God
of my ' joy and ' gladness : and upon the harp will I give
thanks unto ' thee O ' God my ' God.

p 5 Why art thou so heavy ' O my ' soul : and why art thou ' so
dis'quiet · ed with'in me?

f 6 O put thy ' trust in ' God : for I will yet give him thanks,
which is the help of my ' countenance ' and my ' God.

DAY 9 MORNING

PSALM 44

WE have heard with our ears O God our ' fathers have ' told
us : what thou hast done ' in their ' time of ' old;

2 How thou hast driven out the heathen with thy hand,
and ' planted them ' in : how thou hast destroyed the '
nations and ' cast them ' out.

3 For they gat not the land in possession through their '
own ' sword : neither was it their own ' arm that ' help-ed '
them;

4 But thy right hand and thine arm and the ' light of
thy ' countenance : because thou hadst a ' favour ' unto '
them.

5 Thou art my ' King O ' God : send ' help ' unto ' Jacob.

6 Through thee will we over'throw our ' enemies : and in thy
Name will we tread them under that ' rise ' up a'gainst us.

7 For I will not trust ' in my ' bow : it is not my ' sword ' that
shall ' help me;

8 But it is thou that savest us ' from our ' enemies : and puttest ' them · to con'fusion that ' hate us.

2nd Part

9 We make our boast of God ' all day ' long : and will ' praise thy ' Name for ' ever.

10 But now thou art far off, and puttest ' us · to con'fusion : and ' goest not ' forth with our ' armies.

11 Thou makest us to turn our backs up'on our ' enemies : so that they which ' hate us ' spoil our ' goods.

12 Thou lettest us be eaten ' up like ' sheep : and hast ' scattered us a'mong the ' heathen.

13 Thou sellest thy ' people for ' nought : and ' takest no ' money ' for them.

14 Thou makest us to be re'buked of our ' neighbours : to be laughed to scorn, and had in derision of ' them that are ' round a'bout us.

15 Thou makest us to be a by-word a'mong the ' heathen : and that the ' people ' shake their ' heads at us.

16 My confusion is ' daily be'fore me : and the ' shame of my ' face hath ' covered me;

17 For the voice of the slanderer ' and blas'phemer : for the ' enemy ' and a'venger.

18 And though all this be come upon us, yet do we ' not for'get thee : nor behave ourselves ' frowardly ' in thy ' covenant.

19 Our heart is not ' turn-ed ' back : neither our ' steps gone ' out of thy ' way;

2nd Part

20 No not when thou hast smitten us into the ' place of ' dragons : and covered us ' with the ' shadow of ' death.

21 If we have forgotten the Name of our God, and holden up our hands to any ' strange ' god : shall not God search it out? for he knoweth the very ' secrets ' of the ' heart.

22 For thy sake also are we killed ' all the day ' long : and are counted as sheep ap'pointed ' to be ' slain.

23 Up Lord, why ' sleepest ' thou : awake, and be not ' absent from ' us for ' ever.

24 Wherefore hidest ' thou thy ' face : and for'gettest our ' misery and ' trouble?

25 For our soul is brought low, even ' unto the ' dust : our belly ' cleaveth ' unto the ' ground.

26 Arise and ' help ' us : and deliver us ' for thy ' mercy's ' sake.

PSALM 45

Single Chant

My heart is inditing of a ' good ' matter : I speak of the things which I have ' made ' unto the ' King.

½ 2 My tongue is the ' pen : of a ' ready ' writer.

3 Thou art fairer than the ' children of ' men : full of grace are thy lips, because God hath ' bless-ed ' thee for ' ever.

4 Gird thee with thy sword upon thy thigh O ' thou most ' Mighty : according to thy ' worship ' and re'nown.

5 Good luck have thou ' with thine ' honour : ride on because of the word of truth, of meekness and righteousness, and thy right hand shall ' teach thee ' terrible ' things.

2 My tongue ' is the ' pen : of ' — a ' ready ' writer.

327

6 Thy arrows are very sharp, and the people shall be subdued ' unto ' thee : even in the midst a'mong the ' King's '
enemies.

7 Thy seat O God en'dureth for ' ever : the sceptre of thy
kingdom ' is a ' right ' sceptre.

8 Thou hast loved righteousness and ' hated in'iquity :
wherefore God even thy God, hath anointed thee with the
oil of ' gladness a'bove thy ' fellows.

9 All thy garments smell of myrrh ' aloes and ' cassia : out of
the ivory palaces whereby ' they have ' made thee ' glad.

10 Kings' daughters were among thy ' honour · able ' women :
upon thy right hand did stand the queen in a vesture of
gold, wrought a'bout with ' divers ' colours.

11 Hearken O daughter and consider, in'cline thine ' ear :
forget also thine own people ' and thy ' father's ' house.

12 So shall the King have pleasure ' in thy ' beauty : for he is
thy Lord ' God and ' worship thou ' him.

13 And the daughter of Tyre shall be ' there with a ' gift : like
as the rich also among the people shall make their ' suppli'cation be'fore thee.

14 The King's daughter is all ' glorious with'in : her clothing '
is of ' wrought ' gold.

15 She shall be brought unto the King in ' raiment of ' needle-
work : the virgins that be her fellows shall bear her company, and shall be ' brought ' unto ' thee.

16 With joy and gladness shall ' they be ' brought : and shall
enter ' into the ' King's ' palace.

17 Instead of thy fathers thou ' shalt have ' children : whom
thou mayest make ' princes in ' all ' lands.

18 I will remember thy Name from one generation ′ to an′other : therefore shall the people give thanks unto thee ′ world with′out ′ end.

PSALM 46

GOD is our ′ hope and ′ strength : a very ′ present ′ help in ′ trouble.

2 Therefore will we not fear, though the ′ earth be ′ moved : and though the hills be carried ′ into the ′ midst of the ′ sea;

3 Though the waters thereof ′ rage and ′ swell : and though the mountains shake at the ′ tempest ′ of the ′ same.

4 The rivers of the flood thereof shall make glad the ′ city of ′ God : the holy place of the tabernacle ′ of the ′ most ′ Highest.

5 God is in the midst of her, therefore shall she ′ not be re′moved : God shall ′ help her and ′ that right ′ early.

6 The heathen make much ado and the ′ kingdoms are ′ moved : but God hath shewed his voice, and the ′ earth shall ′ melt a′way.

2nd Part Unison

7 The Lord of ′ hosts is ′ with us : the God of ′ Jacob ′ is our ′ refuge.

8 O come hither and behold the ′ works of the ′ Lord : what destruction he hath ′ brought up′on the ′ earth.

9 He maketh wars to cease in ′ all the ′ world : he breaketh the bow, and knappeth the spear in sunder, and burneth the ′ chariots ′ in the ′ fire.

10 Be still then and know that ' I am ' God : I will be exalted among the heathen, and I will be ex'alted ' in the ' earth.

Unison

11 The Lord of ' hosts is ' with us : the God of ' Jacob ' is our ' refuge.

DAY 9 EVENING

PSALM 47

O CLAP your hands together ' all ye ' people : O sing unto ' God with the ' voice of ' melody.

2 For the Lord is high and ' to be ' feared : he is the great ' King upon ' all the ' earth.

3 He shall subdue the ' people ' under us : and the ' nations ' under our ' feet.

4 He shall choose out an ' heritage ' for us : even the worship of ' Jacob ' whom he ' loved.

2nd Part

5 God is gone up with a ' merry ' noise : and the ' Lord with the ' sound of the ' trump.

6 O sing praises sing praises ' unto our ' God : O sing praises sing ' praises ' unto our ' King.

7 For God is the King of ' all the ' earth : sing ye ' praises with ' under ' standing.

8 God reigneth ' over the ' heathen : God sitteth up'on his ' holy ' seat.

9 The princes of the people are joined unto the people of the ' God of ' Abraham : for God which is very high exalted, doth defend the ' earth as it ' were with a ' shield.

PSALM 48

GREAT is the Lord and ' highly · to be ' praised : in the city of our God, even up'on his ' holy ' hill.

2 The hill of Sion is a fair place, and the joy of the ' whole ' earth : upon the north-side lieth the city of the great King, God is well known in her palaces ' as a ' sure ' refuge.

3 For lo the ' kings of the ' earth : are gathered and ' gone ' by to'gether.

4 They marvelled to ' see such ' things : they were astonished and ' suddenly ' cast ' down.

5 Fear came there upon ' them and ' sorrow : as upon a ' woman ' in her ' travail.

* 6 Thou shalt ' break the ' ships of the ' sea : ' through the ' east ' wind.

2nd Part

7 Like as we have heard, so have we seen in the city of the Lord of hosts, in the city of ' our ' God : God up'holdeth the ' same for'ever.

8 We wait for thy loving'kindness O ' God : in the ' midst of ' thy ' temple.

9 O God according to thy Name, so is thy praise unto the ' world's ' end : thy right ' hand is ' full of ' right-eousness.

6 Thou shalt break the ' ships of the ' sea : through ' — the ' east ' wind.

10 Let the mount Sion rejoice, and the daughter of ' Judah be ' glad : be'cause of ' thy ' judgements.

11 Walk about Sion and go ' round a'bout her : and ' tell the ' towers there'of.

12 Mark well her bulwarks, set ' up her ' houses : that ye may tell ' them that ' come ' after.

13 For this God is our God for ' ever and ' ever : he shall be our ' guide ' unto ' death.

PSALM 49

O HEAR ye this ' all ye ' people : ponder it with your ears, all ' ye that ' dwell in the ' world;

* 2 High and ' low ' rich and ' poor : ' one ' with an'other.

3 My mouth shall ' speak of ' wisdom : and my heart shall ' muse of ' under'standing.

4 I will incline mine ' ear to the ' parable : and shew my dark ' speech up'on the ' harp.

5 Wherefore should I fear in the ' days of ' wickedness : and when the wickedness of my heels ' compasseth me ' round a'bout?

6 There be some that put their ' trust in their ' goods : and boast themselves in the ' multitude ' of their ' riches.

7 But no man may de'liver his ' brother : nor make agreement ' unto ' God ' for him;

8 For it cost more to re'deem their ' souls : so that he must let ' that a'lone for ' ever;

9 Yea though he ' live ' long : and ' see ' not the ' grave.

2 High and low ' rich and ' poor : one ' — ' with an'other.

10 For he seeth that wise men also die and ' perish to'gether : as well as the ignorant and foolish and ' leave their ' riches for ' other.

11 And yet they think that their houses shall con'tinue for'ever : and that their dwelling-places shall endure from one generation to another, and call the lands ' after their ' own ' names.

12 Nevertheless man will not a'bide in ' honour : seeing he may be compared unto the beasts that perish, ' this is the ' way of ' them.

13 This ' is their ' foolishness : and their pos'terity ' praise their ' saying.

14 They lie in the hell like sheep, death gnaweth upon them, and the righteous shall have domination over them ' in the ' morning : their beauty shall consume in the ' sepulchre ' out of their ' dwelling.

15 But God hath delivered my soul from the ' place of ' hell : for ' he ' shall re'ceive me.

16 Be not thou afraid though ' one be made ' rich : or if the ' glory · of his ' house · be in'creased;

17 For he shall carry nothing away with him ' when he ' dieth : neither ' shall his ' pomp ' follow him.

18 For while he lived he counted himself an ' happy ' man : and so long as thou doest well unto thyself, ' men will · speak ' good of ' thee.

19 He shall follow the generation ' of his ' fathers : and shall ' never ' see ' light.

20 Man being in honour hath no ' under'standing : but is
   compared ' unto the ' beasts that ' perish.

DAY 10   MORNING

PSALM 50

THE Lord even the most mighty ' God hath ' spoken : and
   called the world, from the rising up of the sun unto the '
   going ' down there'of.

* 2 Out ' of ' Sion ' hath God ap'peared : in ' perfect ' beauty.

3 Our God shall come and shall ' not keep ' silence : there
   shall go before him a consuming fire, and a mighty tempest
   shall be ' stirred up ' round a'bout him.

4 He shall call the heaven ' from a'bove : and the earth that '
   he may ' judge his ' people.

5 Gather my saints together ' unto ' me : those that have
   made a ' covenant with ' me with ' sacrifice.

6 And the heavens shall de'clare his ' righteousness : for '
   God is ' Judge him'self.

7 Hear O my people and ' I will ' speak : I myself will testify
   against thee O Israel, for I am God ' even ' thy ' God.

8 I will not reprove thee because of thy sacrifices, or for
   thy ' burnt'offerings : because they ' were not ' alway
   be'fore me.

9 I will take no bullock ' out of thine ' house : nor ' he-goat '
   out of thy ' folds.

10 For all the beasts of the ' forest are ' mine : and so are the
   cattle up'on a ' thousand ' hills.

   2 Out of Sion hath ' God ap'peared : in ' per'fect ' beauty.

11 I know all the fowls up'on the ' mountains : and the wild beasts of the ' field are ' in my ' sight.

12 If I be hungry I ' will not ' tell thee : for the whole world is mine and ' all that ' is there'in.

13 Thinkest thou that I will ' eat bulls' ' flesh : and ' drink the ' blood of ' goats?

14 Offer unto ' God ' thanksgiving : and pay thy vows ' unto the ' most ' Highest.

2nd Part

15 And call upon me in the ' time of ' trouble : so will I ' hear thee and ' thou shalt ' praise me.

16 But unto the un'godly said ' God : Why dost thou preach my laws, and takest my ' covenant ' in thy ' mouth;

17 Whereas thou hatest to ' be re'formed : and hast ' cast my ' words be'hind thee?

18 When thou sawest a thief thou consentedst ' unto ' him : and hast been par'taker ' with the a'dulterers.

19 Thou hast let thy ' mouth speak ' wickedness : and with thy tongue ' thou hast set ' forth de'ceit.

20 Thou satest and spakest a'gainst thy ' brother : yea and hast slandered thine ' own ' mother's ' son.

21 These things hast thou done and I held my tongue, and thou thoughtest wickedly that I am even such a one ' as thy'self : but I will reprove thee, and set before thee the ' things that ' thou hast ' done.

22 O consider this ye that for'get ' God : lest I pluck you away and ' there be ' none to de'liver you.

23 Whoso offereth me thanks and praise, he ' honoureth '
me : and to him that ordereth his conversation right will I '
shew the sal'vation of ' God.

PSALM 51

HAVE mercy upon me O God after ' thy great ' goodness :
according to the multitude of thy mercies ' do a'way
mine of'fences.

2 Wash me thoroughly ' from my ' wickedness : and ' cleanse
me ' from my ' sin.

3 For I ac'knowledge my ' faults : and my ' sin is ' ever
be'fore me.

4 Against thee only have I sinned, and done this evil ' in thy '
sight : that thou mightest be justified in thy saying, and '
clear when ' thou art ' judged.

5 Behold I was ' shapen in ' wickedness : and in ' sin hath my '
mother con'ceived me.

6 But lo, thou requirest truth in the ' inward ' parts : and shalt
make me to under'stand ' wisdom ' secretly.

7 Thou shalt purge me with hyssop, and ' I shall be ' clean :
thou shalt wash me, and ' I shall be ' whiter than ' snow.

8 Thou shalt make me hear of ' joy and ' gladness : that the
bones which thou hast ' broken ' may re'joice.

9 Turn thy face ' from my ' sins : and ' put out ' all my
mis'deeds.

10 Make me a clean ' heart O ' God : and re'new a right ' spirit
with'in me.

336

11 Cast me not away ' from thy ' presence : and take not thy '
holy ' Spirit ' from me.

12 O give me the comfort of thy ' help a'gain : and stablish
me ' with thy ' free ' Spirit.

2nd Part

13 Then shall I teach thy ways ' unto the ' wicked : and sinners
shall be con'verted ' unto ' thee.

14 Deliver me from blood-guiltiness O God, thou that art
the ' God of my ' health : and my ' tongue shall ' sing of thy '
righteousness.

15 Thou shalt open my ' lips O ' Lord : and my ' mouth shall '
shew thy ' praise.

16 For thou desirest no sacrifice ' else would I ' give it thee :
but thou delightest ' not in ' burnt'offerings.

17 The sacrifice of God is a ' troubled ' spirit : a broken and
contrite heart O God ' shalt thou ' not des'pise.

18 O be favourable and gracious ' unto ' Sion : build ' thou
the ' walls of Je'rusalem.

19 Then shalt thou be pleased with the sacrifice of righteousness, with the burnt-offerings ' and ob'lations : then shall
they offer young ' bullocks up'on thine ' altar.

PSALM 52

Why boastest thou thy'self thou ' tyrant : that ' thou
canst ' do ' mischief;

2 Whereas the ' goodness of ' God : en'dureth ' yet ' daily?

3 Thy tongue im'agineth ' wickedness : and with lies thou
cuttest ' like a ' sharp ' rasor.

4 Thou hast loved unrighteousness ' more than ' goodness :
and to talk of ' lies ' more than ' righteousness.

5 Thou hast loved to speak all words that ' may do ' hurt :
O ' thou ' false ' tongue.

6 Therefore shall God destroy ' thee for ' ever : he shall take
thee and pluck thee out of thy dwelling, and root thee ' out
of the ' land of the ' living.

7 The righteous also shall see ' this and ' fear : and shall '
laugh ' him to ' scorn;

8 Lo this is the man that took not ' God for his ' strength : but
trusted unto the multitude of his riches, and ' strengthened
him'self in his ' wickedness.

9 As for me I am like a green olive-tree in the ' house of '
God : my trust is in the tender mercy of ' God for ' ever
and ' ever.

10 I will always give thanks unto thee for that ' thou hast '
done : and I will hope in thy Name for thy ' saints ' like it '
well.

DAY 10   EVENING

PSALM 53

THE foolish body hath said ' in his ' heart : There ' is ' no ' God.

2 Corrupt are they, and become abominable ' in their '
wickedness : there is ' none that ' doeth ' good.

3 God looked down from heaven upon the ' children of '
men : to see if there were any that would understand and '
seek ' after ' God.

4 But they are all gone out of the way, they are altogether be'come a'bominable : there is also none that doeth ' good ' no not ' one.

5 Are not they without understanding that ' work ' wickedness : eating up my people as if they would eat bread? they ' have not ' called upon ' God.

6 They were afraid where ' no fear ' was : for God hath broken the bones of him that besieged thee, thou hast put them to confusion, because ' God ' hath des'pised them.

7 O that the salvation were given unto Israel ' out of ' Sion : O that the Lord would deliver his ' people ' out of cap'tivity!

8 Then should ' Jacob re'joice : and Israel ' should be ' right ' glad.

PSALM 54

p SAVE me O God for thy ' Name's ' sake : and a'venge me ' in thy ' strength.

2 Hear my ' prayer O ' God : and hearken ' unto the ' words of my ' mouth.

2nd Part

3 For strangers are risen ' up a'gainst me : and tyrants which have not God before their eyes ' seek ' after my ' soul.

f 4 Behold ' God is my ' helper : the Lord is with ' them that up'hold my ' soul.

5 He shall reward evil ' unto mine ' enemies : destroy thou ' them in ' thy ' truth.

6 An offering of a free heart will I give thee, and praise thy ' Name O ' Lord : be'cause it ' is so ' comfortable.

7 For he hath delivered me out of ' all my ' trouble : and mine eye hath seen his de'sire up'on mine ' enemies.

PSALM 55

Hear my ' prayer O ' God : and hide not thy'self from ' my pe'tition.

2 Take heed unto ' me and ' hear me : how I mourn in my ' prayer ' and am ' vexed.

3 The enemy crieth so, and the ungodly cometh ' on so ' fast : for they are minded to do me some mischief, so maliciously ' are they ' set a'gainst me.

4 My heart is dis'quieted with'in me : and the fear of ' death is ' fallen up'on me.

5 Fearfulness and trembling are ' come up'on me : and an horrible ' dread hath ' over'whelmed me.

6 And I said, O that I had ' wings like a ' dove : for then would I flee a'way and ' be at ' rest.

7 Lo then would I get me a'way far ' off : and re'main ' in the ' wilderness.

8 I would make ' haste to es'cape : because of the ' stormy ' wind and ' tempest.

9 Destroy their tongues O Lord ' and di'vide them : for I have spied un'righteousness and ' strife in the ' city.

10 Day and night they go about within the ' walls there'of : mischief also and ' sorrow are ' in the ' midst of it.

11 Wickedness ' is there'in : deceit and guile ' go not ' out of their ' streets.

12 For it is not an open enemy that hath done me ' this dis'honour : for ' then I ' could have ' borne it.

13 Neither was it mine adversary, that did magnify him'self a'gainst me : for then peradventure I would have ' hid my'self ' from him.

14 But it was even thou ' my com'panion : my guide and mine ' own fa'miliar ' friend.

2nd Part

15 We took sweet ' counsel to'gether : and walked in the ' house of ' God as ' friends.

[16 Let death come hastily upon them, and let them go down ' quick into ' hell : for wickedness is in their ' dwellings ' and a'mong them.]

17 As for me, I will ' call upon ' God : and the ' Lord ' shall ' save me.

18 In the evening and morning and at noon-day will I ' pray and that ' instantly : and ' he shall ' hear my ' voice.

19 It is he that hath delivered my soul in peace from the battle that ' was a'gainst me : for ' there were ' many ' with me.

20 Yea even God that endureth for ever shall hear me and ' bring them ' down : for they will not ' turn nor ' fear ' God.

21 He laid his hands upon such as be at ' peace with ' him : and he ' brake ' his ' convenant.

22 The words of his mouth were softer than butter, having ' war in his ' heart : his words were smoother than oil, and yet ' be they ' very ' swords.

23 O cast thy burden upon the Lord, and he shall ' nourish ' thee : and shall not suffer the ' righteous to ' fall for ' ever.

24 And ' as for ' them : thou O God shalt bring them ' into the ' pit of de'struction.

2nd Part

25 The blood-thirsty and deceitful men shall not live out ' half their ' days : nevertheless my trust shall ' be in ' thee O ' Lord.

DAY 11   MORNING
PSALM 56

Be merciful unto me O God, for man goeth a'bout to de'vour me : he is daily ' fighting and ' troubling ' me.

2 Mine enemies are daily in hand to ' swallow me ' up : for they be many that fight against ' me O ' thou most ' Highest.

3 Nevertheless though I am ' sometime a'fraid : yet put ' I my ' trust in ' thee.

4 I will praise God be'cause of his ' word : I have put my trust in God, and will not fear what ' flesh can ' do unto ' me.

5 They daily mis'take my ' words : all that they imagine ' is to ' do me ' evil.

6 They hold all together and ' keep themselves ' close : and mark my steps, when they lay ' wait ' for my ' soul.

7 Shall they escape ' for their ' wickedness : thou O God in thy dis'pleasure shalt ' cast them ' down.

8 Thou tellest my flittings, put my tears ' into thy ' bottle : are not these things ' noted ' in thy ' book?

2nd Part

9 Whensoever I call upon thee, then shall mine enemies be ' put to ' flight : this I know, for ' God is ' on my ' side.

10 In God's word will ' I re'joice : in the ' Lord's word ' will I ' comfort me.

11 Yea in God have I ' put my ' trust : I will not be afraid what '
man can ' do unto ' me.

12 Unto thee O God will I ' pay my ' vows : unto ' thee will ' I
give ' thanks.

13 For thou hast delivered my soul from death and my ' feet
from ' falling : that I may walk before ' God in the ' light of
the ' living.

PSALM 57

BE merciful unto me O God, be merciful unto me, for
my soul ' trusteth in ' thee : and under the shadow of
thy wings shall be my refuge, until this ' tyranny be '
over'past.

2 I will call unto the ' most high ' God : even unto the God
that shall perform the cause ' which I ' have in ' hand.

3 He shall ' send from ' heaven : and save me from the
reproof of ' him that would ' eat me ' up.

4 God shall send forth his ' mercy and ' truth : my ' soul is
a'mong ' lions.

5 And I lie even among the children of men that are ' set on '
fire : whose teeth are spears and arrows, and their ' tongue
a ' sharp ' sword.

Unison

f 6 Set up thyself O God a'bove the ' heavens : and thy glory
a'bove ' all the ' earth.

p 7 They have laid a net for my feet, and press-ed ' down my '
soul : they have digged a pit before me, and are fallen into
the ' midst of ' it them'selves.

f 8 My heart is fixed O God my ' heart is ' fixed : I will ' sing
and ' give ' praise.

9 Awake up my glory, awake ' lute and ' harp : I myself ' will
a'wake right ' early.

10 I will give thanks unto thee O Lord a'mong the ' people :
and I will sing unto ' thee a'mong the ' nations.

11 For the greatness of thy mercy reacheth ' unto the ' heavens : and thy ' truth ' unto the ' clouds.

Unison

12 Set up thyself O God a'bove the ' heavens : and thy glory
a'bove ' all the ' earth.

[PSALM 58

ARE your minds set upon righteousness O ye ' congre'gation : and do ye judge the thing that is right '
O ye ' sons of ' men?

2 Yea ye imagine mischief in your heart up'on the ' earth :
and your ' hands ' deal with ' wickedness.

3 The ungodly are froward, even from their ' mother's '
womb : as soon as they are born, they go a'stray and '
speak ' lies.

4 They are as venomous as the ' poison of a ' serpent : even
like the deaf ' adder that ' stoppeth her ' ears;

5 Which refuseth to hear the ' voice of the ' charmer : charm
he ' never ' so ' wisely.

6 Break their teeth O God in their mouths, smite the jaw-
bones of the ' lions O ' Lord : let them fall away like water
that runneth apace, and when they shoot their arrows ' let
them be ' rooted ' out.

7 Let them consume away like a snail, and be like the untimely ' fruit of a ' woman : and ' let them not ' see the ' sun.

8 Or ever your pots be made ' hot with ' thorns : so let indignation vex him, ' even as a ' thing that is ' raw.

9 The righteous shall rejoice when he ' seeth the ' vengeance : he shall wash his footsteps in the ' blood of ' the un'godly.

10 So that a man shall say, Verily there is a re'ward for the ' righteous : doubtless there is a ' God that ' judgeth the ' earth.]

DAY 11 EVENING
PSALM 59

DELIVER me from mine ' enemies O ' God : defend me from ' them that rise ' up a'gainst me.

2 O deliver me from the ' wicked ' doers : and save me ' from the ' blood-thirsty ' men.

3 For lo they lie waiting ' for my ' soul : the mighty men are gathered against me, without any offence or ' fault of ' me O ' Lord.

4 They run and prepare themselves with'out my ' fault : arise thou therefore to ' help me ' and be'hold.

5 Stand up O Lord God of hosts thou God of Israel, to visit ' all the ' heathen : and be not merciful unto them that offend ' of ma'licious ' wickedness.

6 They go to and fro ' in the ' evening : they grin like a dog, and ' run a'bout through the ' city.

7 Behold they speak with their mouth, and swords are ' in their ' lips : for ' who ' doth ' hear?

8 But thou O Lord shalt have them ' in de'rision : and thou shalt laugh ' all the ' heathen to ' scorn.

9 My strength will I ascribe ' unto ' thee : for ' thou art the ' God of my ' refuge.

10 God sheweth me his ' goodness ' plenteously : and God shall let me see my de'sire up'on mine ' enemies.

11 Slay them not lest my ' people for'get it : but scatter them abroad among the people, and put them down O ' Lord ' our de'fence.

12 For the sin of their mouth and for the words of their lips, they shall be taken ' in their ' pride : and why?, their preaching ' is of ' cursing and ' lies.

13 Consume them in thy wrath, consume them that ' they may ' perish : and know that it is God that ruleth in Jacob and ' unto the ' ends of the ' world.

14 And in the evening they ' will re'turn : grin like a dog and will ' go a'bout the ' city.

15 They will run here and ' there for ' meat : and grudge ' if they ' be not ' satisfied.

16 As for me I will sing of thy power, and will praise thy mercy be'times in the ' morning : for thou hast been my defence and ' refuge in the ' day of my ' trouble.

2nd Part

17 Unto thee O my strength ' will I ' sing : for thou O God art my ' refuge · and my ' merciful ' God.

PSALM 60

p O GOD thou has cast us out and scattered ' us a'broad : thou hast also been displeased, O turn thee ' unto ' us a'gain.

2 Thou hast moved the ' land and di'vided it : heal the ' sores thereof ' for it ' shaketh.

3 Thou hast shewed thy people ' heavy ' things : thou hast given us a ' drink of ' deadly ' wine.

4 Thou hast given a token for ' such as ' fear thee : that they may ' triumph be'cause of the ' truth.

5 Therefore were thy be'loved de'livered : help me with ' thy right ' hand and ' hear me.

6 God hath spoken in his holiness, I will rejoice and di'vide ' Sichem : and mete ' out the ' valley of ' Succoth.

7 Gilead is mine and Ma'nasses is ' mine : Ephraim also is the strength of my head, ' Judah ' is my ' law-giver;

8 Moab is my wash-pot, over Edom will I cast ' out my ' shoe : Philistia ' be thou ' glad of ' me.

9 Who will lead me into the ' strong ' city : who will ' bring me ' into ' Edom?

10 Hast not thou cast us ' out O ' God : wilt not thou O ' God go ' out with our ' hosts?

11 O be thou our ' help in ' trouble : for ' vain is the ' help of ' man.

12 Through God will we ' do great ' acts : for it is he that ' shall tread ' down our ' enemies.

PSALM 61

HEAR my ' crying O ' God : give ' ear ' unto my ' prayer.

2 From the ends of the earth will I ' call upon ' thee : when my ' heart ' is in ' heaviness.

3 O set me up upon the rock that is ' higher than ' I : for thou hast been my hope, and a strong tower for ' me a'gainst the ' enemy.

4 I will dwell in thy ' tabernacle for ' ever : and my trust shall be under the ' covering ' of thy ' wings.

f 5 For thou O Lord hast ' heard my de'sires : and hast given an heritage unto ' those that ' fear thy ' Name.

6 Thou shalt grant the ' King a long ' life : that his years may endure through'out all ' gene'rations.

7 He shall dwell before ' God for ' ever : O prepare thy loving mercy and ' faithfulness that ' they may pre'serve him.

8 So will I alway sing praise ' unto thy ' Name : that I may ' daily per'form my ' vows.

DAY 12   MORNING

PSALM 62

MY soul truly waiteth ' still upon ' God : for of him ' cometh ' my sal'vation.

2 He verily is my strength and ' my sal'vation : he is my defence, so that I ' shall not ' greatly ' fall.

3 How long will ye imagine mischief against ' every ' man : ye shall be slain all the sort of you, yea as a tottering wall shall ye be and ' like a ' broken ' hedge.

4 Their device is only how to put him out whom ' God will ex'alt : their delight is in lies, they give good words with their ' mouth but ' curse with their ' heart.

5 Nevertheless my soul wait thou ' still upon ' God : for my ' hope ' is in ' him.

6 He truly is my strength and ' my sal'vation : he is my defence ' so that I ' shall not ' fall.

7 In God is my ' health and my ' glory : the rock of my might, and in ' God is ' my ' trust.

8 O put your trust in him ' alway ye ' people : pour out your hearts before him, for ' God is ' our ' hope.

9 As for the children of men ' they are but ' vanity : the children of men are deceitful upon the weights, they are altogether ' lighter than ' vanity it'self.

10 O trust not in wrong and robbery, give not yourselves ' unto ' vanity : if riches increase ' set not your ' heart up'on them.

11 God spake once, and twice I have also ' heard the ' same : that power be'longeth ' unto ' God;

12 And that thou ' Lord art ' merciful : for thou rewardest every man ac'cording ' to his ' work.

PSALM 63

O GOD ' thou art my ' God : early ' will I ' seek ' thee.

2 My soul thirsteth for thee, my flesh also longeth ' after ' thee : in a barren and dry land ' where no ' water ' is.

3 Thus have I looked for ' thee in ' holiness : that I might be'hold thy ' power and ' glory.

4 For thy loving-kindness is better than the ' life it'self : my ' lips shall ' praise ' thee.

5 As long as I live will I magnify thee ' on this ' manner : and lift up my ' hands in ' thy ' Name.

6 My soul shall be satisfied, even as it were with ' marrow and ' fatness : when my mouth praiseth ' thee with ' joyful ' lips.

7 Have I not remembered thee ' in my ' bed : and thought upon ' thee when ' I was ' waking?

8 Because thou hast ' been my ' helper : therefore under the shadow of thy ' wings will ' I re'joice.

9 My soul ' hangeth up'on thee : thy ' right hand ' hath up'holden me.

10 These also that seek the ' hurt of my ' soul : they shall ' go ' under the ' earth.

11 Let them fall upon the ' edge of the ' sword : that they may ' be a ' portion for ' foxes.

12 But the King shall rejoice in God, all they also that swear by him shall ' be com'mended : for the mouth of them that speak ' lies ' shall be ' stopped.

PSALM 64

HEAR my voice O God ' in my ' prayer : preserve my ' life from ' fear of the ' enemy.

2 Hide me from the gathering together ' of the ' froward : and from the insur'rection of ' wicked ' doers;

3 Who have whet their tongue ' like a ' sword : and shoot out their arrows ' even ' bitter ' words;

4 That they may privily shoot at ' him that is ' perfect : suddenly do they ' hit him and ' fear ' not.

5 They encourage them'selves in ' mischief : and commune among themselves how they may lay snares, and ' say that ' no man shall ' see them.

6 They imagine ' wickedness and ' practise it : that they keep secret among themselves, every man ' in the ' deep of his ' heart.

7 But God shall suddenly shoot at them with a ' swift ' arrow : that ' they ' shall be ' wounded.

8 Yea their own tongues shall ' make them ' fall : insomuch that whoso ' seeth them shall ' laugh them to ' scorn.

9 And all men that see it shall say, This hath ' God ' done : for they shall perceive that ' it is ' his ' work.

f 10 The righteous shall rejoice in the Lord and put his ' trust in ' him : and all they that are ' true of ' heart shall be ' glad.

DAY 12   EVENING

PSALM 65

THOU O God art ' praised in ' Sion : and unto thee shall the vow be per'form-ed ' in Je'rusalem.

2 Thou that ' hearest the ' prayer : unto ' thee shall ' all flesh ' come.

3 My misdeeds pre'vail a'gainst me : O be thou ' merciful ' unto our ' sins.

4 Blessed is the man whom thou choosest and receivest ' unto ' thee : he shall dwell in thy court, and shall be satisfied with the pleasures of thy house, even ' of thy ' holy ' temple.

5 Thou shalt shew us wonderful things in thy righteousness, O God of ' our sal'vation : thou that art the hope of all the ends of the earth, and of them that re'main in the ' broad ' sea.

6 Who in his strength setteth ' fast the ' mountains : and is '
girded a'bout with ' power.

7 Who stilleth the ' raging · of the ' sea : and the noise of his
waves and the ' madness ' of the ' people.

8 They also that dwell in the uttermost parts of the earth shall
be afraid ' at thy ' tokens : thou that makest the outgoings
of the ' morning and ' evening to ' praise thee.

9 Thou visitest the ' earth and ' blessest it : thou ' makest it '
very ' plenteous.

10 The river of God is ' full of ' water : thou preparest their
corn, for so thou pro'videst ' for the ' earth.

11 Thou waterest her furrows, thou sendest rain into the
little ' valleys there'of : thou makest it soft with the drops of
rain, and ' blessest the ' increase ' of it.

12 Thou crownest the year ' with thy ' goodness : and thy '
clouds ' drop ' fatness.

13 They shall drop upon the ' dwellings · of the ' wilderness :
and the little hills shall re'joice on ' every ' side.

14 The folds shall be ' full of ' sheep : the valleys also shall
stand so thick with corn that ' they shall ' laugh and ' sing.

PSALM 66

O BE joyful in God ' all ye ' lands : sing praises unto the
honour of his Name, make his ' praise ' to be '
glorious.

2 Say unto God, O how wonderful art thou ' in thy ' works :
through the greatness of thy power shall thine enemies be
found ' liars ' unto ' thee.

3 For all the ' world shall ' worship thee : sing of ' thee and '
  praise thy ' Name.

4 O come hither and behold the ' works of ' God : how
  wonderful he is in his doing ' toward the ' children of ' men.

5 He turned the sea into ' dry ' land : so that they went
  through the water on foot, there did ' we re'joice there'of.

6 He ruleth with his power for ever, his eyes be'hold the '
  people : and such as will not believe, shall not be ' able to
  ex'alt them'selves.

7 O praise our ' God ye ' people : and make the ' voice of his '
  praise to be ' heard;

8 Who holdeth our ' soul in ' life : and suffereth ' not our '
  feet to ' slip.

9 For thou O ' God hast ' proved us : thou also hast tried us '
  like as ' silver is ' tried.

10 Thou broughtest us ' into the ' snare : and laidest ' trouble
  up'on our ' loins.

11 Thou sufferedst men to ride ' over our ' heads : we went
  through fire and water, and thou broughtest us out ' into a '
  wealthy ' place.

12 I will go into thine house with ' burnt'offerings : and will
  pay thee my vows, which I promised with my lips and spake
  with my mouth ' when I ' was in ' trouble.

13 I will offer unto thee fat burnt-sacrifices, with the ' incense
  of ' rams : I will ' offer ' bullocks and ' goats.

14 O come hither and hearken, all ye that ' fear ' God : and I
  will tell you what ' he hath ' done for my ' soul.

15 I called unto him ' with my ' mouth : and gave him '
   praises ' with my ' tongue.

16 If I incline unto wickedness ' with mine ' heart : the ' Lord '
   will not ' hear me.

17 But ' God hath ' heard me : and con'sidered the ' voice of
   my ' prayer.

18 Praised be God who hath not cast ' out my ' prayer : nor '
   turned his ' mercy ' from me.

PSALM 67

God be merciful unto ' us and ' bless us : and shew us
   the light of his countenance, and be ' merciful ' unto '
   us :

 2 That thy way may be ' known upon ' earth : thy saving '
   health a'mong all ' nations.

Unison

 3 Let the people ' praise thee O ' God : yea let ' all the '
   people ' praise thee.

 4 O let the nations re'joice and be ' glad : for thou shalt judge
   the folk righteously, and govern the ' nations up'on ' earth.

Unison

 5 Let the people ' praise thee O ' God : let ' all the ' people '
   praise thee.

 6 Then shall the earth bring ' forth her ' increase : and God
   even our own ' God shall ' give us his ' blessing.

2nd Part

7 God ' shall ' bless us : and all the ' ends of the ' world shall ' fear him.

DAY 13 MORNING

PSALM 68

LET God arise and let his ' enemies be ' scattered : let them also that ' hate him ' flee be'fore him.

2 Like as the smoke vanisheth, so shalt thou ' drive them a'way : and like as wax melteth at the fire, so let the ungodly ' perish at the ' presence of ' God.

3 But let the righteous be glad and re'joice before ' God : let them ' also be ' merry and ' joyful.

4 O sing unto God and sing praises ' unto his ' Name : magnify him that rideth upon the heavens as it were upon an horse, praise him in his Name JAH ' and re'joice be'fore him.

5 He is a father of the fatherless, and defendeth the ' cause of the ' widows : even God in his ' holy ' habi'tation.

6 He is the God that maketh men to be of one mind in an house, and bringeth the prisoners ' out of cap'tivity : but letteth the ' runagates con'tinue in ' scarceness.

7 O God when thou wentest forth be'fore the ' people : when thou ' wentest ' through the ' wilderness;

8 The earth shook and the heavens dropped, at the ' presence of ' God : even as Sinai also was moved at the presence of God who ' is the ' God of ' Israel.

9 Thou O God sentest a gracious rain upon ' thine in'heritance : and re'freshedst it ' when it was ' weary.

10 Thy congregation shall ' dwell there'in : for thou O God
hast of thy goodness pre'par-ed ' for the ' poor.

11 The Lord ' gave the ' word : great was the ' company ' of
the ' preachers.

12 Kings with their armies did flee and ' were dis'comfited :
and they of the ' household di'vided the ' spoil.

13 Though ye have lien among the pots, yet shall ye be as the '
wings of a ' dove : that is covered with silver wings ' and
her ' feathers like ' gold.

14 When the Almighty scattered ' kings for their ' sake : then
were they as ' white as ' snow in ' Salmon.

15 As the hill of Basan ' so is ' God's hill : even an high hill ' as
the ' hill of ' Basan.

16 Why hop ye so ye high hills? this is God's hill in the which it
pleaseth ' him to ' dwell : yea the Lord will a'bide in ' it for '
ever.

17 The chariots of God are twenty thousand, even ' thousands
of ' angels : and the Lord is among them, as in the ' holy '
place of ' Sinai.

18 Thou art gone up on high, thou hast led captivity captive,
and received ' gifts for ' men : yea even for thine enemies,
that the Lord ' God might ' dwell a'mong them.

19 Praised be the ' Lord ' daily : even the God who helpeth us,
and ' poureth his ' benefits up'on us.

20 He is our God, even the God of whom ' cometh sal'vation :
God is the Lord by ' whom we es'cape ' death.

[21 God shall wound the ' head of his ' enemies : and the hairy
scalp of such a one as ' goeth on ' still in his ' wickedness.

22 The Lord hath said, I will bring my people again as I ' did from ' Basan : mine own will I bring again, as I did some-time ' from the ' deep of the ' sea.

2nd Part

23 That thy foot may be dipped in the ' blood of thine ' enemies : and that the tongue of thy ' dogs may be ' red through the ' same.]

24 It is well seen O God ' how thou ' goest : how thou my God and King ' goest ' in the ' sanctuary.

25 The singers go before, the minstrels ' follow ' after : in the midst are the damsels ' playing ' with the ' timbrels.

26 Give thanks O Israel unto God the Lord in the ' con-gre'gations : from the ' ground ' of the ' heart.

27 There is little Benjamin their ruler, and the princes of ' Judah their ' counsel : the princes of ' Zabulon · and the ' princes of ' Nephthali.

28 Thy God hath sent forth ' strength for ' thee : stablish the thing O God that ' thou hast ' wrought in ' us,

29 For thy temple's sake ' at Je'rusalem : so shall kings bring ' presents ' unto ' thee.

30 When the company of the spear-men and multitude of the mighty, are scattered abroad among the beasts of the people, so that they humbly bring ' pieces of ' silver : and when he hath scattered the people ' that de'light in ' war;

31 Then shall the princes come ' out of ' Egypt : the Morians' land shall soon stretch ' out her ' hands · unto ' God.

32 Sing unto God O ye ' kingdoms of the ' earth : O sing ' praises ' unto the ' Lord;

33 Who sitteth in the heavens over all ' from the be'ginning : lo he doth send out his voice, yea and ' that a ' mighty ' voice.

34 Ascribe ye the power to God ' over ' Israel : his worship and ' strength is ' in the ' clouds.

35 O God wonderful art thou in thy ' holy ' places : even the God of Israel, he will give strength and power unto his people, ' blessed ' be ' God.

DAY 13   EVENING
PSALM 69

Save ' me O ' God : for the waters are come in ' even ' unto my ' soul.

2 I stick fast in the deep mire ' where no ' ground is : I am come into deep waters ' so that the ' floods run ' over me.

3 I am weary of crying, my ' throat is ' dry : my sight faileth me for ' waiting so ' long upon my ' God.

4 They that hate me without a cause are more than the ' hairs of my ' head : they that are mine enemies, and would de'stroy me ' guiltless are ' mighty.

5 I paid them the things that I ' never ' took : God thou knowest my simpleness, and my faults ' are not ' hid from ' thee.

6 Let not them that trust in thee O Lord God of hosts, be ashamed for ' my ' cause : let not those that seek thee be confounded through me, O ' Lord ' God of ' Israel.

7 And why?, for thy sake have I ' suffered re'proof : shame hath ' covered ' my ' face.

8 I am become a stranger ' unto my ' brethren : even an alien ' unto my ' mother's ' children.

9 For the zeal of thine house hath ' even ' eaten me : and the rebukes of them that rebuked ' thee are ' fallen up'on me.

10 I wept and chastened my'self with ' fasting : and that was ' turned to ' my re'proof.

11 I put on ' sackcloth ' also : and they ' jested up'on ' me.

12 They that sit in the gate ' speak a'gainst me : and the ' drunkards make ' songs up'on me.

13 But Lord I make my prayer ' unto ' thee : in ' an ac'cept-able ' time.

14 Hear me O God in the multitude ' of thy ' mercy : even in the ' truth of ' thy sal'vation.

15 Take me out of the mire ' that I ' sink not : O let me be delivered from them that hate me, and ' out of the ' deep ' waters.

16 Let not the water-flood drown me, neither let the deep ' swallow me ' up : and let not the pit ' shut her ' mouth up'on me.

17 Hear me O Lord, for thy loving'kindness is ' comfortable : turn thee unto me according to the ' multitude ' of thy ' mercies.

18 And hide not thy face from thy servant for ' I am in ' trouble : O ' haste ' thee and ' hear me.

19 Draw nigh unto my ' soul and ' save it : O de'liver me be'cause of mine ' enemies.

20 Thou hast known my reproof my shame and ' my dis'hon-our : mine adversaries are ' all in ' thy ' sight.

21 Thy rebuke hath broken my heart, I am ' full of ' heaviness : I looked for some to have pity on me, but there was no man, neither ' found I ' any to ' comfort me.

22 They gave me ' gall to ' eat : and when I was thirsty they ' gave me ' vinegar to ' drink.

[23 Let their table be made a snare to take them'selves with'al : and let the things that should have been for their wealth, be unto ' them an oc'casion of ' falling.

24 Let their eyes be blinded ' that they ' see not : and ever ' bow thou ' down their ' backs.

25 Pour out thine indig'nation up'on them : and let thy ' wrathful dis'pleasure take ' hold of them.

26 Let their habi'tation be ' void : and ' no man to ' dwell in their ' tents.

27 For they persecute him whom ' thou hast ' smitten : and they talk how they may vex ' them whom ' thou hast ' wounded.

28 Let them fall from one wickedness ' to an'other : and ' not come ' into thy ' righteousness.

2nd Part

29 Let them be wiped out of the ' book of the ' living : and not be ' written a'mong the ' righteous.]

30 As for me, when I am ' poor and in ' heaviness : thy help O ' God shall ' lift me ' up.

31 I will praise the Name of ' God · with a ' song : and ' magni'fy it with ' thanksgiving.

32 This also shall ' please the ' Lord : better than a bullock ' that hath ' horns and ' hoofs.

33 The humble shall consider this ' and be ' glad : seek ye after God ' and your ' soul shall ' live.

34 For the Lord ' heareth the ' poor : and des'piseth ' not his ' prisoners.

35 Let heaven and ' earth ' praise him : the sea and ' all that ' moveth there'in.

36 For God will save Sion, and build the ' cities of ' Judah : that men may dwell there and ' have it ' in pos'session.

37 The posterity also of his servants ' shall in'herit it : and they that love his ' Name shall ' dwell there'in.

PSALM 70

Haste thee O God ' to de'liver me : make ' haste to ' help me O ' Lord.

2 Let them be ashamed and confounded that seek ' after my ' soul : let them be turned backward and put to con'-fusion that ' wish me ' evil.

3 Let them for their reward be soon ' brought to ' shame : that cry ' over me ' There ' there.

4 But let all those that seek thee be joyful and ' glad in ' thee : and let all such as delight in thy salvation say ' alway The ' Lord be ' praised.

5 As for me I am ' poor and in ' misery : haste thee ' unto ' me O ' God.

6 Thou art my helper and ' my re'deemer : O ' Lord make ' no long ' tarrying.

DAY 14 MORNING

PSALM 71

In thee O Lord have I put my trust, let me never be ' put to con'fusion : but rid me and deliver me in thy righteousness, incline thine ear ' unto ' me and ' save me.

2 Be thou my strong hold whereunto I may ' alway re'sort : thou hast promised to help me, for thou art my house of de'fence and ' my ' castle.

3 Deliver me O my God out of the ' hand of · the un'godly : out of the hand of the un'righteous and ' cruel ' man.

4 For thou O Lord God art the ' thing that I ' long for : thou art my hope ' even ' from my ' youth.

5 Through thee have I been holden up ever since ' I was ' born : thou art he that took me out of my mother's womb, my praise ' shall be ' always of ' thee.

6 I am become as it were a monster ' unto ' many : but my ' sure ' trust is in ' thee.

7 O let my mouth be ' filled with thy ' praise : that I may sing of thy glory and ' honour ' all the day ' long.

8 Cast me not away in the ' time of ' age : forsake me not ' when my ' strength ' faileth me.

9 For mine enemies speak against me, and they that lay wait for my soul take their counsel to'gether ' saying : God hath forsaken him, persecute him and take him, for ' there is ' none to de'liver him.

10 Go not far from ' me O ' God : my God ' haste ' thee to ' help me.

11 Let them be confounded and perish that are a'gainst my ' soul : let them be covered with shame and dishonour that ' seek to ' do me ' evil.

12 As for me I will patiently a'bide ' alway : and will ' praise thee ' more and ' more.

13 My mouth shall daily speak of thy righteousness ' and sal'vation : for I ' know no ' end there'of.

14 I will go forth in the strength of the ' Lord ' God : and will make mention of ' thy ' righteousness ' only.

15 Thou O God hast taught me from my youth up ' until ' now : therefore will I ' tell of thy ' wondrous ' works.

16 Forsake me not O God in mine old age, when I am ' gray'headed : until I have shewed thy strength unto this generation, and thy power to all ' them that are ' yet for to ' come.

17 Thy righteousness O God is ' very ' high : and great things are they that thou hast done, O God ' who is ' like unto ' thee?

18 O what great troubles and adversities hast thou shewed me, and yet didst thou ' turn and re'fresh me : yea and broughtest me from the ' deep of the ' earth a'gain.

19 Thou hast brought me to ' great ' honour : and comforted ' me on ' every ' side.

20 Therefore will I praise thee and thy faithfulness O God, playing upon an ' instrument of ' musick : unto thee will I sing upon the harp, O thou ' Holy ' One of ' Israel.

21 My lips will be fain when I sing ' unto ' thee : and so will my soul ' whom thou ' hast de'livered.

22 My tongue also shall talk of thy righteousness ' all the day ' long : for they are confounded and brought unto shame that ' seek to ' do me ' evil.

PSALM 72

GIVE the King thy ' judgements O ' God : and thy right-eousness' unto the 'King's'son.

*   2 Then shall he judge thy people ac'cording ' unto ' right : '
and de'fend the ' poor.

3 The mountains also ' shall bring ' peace : and the little hills '
righteousness ' unto the ' people.

4 He shall keep the simple folk ' by their ' right : defend the
children of the poor and ' punish the ' wrong'doer.

5 They shall fear thee as long as the sun and ' moon
en'dureth : from one gene'ration ' to an'other.

6 He shall come down like the rain into a ' fleece of ' wool :
even as the ' drops that ' water the ' earth.

2nd Part

7 In his time shall the ' righteous ' flourish : yea and abundance of peace so ' long as the ' moon en'dureth.

8 His dominion shall be also from the one ' sea to the ' other :
and from the flood ' unto the ' world's ' end.

9 They that dwell in the wilderness shall ' kneel be'fore him :
his ' enemies shall ' lick the ' dust.

10 The kings of Tharsis and of the isles ' shall give ' presents :
the kings of Arabia and ' Saba ' shall bring ' gifts.

11 All kings shall fall ' down be'fore him : all ' nations shall '
do him ' service.

12 For he shall deliver the poor ' when he ' crieth : the needy
also and ' him that ' hath no ' helper.

13 He shall be favourable to the ' simple and ' needy : and
shall pre'serve the ' souls of the ' poor.

14 He shall deliver their souls from ' falsehood and ' wrong :
and dear shall their ' blood be ' in his ' sight.

2 Then shall he judge thy people according ' unto ' right : and de-'
fend ' the ' poor.

15 He shall live, and unto him shall be given of the ' gold of A'rabia : prayer shall be made ever unto him and ' daily shall ' he be ' praised.

16 There shall be an heap of corn in the earth, high up'on the ' hills : his fruit shall shake like Libanus, and shall be green in the city like ' grass up'on the ' earth.

17 His Name shall endure for ever, his Name shall remain under the sun a'mong the pos'terities : which shall be blessed through him, and ' all the ' heathen shall ' praise him.

18 Blessed be the Lord God, even the ' God of ' Israel : which only ' doeth ' wondrous ' things;

19 And blessed be the Name of his ' majesty for ' ever : and all the earth shall be filled with his majesty. ' Amen ' A'men.

DAY 14 EVENING

PSALM 73

TRULY God is loving ' unto ' Israel : even unto such as ' are of a ' clean ' heart.

2 Nevertheless my feet were ' almost ' gone : my ' treadings had ' well-nigh ' slipt.

3 And why?, I was grieved ' at the ' wicked : I do also see the un'godly in ' such pros'perity.

* 4 For they are ' in no ' peril of ' death : ' but are ' lusty and ' strong.

5 They come in no mis'fortune like ' other folk : neither ' are they ' plagued like ' other men.

4 For they are in no ' peril of ' death : but are ' lusty ' and ' strong.

365

6 And this is the cause that they are so ' holden with ' pride : and ' over'whelmed with ' cruelty.

7 Their eyes ' swell with ' fatness : and they do ' even ' what they ' lust.

8 They corrupt other, and speak of ' wicked ' blasphemy : their talking is a'gainst the ' most ' High.

9 For they stretch forth their mouth ' unto the ' heaven : and their tongue ' goeth ' through the ' world.

10 Therefore fall the ' people ' unto them : and thereout ' suck they no ' small ad'vantage.

11 Tush say they, how should ' God per'ceive it : is there knowledge ' in the ' most ' High?

12 Lo these are the ungodly, these prosper in the world, and these have riches ' in pos'session : and I said, Then have I cleansed my heart in vain and ' washed mine ' hands in ' innocency.

13 All the day long have ' I been ' punished : and ' chastened ' every ' morning.

14 Yea and I had almost said ' even as ' they : but lo then I should have condemned the gene'ration ' of thy ' children.

15 Then thought I to under'stand ' this : but it ' was too ' hard for ' me,

16 Until I went into the ' sanctuary of ' God : then under-' stood I the ' end of ' these men;

17 Namely how thou dost set them in ' slippery ' places : and ' castest them ' down and de'stroyest them.

18 O how suddenly do ' they con'sume : perish and ' come to a ' fearful ' end!

19 Yea even like as a dream ' when one a'waketh : so shalt thou make their image to ' vanish ' out of the ' city.

20 Thus my ' heart was ' grieved : and it went ' even ' through my ' reins.

2nd Part

21 So foolish was ' I and ' ignorant : even as it ' were a ' beast be'fore thee.

22 Nevertheless I am ' alway by ' thee : for thou hast holden me ' by my ' right ' hand.

23 Thou shalt guide me ' with thy ' counsel : and after ' that re'ceive me with ' glory.

24 Whom have I in ' heaven but ' thee : and there is none upon earth that I de'sire in com'parison of ' thee.

25 My flesh and my ' heart ' faileth : but God is the strength of my heart ' and my ' portion for ' ever.

26 For lo they that forsake ' thee shall ' perish : thou hast destroyed all them that com'mit forni'cation a'gainst thee.

27 But it is good for me to hold me fast by God, to put my trust in the ' Lord ' God : and to speak of all thy works in the ' gates of the ' daughter of ' Sion.

PSALM 74

O GOD wherefore art thou absent from ' us so ' long : why is thy wrath so hot a'gainst the ' sheep of thy ' pasture?

2 O think upon thy ' congre'gation : whom thou hast pur-chased ' and re'deemed of ' old.

3 Think upon the tribe of ' thine in'heritance : and mount '
Sion where'in thou hast ' dwelt.

4 Lift up thy feet, that thou mayest utterly destroy ' every '
enemy : which hath done ' evil ' in thy ' sanctuary.

5 Thine adversaries roar in the midst of thy ' congre'gations :
and set ' up their ' banners for ' tokens.

6 He that hewed timber afore out of the ' thick ' trees : was
known to ' bring it to an ' excellent ' work.

7 But now they break down all the carved ' work there'of :
with ' axes ' and ' hammers.

8 They have set fire upon thy ' holy ' places : and have defiled
the dwelling-place of thy Name ' even ' unto the ' ground.

9 Yea they said in their hearts, Let us make havock of them '
alto'gether : thus have they burnt up all the ' houses of '
God in the ' land.

10 We see not our tokens, there is not one ' prophet ' more :
no not one is there among us, that under'standeth ' any '
more.

11 O God how long shall the adversary do ' this dis'honour :
how long shall the enemy blas'pheme thy ' Name for '
ever?

12 Why withdrawest ' thou thy ' hand : why pluckest thou not
thy right hand out of thy bosom ' to con'sume the ' enemy?

13 For God is my ' King of ' old : the help that is done upon
earth he ' doeth ' it him'self.

14 Thou didst divide the sea ' through thy ' power : thou
brakest the heads of the ' dragons ' in the ' waters.

15 Thou smotest the heads of Le'viathan in ' pieces : and
gavest him to be meat for the ' people ' in the ' wilderness.

16 Thou broughtest out fountains and waters out of the '
hard ' rocks : thou ' driedst up ' mighty ' waters.

17 The day is thine and the ' night is ' thine : thou hast
pre'pared the ' light and the ' sun.

18 Thou hast set all the ' borders · of the ' earth : thou ' hast
made ' summer and ' winter.

19 Remember this O Lord, how the enemy ' hath re'buked :
and how the foolish people ' hath blas'phemed thy ' Name.

20 O deliver not the soul of thy turtle-dove, unto the multitude ' of the ' enemies : and forget not the congre'gation ·
of the ' poor for ' ever.

21 Look up'on the ' covenant : for all the earth is full of
darkness and ' cruel ' habi'tations.

22 O let not the simple go a'way a'shamed : but let the poor
and needy give ' praise ' unto thy ' Name.

23 Arise O God maintain thine ' own ' cause : remember how
the foolish man blas'phemeth ' thee ' daily.

24 Forget not the ' voice of thine ' enemies : the presumption
of them that hate thee increaseth ' ever ' more and ' more.

DAY 15   MORNING

PSALM 75

Unto thee O God do ' we give ' thanks : yea unto ' thee do '
we give ' thanks.

2 Thy Name also ' is so ' nigh : and that do thy ' wondrous '
works de'clare.

3 When I receive the ' congre'gation : I shall judge ac'cording ' unto ' right.

4 The earth is weak, and all the in'habiters there'of : I bear ' up the ' pillars ' of it.

5 I said unto the fools, Deal ' not so ' madly : and to the ungodly, ' Set not ' up your ' horn.

6 Set not up your ' horn on ' high : and ' speak not ' with a stiff ' neck.

* 7 For promotion cometh neither ' from the ' east nor ' from the ' west : nor ' yet from the ' south.

8 And why? ' God is the ' Judge : he putteth down one and ' setteth ' up an'other.

9 For in the hand of the Lord there is a cup and the ' wine is ' red : it is full mixed, and he ' poureth ' out of the ' same.

10 As for the ' dregs there'of : all the ungodly of the earth shall ' drink them and ' suck them ' out.

11 But I will talk of the ' God of ' Jacob : and ' praise ' him for ' ever.

12 All the horns of the ungodly also ' will I ' break : and the horns of the ' righteous shall ' be ex'alted.

PSALM 76

In Jewry is ' God ' known : his ' Name is ' great in ' Israel.

2 At Salem ' is his ' tabernacle : and his ' dwelling ' in ' Sion.

3 There brake he the ' arrows of the ' bow : the ' shield the ' sword · and the ' battle.

Ps. 75. vs. 7 For promotion cometh neither from the east nor ' from the ' west : nor ' yet ' from the ' south.

4 Thou art of more ' honour and ' might : than the ' hills ' of the ' robbers.

5 The proud are robbed, they have ' slept their ' sleep : and all the men whose hands were ' mighty have ' found ' nothing.

6 At thy rebuke O ' God of ' Jacob : both the ' chariot and ' horse are ' fallen.

7 Thou even thou ' art to be ' feared : and who may stand in thy ' sight when ' thou art ' angry?

8 Thou didst cause thy judgement to be ' heard from ' heaven : the earth ' trembled ' and was ' still;

9 When God a'rose to ' judgement : and to help ' all the ' meek upon ' earth.

10 The fierceness of man shall ' turn to thy ' praise : and the fierceness of ' them shalt ' thou re'frain.

11 Promise unto the Lord your God and keep it, all ye that are ' round a'bout him : bring presents unto ' him that ' ought to be ' feared.

12 He shall refrain the ' spirit of ' princes : and is wonderful a'mong the ' kings of the ' earth.

PSALM 77

I WILL cry unto God ' with my ' voice : even unto God will I cry with my voice, and he shall ' hearken ' unto 'me.

2 In the time of my trouble I ' sought the ' Lord : my sore ran and ceased not in the night-season, my ' soul re'fus-ed ' comfort.

3 When I am in heaviness I will ' think upon ' God : when my heart is ' vexed I ' will com'plain.

4 Thou holdest mine ' eyes ' waking : I am so feeble ' that I ' cannot ' speak.

5 I have considered the ' days of ' old : and the ' years ' that are ' past.

6 I call to re'membrance my ' song : and in the night I commune with mine own heart and ' search ' out my ' spirits.

7 Will the Lord absent him'self for ' ever : and will he ' be no ' more in'treated?

8 Is his mercy clean ' gone for ' ever : and is his promise come utterly to an ' end for ' ever'more?

9 Hath God forgotten ' to be ' gracious : and will he shut up his loving'kindness ' in dis'pleasure?

10 And I said, It is mine ' own in'firmity : but I will remember the years of the right hand ' of the ' most ' Highest.

11 I will remember the ' works of the ' Lord : and call to mind thy ' wonders of ' old ' time.

12 I will think also of ' all thy ' works : and my talking shall ' be of ' thy ' doings.

13 Thy way O ' God is ' holy : who is so ' great a ' God as ' our God?

14 Thou art the God that ' doeth ' wonders : and hast declared thy ' power a'mong the ' people.

15 Thou hast mightily de'livered thy ' people : even the ' sons of ' Jacob and ' Joseph.

16 The waters saw thee O God, the waters saw thee and ' were a'fraid : the ' depths ' also were ' troubled.

17 The clouds poured out water the ' air ' thundered : and thine ' arrows ' went a'broad.

18 The voice of thy thunder was heard ' round a'bout : the lightnings shone upon the ground, the earth was ' moved and ' shook with'al.

19 Thy way is in the sea, and thy paths in the ' great ' waters : and thy ' footsteps ' are not ' known.

20 Thou leddest thy ' people like ' sheep : by the ' hand of ' Moses and ' Aaron.

DAY 15 EVENING

PSALM 78

HEAR my law ' O my ' people : incline your ears ' unto the ' words of my ' mouth.

2 I will open my ' mouth in a ' parable : I will de'clare hard ' sentences of ' old;

3 Which we have ' heard and ' known : and ' such as our ' fathers have ' told us;

4 That we should not hide them from the children of the gene'rations to ' come : but to shew the honour of the Lord, his mighty and wonderful ' works that ' he hath ' done.

5 He made a covenant with Jacob, and gave ' Israel a ' law : which he commanded our fore'fathers to ' teach their ' children;

6 That their pos'terity might ' know it : and the children ' which were ' yet un'born;

7 To the intent that when ' they came ' up : they might ' shew their ' children the ' same;

8 That they might put their ' trust in ' God : and not to forget the works of God, but to ' keep ' his com'mandments;

9 And not to be as their forefathers, a faithless and ' stubborn · gene'ration : a generation that set not their heart aright, and whose spirit cleaveth not ' stedfastly ' unto ' God;

10 Like as the ' children of ' Ephraim : who being harnessed and carrying bows, turned themselves ' back in the ' day of ' battle.

11 They kept not the ' covenant of ' God : and ' would not ' walk in his ' law;

12 But forgat what ' he had ' done : and the wonderful works that ' he had ' shew-ed ' for them.

13 Marvellous things did he in the sight of our forefathers, in the ' land of ' Egypt : even ' in the ' field of ' Zoan.

14 He divided the sea and ' let them go ' through : he made the ' waters to ' stand on an ' heap.

15 In the day-time also he led them ' with a ' cloud : and all the night through ' with a ' light of ' fire.

16 He clave the hard rocks ' in the ' wilderness : and gave them drink thereof, as it had been ' out of the ' great ' depth.

17 He brought waters out of the ' stony ' rock : so that it ' gush-ed ' out · like the ' rivers.

18 Yet for all this they sin-ned ' more a'gainst him : and provoked the most ' Highest ' in the ' wilderness.

19 They tempted God ' in their ' hearts : and required ' meat ' for their ' lust.

20 They spake against God ' also ' saying : Shall God prepare a ' table ' in the ' wilderness?

2nd Part

21 He smote the stony rock indeed, that the waters gushed out and the streams ' flowed with'al : but can he give bread also, or provide ' flesh for ' his ' people?

22 When the Lord heard this ' he was ' wroth : so the fire was kindled in Jacob, and there came up heavy dis'pleasure a'gainst ' Israel;

23 Because they believed ' not in ' God : and ' put not their ' trust in his ' help.

24 So he commanded the ' clouds a'bove : and ' opened the ' doors of ' heaven.

25 He rained down manna also upon them ' for to ' eat : and ' gave them ' food from ' heaven.

26 So man did eat ' angels' ' food : for he ' sent them ' meat e'nough.

27 He caused the east-wind to blow ' under ' heaven : and through his power he brought ' in the ' south-west'wind.

28 He rained flesh upon them as ' thick as ' dust : and feathered fowls ' like as the ' sand of the ' sea.

29 He let it fall a'mong their ' tents : even round a'bout their ' habi'tation.

30 So they did eat and were well filled, for he gave them their ' own de'sire : they were not disap'pointed ' of their ' lust.

31 But while the meat was yet in their mouths, the heavy wrath of God came upon them, and slew the ' wealthiest ' of them : yea and smote down the chosen ' men that ' were in ' Israel.

32 But for all this they ' sinned yet ' more : and believed ' not his ' wondrous ' works.

* 33 Therefore their days did ' he con'sume in ' vanity : ' and their ' years in ' trouble.

34 When he slew ' them they ' sought him : and turned them early and in'quired ' after ' God.

35 And they remembered that ' God was their ' strength : and that the high ' God was ' their re'deemer.

36 Nevertheless they did but flatter him ' with their ' mouth : and dissembled ' with him ' in their ' tongue.

37 For their heart was not ' whole with ' him : neither continued they ' stedfast ' in his ' covenant.

38 But he was so merciful that he forgave ' their mis'deeds : and de'stroy-ed ' them ' not.

39 Yea many a time turned he his ' wrath a'way : and would not suffer his whole dis'pleasure ' to a'rise.

40 For he considered that they ' were but ' flesh : and that they were even a wind that passeth away and ' cometh ' not a'gain.

41 Many a time did they provoke him ' in the ' wilderness : and ' grieved him ' in the ' desert.

42 They turned back and ' tempted ' God : and moved the ' Holy ' One in ' Israel.

43 They thought not ' of his ' hand : and of the day when he delivered them ' from the ' hand of the ' enemy;

44 How he had wrought his ' miracles in ' Egypt : and his wonders ' in the ' field of ' Zoan.

33 Therefore their days did he con'sume in ' vanity : and their ' years ' in ' trouble.

376

2nd Part

45 He turned their waters ' into ' blood : so that they ' might not ' drink of the ' rivers.

46 He sent lice among them and de'voured them ' up : and ' frogs ' to de'stroy them.

47 He gave their fruit ' unto the ' caterpillar : and their ' labour ' unto the ' grasshopper.

48 He destroyed their ' vines with ' hailstones : and their ' mulberry'trees with the ' frost.

49 He smote their cattle ' also with ' hailstones : and their ' flocks with ' hot ' thunder-bolts.

50 He cast upon them the furiousness of his wrath, anger dis'pleasure and ' trouble : and sent ' evil ' angels a'mong them.

51 He made a way to his indignation, and spared not their ' soul from ' death : but gave their life ' over ' to the ' pestilence;

52 And smote all the ' first-born in ' Egypt : the most principal and mightiest ' in the ' dwellings of ' Ham.

53 But as for his own people, he led them ' forth like ' sheep : and carried them in the ' wilderness ' like a ' flock.

54 He brought them out safely that they ' should not ' fear : and overwhelmed their ' enemies ' with the ' sea.

55 And brought them within the ' borders · of his ' sanctuary : even to his mountain which he purchased ' with his ' right ' hand.

56 He cast out the heathen ' also be'fore them : caused their land to be divided among them for an heritage, and made the tribes of Israel to ' dwell in ' their ' tents.

57 So they tempted and displeased the ' most high ' God :
and ' kept not ' his ' testimonies;

58 But turned their backs and fell away ' like their ' forefathers : starting aside ' like a ' broken ' bow.

2nd Part

59 For they grieved him with their ' hill'altars : and provoked
him to dis'pleasure ' with their ' images.

60 When God heard this ' he was ' wroth : and took ' sore
dis'pleasure at ' Israel.

61 So that he forsook the ' tabernacle in ' Silo : even the tent
that he had ' pitched a'mong ' men.

62 He delivered their power ' into cap'tivity : and their
beauty ' into the ' enemy's ' hand.

63 He gave his people over also ' unto the ' sword : and was '
wroth with ' his in'heritance.

64 The fire consumed their ' young ' men : and their maidens '
were not ' given to ' marriage.

65 Their priests were ' slain with the ' sword : and there were
no ' widows to ' make lamen'tation.

66 So the Lord awaked as one ' out of ' sleep : and like a ' giant
re'freshed with ' wine.

67 He smote his enemies in the ' hinder ' parts : and put them '
to a per'petual ' shame.

68 He refused the ' tabernacle of ' Joseph : and ' chose not
the ' tribe of ' Ephraim;

69 But chose the ' tribe of ' Judah : even the hill of ' Sion '
which he ' loved.

70 And there he built his ' temple on ' high : and laid the
foundation of it, like the ground which ' he hath ' made
con'tinually.

71 He chose David ' also his ' servant : and ' took him a'way
from the ' sheep-folds.

72 As he was following the ewes great with ' young ones he '
took him : that he might feed Jacob his people and ' Israel '
his in'heritance.

73 So he fed them with a faithful and ' true ' heart : and ruled
them ' prudently with ' all his ' power.

DAY 16   MORNING

PSALM 79

O GOD the heathen are come into ' thine in'heritance : thy holy
temple have they defiled, and made Je'rusalem an ' heap
of ' stones.

2 The dead bodies of thy servants have they given, to be meat
unto the ' fowls of the ' air : and the flesh of thy saints ' unto
the ' beasts of the ' land.

3 Their blood have they shed like water on every ' side of
Je'rusalem : and ' there was ' no man to ' bury them.

4 We are become an open shame ' to our ' enemies : a very
scorn and derision unto them ' that are ' round a'bout us.

5 Lord how long wilt ' thou be ' angry : shall thy jealousy '
burn like ' fire for ' ever?

6 Pour out thine indignation upon the heathen that ' have
not ' known thee : and upon the kingdoms that have not '
called up'on thy ' Name.

7 For they have de'vour-ed ' Jacob : and ' laid ' waste
his ' dwelling-place.

8 O remember not our old sins, but have mercy upon us ' and
that ' soon : for we are ' come to ' great ' misery.

9 Help us O God of our salvation, for the glory ' of thy '
Name : O deliver us, and be merciful unto our sins ' for thy '
Name's ' sake.

* 10 Wherefore ' do the ' heathen ' say : ' Where is ' now their '
God?

11 O let the vengeance of thy servants' blood ' that is ' shed :
be openly shewed upon the ' heathen ' in our ' sight.

12 O let the sorrowful sighing of the prisoners ' come be'fore
thee : according to the greatness of thy power, preserve
thou those that ' are ap'pointed to ' die.

13 And for the blasphemy wherewith our neighbours have
blas'phem-ed ' thee : reward thou them O Lord ' seven-
fold ' into their ' bosom.

14 So we that are thy people and sheep of thy pasture, shall
give thee ' thanks for ' ever : and will alway be shewing
forth thy praise from gene'ration to ' gene'ration.

PSALM 80

HEAR O thou Shepherd of Israel, thou that leadest
Joseph ' like a ' sheep : shew thyself also, thou that '
sittest up'on the ' cherubims.

2 Before Ephraim Benjamin ' and Ma'nasses : stir up thy '
strength and ' come and ' help us.

10 Wherefore do the ' heathen ' say : where is ' now ' their ' God?

2nd Part

3 Turn us a'gain O ' God : shew the light of thy countenance '
   and we ' shall be ' whole.

4 O Lord ' God of ' hosts : how long wilt thou be angry ' with
   thy ' people that ' prayeth?

5 Thou feedest them with the ' bread of ' tears : and givest
   them ' plenteousness of ' tears to ' drink.

6 Thou hast made us a very strife ' unto our ' neighbours :
   and our ' enemies ' laugh us to ' scorn.

7 Turn us again thou ' God of ' hosts : shew the light of thy
   countenance ' and we ' shall be ' whole.

8 Thou hast brought a vine ' out of ' Egypt : thou hast cast '
   out the ' heathen and ' planted it.

9 Thou ' madest ' room for it : and when it had taken ' root it '
   filled the ' land.

10 The hills were covered ' with the ' shadow of it : and the
   boughs thereof were ' like the ' goodly ' cedar-trees.

11 She stretched out her branches ' unto the ' sea : and her '
   boughs ' unto the ' river.

12 Why hast thou then broken ' down her ' hedge : that all
   they that go ' by pluck ' off her ' grapes?

13 The wild boar out of the wood doth ' root it ' up : and the
   wild ' beasts of the ' field de'vour it.

2nd Part

14 Turn thee again thou God of hosts, look ' down from '
   heaven : be'hold and ' visit this ' vine;

15 And the place of the vineyard that thy right ' hand hath '
   planted : and the branch that thou ' madest so ' strong for
   thy'self.

16 It is burnt with fire and ' cut ' down · and they shall perish at the re'buke of ' thy ' countenance.

17 Let thy hand be upon the man of thy ' right ' hand : and upon the son of man, whom thou madest so strong ' for thine ' own ' self.

18 And so will not we go ' back from ' thee : O let us live, and we shall ' call up'on thy ' Name.

2nd Part

19 Turn us again O Lord ' God of ' hosts : shew the light of thy countenance ' and we ' shall be ' whole.

PSALM 81

SING we merrily unto ' God our ' strength : make a cheerful noise'unto the'God of'Jacob.

2 Take the psalm bring ' hither the ' tabret : the ' merry ' harp with the ' lute.

3 Blow up the trumpet in the ' new ' moon : even in the time appointed, and up'on our ' solemn ' feast-day.

4 For this was made a ' statute for ' Israel : and a ' law of the ' God of ' Jacob.

5 This he ordained in Joseph ' for a ' testimony : when he came out of the land of Egypt, and had ' heard a ' strange ' language.

6 I eased his shoulder ' from the ' burden : and his hands were ' delivered from ' making the ' pots.

7 Thou calledst upon me in troubles, and ' I de'livered thee : and heard thee what time as the ' storm ' fell up'on thee.

*   8 I ' prov-ed ' thee ' also : ' at the ' waters of ' strife.

   9 Hear O my people, and I will assure ' thee O ' Israel : if
      thou wilt ' hearken ' unto ' me,

  10 There shall no strange god ' be in ' thee : neither shalt thou
      worship ' any ' other ' god.

2nd Part

  11 I am the Lord thy God, who brought thee out of the ' land
      of ' Egypt : open thy mouth ' wide and ' I shall ' fill it.

  12 But my people would not ' hear my ' voice : and ' Israel '
      would not o'bey me.

  13 So I gave them up unto their ' own hearts' ' lusts : and let
      them follow their ' own i'magi'nations.

  14 O that my people would have hearkened ' unto ' me : for if '
      Israel had ' walked in my ' ways,

  15 I should soon have put ' down their ' enemies : and turned
      my ' hand a'gainst their ' adversaries.

  16 The haters of the Lord should have been ' found ' liars : but
      their time ' should have en'dured for ' ever.

  17 He should have fed them also with the ' finest ' wheat-
      flour : and with honey out of the stony rock should '
      I have ' satisfied ' thee.

DAY 16   EVENING

PSALM 82

GOD standeth in the congre'gation of ' princes : he is a ' Judge
a'mong ' gods.

  8 I proved ' thee ' also : at the ' waters ' of ' strife.

2 How long will ye ' give wrong ' judgement : and accept the ' persons ' of the un'godly?

3 Defend the ' poor and ' fatherless : see that such as are in need and ne'cessity ' have ' right.

4 Deliver the ' outcast and ' poor : save them from the ' hand ' of the un'godly.

5 They will not be learned nor understand, but walk on ' still in ' darkness : all the foundations of the ' earth are ' out of ' course.

6 I have said ' Ye are ' gods : and ye are all the ' children ' of the most ' Highest.

7 But ye shall ' die like ' men : and ' fall like ' one of the ' princes.

8 Arise O God, and judge ' thou the ' earth : for thou shalt take all ' heathen to ' thine in'heritance.

PSALM 83

HOLD not thy tongue O God, keep ' not still ' silence : re'frain not thy'self O ' God.

2 For lo thine enemies ' make a ' murmuring : and they that hate thee ' have lift ' up their ' head.

3 They have imagined craftily a'gainst thy ' people : and taken ' counsel a'gainst thy ' secret ones.

4 They have said, Come and let us root them out, that they be no ' more a ' people : and that the name of Israel may be no ' more ' in re'membrance.

5 For they have cast their heads together with ' one con'sent : and ' are con'federate a'gainst thee;

6 The tabernacles of the Edomites ' and the ' Ismaelites :
the ' Moab'ites and ' Hagarenes;

7 Gebal and ' Ammon and ' Amalek : the Philistines with '
them that ' dwell at ' Tyre.

8 Assur also is ' join-ed ' with them : and have ' holpen the '
children of ' Lot.

9 But do thou to them as ' unto the ' Madianites : unto Sisera
and unto Jabin ' at the ' brook of ' Kison;

10 Who ' perished at ' Endor : and be'came · as the ' dung of
the ' earth.

11 Make them and their princes like ' Oreb and ' Zeb : yea
make all their princes like as ' Zeba ' and Sal'mana;

12 Who say Let us ' take to our'selves : the ' houses of ' God ·
in pos'session.

13 O my God make them like ' unto a ' wheel : and as the '
stubble be'fore the ' wind;

14 Like as the fire that burneth ' up the ' wood : and as the '
flame that con'sumeth the ' mountains.

15 Persecute them even so ' with thy ' tempest : and make
them a'fraid ' with thy ' storm.

16 Make their faces a'shamed O ' Lord : that ' they may ' seek
thy ' Name.

17 Let them be confounded and vexed ever ' more and '
more : let them be'put to'shame and'perish.

18 And they shall know that thou whose Name ' is Je'hovah :
art only the most Highest ' over ' all the ' earth.

PSALM 84

O how amiable ' are thy ' dwellings : thou ' Lord ' of '
hosts!

2 My soul hath a desire and longing, to enter into the ' courts
of the ' Lord : my heart and my flesh rejoice ' in the ' living '
God.

3 Yea the sparrow hath found her an house, and the swallow
a nest where she may ' lay her ' young : even thy altars,
O Lord of hosts my ' King and ' my ' God.

4 Blessed are they that ' dwell in thy ' house : they will be '
alway ' praising ' thee.

5 Blessed is the man whose ' strength is in ' thee : in whose '
heart are ' thy ' ways.

6 Who going through the vale of misery, use it ' for a ' well :
and the ' pools are ' filled with ' water.

2nd Part

7 They will go from ' strength to ' strength : and unto the God
of gods appeareth every ' one of ' them in ' Sion.

8 O Lord God of hosts ' hear my ' prayer : hearken ' O ' God
of ' Jacob.

9 Behold O God ' our de'fender : and look upon the ' face
of ' thine A'nointed.

10 For one day ' in thy ' courts : is ' better ' than a ' thousand.

11 I had rather be a door-keeper in the ' house of my ' God :
than to ' dwell in the ' tents of un'godliness.

12 For the Lord God is a ' light and de'fence : the Lord will
give grace and worship, and no good thing shall he with-
hold from them that ' live a ' godly ' life.

13 O Lord ' God of ' hosts : blessed is the man that ' putteth
his ' trust in ' thee.

PSALM 85

LORD thou art become gracious ' unto thy ' land : thou
hast turned a'way the cap'tivity of ' Jacob.

2 Thou hast forgiven the offence of ' thy ' people : and '
   covered ' all their ' sins.

2nd Part

3 Thou hast taken away all ' thy dis'pleasure : and turned
   thyself from thy ' wrathful ' indig'nation.

4 Turn us then O ' God our ' Saviour : and let thine ' anger '
   cease ' from us.

5 Wilt thou be displeased at ' us for ' ever : and wilt thou
   stretch out thy wrath from one gene'ration ' to an'other?

6 Wilt thou not turn again and ' quicken ' us : that thy
   people ' may re'joice in ' thee?

7 Shew us thy ' mercy O ' Lord : and ' grant us ' thy
   sal'vation.

8 I will hearken what the Lord God will ' say con'cerning
   me : for he shall speak peace unto his people and to his
   saints, ' that they ' turn not a'gain.

9 For his salvation is nigh ' them that ' fear him : that ' glory
   may ' dwell in our ' land.

10 Mercy and truth are ' met to'gether : righteousness and '
   peace have ' kissed each ' other.

11 Truth shall flourish ' out of the ' earth : and righteousness
   hath ' look-ed ' down from ' heaven.

12 Yea the Lord shall shew ' loving'kindness : and our ' land
   shall ' give her ' increase.

13 Righteousness shall ' go be'fore him : and he shall direct
   his ' going ' in the ' way.

DAY 17 MORNING
PSALM 86

Bow down thine ear O ' Lord and ' hear me : for ' I am ' poor
   and in ' misery.

2 Preserve thou my soul for ' I am ' holy : my God save thy servant that ' putteth his ' trust in ' thee.

3 Be merciful unto ' me O ' Lord : for I will ' call ' daily up'on thee.

4 Comfort the ' soul of thy ' servant : for unto thee O Lord do ' I lift ' up my ' soul.

5 For thou Lord art ' good and ' gracious : and of great mercy unto all ' them that ' call up'on thee.

6 Give ear Lord ' unto my ' prayer : and ponder the ' voice of my ' humble de'sires.

7 In the time of my trouble I will ' call upon ' thee : for ' thou ' hearest ' me.

8 Among the gods there is none like unto ' thee O ' Lord : there is not one that can ' do as ' thou ' doest.

9 All nations whom thou hast made shall come and worship ' thee O ' Lord : and shall ' glori'fy thy ' Name.

* 10 For thou art great and ' doest ' wondrous ' things : ' thou art ' God a'lone.

11 Teach me thy way O Lord, and I will ' walk in thy ' truth : O knit my heart unto thee that ' I may ' fear thy ' Name.

12 I will thank thee O Lord my God with ' all my ' heart : and will praise thy ' Name for ' ever'more.

2nd Part

13 For great is thy ' mercy ' toward me : and thou hast delivered my soul ' from the ' nethermost ' hell.

Ps. 86. vs. 10 For thou art great and doest ' wondrous ' things : thou ' art ' God a'lone.

14 O God the proud are ' risen a'gainst me : and the congregations of naughty men have sought after my soul, and
have not set ' thee be'fore their ' eyes.

15 But thou O Lord God art full of com'passion and ' mercy :
long-suffering ' plenteous in ' goodness and ' truth.

16 O turn thee then unto me and have ' mercy up'on me : give
thy strength unto thy servant and ' help the ' son of thine '
handmaid.

17 Shew some token upon me for good, that they who hate me
may see it and ' be a'shamed : because thou Lord hast '
holpen ' me and ' comforted me.

PSALM 87

Single Chant

Her foundations are upon the ' holy ' hills : the Lord
loveth the gates of Sion more than ' all the ' dwellings of ' Jacob.

2 Very excellent things are spoken of ' thee : thou ' city of '
God.

3 I will think upon ' Rahab and ' Babylon : with ' them that '
know ' me.

4 Behold ye the ' Philistines ' also : and they of Tyre with the
Morians, lo ' there was ' he ' born.

5 And of Sion it shall be reported that he was ' born in ' her :
and the most ' High shall ' stablish ' her.

6 The Lord shall rehearse it when he writeth ' up the '
people : that ' he was ' born ' there.

Ps. 87. vs. 2 Very excellent things are ' spoken of ' thee : thou ' city '
of ' God.

7 The singers also and trumpeters shall ' he re'hearse : All
   my fresh ' springs shall ' be in ' thee.

PSALM 88

O LORD God of my salvation, I have cried day and '
   night be'fore thee : O let my prayer enter into thy
   presence, incline thine ' ear ' unto my ' calling.

2 For my soul is ' full of ' trouble : and my life draweth '
   nigh ' unto ' hell.

3 I am counted as one of them that go down ' into the ' pit :
   and I have been even as a ' man that ' hath no ' strength.

4 Free among the dead, like unto them that are wounded
   and ' lie in the ' grave : who are out of remembrance, and
   are ' cut a'way from thy ' hand.

5 Thou hast laid me in the ' lowest ' pit : in a place of '
   darkness and ' in the ' deep.

6 Thine indignation lieth ' hard up'on me : and thou hast '
   vexed me with ' all thy ' storms.

7 Thou hast put away mine acquaintance ' far ' from me : and
   made me to ' be ab'hor-red ' of them.

8 I am so ' fast in ' prison : that I ' cannot ' get ' forth.

9 My sight faileth for ' very ' trouble : Lord I have called daily
   upon thee, I have stretched forth my ' hands ' unto ' thee.

10 Dost thou shew wonders a'mong the ' dead : or shall the
   dead rise ' up a'gain and ' praise thee?

11 Shall thy loving-kindness be shewed ' in the ' grave : or thy '
   faithfulness ' in de'struction?

12 Shall thy wondrous works be known ' in the ' dark : and thy
   righteousness in the land where ' all things ' are for'gotten?

13 Unto thee have I ' cried O ' Lord : and early shall my '
prayer ' come be'fore thee.

14 Lord why abhorrest ' thou my ' soul : and hidest ' thou thy '
face ' from me?

15 I am in misery, and like unto him that is at the ' point to '
die : even from my youth up thy terrors have I suffered '
with a ' troubled ' mind.

16 Thy wrathful displeasure ' goeth ' over me : and the ' fear
of thee ' hath un'done me.

17 They came round about me ' daily like ' water : and
compassed me to'gether on ' every ' side.

18 My lovers and friends hast thou ' put a'way from me : and
hid mine ac'quaintance ' out of my ' sight.

DAY 17 EVENING

PSALM 89

MY song shall be alway of the loving-kindness ' of the ' Lord :
with my mouth will I ever be shewing thy truth from one
gene'ration ' to an'other.

 2 For I have said, Mercy shall be set ' up for ' ever : thy truth
shalt thou ' stablish ' in the ' heavens.

 3 I have made a covenant ' with my ' chosen : I have sworn '
unto ' David my ' servant;

 4 Thy seed will I ' stablish for ' ever : and set up thy throne
from one gene'ration ' to an'other.

 5 O Lord the very heavens shall praise thy ' wondrous '
works : and thy truth in the congre'gation ' of the ' saints.

6 For who is he a'mong the ' clouds : that shall be com-'
pared'unto the ' Lord?

7 And what is he a'mong the ' gods : that shall be ' like ' unto
the ' Lord?

8 God is very greatly to be feared in the council ' of the '
saints : and to be had in reverence of all ' them that are '
round a'bout him.

9 O Lord God of hosts, who is ' like unto ' thee : thy truth
most mighty Lord ' is on ' every ' side.

10 Thou rulest the ' raging · of the ' sea : thou stillest the waves
there'of when ' they a'rise.

11 Thou hast subdued Egypt ' and de'stroyed it : thou hast
scattered thine enemies abroad ' with thy ' mighty ' arm.

12 The heavens are thine, the earth ' also is ' thine : thou hast
laid the foundation of the round world and ' all that '
therein ' is.

13 Thou hast made the ' north and the ' south : Tabor and
Hermon shall re'joice in ' thy ' Name.

14 Thou hast a ' mighty ' arm : strong is thy hand and ' high is '
thy right ' hand.

15 Righteousness and equity are the habitation ' of thy ' seat :
mercy and truth shall ' go be'fore thy ' face.

16 Blessed is the people O Lord that can re'joice in ' thee :
they shall ' walk in the ' light of thy ' countenance.

17 Their delight shall be daily ' in thy ' Name : and in thy
righteousness ' shall they ' make their ' boast.

18 For thou art the glory ' of their ' strength : and in thy loving-
kindness thou ' shalt lift ' up our ' horns.

2nd Part

19 For the Lord is ' our de'fence : the Holy One of ' Israel ' is our ' King.

20 Thou spakest sometime in visions unto thy ' saints and ' saidst : I have laid help upon one that is mighty, I have exalted one ' chosen ' out of the ' people.

21 I have found ' David my ' servant : with my holy oil have ' I a'nointed ' him.

22 My hand shall ' hold him ' fast : and my ' arm shall ' strengthen ' him.

23 The enemy shall not be able to ' do him ' violence : the son of ' wickedness ' shall not ' hurt him.

24 I will smite down his foes be'fore his ' face : and ' plague ' them that ' hate him.

25 My truth also and my mercy ' shall be ' with him : and in my Name shall his ' horn ' be ex'alted.

26 I will set his dominion also ' in the ' sea : and his ' right hand ' in the ' floods.

27 He shall call me, Thou ' art my ' Father : my God ' and my ' strong sal'vation.

28 And I will make ' him my ' first-born : higher than the ' kings ' of the ' earth.

29 My mercy will I keep for him for ' ever'more : and my covenant ' shall stand ' fast with ' him.

2nd Part

30 His seed also will I make to en'dure for ' ever : and his ' throne as the ' days of ' heaven.

31 But if his children for'sake my ' law : and ' walk not ' in my ' judgements;

32 If they break my statutes, and keep not ' my com'mandments : I will visit their offences with the rod ' and their ' sin
with ' scourges.

33 Nevertheless my loving-kindness will I not utterly ' take '
from him : nor ' suffer my ' truth to ' fail.

34 My covenant will I not break, nor alter the thing that is
gone ' out of my ' lips : I have sworn once by my holiness,
that I ' will not ' fail ' David.

35 His seed shall en'dure for ' ever : and his seat is ' like as
the ' sun be'fore me.

36 He shall stand fast for evermore ' as the ' moon : and as
the ' faithful ' witness in ' heaven.

37 But thou hast abhorred and forsaken ' thine A'nointed :
and ' art dis'pleased ' at him.

38 Thou hast broken the covenant ' of thy ' servant : and ' cast
his ' crown · to the ' ground.

39 Thou hast overthrown ' all his ' hedges : and ' broken '
down his ' strong holds.

40 All they that go ' by ' spoil him : and he is be'come a
re'proach to his ' neighbours.

41 Thou hast set up the right hand ' of his ' enemies : and made
all his ' adversaries ' to re'joice.

42 Thou hast taken away the ' edge of his ' sword : and givest
him not ' victory ' in the ' battle.

43 Thou hast put ' out his ' glory : and cast his ' throne ' down
to the ' ground.

44 The days of his youth ' hast thou ' shortened : and ' covered
him ' with dis'honour.

45 Lord how long wilt thou hide thy'self for ' ever : and shall thy ' wrath ' burn like ' fire?

46 O remember how ' short my ' time is : wherefore hast thou made ' all ' men for ' nought?

47 What man is he that liveth and shall ' not see ' death : and shall he deliver his soul ' from the ' hand of ' hell?

48 Lord where are thy old ' loving'kindnesses : which thou swarest unto ' David ' in thy ' truth?

49 Remember Lord the rebuke that thy ' servants ' have : and how I do bear in my bosom the re'bukes of ' many ' people;

50 Wherewith thine enemies have blas'phem-ed ' thee : and slandered the ' footsteps of ' thine A'nointed.

Unison 2nd Part

50a Praised be the Lord for ' ever'more : A'men and ' A'men.

DAY 18 MORNING

PSALM 90

LORD thou hast ' been our ' refuge : from one gene'ration ' to an'other.

2 Before the mountains were brought forth, or ever the earth and the ' world were ' made : thou art God from ever'lasting and ' world without ' end.

3 Thou turnest ' man to de'struction : again thou sayest, Come a'gain ye ' children of ' men.

50 Wherewith thine enemies have blasphemed thee, and slandered the footsteps of ' thine A'nointed : Praised be the Lord for evermore ' Amen and ' A'men.

395

4 For a thousand years in thy sight ' are but as ' yesterday : seeing that is ' past · as a ' watch in the ' night.

5 As soon as thou scatterest them they are ' even as a ' sleep : and fade away ' suddenly ' like the ' grass.

6 In the morning it is green and ' groweth ' up : but in the evening it is cut down ' dri-ed ' up and ' withered.

7 For we consume away in ' thy dis'pleasure : and are afraid at thy ' wrathful ' indig'nation.

8 Thou hast set our mis'deeds be'fore thee : and our secret ' sins in the ' light of thy ' countenance.

9 For when thou art angry all our ' days are ' gone : we bring our years to an end, as it ' were a ' tale that is ' told.

10 The days of our age are threescore years and ten, and though men be so strong that they come to ' fourscore ' years : yet is their strength then but labour and sorrow, so soon passeth it a'way and ' we are ' gone.

11 But who regardeth the ' power of thy ' wrath : for even thereafter as a man feareth ' so is ' thy dis'pleasure.

12 So teach us to ' number our ' days : that we may ap'ply our ' hearts unto ' wisdom.

13 Turn thee again O Lord ' at the ' last : and be ' gracious ' unto thy ' servants.

14 O satisfy us with thy mercy ' and that ' soon : so shall we rejoice and be glad ' all the ' days of our ' life.

15 Comfort us again now, after the time that ' thou hast ' plagued us : and for the years where'in we have ' suffered ad'versity.

16 Shew thy ' servants thy ' work : and their ' children ' thy ' glory.

2nd Part

17 And the glorious majesty of the Lord our God ' be up'on us : prosper thou the work of our hands upon us, O ' prosper ' thou our ' handy-work.

PSALM 91

WHOSO dwelleth under the defence of the ' most ' High : shall abide under the ' shadow ' of the Al'mighty.

2 I will say unto the Lord, Thou art my ' hope and my ' strong hold : my God in ' him will ' I ' trust.

3 For he shall deliver thee from the ' snare · of the ' hunter : and ' from the ' noisome ' pestilence.

4 He shall defend thee under his wings, and thou shalt be safe ' under his ' feathers : his faithfulness and truth shall ' be thy ' shield and ' buckler.

5 Thou shalt not be afraid for any ' terror by ' night : nor for the ' arrow that ' flieth by ' day;

6 For the pestilence that ' walketh in ' darkness : nor for the sickness that de'stroyeth ' in the ' noon-day.

7 A thousand shall fall beside thee, and ten thousand at ' thy right ' hand : but it shall ' not come ' nigh ' thee.

8 Yea with thine eyes shalt ' thou be'hold : and see the re'ward of ' the un'godly.

9 For thou Lord ' art my ' hope : thou hast set thine house of de'fence ' very ' high.

10 There shall no evil happen ' unto ' thee : neither shall any ' plague come ' nigh thy ' dwelling.

11 For he shall give his angels charge ' over ' thee : to ' keep thee in ' all thy ' ways.

12 They shall bear thee ' in their ' hands : that thou hurt not thy ' foot a'gainst a ' stone.

13 Thou shalt go upon the ' lion and ' adder : the young lion and the dragon shalt thou ' tread ' under thy ' feet.

14 Because he hath set his love upon me, therefore will ' I de'liver him : I will set him up, because ' he hath ' known my ' Name.

15 He shall call upon me and ' I will ' hear him : yea I am with him in trouble, I will de'liver him and ' bring him to ' honour.

16 With long ' life will I ' satisfy him : and ' shew him ' my sal'vation.

PSALM 92

It is a good thing to give thanks ' unto the ' Lord : and to sing praises unto thy ' Name ' O most ' Highest;

2 To tell of thy loving-kindness early ' in the ' morning : and of thy ' truth in the ' night'season;

3 Upon an instrument of ten strings, and up'on the ' lute : upon a loud instrument ' and up'on the ' harp.

4 For thou Lord hast made me glad ' through thy ' works : and I will rejoice in giving praise for the ope'rations ' of thy ' hands.

5 O Lord how glorious ' are thy ' works : thy ' thoughts are ' very ' deep.

6 An unwise man doth not well con'sider ' this : and a fool ' doth not ' under'stand it.

7 When the ungodly are green as the grass, and when all the workers of ' wickedness do ' flourish : then shall they be destroyed for ever, but thou Lord art the most ' Highest for ' ever'more.

8 For lo thine enemies O Lord, lo thine ' enemies shall ' perish : and all the workers of ' wickedness shall ' be de'stroyed.

9 But mine horn shall be exalted like the ' horn of an ' unicorn : for I am a'nointed with ' fresh ' oil.

10 Mine eye also shall see his ' lust of mine ' enemies : and mine ear shall hear his desire of the wicked that a'rise ' up a'gainst me.

11 The righteous shall flourish ' like a ' palm-tree : and shall spread abroad ' like a ' cedar in ' Libanus.

12 Such as are planted in the ' house of the ' Lord : shall flourish in the ' courts of the ' house of our ' God.

13 They also shall bring forth more ' fruit in their ' age : and shall be ' fat and ' well'liking.

14 That they may shew how true the Lord my ' strength ' is : and that there is ' no un'righteousness in ' him.

DAY 18   EVENING

PSALM 93

The Lord is King, and hath put on ' glorious ap'parel : the Lord hath put on his apparel and ' girded him'self with ' strength.

2 He hath made the round ' world so ' sure : that it ' cannot ' be ' moved.

3 Ever since the world began hath thy seat ' been pre'pared : thou ' art from ' ever'lasting.

4 The floods are risen O Lord, the floods have lift ' up their ' voice : the ' floods lift ' up their ' waves.

5 The waves of the sea are mighty and ' rage ' horribly : but yet the Lord who ' dwelleth on ' high is ' mightier.

6 Thy testimonies O Lord are ' very ' sure : holiness be'cometh thine ' house for ' ever.

PSALM 94

O LORD God to whom ' vengeance be'longeth : thou God to whom vengeance be'longeth ' shew thy ' self.

2 Arise thou ' Judge of the ' world : and reward the proud ' after ' their de'serving.

3 Lord how long ' shall the un'godly : how long ' shall the un'godly ' triumph?

4 How long shall all wicked doers speak ' so dis'dainfully : and ' make such ' proud ' boasting?

5 They smite down thy ' people O ' Lord : and ' trouble ' thine ' heritage.

6 They murder the ' widow · and the ' stranger : and ' put the ' fatherless to ' death.

7 And yet they say, Tush the ' Lord shall not ' see : neither shall the ' God of ' Jacob re'gard it.

8 Take heed ye unwise a'mong the ' people : O ye fools ' when will ye ' under'stand?

9 He that planted the ear shall ' he not ' hear : or he that made the ' eye shall ' he not ' see?

10 Or he that ' nurtureth the ' heathen : it is he that teacheth man knowledge , ' shall not ' he ' punish?

2nd Part

11 The Lord knoweth the ' thoughts of ' man : that ' they ' are but ' vain.

12 Blessed is the man whom thou ' chastenest O ' Lord : and ' teachest him ' in thy ' law;

13 That thou mayest give him patience in ' time of ad'versity : until the pit be digged ' up for ' the un'godly.

14 For the Lord will not ' fail his ' people : neither will he for'sake ' his in'heritance;

15 Until righteousness turn again ' unto ' judgement : all such as are ' true in ' heart shall ' follow it.

16 Who will rise up with me a'gainst the ' wicked : or who will take my part a'gainst the ' evil'doers?

17 If the Lord ' had not ' helped me : it had not failed but my ' soul had been ' put to ' silence.

18 But when I said My ' foot hath ' slipt : thy mercy O ' Lord ' held me ' up.

19 In the multitude of the sorrows that I had ' in my ' heart : thy comforts ' have re'fresh-ed my ' soul.

20 Wilt thou have any thing to do with the ' stool of ' wickedness : which imagineth ' mischief ' as a ' law?

21 They gather them together against the ' soul of the ' righteous : and con'demn the ' innocent ' blood.

22 But the Lord ' is my ' refuge : and my ' God is the ' strength of my ' confidence.

23 He shall recompense them their wickedness, and destroy
   them in their ' own ' malice : yea the ' Lord our ' God shall
   de'stroy them.

DAY 19 MORNING

PSALM 95

f O COME let us ' sing unto the ' Lord : let us heartily rejoice in
   the ' strength of ' our sal'vation.

2 Let us come before his ' presence with ' thanksgiving : and
   shew ourselves ' glad in ' him with ' psalms.

3 For the Lord is a ' great ' God : and a great ' King above '
   all ' gods.

4 In his hand are all the ' corners · of the ' earth : and the
   strength of the ' hills is ' his ' also.

2nd Part

5 The sea is his and ' he ' made it : and his hands pre'pared
   the ' dry ' land.

p 6 O come let us worship and ' fall ' down : and kneel be'fore
   the ' Lord our ' Maker.

7 For he is the ' Lord our ' God : and we are the people of his
   pasture, and the ' sheep of ' his ' hand.

mf 8 To-day if ye will hear his voice, harden ' not your ' hearts :
   as in the provocation, and as in the day of temp'tation ' in
   the ' wilderness;

* 9 When your ' fathers ' tempted ' me : ' proved me and ' saw
   my ' works.

   Ps. 95. vs. 9 When your fathers ' tempted ' me : proved ' me and ' saw
   my ' works.

10 Forty years long was I grieved with this gene′ration and ′
said : It is a people that do err in their hearts, for they ′ have
not ′ known my ′ ways;

11 Unto whom I ′ sware · in my ′ wrath : that they should not ′
enter ′ into my ′ rest.

PSALM 96

O SING unto the Lord a ′ new ′ song : sing unto the Lord ′
all the ′ whole ′ earth.

2 Sing unto the Lord and ′ praise his ′ Name : be telling of his
sal′vation from ′ day to ′ day.

3 Declare his honour ′ unto the ′ heathen : and his wonders ′
unto ′ all ′ people.

4 For the Lord is great, and cannot ′ worthily be ′ praised : he
is more to be ′ feared than ′ all ′ gods.

5 As for all the gods of the heathen, they ′ are but ′ idols : but
it is the ′ Lord that ′ made the ′ heavens.

6 Glory and worship ′ are be′fore him : power and ′ honour
are ′ in his ′ sanctuary.

7 Ascribe unto the Lord O ye ′ kindreds of the ′ people :
ascribe unto the ′ Lord ′ worship and ′ power.

8 Ascribe unto the Lord the honour due ′ unto his ′ Name :
bring presents and ′ come ′ into his ′ courts.

9 O worship the Lord in the ′ beauty of ′ holiness : let the ′
whole earth ′ stand in ′ awe of him.

10 Tell it out among the heathen that the ′ Lord is ′ King : and
that it is he who hath made the round world so fast that it
cannot be moved, and how that he shall ′ judge the ′
people ′ righteously.

11 Let the heavens rejoice and let the ' earth be ' glad : let the
sea make a noise and ' all that ' therein ' is.

12 Let the field be joyful and ' all that is ' in it : then shall all
the trees of the wood re'joice be'fore the ' Lord.

2nd Part

13 For he cometh, for he cometh to ' judge the ' earth : and
with righteousness to judge the world, and the ' people '
with his ' truth.

PSALM 97

THE Lord is King, the earth may be ' glad there'of : yea
the multitude of the isles ' may be ' glad there'of.

2 Clouds and darkness are ' round a'bout him : righteousness and judgement are the habi'tation ' of his ' seat.

3 There shall go a ' fire be'fore him : and burn up his '
enemies on ' every ' side.

4 His lightnings gave shine ' unto the ' world : the earth ' saw
it and ' was a'fraid.

5 The hills melted like wax at the ' presence of the ' Lord : at
the presence of the ' Lord of the ' whole ' earth.

6 The heavens have de'clared his ' righteousness : and all
the ' people have ' seen his ' glory.

7 Confounded be all they that worship carved images, and
that delight in ' vain ' gods : worship ' him ' all ye ' gods.

8 Sion heard of it ' and re'joiced : and the daughters of Judah
were glad be'cause of thy ' judgements O ' Lord.

9 For thou Lord art higher than all that are ' in the ' earth :
thou art exalted ' far above ' all ' gods.

404

10 O ye that love the Lord, see that ye hate the ' thing which is ' evil : the Lord preserveth the souls of his saints, he shall deliver them ' from the ' hand of the un'godly.

11 There is sprung up a ' light for the ' righteous : and joyful gladness for ' such as are ' true'hearted.

12 Rejoice in the ' Lord ye ' righteous : and give thanks for a re'membrance ' of his ' holiness.

DAY 19   EVENING

PSALM 98

O SING unto the Lord a ' new ' song : for he hath ' done ' marvellous ' things.

 2 With his own right hand and with his ' holy ' arm : hath he ' gotten him'self the ' victory.

 3 The Lord declared ' his sal'vation : his righteousness hath he openly ' shewed in the ' sight of the ' heathen.

 4 He hath remembered his mercy and truth, toward the ' house of ' Israel : and all the ends of the world have seen the sal'vation of ' our ' God.

 5 Shew yourselves joyful unto the Lord ' all ye ' lands : sing re'joice and ' give ' thanks.

 6 Praise the Lord up'on the ' harp : sing to the ' harp with a ' psalm of ' thanksgiving.

 7 With trumpets ' also and ' shawms : O shew yourselves joyful be'fore the ' Lord the ' King.

 8 Let the sea make a noise, and all that ' therein ' is : the round world and ' they that ' dwell there'in.

9 Let the floods clap their hands, and let the hills be joyful together be'fore the ' Lord : for he is ' come to ' judge the ' earth.

10 With righteousness shall he ' judge the ' world : and the ' people ' with ' equity.

PSALM 99

THE Lord is King, be the people never ' so un'patient : he sitteth between the cherubims, be the earth ' never' so un'quiet.

2 The Lord is ' great in ' Sion : and ' high a'bove all ' people.

3 They shall give thanks ' unto thy ' Name : which is great ' wonder'ful and ' holy.

4 The King's power loveth judgement, thou hast pre'par-ed ' equity : thou hast executed ' judgement and ' righteousness in ' Jacob.

Unison 2nd Part

5 O magnify the ' Lord our ' God : and fall down before his ' footstool for ' he is ' holy.

6 Moses and Aaron among his priests, and Samuel among such as call up'on his ' Name : these called upon the ' Lord and ' he ' heard them.

7 He spake unto them out of the ' cloudy ' pillar : for they kept his testimonies, and the ' law that ' he ' gave them.

8 Thou heardest them O ' Lord our ' God : thou forgavest them O God, and ' punishedst their ' own in'ventions.

Unison

9 O magnify the Lord our God, and worship him upon his '
   holy ' hill : for the ' Lord our ' God is ' holy.

PSALM 100

O be joyful in the Lord ' all ye ' lands : serve the Lord
   with gladness, and come before his ' presence ' with
   a ' song.

2 Be ye sure that the Lord ' he is ' God : it is he that hath
   made us and not we ourselves, we are his ' people · and the '
   sheep of his ' pasture.

3 O go your way into his gates with thanksgiving, and into
   his ' courts with ' praise : be thankful unto him and ' speak
   good ' of his ' Name.

4 For the Lord is gracious, his mercy is ' ever'lasting : and his
   truth endureth from gene'ration to ' gene'ration.

† PSALM 101

My song shall be of ' mercy and ' judgement : unto '
   thee O ' Lord will I ' sing.

* 2 O ' let me have ' under'standing : ' in the ' way of '
   godliness.

3 When wilt thou come ' unto ' me : I will walk in my house '
   with a ' perfect ' heart.

† For alternative setting to Psalm 101 see Appendix.
Ps. 101. vs. 2 O let me have ' under'standing : in the ' way of '
godli'ness.

4 I will take no wicked thing in hand, I hate the ' sins of un'faithfulness : there shall ' no such ' cleave unto ' me.

5 A froward heart shall de'part ' from me : I will not ' know a ' wicked ' person.

* 6 Whoso ' privily ' slandereth his ' neighbour : ' him will ' I de'stroy.

7 Whoso hath also a proud look and ' high ' stomach : I ' will not ' suffer ' him.

8 Mine eyes look upon such as are faithful ' in the ' land : that ' they may ' dwell with ' me.

* 9 Whoso ' leadeth a ' godly ' life : ' he shall ' be my ' servant.

10 There shall no deceitful person ' dwell in my ' house : he that telleth lies shall not ' tarry ' in my ' sight.

2nd Part

11 I shall soon destroy all the ungodly that are ' in the ' land : that I may root out all wicked doers from the ' city ' of the ' Lord.

DAY 20   MORNING
PSALM 102

HEAR my ' prayer O ' Lord : and let my ' crying ' come unto ' thee.

2 Hide not thy face from me in the ' time of my ' trouble : incline thine ear unto me when I call, O ' hear me and ' that right ' soon.

6 Whoso privily ' slandereth his ' neighbour : him ' — will ' I de'stroy.
Ps. 101 vs. 9 Whoso leadeth a ' godly ' life : he ' shall be ' my ' servant.

3 For my days are consumed a'way like ' smoke : and my
bones are burnt up ' as it ' were a ' fire-brand.

4 My heart is smitten down and ' withered like ' grass : so that
I for'get to ' eat my ' bread.

5 For the ' voice of my ' groaning : my bones will scarce '
cleave ' to my ' flesh.

6 I am become like a pelican ' in the ' wilderness : and like an
owl ' that is ' in the ' desert.

7 I have watched, and am even as it ' were a ' sparrow : that
sitteth a'lone up'on the ' house-top.

8 Mine enemies revile me ' all the day ' long : and they that
are mad upon me are ' sworn to'gether a'gainst me.

9 For I have eaten ashes ' as it were ' bread : and ' mingled
my ' drink with ' weeping;

10 And that because of thine indig'nation and ' wrath : for
thou hast taken me ' up and ' cast me ' down.

2nd Part

11 My days are ' gone · like a ' shadow : and ' I am ' withered
like ' grass.

12 But thou O Lord shalt en'dure for'ever : and thy
remembrance ' throughout ' all gene'rations.

13 Thou shalt arise and have ' mercy upon ' Sion : for it is time
that thou have mercy upon her ' yea the ' time is ' come.

2nd Part

14 And why? thy servants think up'on her ' stones : and it
pitieth them to ' see her ' in the ' dust.

15 The heathen shall fear thy ' Name O ' Lord : and all the '
kings of the ' earth thy ' majesty;

16 When the Lord shall ' build up ' Sion : and when his ' glory '
shall ap'pear;

17 When he turneth him unto the prayer of the ' poor '
destitute : and des'piseth not ' their de'sire.

18 This shall be written for ' those that come ' after : and the
people which shall be ' born shall ' praise the ' Lord.

19 For he hath looked ' down from his ' sanctuary : out of the
heaven did the ' Lord be'hold the ' earth;

20 That he might hear the mournings of such as are ' in
cap'tivity : and deliver the children ap'pointed ' unto '
death;

21 That they may declare the Name of the ' Lord in ' Sion :
and his ' worship ' at Je'rusalem;

22 When the people are ' gathered to'gether : and the kingdoms ' also to ' serve the ' Lord.

23 He brought down my strength ' in my ' journey : and '
shortened ' my ' days.

24 But I said, O my God take me not away in the ' midst of
mine ' age : as for thy years they endure ' throughout ' all
gene'rations.

25 Thou Lord in the beginning hast laid the foundation ' of
the ' earth : and the ' heavens are the ' work of thy ' hands.

26 They shall perish but ' thou shalt en'dure : they all shall
wax ' old as ' doth a ' garment;

27 And as a vesture shalt thou change them, and they ' shall
be ' changed : but thou art the same and thy ' years ' shall
not ' fail.

28 The children of thy servants ' shall con'tinue : and their
seed shall stand ' fast in ' thy ' sight.

PSALM 103

Praise the Lord ' O my ' soul : and all that is within me '
praise his ' holy ' Name.

2 Praise the Lord ' O my ' soul : and for'get not ' all his '
benefits;

3 Who forgiveth ' all thy ' sin : and ' healeth ' all thine
in'firmities;

4 Who saveth thy ' life from de'struction : and crowneth thee
with ' mercy and ' loving ' kindness;

5 Who satisfieth thy mouth with ' good ' things : making thee
young and ' lusty ' as an ' eagle.

6 The Lord executeth ' righteousness and ' judgement : for
all ' them that are op'pressed with ' wrong.

7 He shewed his ways ' unto ' Moses : his works ' unto the '
children of ' Israel.

8 The Lord is full of com'passion and ' mercy : long-
suffering ' and of ' great ' goodness.

9 He will not ' alway be ' chiding : neither ' keepeth he his '
anger for ' ever.

10 He hath not dealt with us ' after our ' sins : nor rewarded us
ac'cording ' to our ' wickednesses.

11 For look how high the heaven is, in comparison ' of the '
earth : so great is his mercy also ' toward ' them that ' fear
him.

12 Look how wide also the east is ' from the ' west : so far hath
he ' set our ' sins ' from us.

13 Yea like as a father pitieth his ' own ' children : even so is the Lord merciful ' unto ' them that ' fear him.

14 For he knoweth whereof ' we are ' made : he re'membereth that ' we are but ' dust.

15 The days of man ' are but as ' grass : for he flourisheth ' as a ' flower of the ' field.

16 For as soon as the wind goeth over it ' it is ' gone : and the ' place thereof shall ' know it no ' more.

17 But the merciful goodness of the Lord endureth for ever and ever, upon ' them that ' fear him : and his righteousness up'on ' children's ' children;

18 Even upon such as ' keep his ' covenant : and think upon ' his com'mandments to ' do them.

19 The Lord hath prepared his ' seat in ' heaven : and his kingdom ' ruleth ' over ' all.

20 O praise the Lord ye angels of his, ye that ex'cel in ' strength : ye that fulfil his commandment, and hearken ' unto the ' voice of his ' words.

21 O praise the Lord all ' ye his ' hosts : ye servants of ' his that ' do his ' pleasure.

22 O speak good of the Lord all ye works of his, in all places of ' his do'minion : praise thou the ' Lord ' O my ' soul.

DAY 20   EVENING
PSALM 104

PRAISE the Lord ' O my ' soul : O Lord my God thou art become exceeding glorious, thou art ' clothed with ' majesty and ' honour.

2 Thou deckest thyself with light as it ' were with a ' garment : and spreadest out the ' heavens ' like a ' curtain.

3 Who layeth the beams of his chambers ' in the ' waters : and maketh the clouds his chariot, and walketh up'on the ' wings of the ' wind.

4 He maketh his ' angels ' spirits : and his ' ministers a ' flaming ' fire.

5 He laid the foundations ' of the ' earth : that it never should ' move at ' any ' time.

6 Thou coveredst it with the deep, like as ' with a ' garment : the ' waters ' stand in the ' hills.

7 At thy re'buke they ' flee : at the voice of thy ' thunder ' they are a'fraid.

8 They go up as high as the hills, and down to the ' valleys be'neath: even unto the place which ' thou hast ap'pointed ' for them.

9 Thou hast set them their bounds which they ' shall not ' pass : neither turn a'gain to ' cover the ' earth.

10 He sendeth the springs ' into the ' rivers : which ' run a'mong the ' hills.

11 All beasts of the field ' drink there'of : and the wild ' asses ' quench their ' thirst.

12 Beside them shall the fowls of the air have their ' habi'tation : and ' sing a'mong the ' branches.

13 He watereth the hills ' from a'bove : the earth is ' filled with the ' fruit of thy ' works.

14 He bringeth forth ' grass for the ' cattle : and green ' herb for the ' service of ' men;

15 That he may bring food out of the earth, and wine that maketh glad the ' heart of ' man : and oil to make him a cheerful countenance, and ' bread to ' strengthen man's ' heart.

16 The trees of the Lord also are ' full of ' sap : even the cedars of ' Libanus which ' he hath ' planted;

17 Wherein the birds ' make their ' nests : and the fir-trees are a ' dwelling ' for the ' stork.

18 The high hills are a refuge ' for the wild ' goats : and so are the ' stony ' rocks for the ' conies.

19 He appointed the moon for ' certain ' seasons : and the sun ' knoweth his ' going ' down.

20 Thou makest darkness that it ' may be ' night : wherein all the ' beasts of the ' forest do ' move.

21 The lions roaring ' after their ' prey : do ' seek their ' meat from ' God.

22 The sun ariseth, and they get them a'way to'gether : and ' lay them ' down in their ' dens.

2nd Part

* 23 Man goeth ' forth to his ' work and ' to his ' labour : un'til the ' evening.

24 O Lord how manifold ' are thy ' works : in wisdom hast thou made them all, the ' earth is ' full of thy ' riches.

25 So is the great and ' wide sea ' also : wherein are things creeping innumerable, both ' small and ' great ' beasts.

26 There go the ships, and there is ' that Le'viathan : whom thou hast made to ' take his ' pastime there'in.

23 Man goeth forth to his work and ' to his ' labour : un'til the ' eve'ning.

27 These wait ' all upon ' thee : that thou mayest give them '
   meat in ' due ' season.

28 When thou givest it ' them they ' gather it : and when thou
   openest thy hand ' they are ' filled with ' good.

29 When thou hidest thy face ' they are ' troubled : when thou
   takest away their breath they die, and are ' turned a'gain to
   their ' dust.

30 When thou lettest thy breath go forth they ' shall be '
   made : and thou shalt re'new the ' face of the ' earth.

31 The glorious majesty of the Lord shall en'dure for ' ever :
   the ' Lord shall re'joice in his ' works.

32 The earth shall ' tremble · at the ' look of him : if he do but '
   touch the ' hills · they shall ' smoke.

33 I will sing unto the Lord as ' long as I ' live : I will praise my
   God ' while I ' have my ' being.

34 And so shall my ' words ' please him : my ' joy shall ' be in
   the ' Lord.

35 As for sinners, they shall be consumed ' out of the ' earth :
   and the un'godly shall ' come to an ' end.

2nd Part

35a Praise ' thou the ' Lord : O my ' soul ' praise the ' Lord.

DAY 21   MORNING

PSALM 105

O Give thanks unto the Lord, and call up'on his ' name : tell
   the ' people what ' things he hath ' done.

35 As for sinners they shall be consumed out of the earth, and the
ungodly shall ' come to an ' end : praise thou the Lord O my '
soul ' praise the ' Lord.

2 O let your songs be of ' him and ' praise him : and let your talking be of ' all his ' wondrous ' works.

3 Rejoice in his ' holy ' Name : let the heart of them re'joice that ' seek the ' Lord.

4 Seek the ' Lord and his ' strength : seek his ' face ' ever'more.

5 Remember the marvellous works that ' he hath ' done : his wonders and the ' judgements ' of his ' mouth.

6 O ye seed of ' Abraham his ' servant : ye ' children of ' Jacob his ' chosen.

7 He is the ' Lord our ' God : his judgements ' are in ' all the ' world.

8 He hath been alway mindful of his ' covenant`and ' promise : that he made to a ' thousand ' gene'rations;

9 Even the covenant that he ' made with ' Abraham : and the ' oath that he ' sware unto ' Isaac;

10 And appointed the same unto ' Jacob for a ' law : and to Israel for an ' ever'lasting ' testament;

11 Saying Unto thee will I give the ' land of ' Canaan : the ' lot of ' your in'heritance;

12 When there were ' yet but a ' few of them : and they ' strangers ' in the ' land;

13 What time as they went from one nation ' to an'other : from one kingdom ' to an'other ' people;

14 He suffered no man to ' do them ' wrong : but reproved even ' kings for ' their ' sakes;

2nd Part

15 Touch not ' mine A'nointed : and ' do my ' prophets no ' harm.

16 Moreover he called for a dearth up'on the ' land : and destroyed ' all the pro'vision of ' bread.

17 But he had sent a ' man be'fore them : even Joseph who was ' sold to ' be a ' bond-servant;

18 Whose feet they ' hurt in the ' stocks : the iron ' entered ' into his ' soul;

19 Until the time came that his ' cause was ' known : the ' word of the ' Lord ' tried him.

20 The king ' sent and de'livered him : the prince of the ' people ' let him go ' free.

21 He made him lord also ' of his ' house : and ' ruler of ' all his ' substance;

2nd Part

22 That he might inform his princes ' after his ' will : and ' teach his ' senators ' wisdom.

23 Israel also came ' into ' Egypt : and Jacob was a stranger ' in the ' land of ' Ham.

24 And he increased his ' people ex'ceedingly : and made them ' stronger ' than their ' enemies;

2nd Part

25 Whose heart turned, so that they ' hated his ' people : and dealt un'truly ' with his ' servants.

26 Then sent he ' Moses his ' servant : and ' Aaron whom ' he had ' chosen.

27 And these shewed his ' tokens a'mong them : and wonders ' in the ' land of ' Ham.

28 He sent darkness ' and it was ' dark : and they were not o'bedient ' unto his ' word.

29 He turned their waters ' into ' blood : and ' slew ' their ' fish.

30 Their land ' brought forth ' frogs : yea even ' in their ' kings' ' chambers.

31 He spake the word, and there came all ' manner of ' flies : and ' lice in ' all their ' quarters.

32 He gave them ' hail-stones for ' rain : and ' flames of ' fire in their ' land.

33 He smote their vines ' also and ' fig-trees : and destroyed the ' trees that were ' in their ' coasts.

34 He spake the word and the grass-hoppers came, and cater'pillars in'numerable : and did eat up all the grass in their land, and de'voured the ' fruit of their ' ground.

35 He smote all the first-born ' in their ' land : even the ' chief of ' all their ' strength.

36 He brought them forth also with ' silver and ' gold : there was not one feeble ' person a'mong their ' tribes.

37 Egypt was glad at ' their de'parting : for they ' were a'fraid of ' them.

38 He spread out a cloud to ' be a ' covering : and fire to give light ' in the ' night'season.

39 At their desire he ' brought ' quails : and he filled them ' with the ' bread of ' heaven.

40 He opened the rock of stone, and the waters ' flow-ed ' out : so that rivers ' ran in the ' dry ' places.

41 For why? he remembered his ' holy ' promise : and ' Abra'ham his ' servant.

42 And he brought forth his ' people with ' joy : and his ' chosen ' with ' gladness;

43 And gave them the ' lands of the ' heathen : and they took the labours of the ' people ' in pos'session;

2nd Part

44 That they might ' keep his ' statutes : and ob'serve ' his ' laws.

DAY 21 EVENING
PSALM 106

O GIVE thanks unto the Lord for ' he is ' gracious : and his ' mercy en'dureth for ' ever.

2 Who can express the noble ' acts of the ' Lord : or ' shew forth ' all his ' praise?

* 3 Blessed ' are ' they that ' alway keep ' judgement : ' and do ' righteousness.

4 Remember me O Lord, according to the favour that thou bearest ' unto thy ' people : O ' visit me with ' thy sal'vation;

5 That I may see the felicity ' of thy ' chosen : and rejoice in the gladness of thy people, and give ' thanks with ' thine in'heritance.

6 We have sinned ' with our ' fathers : we have done a'miss and ' dealt ' wickedly.

7 Our fathers regarded not thy wonders in Egypt, neither kept they thy great goodness ' in re'membrance : but were disobedient at the sea, even ' at the ' Red ' sea.

3 Blessed are they that ' alway keep ' judgement : and ' do ' righteous'ness.

419

8 Nevertheless he helped them for his ' Name's ' sake : that he might make his ' power ' to be ' known.

9 He rebuked the Red sea also, and it was ' dried ' up : so he led them through the ' deep as ' through a ' wilderness.

10 And he saved them from the ' adversaries' ' hand : and delivered them ' from the ' hand of the ' enemy.

11 As for those that troubled them, the waters ' over-' whelmed them : there ' was not ' one of them ' left.

12 Then believed ' they his ' words : and sang ' praise ' unto ' him.

13 But within a while they for'gat his ' works : and would ' not a'bide his ' counsel.

14 But lust came upon them ' in the ' wilderness : and they ' tempted ' God · in the ' desert.

15 And he gave them ' their de'sire : and sent leanness with'al ' into their ' soul.

16 They angered Moses also ' in the ' tents : and ' Aaron the ' saint of the ' Lord.

17 So the earth opened and ' swallowed up ' Dathan : and covered the congre'gation ' of A'biram.

18 And the fire was kindled ' in their ' company : the ' flame burnt ' up the un'godly.

19 They made a ' calf in ' Horeb : and ' worshipped the ' molten ' image.

20 Thus they ' turned their ' glory : into the similitude of a ' calf that ' eateth ' hay.

21 And they forgat ' God their ' Saviour : who had done so ' great ' things in ' Egypt;

22 Wondrous works in the ' land of ' Ham : and fearful things '
   by the ' Red ' sea.

2nd Part

23 So he said he would have destroyed them, had not Moses
   his chosen stood before him ' in the ' gap : to turn away his
   wrathful indignation ' lest he ' should de'stroy them.

24 Yea they thought scorn of that ' pleasant ' land : and gave
   no ' credence ' unto his ' word;

25 But murmured ' in their ' tents : and hearkened not ' unto
   the ' voice of the ' Lord.

26 Then lift he up his ' hand a'gainst them : to over'throw
   them ' in the ' wilderness;

27 To cast out their seed a'mong the ' nations : and to ' scatter
   them ' in the ' lands.

28 They joined themselves unto ' Baal'peor : and ate the '
   offerings ' of the ' dead.

29 Thus they provoked him to anger with their ' own in'ventions : and the ' plague was ' great a'mong them.

30 Then stood up ' Phinees and ' prayed : and ' so the '
   plague ' ceased.

31 And that was counted unto ' him for ' righteousness :
   among all pos'terities for ' ever'more.

32 They angered him also at the ' waters of ' strife : so that he
   punished ' Moses for ' their ' sakes;

33 Because they pro'voked his ' spirit : so that he spake
   unad'visedly ' with his ' lips.

34 Neither destroyed ' they the ' heathen : as the ' Lord
   com'manded ' them;

421

35 But were mingled a'mong the ' heathen : and ' learn-ed ' their ' works.

36 Insomuch that they worshipped their idols, which turned to their ' own de'cay : yea they offered their sons and their ' daughters ' unto ' devils;

37 And shed innocent blood, even the blood of their sons and ' of their ' daughters : whom they offered unto the idols of Canaan, and the ' land was de'filed with ' blood.

2nd Part

38 Thus were they stained with their ' own ' works : and went a whoring ' with their ' own in'ventions.

39 Therefore was the wrath of the Lord kindled a'gainst his ' people : insomuch that he ab'horred his ' own in'heritance.

40 And he gave them over into the ' hands of the ' heathen : and they that ' hated them were ' lords ' over them.

41 Their ' enemies op'pressed them : and ' had them ' in sub'jection.

42 Many a time did ' he de'liver them : but they rebelled against him with their own inventions, and were brought ' down in ' their ' wickedness.

43 Nevertheless, when he saw ' their ad'versity : he ' heard ' their com'plaint.

44 He thought upon his covenant and pitied them, according unto the multitude ' of his ' mercies : yea he made all those that led them away ' captive to ' pity ' them.

45 Deliver us O Lord our God, and gather us from a'mong the ' heathen : that we may give thanks unto thy holy Name, and ' make our ' boast of thy ' praise.

46 Blessed be the Lord God of Israel from everlasting and '
world without ' end : and let all the ' people ' say A'men.

DAY 22   MORNING
PSALM 107

O GIVE thanks unto the Lord for ' he is ' gracious : and his '
mercy en'dureth for ' ever.

  2 Let them give thanks whom the ' Lord hath re'deemed :
and delivered ' from the ' hand of the ' enemy;

2nd Part

  3 And gathered them out of the lands, from the east and '
from the ' west : from the ' north and ' from the ' south.

  4 They went astray in the wilderness ' out of the ' way : and '
found no ' city to ' dwell in;

  5 Hungry ' and ' thirsty : their ' soul ' fainted in ' them.

p 6 So they cried unto the Lord ' in their ' trouble : and he
delivered them ' from ' their dis'tress.

  7 He led them forth by the ' right ' way : that they might go to
the ' city ' where they ' dwelt.

f 8 O that men would therefore praise the ' Lord for his '
goodness : and declare the wonders that he ' doeth for the '
children of ' men!

  9 For he satisfieth the ' empty ' soul : and filleth the ' hungry '
soul with ' goodness.

10 Such as sit in darkness, and in the ' shadow of ' death :
being fast ' bound in ' misery and ' iron;

11 Because they rebelled against the ' words of the ' Lord :
and lightly regarded the counsel ' of the ' most ' Highest;

423

2nd Part

12 He also brought down their ' heart through ' heaviness : they fell down and ' there was ' none to ' help them.

p 13 So when they cried unto the Lord ' in their ' trouble : he delivered them ' out of ' their dis'tress.

14 For he brought them out of darkness, and out of the ' shadow of ' death : and ' brake their ' bonds in ' sunder.

f 15 O that men would therefore praise the ' Lord for his ' goodness : and declare the wonders that he ' doeth for the ' children of ' men!

16 For he hath broken the ' gates of ' brass : and smitten the ' bars of ' iron in sunder.

17 Foolish men are plagued for ' their of'fence : and be'cause of ' their ' wickedness.

18 Their soul abhorred all ' manner of ' meat : and they were even ' hard at ' death's ' door.

p 19 So when they cried unto the Lord ' in their ' trouble : he delivered them ' out of ' their dis'tress.

20 He sent his ' word and ' healed them : and they were ' saved from ' their de'struction.

f 21 O that men would therefore praise the ' Lord for his ' goodness : and declare the wonders that he ' doeth for the ' children of ' men!

22 That they would offer unto him the ' sacrifice of ' thanksgiving : and tell ' out his ' works with ' gladness!

23 They that go down to the ' sea in ' ships : and occupy their ' business in ' great ' waters;

24 These men see the ' works of the ' Lord : and his ' wonders ' in the ' deep.

25 For at his word the stormy ' wind a'riseth : which lifteth ' up the ' waves there'of.

26 They are carried up to the heaven, and down a'gain to the ' deep : their soul melteth a'way be'cause of the ' trouble.

27 They reel to and fro, and stagger like a ' drunken ' man : and are ' at their ' wits' ' end.

p 28 So when they cry unto the Lord ' in their ' trouble : he delivereth them ' out of ' their dis'tress.

29 For he maketh the ' storm to ' cease : so that the ' waves there'of are ' still.

30 Then are they glad, because they ' are at ' rest : and so he bringeth them unto the ' haven where ' they would ' be.

f 31 O that men would therefore praise the ' Lord for his ' goodness : and declare the wonders that he ' doeth for the ' children of ' men!

32 That they would exalt him also in the congre'gation of the ' people : and praise him ' in the ' seat of the ' elders!

33 Who turneth the floods ' into a ' wilderness : and ' drieth ' up the ' water-springs.

34 A fruitful land ' maketh he ' barren : for the wickedness of ' them that ' dwell there'in.

35 Again he maketh the wilderness a ' standing ' water : and water-springs ' of a ' dry ' ground.

36 And there he ' setteth the ' hungry : that they may ' build them a ' city to ' dwell in;

37 That they may sow their land and ' plant ' vineyards : to ' yield them ' fruits of ' increase.

38 He blesseth them, so that they ' multiply ex'ceedingly : and suffereth not their ' cattle ' to de'crease.

39 And again, when they are minished and ' brought ' low :
through oppression through ' any ' plague or ' trouble;

40 Though he suffer them to be evil in'treated through '
tyrants : and let them wander out of the ' way ' in the '
wilderness;

2nd Part

41 Yet helpeth he the poor ' out of ' misery : and maketh him
house-holds ' like a ' flock of ' sheep.

42 The righteous will consider this ' and re'joice : and the
mouth of all ' wickedness ' shall be ' stopped.

43 Whoso is wise will ' ponder these ' things : and they shall
understand the loving'kindness ' of the ' Lord.

DAY 22   EVENING
PSALM 108

O GOD, my heart is ready my ' heart is ' ready : I will sing and
give praise with the best ' member ' that I ' have.

2 Awake thou ' lute and ' harp : I myself ' will a'wake right '
early.

3 I will give thanks unto thee O Lord a'mong the ' people : I
will sing praises unto ' thee a'mong the ' nations.

4 For thy mercy is greater ' than the ' heavens : and thy truth '
reacheth ' unto the ' clouds.

5 Set up thyself O God a'bove the ' heavens : and thy glory
a'bove ' all the ' earth.

6 That thy beloved may ' be de'livered : let thy right hand
save ' them and ' hear thou ' me.

7 God hath spoken ' in his ' holiness : I will rejoice therefore
and divide Sichem, and mete ' out the ' valley of ' Succoth.

8 Gilead is mine and Ma'nasses is ' mine : Ephraim also is
the ' strength of ' my ' head.

2nd Part

9 Judah is my law-giver, Moab ' is my ' wash-pot : over Edom
will I cast out my shoe, upon Phi'listia ' will I ' triumph.

10 Who will lead me into the ' strong ' city : and who will '
bring me ' into ' Edom?

11 Hast not thou forsaken ' us O ' God : and wilt not thou O '
God go ' forth with our ' hosts?

12 O help us a'gainst the ' enemy : for ' vain is the ' help of '
man.

13 Through God we shall ' do great ' acts : and it is he that '
shall tread ' down our ' enemies.

PSALM 109

HOLD not thy tongue O ' God of my ' praise : for the
mouth of the ungodly, yea the mouth of the de'ceitful is ' opened up'on me.

2 And they have spoken against me with ' false ' tongues :
they compassed me about also with words of hatred, and
fought a'gainst me with'out a ' cause.

3 For the love that I had unto them, lo they take now my '
contrary ' part : but I ' give myself ' unto ' prayer.

4 Thus have they rewarded me ' evil for ' good : and ' hatred
for ' my good ' will.

427

[5 Set thou an ungodly man to be ' ruler ' over him : and let Satan ' stand at ' his right ' hand.

6 When sentence is given upon him, let him ' be con'-demned : and let his ' prayer be ' turned into ' sin.

7 Let his ' days be ' few : and let an'other ' take his ' office.

8 Let his ' children be ' fatherless : and ' his ' wife a ' widow.

9 Let his children be vagabonds and ' beg their ' bread : let them seek it also ' out of ' desolate ' places.

10 Let the extortioner consume ' all that he ' hath : and let the ' stranger ' spoil his ' labour.

11 Let there be ' no man to ' pity him : nor to have compassion up'on his ' fatherless ' children.

12 Let his posterity ' be de'stroyed : and in the next genera-tion let his ' name be ' clean put ' out.

13 Let the wickedness of his fathers be had in remembrance in the ' sight of the ' Lord : and let not the sin of his ' mother be ' done a'way.

14 Let them alway be be'fore the ' Lord : that he may root out the memorial of ' them from ' off the ' earth.

15 And that, because his mind was ' not to do ' good : but persecuted the poor helpless man, that he might slay him that was ' vex-ed ' at the ' heart.

16 His delight was in cursing, and it shall happen ' unto ' him : he loved not blessing, therefore shall ' it be ' far ' from him.

17 He clothed himself with cursing, like as ' with a ' raiment : and it shall come into his bowels like water, and like ' oil ' into his ' bones.

18 Let it be unto him as the cloke that he ' hath up'on him : and as the girdle that he is ' alway ' girded with'al.

2nd Part

19 Let it thus happen from the Lord ' unto mine ' enemies :
and to those that speak ' evil a'gainst my ' soul.]

20 But deal thou with me O Lord God, according ' unto thy '
Name : for ' sweet ' is thy ' mercy.

21 O deliver me for I am ' helpless and ' poor : and my ' heart
is ' wounded with'in me.

22 I go hence like the shadow ' that de'parteth : and am driven
a'way ' as the ' grasshopper.

23 My knees are ' weak through ' fasting : my flesh is dried ' up
for ' want of ' fatness.

24 I became also a reproach ' unto ' them : they that looked
up'on me ' shaked their ' heads.

25 Help me O ' Lord my ' God : O save me ac'cording ' to thy '
mercy.

26 And they shall know how that this is ' thy ' hand : and that '
thou ' Lord hast ' done it.

27 Though they curse yet ' bless ' thou : and let them be
confounded that rise up against me, but ' let thy ' servant
re'joice.

2nd Part

28 Let mine adversaries be ' clothed with ' shame : and let
them cover themselves with their own con'fusion ' as with
a ' cloke.

29 As for me, I will give great thanks unto the Lord ' with my '
mouth : and ' praise him a'mong the ' multitude.

30 For he shall stand at the right ' hand of the ' poor : to save his soul ' from un'righteous ' judges.

DAY 23   MORNING
PSALM 110

The Lord said unto ' my ' Lord : Sit thou on my right hand until I ' make thine ' enemies thy ' footstool.

2 The Lord shall send the rod of thy power ' out of ' Sion : be thou ruler, even in the ' midst a'mong thine ' enemies.

3 In the day of thy power shall the people offer thee free-will offerings, with an ' holy ' worship : the dew of thy birth is ' of the ' womb of the ' morning.

4 The Lord sware and will ' not re'pent : Thou art a priest for ever after the ' order ' of Mel'chisedech.

5 The Lord upon ' thy right ' hand : shall wound even ' kings in the ' day of his ' wrath.

6 He shall judge among the heathen, he shall fill the places with the ' dead ' bodies : and smite in sunder the heads ' over ' divers ' countries.

2nd Part

7 He shall drink of the ' brook in the ' way : therefore ' shall he · lift ' up his ' head.

PSALM 111

I will give thanks unto the Lord with my ' whole ' heart : secretly among the faithful and ' in the ' con-gre'gation.

2 The works of the ' Lord are ' great : sought out of all ' them that have ' pleasure there'in.

3 His work is worthy to be praised and ' had in ' honour : and his ' righteousness en'dureth for ' ever.

4 The merciful and gracious Lord hath so done his ' marvellous ' works : that they ' ought to be ' had in re'membrance.

5 He hath given meat unto ' them that ' fear him : he shall ever be ' mindful ' of his ' covenant.

6 He hath shewed his people the ' power of his ' works : that he may give them the ' heritage ' of the ' heathen.

7 The works of his hands are ' verity and ' judgement : all ' his com'mandments are ' true.

8 They stand fast for ' ever and ' ever : and are ' done in ' truth and ' equity.

9 He sent redemption ' unto his ' people : he hath commanded his covenant for ever, holy and ' reverend ' is his ' Name.

10 The fear of the Lord is the be'ginning of ' wisdom : a good understanding have all they that do thereafter, the ' praise of it en'dureth for ' ever.

PSALM 112

BLESSED is the man that ' feareth the ' Lord : he hath great de'light in ' his com'mandments.

2 His seed shall be ' mighty upon ' earth : the generation of the ' faithful ' shall be ' blessed.

3 Riches and plenteousness shall be ' in his ' house : and his ' righteousness en'dureth for ' ever.

4 Unto the godly there ariseth up ' light in the ' darkness : he is ' merciful ' loving and ' righteous.

5 A good man is ' merciful and ' lendeth : and will ' guide his ' words with dis'cretion.

6 For he shall ' never be ' moved : and the righteous shall be had in ' ever'lasting re'mèmbrance.

7 He will not be afraid of any ' evil ' tidings : for his heart standeth fast and be'lieveth ' in the ' Lord.

8 His heart is established and ' will not ' shrink : until he see his de'sire up'on his ' enemies.

9 He hath dispersed abroad and given ' to the ' poor : and his righteousness remaineth for ever, his horn shall ' be ex'alted with ' honour.

10 The ungodly shall see it and ' it shall ' grieve him : he shall gnash with his teeth and consume away, the de'sire of the un'godly shall ' perish.

PSALM 113

PRAISE the ' Lord ye ' servants : O ' praise the ' Name of the ' Lord.

2 Blessed be the ' Name of the ' Lord : from this time ' forth for ' ever'more.

3 The Lord's ' Name is ' praised : from the rising up of the sun unto the ' going ' down of the ' same.

4 The Lord is high a'bove all ' heathen : and his ' glory a'bove the ' heavens.

5 Who is like unto the Lord our God, that hath his ' dwelling so ' high : and yet humbleth himself to behold the things that ' are in ' heaven and ' earth?

6 He taketh up the simple ' out of the ' dust : and lifteth the '
  poor ' out of the ' mire;

7 That he may set him ' with the ' princes : even with the '
  princes ' of his ' people.

8 He maketh the barren woman to ' keep ' house : and to be
  a ' joyful ' mother of ' children.

DAY 23   EVENING

PSALM 114

WHEN Israel came ' out of ' Egypt : and the house of Jacob
  from a'mong the ' strange ' people,

2 Judah ' was his ' sanctuary : and ' Israel ' his do'minion.

3 The sea saw ' that and ' fled : Jordan ' was ' driven ' back.

4 The mountains ' skipped like ' rams : and the little ' hills
  like ' young ' sheep.

5 What aileth thee O thou sea ' that thou ' fleddest : and thou
  Jordan that ' thou wast ' driven ' back?

6 Ye mountains that ye ' skipped like ' rams : and ye little '
  hills like ' young ' sheep?

7 Tremble thou earth at the presence ' of the ' Lord : at the
  presence ' of the ' God of ' Jacob;

8 Who turned the hard rock into a ' standing ' water : and the
  flintstone ' into a ' springing ' well.

† PSALM 115

NOT unto us O Lord, not unto us, but unto thy Name '
  give the ' praise : for thy loving mercy and ' for thy '
  truth's ' sake.

  † For alternative setting to Psalm 115 see Appendix.

433

*   2 Wherefore ' shall the ' heathen ' say : ' Where is ' now
    their ' God?

  3 As for our God ' he is in ' heaven : he hath done what-
    so'ever ' pleas-ed ' him.

  4 Their idols are ' silver and ' gold : even the ' work of '
    men's ' hands.

*   5 They have ' mouths and ' speak ' not : ' eyes have ' they
    and ' see not.

*   6 They have ' ears and ' hear ' not : ' noses have ' they and '
    smell not.

  7 They have hands and handle not, feet have ' they and '
    walk not : neither ' speak they ' through their ' throat.

  8 They that make them are ' like unto ' them : and so are all
    such as ' put their ' trust in ' them.

  9 But thou house of Israel ' trust thou · in the ' Lord : he is
    their ' succour ' and de'fence.

  10 Ye house of Aaron, put your ' trust · in the ' Lord : he is
    their ' helper ' and de'fender.

  11 Ye that fear the Lord, put your ' trust · in the ' Lord : he is
    their ' helper ' and de'fender.

  12 The Lord hath been mindful of us and ' he shall ' bless us :
    even he shall bless the house of Israel, he shall ' bless the '
    house of ' Aaron.

  13 He shall bless them that ' fear the ' Lord : both ' small '
    and ' great.

  2 Wherefore shall the ' heathen ' say : where is ' now ' their ' God?
  5 They have ' mouths and ' speak not : eyes ' have ' they and ' see not.
  6 They have ' ears and ' hear not : noses ' have ' they and ' smell not.

* 14 The Lord shall in'crease you ' more and ' more : ' you and '
  your ' children.

  15 Ye are the ' blessed of the ' Lord : who ' made ' heaven
  and ' earth.

  16 All the whole heavens ' are the ' Lord's : the earth hath he '
  given to the ' children of ' men.

  17 The dead praise not ' thee O ' Lord : neither all they that
  go ' down ' into ' silence.

  18 But we will ' praise the ' Lord : from this time forth for
  evermore. ' Praise '—the ' Lord.

DAY 24   MORNING
PSALM 116

I AM ' well ' pleased : that the Lord hath ' heard the ' voice of
my ' prayer;

  2 That he hath inclined his ear ' unto ' me : therefore will I
  call upon ' him as ' long as I ' live.

  3 The snares of death compassed me ' round a'bout : and the
  pains of ' hell gat ' hold up'on me.

  4 I shall find trouble and heaviness, and I will call upon the '
  Name of the ' Lord : O Lord I be'seech thee de'liver my '
  soul.

  5 Gracious is the ' Lord and ' righteous : yea ' our ' God is '
  merciful.

  6 The Lord pre'serveth the ' simple : I was in ' misery ' and
  he ' helped me.

  14 The Lord shall increase you ' more and ' more : you ' and ' your '
  children.

7 Turn again then unto thy rest ' O my ' soul : for the ' Lord '
hath re'warded thee.

8 And why? thou hast delivered my ' soul from ' death : mine
eyes from tears ' and my ' feet from ' falling.

9 I will walk be'fore the ' Lord : in the ' land ' of the ' living.

10 I believed and therefore will I speak, but I was ' sore '
troubled : I said in my haste, ' All ' men are ' liars.

11 What reward shall I give ' unto the ' Lord : for all the
benefits that ' he hath ' done unto ' me?

12 I will receive the ' cup of sal'vation : and call up'on the '
Name of the ' Lord.

13 I will pay my vows now in the presence of ' all his ' people :
right dear in the sight of the ' Lord · is the ' death of his '
saints.

14 Behold O Lord how that ' I am thy ' servant : I am thy
servant and the son of thine handmaid, thou hast ' broken
my ' bonds in ' sunder.

15 I will offer to thee the ' sacrifice of ' thanksgiving : and will
call up'on the ' Name of the ' Lord.

16 I will pay my vows unto the Lord, in the sight of ' all his '
people : in the courts of the Lord's house, even in the midst
of thee O Jerusalem. ' Praise '—the ' Lord.

PSALM 117

O PRAISE the Lord ' all ye ' heathen : praise ' him ' all ye '
nations.

2 For his merciful kindness is ever more and more ' towards '
   us : and the truth of the Lord endureth for ever. '
   Praise '—the ' Lord.

PSALM 118

O GIVE thanks unto the Lord for ' he is ' gracious :
   because his ' mercy en'dureth for ' ever.

2 Let Israel now confess that ' he is ' gracious : and that his '
   mercy en'dureth for ' ever.

3 Let the house of Aaron ' now con'fess : that his ' mercy
   en'dureth for ' ever.

4 Yea let them now that fear the ' Lord con'fess : that his '
   mercy en'dureth for ' ever.

5 I called upon the ' Lord in ' trouble : and the Lord ' heard '
   me at ' large.

6 The Lord is ' on my ' side : I will not ' fear what ' man
   doeth ' unto me.

7 The Lord taketh my part with ' them that ' help me :
   therefore shall I see my de'sire up'on mine ' enemies.

8 It is better to ' trust in the ' Lord : than to ' put · any '
   confidence in ' man.

9 It is better to ' trust in the ' Lord : than to ' put · any '
   confidence in ' princes.

10 All nations compassed me ' round a'bout : but in the Name
   of the ' Lord will ' I de'stroy them.

11 They kept me in on every side, they kept me in I say on '
   every ' side : but in the Name of the ' Lord will ' I de'stroy
   them.

12 They came about me like bees, and are extinct even as the fire a'mong the ' thorns : for in the Name of the ' Lord I ' will de'stroy them.

13 Thou hast thrust sore at me that ' I might ' fall : but the ' Lord was ' my ' help.

14 The Lord is my ' strength and my ' song : and is be'come ' my sal'vation.

15 The voice of joy and health is in the dwellings ' of the ' righteous : the right hand of the Lord bringeth ' mighty ' things to ' pass.

16 The right hand of the Lord ' hath the pre'eminence : the right hand of the Lord bringeth ' mighty ' things to ' pass.

17 I shall not ' die but ' live : and de'clare the ' works of the ' Lord.

18 The Lord hath chastened and cor'rected ' me : but he hath not given me ' over ' unto ' death.

19 Open me the ' gates of ' righteousness : that I may go into them and give ' thanks ' unto the ' Lord.

20 This is the ' gate of the ' Lord : the ' righteous shall ' enter ' into it.

21 I will thank thee for ' thou hast ' heard me : and art be'come ' my sal'vation.

22 The same stone which the ' builders re'fused : is become the ' headstone ' in the ' corner.

2nd Part

23 This is the ' Lord's ' doing : and it is ' marvellous ' in our ' eyes.

24 This is the day which the ' Lord hath ' made : we will re'joice and be ' glad in ' it.

25 Help me ' now O ' Lord : O Lord ' send us ' now pros'perity.

26 Blessed be he that cometh in the ' Name of the ' Lord : we have wished you good luck, ye that ' are of the ' house of the ' Lord.

27 God is the Lord who hath ' shewed us ' light : bind the sacrifice with cords, yea even ' unto the ' horns of the ' altar.

28 Thou art my God and ' I will ' thank thee : thou art my ' God and ' I will ' praise thee.

29 O give thanks unto the Lord for ' he is ' gracious : and his ' mercy en'dureth for ' ever.

DAY 24 EVENING

PSALM 119

BLESSED are those that are undefiled ' in the ' way : and ' walk in the ' law of the ' Lord.

2 Blessed are they that ' keep his ' testimonies : and seek him ' with their ' whole ' heart.

3 For they who ' do no ' wickedness : walk ' in ' his ' ways.

4 Thou ' hast ' charged : that we shall ' diligently ' keep thy com'mandments.

5 O that my ways were made ' so di'rect : that ' I might ' keep thy ' statutes!

6 So shall I not ' be con'founded : while I have re'spect unto ' all thy com'mandments.

7 I will thank thee with an un'feign-ed ' heart : when I shall have learned the ' judgements ' of thy ' righteousness.

8 I will ' keep thy ' ceremonies : O for'sake me ' not ' utterly.

Wherewithal shall a young man ' cleanse his ' way : even by ruling him'self ' after thy ' word.

10 With my whole heart ' have I ' sought thee : O let me not go wrong ' out of ' thy com'mandments.

11 Thy words have I hid with'in my ' heart : that I ' should not ' sin a'gainst thee.

12 Blessed art ' thou O ' Lord : O ' teach me ' thy ' statutes.

13 With my lips have ' I been ' telling : of all the ' judgements ' of thy ' mouth.

14 I have had as great delight in the ' way of thy ' testimonies : as in ' all ' manner of ' riches.

15 I will talk of ' thy com'mandments : and have re'spect ' unto thy ' ways.

16 My delight shall be ' in thy ' statutes : and I will ' not for'get thy ' word.

O do well ' unto thy ' servant : that I may ' live and ' keep thy ' word.

18 Open ' thou mine ' eyes : that I may see the ' wondrous ' things of thy ' law.

19 I am a stranger up'on ' earth : O hide not ' thy com'mandments ' from me.

20 My soul breaketh out for the very ' fervent de'sire : that it hath ' alway ' unto thy ' judgements.

21 Thou hast re'buked the ' proud : and cursed are they that do ' err from ' thy com'mandments.

22 O turn from me ' shame and re'buke : for ' I have ' kept thy ' testimonies.

23 Princes also did sit and ' speak a'gainst me : but thy servant is ' occupied ' in thy ' statutes.

* 24 For ' thy ' testimonies ' are my de'light : and ' my ' counsellors.

MY soul cleaveth ' to the ' dust : O quicken thou me ac'cording ' to thy ' word.

26 I have acknowledged my ways ' and thou ' heardest me : O ' teach me ' thy ' statutes.

27 Make me to understand the way of ' thy com'mandments : and so shall I ' talk of thy ' wondrous ' works.

28 My soul melteth away for ' very ' heaviness : comfort thou me ac'cording ' unto thy ' word.

29 Take from me the ' way of ' lying : and cause thou me to make ' much of ' thy ' law.

30 I have chosen the ' way of ' truth : and thy judgements ' have I ' laid be'fore me.

31 I have stuck ' unto thy ' testimonies : O ' Lord con'found me ' not.

32 I will run the way of ' thy com'mandments : when thou hast ' set my ' heart at ' liberty.

DAY 25   MORNING

TEACH me O Lord the ' way of thy ' statutes : and I shall ' keep it ' unto the ' end.

34 Give me understanding and I shall ' keep thy ' law : yea I shall keep it ' with my ' whole ' heart.

24 For thy testimonies are ' my de'light : and ' my '—'counsellors.

441

35 Make me to go in the path of ' thy com'mandments : for there'in is ' my de'sire.

* 36 In'cline my ' heart ' unto thy ' testimonies : and ' not to ' covetousness.

37 O turn away mine eyes, lest they be'hold ' vanity : and quicken thou ' me in ' thy ' way.

38 O stablish thy word ' in thy ' servant : that ' I may ' fear ' thee.

39 Take away the rebuke that ' I am a'fraid of : for thy ' judgements are ' good.

40 Behold my delight is in ' thy com'mandments : O ' quicken me ' in thy ' righteousness.

LET thy loving mercy come also unto ' me O ' Lord : even thy salvation ac'cording ' unto thy ' word.

42 So shall I make answer unto ' my blas'phemers : for my ' trust is ' in thy ' word.

43 O take not the word of thy truth utterly ' out of my ' mouth : for my ' hope is ' in thy ' judgements.

* 44 So shall I ' alway ' keep thy ' law : ' yea for ' ever and ' ever.

45 And I will ' walk at ' liberty : for I ' seek ' thy com'mandments.

46 I will speak of thy testimonies also, even be'fore ' kings : and ' will not ' be a'shamed.

36 Incline my heart ' unto thy ' testimonies : and ' not to ' covetous'ness.
44 So shall I alway ' keep thy ' law : yea for ' ever ' and ' ever.

* 47 And my de'light shall ' be in ' thy com'mandments : ' which I have ' loved.

48 My hands also will I lift up unto thy commandments ' which I have ' loved : and my ' study · shall ' be in thy ' statutes.

O THINK upon thy servant as con'cerning thy ' word : wherein thou hast caused ' me to ' put my ' trust.

50 The same is my comfort ' in my ' trouble : for thy ' word hath ' quickened ' me.

51 The proud have had me exceedingly ' in de'rision : yet have I not ' shrink-ed ' from thy ' law.

* 52 For I remembered thine ever'lasting ' judgements O ' Lord : ' and re'ceiv-ed ' comfort.

53 I am ' horribly a'fraid : for the ungodly ' that for'sake thy ' law.

54 Thy statutes have ' been my ' songs : in the ' house ' of my ' pilgrimage.

55 I have thought upon thy Name O Lord in the ' night'season : and have ' kept ' thy ' law.

56 This ' I ' had : be'cause I ' kept thy com'mandments.

THOU art my ' portion O ' Lord : I have ' promised to ' keep thy ' law.

58 I made my humble petition in thy presence with my ' whole ' heart: O be merciful unto me ac'cording ' to thy ' word.

47 And my delight shall be in ' thy com'mandments : which ' I ' have ' loved.
52 For I remembered thine everlasting ' judgements O ' Lord : and ' —re'ceived ' comfort.

59 I called mine own ' ways to re'membrance : and turned my ' feet ' unto thy ' testimonies.

60 I made haste and prolonged ' not the ' time : to ' keep ' thy com'mandments.

61 The congregations of the un'godly have ' robbed me : but I have ' not for'gotten thy ' law.

62 At midnight I will rise to give ' thanks unto ' thee : be'cause of thy ' righteous ' judgements.

63 I am a companion of all ' them that ' fear thee : and ' keep ' thy com'mandments.

64 The earth O Lord is ' full of thy ' mercy : O ' teach me ' thy ' statutes.

O LORD thou hast dealt graciously ' with thy ' servant : ac'cording ' unto thy ' word.

66 O learn me true under'standing and ' knowledge : for I have be'liev-ed ' thy com'mandments.

67 Before I was troubled ' I went ' wrong : but ' now. have I ' kept thy ' word.

68 Thou art ' good and ' gracious : O ' teach me ' thy ' statutes.

69 The proud have imagined a ' lie a'gainst me : but I will keep thy commandments ' with my ' whole ' heart.

70 Their heart is as ' fat as ' brawn : but my delight hath ' been in ' thy ' law.

71 It is good for me that I have ' been in ' trouble : that ' I may ' learn thy ' statutes.

72 The law of thy mouth is dearer ' unto ' me : than ' thousands of ' gold and ' silver.

DAY 25 EVENING

THY hands have ' made me and ' fashioned me : O give me understanding, that I may ' learn ' thy com'-mandments.

74 They that fear thee will be glad ' when they ' see me : because I have ' put my ' trust in thy ' word.

75 I know O Lord that thy ' judgements are ' right : and that thou of very faithfulness hast ' caused me ' to be ' troubled.

76 O let thy merciful kindness ' be my ' comfort : according to thy ' word ' unto thy ' servant.

77 O let thy loving mercies come unto me that ' I may ' live : for thy ' law is ' my de'light.

78 Let the proud be confounded, for they go wickedly about ' to de'stroy me : but I will be ' occupied in ' thy com'mandments.

79 Let such as fear thee and have ' known thy ' testimonies : be ' turn-ed ' unto ' me.

80 O let my heart be sound ' in thy ' statutes : that ' I be ' not a'shamed.

MY soul hath longed for ' thy sal'vation : and I have a good ' hope be'cause of thy ' word.

82 Mine eyes long sore ' for thy ' word : saying ' O when ' wilt thou ' comfort me?

83 For I am become like a bottle ' in the ' smoke : yet do I ' not for'get thy ' statutes.

84 How many are the ' days of thy ' servant : when wilt thou
be ' avenged of ' them that ' persecute me?

85 The proud have ' dig-ged ' pits for me : which ' are not '
after thy ' law.

86 All thy com'mandments are ' true : they persecute me
falsely ' O be ' thou my ' help.

87 They had almost made an end of me up'on ' earth : but I
for'sook not ' thy com'mandments.

88 O quicken me after thy ' loving'kindness : and so shall I
keep the ' testimonies ' of thy ' mouth.

O LORD ' thy ' word : en'dureth for ' ever in ' heaven.

90 Thy truth also remaineth from one generation ' to
an'other : thou hast laid the foundation of the ' earth and '
it a'bideth.

91 They continue this day according ' to thine ' ordinance :
for ' all things ' serve ' thee.

92 If my delight had not been ' in thy ' law : I should have '
perished ' in my ' trouble.

93 I will never forget ' thy com'mandments : for with them '
thou hast ' quickened ' me.

94 I am ' thine O ' save me : for I have ' sought ' thy
com'mandments.

95 The ungodly laid wait for me ' to de'stroy me : but ' I will
con'sider thy ' testimonies.

96 I see that all things ' come to an ' end : but thy commandment ' is ex'ceeding ' broad.

LORD what love have I ' unto thy ' law : all the day long ' is my '
study ' in it.

98 Thou through thy commandments hast made me wiser ' than mine ' enemies : for ' they are ' ever ' with me.

99 I have more understanding ' than my ' teachers : for thy ' testimonies ' are my ' study.

100 I am wiser ' than the ' ag-ed : because I ' keep ' thy com'mandments.

101 I have refrained my feet from every ' evil ' way : that ' I may ' keep thy ' word.

102 I have shrunk ' from thy ' judgements : for ' thou ' teachest ' me.

103 O how sweet are thy words ' unto my ' throat : yea sweeter than ' honey ' unto my ' mouth.

104 Through thy commandments I get ' under'standing : therefore I ' hate all ' evil ' ways.

DAY 26   MORNING

THY word is a lantern ' unto my ' feet : and a ' light ' unto my ' paths.

106 I have sworn and am ' stedfastly ' purposed : to ' keep thy ' righteous ' judgements.

107 I am troubled a'bove ' measure : quicken me O Lord ac'cording ' to thy ' word.

108 Let the free-will offerings of my mouth please ' thee O ' Lord : and ' teach me ' thy ' judgements.

109 My soul is alway ' in my ' hand : yet do I ' not for'get thy ' law.

110 The ungodly have ' laid a ' snare for me : but yet I swerved ' not from ' thy com'mandments.

111 Thy testimonies have I claimed as mine ' heritage for-' ever : and why?, they are the ' very ' joy of my ' heart.

* 112 I have applied my heart to ful'fil thy ' statutes ' alway : ' even ' unto the ' end.

I HATE them that imagine ' evil ' things : but thy ' law ' do I ' love.

114 Thou art my de'fence and ' shield : and my ' trust is ' in thy ' word.

115 Away from ' me ye ' wicked : I will keep the com'mand-ments ' of my ' God.

116 O stablish me according to thy word that ' I may ' live : and let me not be disap'pointed ' of my ' hope.

117 Hold thou me up and ' I shall be ' safe : yea my delight shall be ' ever ' in thy ' statutes.

118 Thou hast trodden down all them that depart ' from thy ' statutes : for they im'agine ' but de'ceit.

119 Thou puttest away all the ungodly of the ' earth like ' dross : therefore I ' love ' thy ' testimonies.

120 My flesh trembleth for ' fear of ' thee : and I am a'fraid of ' thy ' judgements.

I DEAL with the thing that is ' lawful and ' right : O give me not over ' unto ' mine op'pressors.

122 Make thou thy servant to delight in ' that which is ' good : that the proud ' do me ' no ' wrong.

123 Mine eyes are wasted away with looking ' for thy ' health : and for the ' word of ' thy ' righteousness.

112 I have applied my heart to fulfil thy ' statutes ' alway : even ' un'to the ' end.

124 O deal with thy servant according unto thy ' loving ' mercy : and ' teach me ' thy ' statutes.

125 I am thy servant, O grant me ' under'standing : that ' I may ' know thy ' testimonies.

126 It is time for thee Lord to lay ' to thine ' hand : for ' they have de'stroyed thy ' law.

127 For I love ' thy com'mandments : above ' gold and ' precious ' stone.

128 Therefore hold I straight all ' thy com'mandments : and all false ' ways I ' utterly ab'hor.

THY testimonies ' are ' wonderful : therefore ' doth my ' soul ' keep them.

130 When thy word ' goeth ' forth : it giveth light and under'-standing ' unto the ' simple.

131 I opened my mouth and drew ' in my ' breath : for my de'light was in ' thy com'mandments.

132 O look thou upon me and be ' merciful ' unto me : as thou usest to do unto ' those that ' love thy ' Name.

133 Order my ' steps in thy ' word : and so shall no wicked-ness ' have do'minion ' over me.

134 O deliver me from the wrongful ' dealings of ' men : and so shall I ' keep ' thy com'mandments.

135 Shew the light of thy countenance up'on thy ' servant : and ' teach me ' thy ' statutes.

136 Mine eyes gush ' out with ' water : because men ' keep not ' thy ' law.

RIGHTEOUS art ' thou O ' Lord : and ' true is ' thy ' judgement.

138 The testimonies that thou ' hast com'manded : are ex'ceeding ' righteous and ' true.

139 My zeal hath ' even con'sumed me : because mine enemies ' have for'gotten thy ' words.

140 Thy word is ' tried to the ' uttermost : and thy ' servant ' loveth ' it.

141 I am small and of no ' repu'tation : yet do I ' not for'get thy com'mandments.

142 Thy righteousness is an ever'lasting ' righteousness : and thy ' law ' is the ' truth.

143 Trouble and heaviness have taken ' hold up'on me · yet is my de'light in ' thy com'mandments.

144 The righteousness of thy testimonies is ' ever'lasting : O grant me under'standing and ' I shall ' live.

DAY 26   EVENING

I CALL with my ' whole ' heart : hear me O Lord ' I will ' keep thy ' statutes.

146 Yea even unto thee ' do I ' call : help me and ' I shall ' keep thy ' testimonies.

147 Early in the morning do I ' cry unto ' thee : for ' in thy ' word is my ' trust.

148 Mine eyes prevent the ' night'watches : that I might be ' occupied ' in thy ' words.

149 Hear my voice O Lord, according unto thy ' loving'kindness : quicken me ac'cording as ' thou art ' wont.

150 They draw nigh that of ' malice ' persecute me : and are ' far ' from thy ' law.

151 Be thou nigh at ' hand O ' Lord : for all ' thy com-' mandments are ' true.

152 As concerning thy testimonies I have ' known long ' since : that thou hast ' grounded ' them for ' ever.

O CONSIDER mine adversity ' and de'liver me : for I do ' not for'get thy ' law.

154 Avenge thou my cause ' and de'liver me : quicken me ac'cording ' to thy ' word.

155 Health is far ' from the un'godly : for ' they re'gard not thy ' statutes.

156 Great is thy ' mercy O ' Lord : quicken ' me as ' thou art ' wont.

157 Many there are that ' trouble · me and ' persecute me : yet do I not ' swerve ' from thy ' testimonies.

158 It grieveth me when I ' see the trans'gressors : be'cause they ' keep not thy ' law.

159 Consider O Lord how I love ' thy com'mandments : O quicken me ac'cording · to thy ' loving ' kindness.

160 Thy word is true from ever'lasting : all the judgements of thy righteousness en'dure for ' ever'more.

PRINCES have persecuted me with'out a ' cause : but my heart ' standeth in ' awe of thy ' word.

162 I am as ' glad of thy ' word : as one that ' findeth ' great ' spoils.

163 As for lies I ' hate and ab'hor them : but thy ' law 'do I ' love.

164 Seven times a ' day do I ' praise thee : be'cause of thy ' righteous ' judgements.

165 Great is the peace that they have who ' love thy ' law : and they are ' not of'fended ' at it.

166 Lord I have looked for thy ' saving ' health : and done ' after ' thy com'mandments.

167 My soul hath ' kept thy ' testimonies : and ' lov-ed ' them ex'ceedingly.

168 I have kept thy com'mandments and ' testimonies : for ' all my ' ways are be'fore thee.

LET my complaint come before ' thee O ' Lord : give me understanding ac'cording ' to thy ' word.

170 Let my supplication ' come be'fore thee : deliver me ac'cording ' to thy ' word.

171 My lips shall ' speak of thy ' praise : when thou hast ' taught me ' thy ' statutes.

172 Yea my tongue shall ' sing of thy ' word : for ' all thy com'mandments are ' righteous.

173 Let thine ' hand ' help me : for I have ' chosen ' thy com'mandments.

174 I have longed for thy saving ' health O ' Lord : and in thy ' law is ' my de'light.

175 O let my soul live and ' it shall ' praise thee : and thy ' judgements ' shall ' help me.

176 I have gone astray like a ' sheep that is ' lost : O seek thy servant, for I ' do not for'get thy com'mandments.

DAY 27   MORNING

PSALM 120

* When I ' was in ' trouble ' I called upon the ' Lord : and ' he ' heard me.

Ps. 120. vs. 1 when I was in trouble I called up'on the ' Lord : and ' he ' heard ' me.

2 Deliver my soul O Lord from ' lying ' lips : and ' from a de'ceitful ' tongue.

3 What reward shall be given or done unto thee thou ' false ' tongue: even mighty and sharp ' arrows with ' hot burning ' coals.

4 Woe is me that I am constrained to ' dwell with ' Mesech : and to have my habitation a'mong the ' tents of ' Kedar.

5 My soul hath long ' dwelt a'mong them : that are ' enemies ' unto ' peace.

6 I labour for peace, but when I speak unto ' them there'of : they ' make them ' ready to ' battle.

PSALM 121

I WILL lift up mine eyes ' unto the ' hills : from ' whence ' cometh my ' help.

2 My help cometh even ' from the ' Lord : who ' hath made ' heaven and ' earth.

3 He will not suffer thy ' foot to be ' moved : and he that ' keepeth thee ' will not ' sleep.

4 Behold he that ' keepeth ' Israel : shall ' neither ' slumber nor ' sleep.

5 The Lord himself ' is thy ' keeper : the Lord is thy de'fence upon ' thy right ' hand;

* 6 So that the ' sun shall not ' burn thee by ' day : ' neither the ' moon by ' night.

7 The Lord shall preserve thee from ' all ' evil : yea it is even he ' that shall ' keep thy ' soul.

Ps. 121. vs. 6 So that the sun shall not burn ' thee by ' day : neither the ' moon ' by ' night.

8 The Lord shall preserve thy going out and thy ' coming ' in :
from this time ' forth for ' ever'more.

PSALM 122

I was glad when they said ' unto ' me : We will ' go into
the ' house of the ' Lord.

* 2 Our ' feet shall ' stand ' in thy ' gates : ' O Je'rusalem.

3 Jerusalem is ' built as a ' city : that is at ' unity ' in it'self.

4 For thither the tribes go up, even the ' tribes of the ' Lord :
to testify unto Israel, to give thanks ' unto the ' Name of
the ' Lord.

2nd Part

5 For there is the ' seat of ' judgement : even the ' seat of the '
house of ' David.

6 O pray for the ' peace of Je'rusalem : they shall ' prosper
that ' love ' thee.

7 Peace be with'in thy ' walls : and ' plenteousness with'in
thy ' palaces.

8 For my brethren and com'panions' ' sakes : I will ' wish '
thee pros'perity.

9 Yea because of the house of the ' Lord our ' God : I will '
seek to ' do thee ' good.

PSALM 123

Unto thee lift I ' up mine ' eyes : O thou that ' dwellest '
in the ' heavens.

Ps. 122. vs. 2 Our feet shall stand ' in thy ' gates : O ' —Je'rusa'lem.

2 Behold, even as the eyes of servants look unto the hand of their masters, and as the eyes of a maiden unto the ' hand of her ' mistress : even so our eyes wait upon the Lord our God, until ' he have ' mercy up'on us.

3 Have mercy upon us, O Lord have ' mercy up'on us : for ' we are ' utterly des'pised.

4 Our soul is filled with the scornful re'proof of the ' wealthy : and with the de'spitefulness ' of the ' proud.

PSALM 124

If the Lord himself had not been on our side, now may ' Israel ' say : if the Lord himself had not been on our side when ' men rose ' up a'gainst us;

2 They had swallowed ' us up ' quick : when they were so ' wrathfully dis'pleas-ed ' at us.

3 Yea the ' waters had ' drowned us : and the ' stream had gone ' over our ' soul.

4 The deep ' waters · of the ' proud : had gone ' even ' over our ' soul.

5 But praised ' be the ' Lord : who hath not given us over for a ' prey ' unto their ' teeth.

6 Our soul is escaped, even as a bird out of the ' snare of the ' fowler : the snare is ' broken and ' we · are de'livered.

2nd Part

7 Our help standeth in the ' Name of the ' Lord : who hath ' made ' heaven and ' earth.

PSALM 125

They that put their trust in the Lord shall be even ' as the mount ' Sion : which may not be removed but ' standeth ' fast for ' ever.

2 The hills stand a'bout Je'rusalem : even so standeth the Lord round about his people, from this time ' forth for ' ever'more.

2nd Part

3 For the rod of the ungodly, cometh not into the ' lot of the ' righteous : lest the righteous ' put their ' hand unto ' wickedness.

4 Do ' well O ' Lord : unto those that are ' good and 'true of ' heart.

5 As for such as turn back into their ' own ' wickedness : the Lord shall lead them forth with the evil-doers, but ' peace shall ' be upon ' Israel.

DAY 27 EVENING
PSALM 126

WHEN the Lord turned again the cap'tivity of ' Sion : then were we ' like unto ' them that ' dream.

2 Then was our mouth ' filled with ' laughter : and ' our ' tongue with ' joy.

3 Then said they a'mong the ' heathen : The ' Lord hath done' great things ' for them.

4 Yea, the Lord hath done great things ' for us al'ready : where'of ' we re'joice.

5 Turn our cap'tivity O ' Lord : as the ' rivers ' in the ' south.

6 They that ' sow in ' tears : shall ' reap ' in ' joy.

2nd Part

7 He that now goeth on his way weeping, and beareth ' forth
good ' seed : shall doubtless come again with joy and ' bring
his ' sheaves ' with him.

PSALM 127

EXCEPT the Lord ' build the ' house : their labour ' is
but ' lost that ' build it.

2 Except the Lord ' keep the ' city : the watchman ' waketh '
but in ' vain.

3 It is but lost labour that ye haste to rise up early, and so late
take rest, and eat the ' bread of ' carefulness : for so he
giveth ' his be'lov-ed ' sleep.

4 Lo children and the ' fruit of the ' womb : are an heritage
and gift that ' cometh ' of the ' Lord.

5 Like as the arrows in the ' hand of the ' giant : even so 'are
the ' young ' children.

6 Happy is the man that hath his quiver ' full of ' them :
they shall not be ashamed, when they speak with their '
enemies ' in the ' gate.

PSALM 128

BLESSED are all they that ' fear the ' Lord : and ' walk in '
his ' ways.

2 For thou shalt eat the labours ' of thine ' hands : O well is
thee and ' happy ' shalt thou ' be.

3 Thy wife shall be as the ' fruitful ' vine : up'on the 'walls of
thine ' house.

* 4 Thy children ' like the ' olive ' branches : ' round a'bout thy ' table.

5 Lo thus shall the ' man be ' blessed : that ' fear'eth the ' Lord.

6 The Lord from out of Sion shall ' so ' bless thee : that thou shalt see Jerusalem in prosperity ' all thy ' life ' long.

2nd Part

7 Yea that thou shalt see thy ' children's ' children : and ' peace up'on ' Israel.

PSALM 129

MANY a time have they found against me from my ' youth ' up : may ' Israel ' now ' say.

2 Yea many a time have they vexed me from my ' youth ' up : but they have ' not pre'vailed a'gainst me.

3 The plowers plowed up'on my ' back : and ' made ' long ' furrows.

4 But the ' righteous ' Lord : hath hewn the ' snares of · the un'godly in ' pieces.

5 Let them be confounded and ' turned ' backward : as many as have ' evil ' will at ' Sion.

6 Let them be even as the grass growing up'on the ' house-tops : which withereth a'fore it be ' pluck-ed ' up;

7 Whereof the mower filleth ' not his ' hand : neither he that bindeth'up the ' sheaves his ' bosom.

Ps. 128. vs. 4 Thy children like the ' olive ' branches : round ' — a'bout thy ' table.

8 So that they who go by, say not so much as The ' Lord '
prosper you : we wish you good ' luck in the ' Name of the '
Lord.

PSALM 130

Slow

OUT of the deep have I called unto ' thee O ' Lord :
Lord ' hear ' my ' voice.

2 O let thine ears con'sider ' well : the ' voice of ' my
com'plaint.

3 If thou Lord wilt be extreme to mark what is ' done a'miss :
O ' Lord who ' may a'bide it?

4 For there is ' mercy with ' thee : therefore ' shalt ' thou be '
feared.

5 I look for the Lord, my ' soul doth ' wait for him : in his '
word is ' my ' trust.

6 My soul fleeth ' unto the ' Lord : before the morning watch,
I say be'fore the ' morning ' watch.

7 O Israel trust in the Lord, for with the Lord ' there is '
mercy : and with ' him is ' plenteous re'demption.

8 And he shall re'deem ' Israel : from ' all ' his ' sins.

PSALM 131

Slow

LORD I am ' not high'minded : I have ' no ' proud ' looks.

2 I do not exercise myself in ' great ' matters : which ' are
too ' high for ' me.

459

3 But I refrain my soul and keep it low, like as a child that is wean-ed ' from his ' mother : yea my soul is even ' as a ' wean-ed ' child.

f 4 O Israel ' trust in the ' Lord : from this time ' forth for ' ever'more.

DAY 28   MORNING
PSALM 132

LORD re'member ' David : and ' all ' his ' trouble;

2 How he sware ' unto the ' Lord : and vowed a vow unto the Al'mighty ' God of ' Jacob;

3 I will not come within the tabernacle ' of mine ' house : nor ' climb up ' into my ' bed;

4 I will not suffer mine eyes to sleep nor mine ' eye-lids to ' slumber : neither the temples of my ' head to ' take · any ' rest;

2nd Part

5 Until I find out a place for the ' temple of the ' Lord : an habitation for the ' mighty ' God of ' Jacob.

6 Lo we heard of the ' same at ' Ephrata : and ' found it ' in the ' wood.

7 We will go ' into his ' tabernacle : and fall low on our ' knees be'fore his ' footstool.

8 Arise O Lord ' into thy ' resting-place : thou and the ' ark of ' thy ' strength.

9 Let thy priests be ' clothed with ' righteousness : and let thy ' saints ' sing with ' joyfulness.

460

10 For thy servant ' David's ' sake : turn not away the ' presence of ' thine A'nointed.

11 The Lord hath made a faithful ' oath unto ' David : and he ' shall not ' shrink ' from it;

12 Of the fruit ' of thy ' body : shall I ' set up'on thy ' seat.

13 If thy children will keep my covenant, and my testimonies that ' I shall ' learn them : their children also shall sit upon thy ' seat for ' ever'more.

14 For the Lord hath chosen Sion to be an habitation ' for him'self : he hath ' long-ed ' for ' her.

15 This shall be my ' rest for'ever : here will I dwell, for I ' have a de'light there'in.

16 I will bless her ' victuals with ' increase : and will ' satisfy her ' poor with ' bread.

17 I will deck her ' priests with ' health : and her ' saints shall re'joice and ' sing.

18 There shall I make the horn of ' David to ' flourish : I have ordained a ' lantern for ' mine A'nointed.

19 As for his enemies, I shall ' clothe them with ' shame : but upon him'self shall his ' crown ' flourish.

PSALM 133

BEHOLD how good and joyful a ' thing it ' is : brethren to ' dwell to'gether in ' unity!

2 It is like the precious ointment upon the head, that ran down 'unto the ' beard : even unto Aaron's beard, and went ' down to the 'skirts of his ' clothing.

3 Like as the ' dew of ' Hermon : which fell up'on the 'hill of ' Sion.

461

4 For there the Lord ' promised his ' blessing : and ' life for '
ever'more.

PSALM 134

BEHOLD now ' praise the ' Lord : all ye ' servants ' of
the ' Lord;

2 Ye that by night stand in the ' house of the ' Lord : even in
the courts of the ' house of ' our ' God.

3 Lift up your hands ' in the ' sanctuary : and ' praise '—the '
Lord.

Unison

4 The Lord that made ' heaven and ' earth : give thee '
blessing ' out of ' Sion.

PSALM 135

O PRAISE the Lord, laud ye the ' Name of the ' Lord :
praise it O ye ' servants ' of the ' Lord;

2 Ye that stand in the ' house of the ' Lord : in the ' courts of
the ' house of our ' God.

3 O praise the Lord for the ' Lord is ' gracious : O sing praises
unto his ' Name for ' it is ' lovely.

4 For why? the Lord hath chosen Jacob ' unto him'self : and
Israel ' for his ' own pos'session.

2nd Part

5 For I know that the ' Lord is ' great : and that our Lord ' is
a'bove all ' gods.

6 Whatsoever the Lord pleased, that did he in heaven ' and
in ' earth : and in the sea ' and in ' all deep ' places.

7 He bringeth forth the clouds from the ' ends of the ' world : and sendeth forth lightnings with the rain, bringing the ' winds ' out of his ' treasures.

8 He smote the ' first-born of ' Egypt : both of ' man ' and ' beast.

9 He hath sent tokens and wonders into the midst of thee, O thou ' land of ' Egypt : upon ' Pharaoh and ' all his ' servants.

10 He smote ' divers ' nations : and ' slew ' mighty ' kings;

11 Sehon king of the Amorites, and Og the ' king of ' Basan : and ' all the ' kingdoms of ' Canaan;

2nd Part

12 And gave their land to ' be an ' heritage : even an heritage ' unto ' Israel his ' people.

13 Thy Name O Lord en'dureth for'ever : so doth thy memorial O Lord, from one gene'ration ' to ano'ther.

14 For the Lord will a'venge his ' people : and be ' gracious ' unto his ' servants.

15 As for the images of the heathen, they are but ' silver and ' gold : the ' work of ' men's ' hands.

16 They have ' mouths and ' speak not : eyes ' have they ' but they ' see not.

17 They have ears and ' yet they ' hear not : neither is there ' any ' breath in their ' mouths.

18 They that make them are like ' unto ' them : and so are all ' they that ' put their ' trust in them.

19 Praise the Lord ye ' house of ' Israel : praise the ' Lord ye ' house of ' Aaron.

20 Praise the Lord ye ' house of ' Levi : ye that fear the ' Lord '
praise the ' Lord.

2nd Part

21 Praised be the Lord ' out of ' Sion : who ' dwelleth ' at
Je'rusalem.

DAY 28 EVENING
PSALM 136

Single Chant

O GIVE thanks unto the Lord for ' he is ' gracious : and his '
mercy en'dureth for ' ever.

2 O give thanks unto the God of ' all ' gods : for his ' mercy
en'dureth for ' ever.

3 O thank the Lord of ' all ' lords : for his ' mercy en'dureth
for ' ever.

4 Who only ' doeth great ' wonders : for his ' mercy
en'dureth for ' ever.

5 Who by his excellent wisdom ' made the ' heavens : for his '
mercy en'dureth for ' ever.

6 Who laid out the earth a'bove the ' waters : for his ' mercy
en'dureth for ' ever.

7 Who hath ' made great ' lights : for his ' mercy en'dureth
for ' ever;

8 The sun to ' rule the ' day : for his ' mercy en'dureth for '
ever;

9 The moon and the stars to ' govern the ' night : for his '
mercy en'dureth for ' ever.

10 Who smote Egypt '. with their ' first-born : for his ' mercy en'dureth for ' ever;

11 And brought out Israel ' from a'mong them : for his ' mercy en'dureth for ' ever;

12 With a mighty hand and ' stretched out ' arm : for his ' mercy en'dureth for ' ever.

13 Who divided the Red sea in ' two ' parts : for his ' mercy en'dureth for ' ever;

14 And made Israel to ' go through the ' midst of it : for his ' mercy en'dureth for ' ever.

15 But as for Pharaoh and his host, he overthrew them in the ' Red ' sea : for his ' mercy en'dureth for ' ever.

16 Who led his people ' through the ' wilderness : for his ' mercy en'dureth for ' ever.

17 Who smote ' great ' kings : for his ' mercy en'dureth for ' ever;

18 Yea and slew ' mighty ' kings : for his ' mercy en'dureth for ' ever;

19 Sehon ' king of the ' Amorites : for his ' mercy en'dureth for ' ever;

20 And Og the ' king of ' Basan : for his ' mercy en'dureth for ' ever;

21 And gave away their ' land · for an ' heritage : for his ' mercy en'dureth for ' ever;

22 Even for an heritage unto ' Israel his ' servant : for his ' mercy en'dureth for ' ever.

23 Who remembered us when we ' were in ' trouble : for his ' mercy en'dureth for ' ever;

24 And hath delivered us ' from our ' enemies : for his ' mercy en'dureth for ' ever.

25 Who giveth food to ' all ' flesh : for his ' mercy en'dureth for ' ever.

26 O give thanks unto the ' God of ' heaven : for his ' mercy en'dureth for ' ever.

27 O give thanks unto the ' Lord of ' lords : for his ' mercy en'dureth for ' ever.

PSALM 137

Slow. Single Chant.

p By the waters of Babylon we sat ' down and ' wept : when we re'membered ' thee O ' Sion.

2 As for our harps we ' hanged them ' up : upon the ' trees that ' are there'in.

3 For they that led us away captive required of us then a song, and melody ' in our ' heaviness : Sing us ' one of the ' songs of ' Sion.

* 4 How shall we ' sing the ' Lord's ' song : ' in a ' strange ' land?

5 If I forget thee ' O Je'rusalem : let my right ' hand for'get her ' cunning.

6 If I do not remember thee, let my tongue cleave to the ' roof of my ' mouth : yea if I prefer not Je'rusalem ' in my ' mirth.

4 How shall we sing the ' Lord's ' song : in'—a ' strange ' land?

7 [Remember the children of Edom O Lord, in the ' day of
  Je'rusalem : how they said, Down with it, down with it, '
  even ' to the ' ground.

8 O daughter of Babylon ' wasted with ' misery : yea happy
  shall he be that rewardeth thee, as ' thou hast ' serv-ed ' us.

9 Blessed shall he be that ' taketh thy ' children : and '
  throweth them a'gainst the ' stones.]

PSALM 138

I WILL give thanks unto thee O Lord, with my ' whole '
  heart : even before the gods will I sing ' praise ' unto '
  thee.

2 I will worship toward thy holy temple and praise thy Name,
  because of thy loving'kindness and ' truth : for thou hast
  magnified thy Name and thy ' word a'bove ' all things.

3 When I called upon ' thee thou ' heardest me : and
  enduedst my ' soul with ' much ' strength.

4 All the kings of the earth shall ' praise thee O ' Lord : for
  they have ' heard the ' words of thy ' mouth.

5 Yea they shall sing in the ' ways of the ' Lord : that great is
  the ' glory ' of the ' Lord.

6 For though the Lord be high, yet hath he respect ' unto
  the ' lowly : as for the proud, he beholdeth ' them a'far '
  off.

7 Though I walk in the midst of trouble, yet shalt ' thou
  re'fresh me : thou shalt stretch forth thy hand upon the
  furiousness of mine enemies, and thy ' right ' hand shall '
  save me.

8 The Lord shall make good his loving'kindness ' toward
me : yea thy mercy O Lord endureth for ever, despise not
then the ' works of thine ' own ' hands.

DAY 29   MORNING
PSALM 139

O LORD thou hast searched me ' out and ' known me : thou
knowest my down-sitting and mine up-rising, thou under-
standest my ' thoughts ' long be'fore.

2 Thou art about my path and a'bout my ' bed : and ' spiest
out ' all my ' ways.

3 For lo there is not a word ' in my ' tongue : but thou O
Lord ' knowest it ' alto'gether.

4 Thou hast fashioned me be'hind and be'fore : and ' laid
thine ' hand up'on me.

2nd Part

5 Such knowledge is too wonderful and ' excellent ' for me :
I ' cannot at'tain unto ' it.

6 Whither shall I go then ' from thy ' Spirit : or whither shall
I ' go then ' from thy ' presence?

7 If I climb up into heaven ' thou art ' there : if I go down to
hell ' thou art ' there ' also.

8 If I take the ' wings of the ' morning : and remain in the '
uttermost ' parts of the ' sea;

9 Even there also shall ' thy hand ' lead me : and ' thy right '
hand shall ' hold me.

10 If I say, Peradventure the ' darkness shall ' cover me : then
shall my ' night be ' turned to ' day.

11 Yea the darkness is no darkness with thee, but the night is as ' clear as the ' day : the darkness and light to ' thee are ' both a'like.

12 For my ' reins are ' thine : thou hast covered me ' in my ' mother's ' womb.

13 I will give thanks unto thee, for I am fearfully and ' wonderfully ' made : marvellous are thy works, and that my ' soul ' knoweth right ' well.

14 My bones are not ' hid from ' thee : though I be made secretly, and ' fashioned be'neath in the ' earth.

15 Thine eyes did see my substance yet ' being un'perfect : and in thy book were ' all my ' members ' written;

2nd Part

16 Which day by ' day were ' fashioned : when as yet ' there was ' none of ' them.

17 How dear are thy counsels unto ' me O ' God : O how ' great is the ' sum of ' them!

18 If I tell them, they are more in number ' than the ' sand : when I wake up ' I am ' present with ' thee.

19 Wilt thou not slay the ' wicked O ' God : depart from ' me ye ' blood-thirsty ' men.

20 For they speak un'righteously a'gainst thee : and thine enemies ' take thy ' Name in ' vain.

21 Do not I hate them O Lord that ' hate ' thee : and am not I grieved with those that ' rise ' up a'gainst thee?

22 Yea I ' hate them right ' sore : even as ' though they ' were mine ' enemies.

23 Try me O God, and seek the ' ground of my ' heart : prove me ' and ex'amine my ' thoughts.

24 Look well if there be any way of ' wickedness ' in me : and
   lead me in the ' way ' ever'lasting.

PSALM 140

DELIVER me O Lord from the ' evil ' man : and preserve
me ' from the ' wicked ' man.

2 Who imagine mischief ' in their ' hearts : and stir up '
   strife ' all the day ' long.

3 They have sharpened their tongues ' like a ' serpent :
   adders' ' poison is ' under their ' lips.

4 Keep me O Lord from the ' hands of · the un'godly :
   preserve me from the wicked men, who are purposed to '
   over'throw my ' goings.

2nd Part

5 The proud have laid a snare for me, and spread a net
   a'broad with ' cords : yea and set ' traps in ' my ' way.

6 I said unto the Lord, Thou ' art my ' God : hear the ' voice
   of my ' prayers O ' Lord.

7 O Lord God, thou strength ' of my ' health : thou hast
   covered my ' head in the ' day of ' battle.

8 Let not the ungodly have his de'sire O ' Lord : let not his
   mischievous imagination prosper ' lest they ' be too '
   proud.

[9 Let the mischief of their own lips fall upon the ' head of '
   them : that ' compass ' me a'bout.

10 Let hot burning coals ' fall up'on them : let them be cast
   into the fire and into the pit, that they ' never rise ' up
   a'gain.]

11 A man full of words shall not prosper up'on the ' earth : evil shall hunt the wicked ' person to ' over'throw him.

12 Sure I am that the Lord will a'venge the ' poor : and main'tain the ' cause of the ' helpless.

13 The righteous also shall give thanks ' unto thy ' Name : and the just shall con'tinue in ' thy ' sight.

PSALM 141

LORD I call upon thee, haste thee ' unto ' me : and consider my voice when I ' cry ' unto ' thee.

2 Let my prayer be set forth in thy sight ' as the ' incense : and let the lifting up of my hands ' be an ' evening ' sacrifice.

3 Set a watch O Lord be'fore my ' mouth : and ' keep the ' door of my ' lips.

4 O let not mine heart be inclined to any ' evil ' thing : let me not be occupied in ungodly works with the men that work wickedness, lest I ' eat of such ' things as ' please them.

* 5 Let the righteous ' rather ' smite me ' friendly : ' and re'prove ' me.

6 But let not their precious balms ' break my ' head : yea I will pray ' yet a'gainst their ' wickedness.

[7 Let their judges be overthrown in ' stony ' places : that they may hear my ' words for ' they are ' sweet.

8 Our bones lie scattered be'fore the ' pit : like as when one breaketh and heweth ' wood up'on the ' earth.]

5 Let the righteous rather ' smite me ' friendly : and ' — re'prove ' me.

9 But mine eyes look unto thee O ' Lord ' God : in thee is my
   trust O ' cast not ' out my ' soul.

10 Keep me from the snare that ' they have ' laid for me : and
   from the ' traps of the ' wicked ' doers.

2nd Part

11 Let the ungodly fall into their own ' nets to'gether : and ' let
   me ' ever es'cape them.

DAY 29   EVENING
PSALM 142

Slow

I CRIED unto the Lord ' with my ' voice : yea even unto the Lord
   did I ' make my ' suppli'cation.

2 I poured out my com'plaints be'fore him : and ' shewed
   him ' of my ' trouble.

3 When my spirit was in heaviness thou ' knewest my ' path :
   in the way wherein I walked have they ' privily ' laid a '
   snare for me.

4 I looked also upon my ' right ' hand : and saw there was ' no
   man ' that would ' know me.

2nd Part

5 I had no place to ' flee ' unto : and no man ' car-ed ' for my '
   soul.

6 I cried unto thee O ' Lord and ' said : Thou art my hope,
   and my portion ' in the ' land of the ' living.

7 Consider ' my com'plaint : for I am ' brought ' very ' low.

8 O deliver me ' from my ' persecutors : for ' they are too ' strong for ' me.

9 Bring my soul out of prison, that I may give thanks ' unto thy ' Name : which thing if thou wilt grant me, then shall the righteous re'sort ' unto my ' company.

PSALM 143

HEAR my prayer O Lord, and consider ' my de'sire : hearken unto me for thy ' truth and ' righteous-ness' ' sake.

2 And enter not into judgement ' with thy ' servant : for in thy sight shall ' no man ' living be ' justified.

3 For the enemy hath persecuted my soul, he hath smitten my life ' down to the ' ground : he hath laid me in the darkness, as the ' men that have ' been long ' dead.

4 Therefore is my spirit ' vexed with'in me : and my ' heart with'in me is ' desolate.

5 Yet do I remember the time past, I muse upon ' all thy ' works : yea, I exercise myself in the ' works of ' thy ' hands.

6 I stretch forth my hands ' unto ' thee : my soul gaspeth unto thee ' as a ' thirsty ' land.

7 Hear me O Lord and that soon, for my spirit ' waxeth ' faint : hide not thy face from me, lest I be like unto them that go ' down ' into the ' pit.

8 O let me hear thy loving-kindness betimes in the morning, for in thee ' is my ' trust : shew thou me the way that I should walk in, for I lift up my ' soul ' unto ' thee.

9 Deliver me O Lord ' from mine ' enemies : for I flee ' unto ' thee to ' hide me.

10 Teach me to do the thing that pleaseth thee, for thou ' art my ' God : let thy loving Spirit lead me forth ' into the ' land of ' righteousness.

11 Quicken me O Lord for thy ' Name's ' sake : and for thy righteousness' sake bring my ' soul ' out of ' trouble.

12 And of thy goodness ' slay mine ' enemies : and destroy all them that vex my soul, for ' I am ' thy ' servant.

DAY 30 MORNING

PSALM 144

BLESSED be the ' Lord my ' strength : who teacheth my hands to war ' and my ' fingers to ' fight;

2 My hope and my fortress, my castle and deliverer, my defender in ' whom I ' trust : who subdueth my ' people ' that is ' under me.

3 Lord what is man, that thou hast such respect ' unto ' him : or the son of man, that thou ' so re'gardest ' him?

4 Man is like a ' thing of ' nought : his time ' passeth a'way like a ' shadow.

5 Bow thy heavens O Lord ' and come ' down : touch the ' mountains and ' they shall ' smoke.

6 Cast forth thy ' lightning and ' tear them : shoot out thine ' arrows ' and con'sume them.

7 Send down thine hand ' from a'bove : deliver me and take me out of the great waters, from the ' hand of ' strange ' children;

8 Whose mouth ' talketh of ' vanity : and their right hand ' is
   a right ' hand of ' wickedness.

9 I will sing a new song unto ' thee O ' God : and sing praises
   unto thee up'on a ' ten-stringed ' lute.

10 Thou hast given victory ' unto ' kings : and hast delivered
   David thy servant from the ' peril ' of the ' sword.

2nd Part

11 Save me and deliver me from the hand of ' strange '
   children : whose mouth talketh of vanity, and their right
   hand ' is a right ' hand of in'iquity.

12 That our sons may grow up as the ' young ' plants : and that
   our daughters may be as the polished ' corners ' of the '
   temple.

13 That our garners may be full and plenteous, with all '
   manner of ' store : that our sheep may bring forth thousands, and ten ' thousands ' in our ' streets.

14 That our oxen may be strong to labour, that there be ' no
   de'cay : no leading into captivity, and no com'plaining ' in
   our ' streets.

15 Happy are the people that are in ' such a ' case : yea blessed
   are the people who have the ' Lord for ' their ' God.

PSALM 145

I WILL magnify thee O ' God my ' King : and I will praise
   thy ' Name for ' ever and ' ever.

2 Every day will I give thanks ' unto ' thee : and praise thy '
   Name for ' ever and ' ever.

3 Great is the Lord, and marvellous worthy ' to be ' praised :
   there ' is no ' end of his ' greatness.

4 One generation shall praise thy works ' unto an'other : and de'clare ' thy ' power.

5 As for me, I will be talking ' of thy ' worship : thy glory thy ' praise and ' wondrous ' works;

6 So that men shall speak of the might of thy ' marvellous ' acts : and I will ' also ' tell of thy ' greatness.

2nd Part

7 The memorial of thine abundant kindness ' shall be ' shewed : and ' men shall ' sing of thy ' righteousness.

8 The Lord is ' gracious and ' merciful : long-suffering ' and of ' great ' goodness.

9 The Lord is loving ' unto ' every man : and his mercy is ' over ' all his ' works.

10 All thy works praise ' thee O ' Lord : and thy ' saints give ' thanks unto ' thee.

11 They shew the glory ' of thy ' kingdom : and ' talk of ' thy ' power;

12 That thy power thy glory and mightiness ' of thy ' kingdom : might be ' known ' unto ' men.

13 Thy kingdom is an ever'lasting ' kingdom : and thy domin-ion en'dureth through'out all ' ages.

14 The Lord upholdeth all ' such as ' fall : and lifteth up all ' those ' that are ' down.

15 The eyes of all wait upon ' thee O ' Lord : and thou givest them their ' meat in ' due ' season.

16 Thou openest ' thine ' hand : and fillest ' all things ' living with ' plenteousness.

17 The Lord is righteous in ' all his ' ways : and ' holy in ' all his ' works.

18 The Lord is nigh unto all them that ' call up'on him : yea all such as ' call up'on him ' faithfully.

19 He will fulfil the desire of ' them that ' fear him : he also will hear their ' cry ' and will ' help them.

20 The Lord preserveth all ' them that ' love him : but scattereth a'broad ' all the un'godly.

21 My mouth shall speak the ' praise · of the ' Lord : and let all flesh give thanks unto his holy ' Name for ' ever and ' ever.

PSALM 146

PRAISE the Lord O my soul, while I live will I ' praise the ' Lord : yea, as long as I have any being, I will sing ' praises ' unto my ' God.

2 O put not your trust in princes, nor in any ' child of ' man : for there ' is no ' help in ' them.

3 For when the breath of man goeth forth, he shall turn a'gain to his ' earth : and then ' all his ' thoughts ' perish.

4 Blessed is he that hath the God of Jacob ' for his ' help : and whose hope is ' in the ' Lord his ' God;

5 Who made heaven and earth, the sea and all that ' therein ' is : who ' keepeth his ' promise for ' ever;

6 Who helpeth them to right that ' suffer ' wrong : who ' feed'eth the ' hungry.

7 The Lord looseth men ' out of ' prison : the Lord giveth ' sight ' to the ' blind.

8 The Lord helpeth ' them that are ' fallen : the Lord ' careth ' for the ' righteous.

9 The Lord careth for the strangers, he defendeth the '
   fatherless and ' widow : as for the way of the ungodly he '
   turneth it ' upside ' down.

10 The Lord thy God O Sion, shall be King for ' ever'more :
   and through'out all ' gene'rations.

DAY 30   EVENING

PSALM 147

O PRAISE the Lord, for it is a good thing to sing praises '
   unto our ' God : yea a joyful and pleasant ' thing it ' is to be '
   thankful.

2 The Lord doth build ' up Je'rusalem : and gather to'gether
   the ' out-casts of ' Israel.

3 He healeth those that are ' broken in ' heart : and giveth '
   medicine to ' heal their ' sickness.

4 He telleth the ' number · of the ' stars : and ' calleth them '
   all by their ' names.

5 Great is our Lord and ' great is his ' power : yea ' and his '
   wisdom is ' infinite.

6 The Lord setteth ' up the ' meek : and bringeth the
   un'godly ' down to the ' ground.

7 O sing unto the ' Lord with ' thanksgiving : sing praises
   upon the ' harp ' unto our ' God;

8 Who covereth the heaven with clouds, and prepareth ' rain
   for the ' earth : and maketh the grass to grow upon the
   mountains, and ' herb · for the ' use of ' men;

9 Who giveth fodder ' unto the ' cattle : and feedeth the
   young ' ravens that ' call up'on him.

10 He hath no pleasure in the ' strength of an ' horse : neither delighteth ' he in ' any man's ' legs.

2nd Part

11 But the Lord's delight is in ' them that ' fear him : and ' put their ' trust in his ' mercy.

12 Praise the Lord ' O Je'rusalem : praise thy ' God ' O ' Sion.

13 For he hath made fast the ' bars of thy ' gates : and hath ' blessed thy ' children with'in thee.

14 He maketh ' peace in thy ' borders : and filleth thee ' with the ' flour of ' wheat.

15 He sendeth forth his commandment up'on ' earth : and his word ' runneth ' very ' swiftly.

16 He giveth ' snow like ' wool : and scattereth the ' hoar'frost like ' ashes.

17 He casteth forth his ' ice like ' morsels : who is ' able to a'bide his ' frost?

18 He sendeth out his ' word and ' melteth them : he bloweth with his wind ' and the ' waters ' flow.

19 He sheweth his word ' unto ' Jacob : his statutes and ' ordinances ' unto ' Israel.

2nd Part

20 He hath not dealt so with ' any ' nation : neither have the heathen ' knowledge ' of his ' laws.

* PSALM 148

O PRAISE the ' Lord of ' heaven : praise ' him ' in the ' height.

* For alternative setting to Psalm 148 see Appendix.

2 Praise him all ye ' angels of ' his : praise ' him ' all his ' host.

3 Praise him ' sun and ' moon : praise him ' all ye ' stars and ' light.

4 Praise him ' all ye ' heavens : and ye waters that ' are a'bove the ' heavens.

5 Let them praise the ' Name of the ' Lord : for he spake the word and they were made, he commanded ' and they ' were cre'ated.

6 He hath made them fast for ' ever and ' ever : he hath given them a law ' which shall ' not be ' broken.

7 Praise the ' Lord upon ' earth : ye ' dragons and ' all ' deeps;

8 Fire and hail ' snow and ' vapours : wind and ' storm ful'filling his ' word;

9 Mountains and ' all ' hills : fruitful ' trees and ' all ' cedars;

10 Beasts and ' all ' cattle : worms and ' feath'ered ' fowls;

11 Kings of the earth and ' all ' people : princes and all ' judges ' of the ' world;

12 Young men and maidens, old men and children, praise the ' Name of the ' Lord : for his Name only is excellent, and his ' praise above ' heaven and ' earth.

2nd Part

13 He shall exalt the horn of his people, all his ' saints shall ' praise him : even the children of Israel, even the ' people that ' serveth ' him.

PSALM 149

O SING unto the Lord a ' new ' song : let the con-gre'gation of ' saints ' praise him.

2 Let Israel rejoice in ' him that ' made him : and let the children of Sion be ' joyful ' in their ' King.

3 Let them praise his ' Name in the ' dance : let them sing praises unto ' him with ' tabret and ' harp.

4 For the Lord hath pleasure ' in his ' people : and ' helpeth the ' meek-'hearted.

5 Let the saints be ' joyful with ' glory : let them re'joice ' in their ' beds.

6 Let the praises of God be ' in their ' mouth : and a ' two-edged ' sword in their ' hands;

7 To be avenged ' of the ' heathen : and ' to re'buke the ' people;

8 To bind their ' kings in ' chains : and their ' nobles with ' links of ' iron.

2nd Part

9 That they may be avenged of them, ' as it is ' written : Such ' honour have ' all his ' saints.

PSALM 150

O PRAISE God ' in his ' holiness : praise him in the ' firmament ' of his ' power.

2 Praise him in his ' noble ' acts : praise him ac'cording to his ' excellent ' greatness.

3 Praise him in the ' sound of the ' trumpet : praise him up'on the ' lute and ' harp.

4 Praise him in the ' cymbals and ' dances : praise him up'on the ' strings and ' pipe.

5 Praise him upon the ' well-tuned ' cymbals : praise him
up'on the ' loud ' cymbals.

Unison

6 Let everything ' that hath ' breath : praise ' — ' — the '
Lord.

Appendix

Psalm 101

Psalm 101.   (Alternative Setting.)

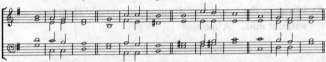

MY song shall be of ' mercy and ' judgement : unto thee O
  Lord ' will I ' sing.

2 O let me have ' under'standing : in the ' way of ' godliness.

3 When wilt thou come ' unto ' me : I will walk in my house with
  a ' perfect ' heart.

4 I will take no wicked thing in hand, I hate the ' sins of
  un'faithfulness : there shall no such cleave ' unto ' me.

5 A froward heart shall de'part from ' me : I will not know a '
  wicked ' person.

6 Whoso privily ' slandereth his ' neighbour : his will ' I de'stroy.

7 Whoso hath also a proud look and ' high ' stomach : I will not '
  suffer ' him.

8 Mine eyes look upon such as are faithful ' in the ' land : that
  they may ' dwell with ' me.

9 Whoso leadeth a ' godly ' life : he shall ' be my ' servant.

10 There shall no deceitful person ' dwell in my ' house : he that
   telleth lies shall not tarry ' in my ' sight.

2nd Part

11 I shall soon destroy all the ungodly that are ' in the ' land : that I may root out all wicked doers from the city ' of the ' Lord.

Glory be to the Father, and ' to the ' Son : and to the ' Holy ' Ghost.

As it was in the beginning, is now and ' ever ' shall be : world without end. ' A'men.

PSALM 115

Psalm 115. (Alternative Setting.) Verses 1–8.

Not unto us O Lord, not unto us, but unto thy Name ' give the ' praise : for thy loving mercy and for thy ' truth's ' sake.

2 Wherefore shall the ' heathen ' say : Where is ' now their ' God?

3 As for our God ' he is in ' heaven : he hath done whatsoever ' pleas-ed ' him.

4 Their idols are ' silver and ' gold : even the work of ' men's ' hands.

5 They have ' mouths and ' speak not : eyes have ' they and ' see not.

6 They have ' ears and ' hear not : noses have ' they and ' smell not.

7 They have hands and handle not, feet have ' they and ' walk not : neither speak they ' through their ' throat.

8 They that make them are ' like unto ' them : and so are all such as put their ' trust in ' them.

Verses 9 to end.

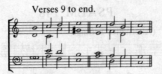

9 But thou house of Israel ' trust thou · in the ' Lord : he is their succour ' and de'fence.

10 Ye house of Aaron, put your ' trust in the ' Lord : he is their ' helper · and de'fender.

11 Ye that fear the Lord, put your ' trust in the ' Lord : he is their ' helper · and de'fender.

12 The Lord hath been mindful of us and ' he shall ' bless us : even he shall bless the house of Israel, he shall bless the ' house of ' Aaron.

13 He shall bless them that ' fear the ' Lord : both ' small and ' great.

14 The Lord shall increase you ' more and ' more : you ' and your ' children.

15 Ye are the blessed ' of the ' Lord : who made ' heaven and ' earth.

16 All the whole heavens ' are the ' Lord's : the earth hath he given to the ' children of ' men.

17 The dead praise not ' thee O ' Lord : neither all they that go ' down into ' silence.

18 But we will ' praise the ' Lord : from this time forth for evermore. ' Praise the ' Lord.

Glory be to the Father, and ' to the ' Son : and to the ' Holy ' Ghost.

As it was in the beginning, is now and ' ever ' shall be : world without end. ' A'men.

PSALM 148

Psalm 148. (Alternative Setting.)

O PRAISE the ' Lord of ' heaven : praise him ' in the ' height.

2 Praise him all ye ' angels of ' his : praise him ' all his ' host.

3 Praise him ' sun and ' moon : praise him all ye ' stars and ' light.

4 Praise him ' all ye ' heavens : and ye waters that are a'bove the ' heavens.

5 Let them praise the ' Name of the ' Lord : for he spake the word and they were made, he commanded and they ' were cre'ated.

6 He hath made them fast for ' ever and ' ever : he hath given them a law which shall ' not be ' broken.

7 Praise the ' Lord upon ' earth : ye dragons and ' all ' deeps;

8 Fire and hail ' snow and ' vapours : wind and storm ful'fil-ling his ' word;

9 Mountains and ' all ' hills : fruitful trees and ' all ' cedars;

10 Beasts and ' all ' cattle : worms and ' feathered ' fowls;

11 Kings of the earth and ' all ' people : princes and all judges ' of the ' world;

12 Young ' men and ' maidens : old ' men and ' children.

13 Praise the ' Name · of the ' Lord : for his Name only is excellent, and his praise above ' heaven and ' earth.

14 He shall exalt the ' horn of his ' people : all his ' saints shall '
praise him.

Psalm 148   (Alternative Setting.)

2nd Part

15 Even the ' children of ' Israel : even the people that '
serveth ' him.

Glory be to the Father, and ' to the ' Son : and to the ' Holy '
Ghost.

As it was in the beginning, is now and ' ever ' shall be : world
without end. ' A'men.

ACKNOWLEDGEMENTS

The services and prayers from *The Alternative Service Book 1980* are reproduced by permission of The Central Board of Finance of the Church of England. They include the following material (some in adapted form) which belongs to other copyright owners and is reproduced with permission.

Venite, Jubilate, and Psalm 134 are from *The Liturgical Psalter*, published separately as *The Psalms: a new translation for worship,* © English text 1976, 1977, David L. Frost, John A. Emerton, Andrew A. Macintosh, all rights reserved, © pointing 1976, 1977 William Collins Sons & Co Ltd.

The texts of the Nicene Creed (adapted), the Gloria in Excelsis, the Sanctus and Benedictus, and the Agnus Dei, as they appear in the Order for Holy Communion Rite A, and the texts of the Apostles' Creed and the Canticles Benedictus, Te Deum (adapted), Magnificat and Nunc Dimittis, as printed in Morning Prayer and Evening Prayer, are copyright © 1970, 1971, 1975 International Consultation on English Texts (ICET). The Lord's Prayer in its modern form is adapted from the ICET version.

The Song of Christ's Glory is from the *South African Daily Office*, the copyright of which is held by the Church of the Province of Southern Africa.

Material from *The Book of Common Prayer*, some in adapted form, was included in *The Alternative Service Book 1980* by permission of Eyre & Spottiswoode (Publishers) Ltd, Her Majesty's Printers.

The Parish Psalter (published separately by Addington Press: RSCM/ Mowbray), with pointing by Sydney H. Nicholson, 1928. A Selection of Prayers (pp. 231–48) include items from *The Oxford and Cambridge Office Book*, published by and © Oxford University Press and Cambridge University Press 1986, and from *Prayers in Church*, edited by John Conacher © Oxford University Press 1987, published by Oxford University Press.

We gratefully acknowledge permissions in respect of the following items:

Bernard SSF: Used by permission of the author.

National Pastoral Congress, Liverpool, 1980: Used by permission of the Archbishop of Liverpool.

From *Contemporary Prayers for Public Worship*, edited Caryl Micklem (1967): Reprinted by permission of SCM Press Ltd.

George Appleton: From *One Man's Prayers*. Reprinted by permission of SPCK.

Edward Dering: Reproduced by permission of Lutterworth Press from *Daily Prayers and Praise*, edited by George Appleton.

Frank Colquhoun: Reproduced by permission of Hodder & Stoughton from *Contemporary Parish Prayers*.

George Appleton: Reproduced by kind permission of the author from *Contemporary Parish Prayers* (Hodder & Stoughton, 1974).

ACKNOWLEDGEMENTS

Timothy Dudley-Smith: Reproduced by kind permission of the author.

John Conacher: © John Conacher 1987. Used with permission.

Liturgy of the Reformed Church of France: Reproduced by permission of Hodder & Stoughton from *Contemporary Parish Prayers*, © 1974 by Frank Colquhoun.

Frank Colquhoun: Reproduced by permission of Hodder & Stoughton from *New Parish Prayers*, © 1981 by Frank Colquhoun.

Bishop Theodore Woods: Reproduced from *Prayer by Prayer* by J. Eddison by permission of Henry E. Walter Ltd.

John Eddison: Reproduced from *Prayer by Prayer* by J. Eddison by permission of Henry E. Walter Ltd.

John D. Searle: Reproduced by permission of the author from *More Prayers for Today's Church*.

William Temple: Reproduced by permission of Macmillan, London & Basingstoke on behalf of the Executors of the Estate of William Temple.

Jamie Wallace: Reproduced by permission of Hodder & Stoughton from *A Month of Sundays*, © 1983 Jamie Wallace.

Mother's Union: Reproduced by permission, from *The Mother's Union Prayer Book* and from *The Mother's Union Service Book*.

Dick Williams: Reproduced by kind permission of the author from *Prayers for Todays Church*.